Negotiating India's Landmark Agreements

ADVANCE PRAISE FOR THE BOOK

'A meticulously researched and carefully presented account of key moments in India's external negotiations. It will be indispensable for analysts and practitioners alike'—**Srinath Raghavan, professor of international relations and history, Ashoka University**

'A.S. Bhasin, the archivist–scholar who has painstakingly documented India's bilateral relationships with neighbours, brings a detailed account in his new book of how India crafted five landmark agreements that transformed its foreign policy. Using a wealth of primary sources, he analyses the complex factors that determined the course of action that India adopted with China, the Soviet Union, the United States, Pakistan and Sri Lanka, and the compromises it made to secure agreements in pursuance of national security interests. The insightful observations on why missteps happened in the case of China and Sri Lanka, and the reasons for success in the case of the Soviet Union and America, make this book mandatory reading for all those who are interested in the mechanics of international diplomacy and negotiation'—**Vijay Gokhale, former ambassador to China and former foreign secretary**

'Young scholars and the intelligent Indian reader alike, curious about India's diplomatic navigation and achievements, can now make A.S. Bhasin's latest book [*Negotiating India's Landmark Agreements*] their first stop. This judicious selection of agreements, historicized and recounted objectively by one of the most experienced handlers of official Indian documentation, is truly commendable'—**Alka Acharya, chairperson, Centre for East Asian Studies, School of International Studies, JNU, and honorary director, Institute of Chinese Studies, Delhi**

Negotiating India's Landmark Agreements

A.S. BHASIN

PENGUIN
VIKING
An imprint of Penguin Random House

VIKING

Viking is an imprint of the Penguin Random House group of companies
whose addresses can be found at global.penguinrandomhouse.com

Published by Penguin Random House India Pvt. Ltd
4th Floor, Capital Tower 1, MG Road,
Gurugram 122 002, Haryana, India

First published in Viking by Penguin Random House India 2024

ISBN 9780143464983

Typeset in Adobe Garamond Pro MAP Systems, Bengaluru, India
Printed at Thomson Press India Ltd, New Delhi

www.penguin.co.in

To my late wife
Mandip Kaur
(1941–96)

Contents

Introduction

A treaty or an agreement is an instrument negotiated between two sovereign states on a particular subject to arrive at a common position to forge a relationship of mutual understanding and trust considered important for their future relations. Unless signed at the conclusion of armed hostilities, it represents the states' reconciled national aspirations. It is a prerequisite for harmony between them. To be meaningful, it must ensure equal benefits to both parties and that the parties involved dilute some of their sovereignty on the subject of the agreement. It is also important that the contours of the problem sought to be resolved, or the objective to be achieved, are clear to both.

India, since Independence, has signed several treaties/agreements with many countries—some routinely to create goodwill—like friendship treaties, some for protocol, and still more for promotion of trade, or cooperation in the economy, or in science and technology. Boundary agreements between neighbours are a category apart and a fundamental requirement for peaceful coexistence between them. Well-defined and mutually agreed upon boundaries between neighbours have intrinsic value and come into being as a result of an understanding between them by adjustment of rival claims, interests and ambitions at points of intersection.

Some agreements have their roots in history. The relations forged between nations in the past become anachronistic with lapse of time by the forces of history. It makes it necessary to update the past relationships to meet the requirements of contemporary realities. In such cases the nations have to give up the past advantages, if any, which history may have bestowed on either of them. The adjustment so made, usually has a long-lasting benefit in their relations.

Of course, the role of the political leadership is crucial. The brief that is given to the negotiator(s) should be balanced and must take care of the minimum interest of both the parties. No agreement can be successfully negotiated unless both parties are sensitive to each other's interests. The flexibility of the brief is an equally important element for successful negotiations. Also, the negotiator's own role in working out an agreed document cannot be minimized. Within the limits set by his mandate, the negotiator should have a clear understanding of his minimum position, and be flexible and amiable while being skilful and audacious.

The author has selected the following five agreements as being outstanding for their beneficial or baneful impact on the future among the several agreements that India has signed in the last three-quarters of a century since its Independence. The agreements which the author dwells upon are:

1. India–China Agreement on Tibet, 1954
2. India–Soviet Treaty of Peace, Friendship and Cooperation, 1971
3. India–Pakistan Simla Agreement, 1972
4. India–Sri Lanka Accord, 1987, and
5. India–US Civil Nuclear Energy Agreement, 2008

Of the above five, two agreements were with the two superpowers of those days—the Soviet Union and the United States (US). It is evident that both were keen to engage India in their new policy framework for their own reasons.

In 1969, the Soviet Union had a long-term agenda in offering India a treaty suo moto. The ideological differences between Moscow and Peking had by then turned into a political slugfest. India's relations with China since the 1962 war were antagonistic and had soured to such an extent that there was hardly any interaction between them. Moscow was anxious to encircle China and felt India could be drawn into an alliance against China. But Moscow perceived one difficulty. India since Independence had pursued a foreign policy in which alliances against a third country and that too of a hostile nature were considered an abomination. The initial attempts of Moscow toward the offer of a treaty were unwelcome to India, but as relations with West Pakistan turned increasingly hostile due to revolt in East Pakistan and the surge of refugees into India, there was a perceptible change in New Delhi's mood. Though grudgingly, India accepted the offer of a treaty from the Soviet Union. Moscow calculated that if India signed the treaty in view of its circumstances, its firmness against an alliance would be breached and would then be easier to make India accept a treaty which would be a little more demanding. But Moscow was disappointed when it tried to foist another definitive treaty to bind India in an anti-China alliance. For its reluctance, of course, India had to face some immediate disappointment.

The US, at the turn of the millennium, decided to reverse its Cold War policies that it had pursued to punish India for its audacity not only in not signing the Nuclear Non-Proliferation Treaty (NPT) but also conducting a nuclear test in 1974, though dubbed as 'peaceful'. Treating India as a pariah, the US neither shared high-tech dual-use technologies nor equipment, which retarded India's economic growth. On the other hand, the US, to India's dismay, provided China with the most sophisticated technologies and capital which had taken China's economy and consequently its political profile to great heights. China, now pretending to project the image of a peaceful nation sought to dominate the virgin region in its vicinity. When the Soviet Union collapsed in 1991, the US perceived a rising China, in the long run, would threaten its 'sole superpower' status. Washington was also worried at the threats that Japan, its biggest allay in Asia, was facing from China, besides China's monetary policies were worrying. For the US, an unbridled China had become menacing. So to serve its own long-term interests and stem Chinese progress, or at least retard it, the US looked for a solution. India had come a long way since the disastrous defeat in the 1962 war with China. It had not only become economically stronger since then but had also successfully built a modern military force capable of standing up to China. Washington calculated that by further bolstering India's capabilities, the largest country in China's neighbourhood which had a score to settle, India would be capable of arresting China's influence in the Indian Ocean Rimland. That was the trigger for Washington to embrace New Delhi.

And India, giving up the hesitations of the past, clinched the historic opportunity to tread the path which its negotiators smoothened with their American counterparts in long and arduous diplomatic duels. The US was anxious to engage India and it reflected not only in dumping its own laws and regulations but also in using its all-round influence to prevail upon the high priests of non-proliferation of other countries to engage India in nuclear trade.

Of the three other agreements, the India–China Agreement on Tibet had become necessary as India's inheritance from the British in Tibet were now considered as gains of imperialism and, therefore, archaic and needing updating. Besides, China had made the functioning of Indian trade agencies almost impossible and had given enough hints that the old regime had ceased to exist and, therefore, it was the time to give them up. India knew but refused to accept that India's boundaries with Tibet were an imperialist inheritance and suffered from infirmities. While giving up its privileges in Tibet, India did not consider it necessary to negotiate the boundaries as quid pro quo. The timidity that marked New Delhi's approach to the agreement of 1954 set the agenda for future Sino–Indian relations with tragic and disastrous consequences.

The India–Pakistan Simla Agreement was essentially a follow-up of the India–Pakistan War of 1971 and was expected to start a fresh chapter in India–Pakistan relations. India's magnanimous approach in not treating Pakistan as a defeated country was primarily to make it look upon India as a friend in its neighbourhood in future. It is a different matter that these hopes were unfortunately belied. India split Pakistan, which was inherent with Pakistan's geography and the narrative of the past returned after the Simla Agreement had been signed and the prisoners of war went home.

The India–Sri Lanka Accord of 1987 with its attendant ethnic story is an unfortunate chapter in the history of Indian diplomacy in the last seventy-five years of Independence. Mrs Indira Gandhi and her son Rajiv Gandhi flexed India's muscles against a small neighbour, allying with Lankan Tamils without due diligence—whether the Tamils' demands were reasonable or even desirable. It was superciliousness of 12 per cent Tamils in the island in demanding language parity with the 74 per cent Sinhalese, whose language, Sinhala had been declared the official language of the island. Similarly, their demand for merger of two Tamil majority regions, the Northern Province and the Eastern Province, to create a Tamil 'homeland' was repugnant to the concept of a nation state and was naturally unacceptable to Sri Lanka. India, instead of advising the Lankan Tamils to moderate their demands and adjust to the ground realities, went all out to support them under pressure from the state of Tamil Nadu, and rushed in where angles would fear to tread. This not only created complications but bloodied the relations between the countries. India emerged from Sri Lanka with its face besmirched adversely affecting its relations with its neighbours.

It would not be wrong to conclude that while agreements per se do help in resolving outstanding problems and building new relationships, finally it is the intentions of the parties that are the tipping factors.

Before writing this book, the author had published the following series which provide the bulk of material for this book:

1. *India–Sri Lanka Relations and Sri Lanka's Ethnic Conflict: 1947–2000*
   (Five Volumes)
2. *India–Bangladesh Relations: 1971–2002*
   (Five Volumes)
3. *Nepal–India, Nepal–China Relations: 1947–2005*
   (Five Volumes)
4. *India–Pakistan Relations: 1947–2007*
   (Ten Volumes)
5. *India–China Relations: 1947–2000*
   (Five Volumes)

The present study is primarily based in the above volumes. These volumes contain official documents, classified and other accessed by the author from various sources, including the archives of the Ministry of External Affairs.

The study India–China Relations is based on Nehru Papers accessed from the Prime Ministers' Museum and Library with the permission of the Ministry of Culture after 2014.

Chapter 1 particularly is based on *Nehru Papers* mentioned at Serial No. 5 (*India–China Relations*).

Between 2002 and 2013, he published an annual series for the Ministry of External Affairs under the title *India's Foreign Relations in 12 Annual Volumes.*

I

The India–China Agreement on Tibet, 1954[*]

On 29 April 1954, India and the People's Republic of China had signed an agreement on 'Trade and Intercourse between Tibet Region of China and India' which redefined the Indian position in Tibet from the one it had inherited from the British, when they demitted power in India in 1947, to the new one which emerged as a result of this agreement. Though the agreement apparently pertained to trade and cultural intercourse and facilitating pilgrimage to Kailash and Mansarovar, its actual impact on political relations was far beyond its scope. India in 1952 agreed to convert its representative office in Lhasa into a consulate had implicitly accepted Tibet as part of China. The present agreement only reconfirmed that status.[1] However, by giving up all the facilities enjoyed earlier, India lost its right to speak for Tibet or even to have direct contacts with the Lhasa government.

India's contacts with Tibet were guided by the various agreements that the British had entered into with Tibet since 1904 leading to the Simla Convention, 1914. If China did not sign the Simla Convention, it was primarily due to its objection to Article 9 which defined the boundary between India and Tibet and between Outer and Inner Tibet, by red and yellow lines respectively, on the map that was attached to the Convention. China insisted that since the borders were not discussed at the conference table, it would

---

[*] This chapter is based on A.S. Bhasin's book *India–China Relations, 1947–2000* (Geetika Publishers, New Delhi, 2018) and referred to as *India–China* in the Notes section.

1

not accept Article 9, but otherwise it had no objection in signing the Convention. The red line which defined the India–Tibet border came to be known by the name of the British officer, Henry McMahon, former Indian foreign secretary, who at the conference represented the British–Indian government.

The Simla Conference was essentially set up to redefine the relationship between China and Tibet which was the central point of Himalayan politics. Historically, the Himalayas had dominated the culture, politics and religion of the area, whereas twentieth-century politics centred around the commercial interests of the British. They had discovered that Tawang was a place of some importance as the distribution centre of goods from Lhasa and Eastern Tibet, from Bhutan, India and Assam from the fertile districts of north-eastern Tibet and the expectation that the commerce of this place would someday assume fairly large proportions.

China, however, had set its covetous eyes on Tibet for centuries in its attempt to make it part of the Chinese empire until it succeeded in occupying it for the first time in 1720. China maintained a resident mission in Lhasa headed by an Amban, who had a fairly large military escort stationed in Lhasa. His role was more than that of an envoy or ambassador. He was more akin to a governor since he assumed the authority to interfere in the day-to-day administration of the Tibetan government. It was not uncommon for the Tibetan officials to vie with each other in seeking his favours. However, his influence and authority varied from time to time, depending on the strength of the imperial court and his own propensity to pecuniary attractions. Sometimes his authority enhanced to an extent that he became the final arbiter in all matters of Tibetan administration including the Dalai Lama's succession.

In 1774, the governor general of India, Warren Hastings, had sent a mission under George Bogle to enter China via Tibet. While Bogle succeeded in persuading the Panchen Lama, the second-most important lama in Tibetan hierarchy heading the Tashilhunpo Monastery at Shigatse, China, to help him in his mission, he found the doors of China firmly locked and, thus, returned home without accomplishing his mission.

In 1876, after signing the Chefoo Convention or Yantai Treaty, which opened more Chinese ports for the British trade, the British made China agree to include a provision in the treaty authorising them to send an exploration mission from China to Tibet via India. But this failed since the Tibetan government had refused to accept the authority of China and so did not allow any British mission to enter Tibet. The British came face-to-face with the reality that Chinese writ did not run in Lhasa. To prevent the entry of foreigners in Tibet, Lhasa swore never to allow any foreign mission to enter its territory.[2]

The British were bent upon opening Tibet to their trade after establishing a protectorate over Sikkim and had no qualms in using coercion. This was also the time when the Russians were trying to penetrate into Tibet through their Buddhist contacts. The British were, however, determined to prevent it. It was Lord Curzon who had proposed direct relations with Tibet in 1903, disregarding China's supposed authority or its suzerainty over Tibet, which he characterized as 'constitutional fiction'—a political affectation which had only been maintained because of its convenience to both parties and insisted that relations should be established with the Dalai Lama. Lord Curzon noted:

> There are in the present circumstances of Tibet a special reason for insisting that Tibet herself shall be a prominent party to any new agreement. For the first time for nearly a century the country is under the rule of a Dalai Lama, who is neither an infant nor a puppet, but a young man, some twenty-eight years of age, who having survived the vicissitudes of a childhood, is believed to exercise a greater personal authority that any of his predecessors and to be de facto as well as de jure sovereign of the country. In other words, there is for the first time in modern history a ruler in Tibet with whom it is possible to deal instead of an obscure junta masked by the Chinese Amban.[3]

Colonel Younghusband's expedition in 1904 succeeded in breaking the Tibetan cordon sanitaire, but when the British occupied Lhasa, the Dalai Lama had to flee to Mongolia. The British did prevail but failed to get the Dalai Lama's signature on the Anglo–Tibetan Convention. Even the Chinese Amban refused to cooperate and sign. The British calculated that without the signature of either of them their control would remain fictional. Since the Dalai Lama had fled Tibet and was not available, a fresh agreement with China had become necessary which resulted in the Anglo–Chinese Convention of 1906. This Convention besides revising the terms of the Anglo–Tibetan Convention of 1904, set the terms afresh of British position in Lhasa. The most important part of this Convention was China's agreement not to permit any other power to interfere in Tibet, clarifying that while China was not a foreign power in relation to Tibet, Britain definitely was.[4] However, Viceroy Lord Minto had informed the Secretary of State on 13 July 1906 that 'in our view Tibet is a feudatory state under the suzerainty of China, but also possessed wide autonomous powers together with power to make treaties in respect of its frontiers, mutual trade and similar matters with coterminous states'.[5]

In the meantime, in the Anglo–Russian Convention of 1907 there was an agreement between the British and the Russians on their European spheres of influence. It too set their spheres of influence in Asia which was to China's advantage. Both the European powers agreed between them to deal with Tibet only through China, endorsing China's preeminent position in Tibet. The British officials posted in Tibet did demur but were rebuked by His Majesty's Government who insisted that 'Britain cannot have two foreign policies . . . be we right or wrong that is our policy'.[6]

The British policy of respecting the Chinese position in Tibet was largely influenced by British commercial interests in China, since the British minister in Peking (now Beijing), John Jordan, had advised London that undermining China in Tibet would prejudice British interest in China which would 'probably produce greater damage to their commercial interests in China than could ever be compensated by an increase in the value of Indo–Tibetan trade'.[7] That gave China full control of Tibet, free from any interference, from any of the two competing European powers.

The British officials posted in Tibet felt suffocated at the Chinese control, and in a change of strategy and taking advantage of the Dalai Lama's absence, they promoted the Panchen Lama. However, they did not get enough support from London and were rebuked by His

Majesty's Government (HMG) who called their action 'thoroughly dubious or even obnoxious'.[8]

The new Secretary of State for India, Lord Morley, further strengthened China's position in Tibet tying in with Viceroy Lord Minto's position that HMG were bound not to interfere in the internal administration of Tibet.[9]

Meanwhile, the Dalai Lama, in exile in Mongolia, felt homesick and was anxious to return to Lhasa. He went to Beijing to negotiate his return to Tibet. Empress Dowager issued an edict conferring upon him a new title and imperial instructions that he 'must be careful to obey the laws and ordinances of the Sovereign State and make known to all the goodwill of the Chinese Court; and he must admonish the Tibetan respectfully to observe the laws and learn the ways of rectitude.'[10]

As luck would have it, the Dalai Lama on return found a Chinese expeditionary force under General Zhao Er-Feng in Lhasa and fled again, this time to India. The British feared that China's occupation of Tibet would deprive them of a buffer between China and India. The Chinese were now deployed along the Himalayan ranges across the Indian border. Lord Minto made a recommendation to London to make a demarche in China, but was countermand by the British minister in Beijing, John Jordan, who said, 'Neither the facts as at present known to us nor the terms of the 1906 Convention would warrant a protest against possible change in the status quo or infringement of the spirit of our agreement with China or Tibet.'[11]

London's foreign policy had made China more assertive than before which created misgivings among the British in India, who now reacted with alarm, particularly when they found in May 1910 that China had occupied Rima and demanded taxes from the people. China too had ordered cutting a road through the tribal belt of Assam. Britain now saw the developments of a strategic threat to Assam, a noxious effect of 1907 Anglo–Russian Convention which had left Tibet at the mercy of China.[12]

The administrative changes that came about around this time favoured reconsideration of the old policy of leaving Tibet at the mercy of China. Viceroy Minto was replaced by Lord Hardinge in Calcutta and Marquess of Crewe replaced Secretary of State Lord Morley in

London. Both had found themselves quite uncomfortable with the policy followed by HMG so far. In a policy reappraisal, it was decided to use Tibet as a buffer between China and India, undoing the earlier policy of allowing China a free hand in Tibet.[13]

To initiate the desired changes, HMG in a memorandum on 12 August 1912, reminded Beijing of Yuan Shih-kai's assurance, when he was sworn as President of the newly promulgated Republic of China in 1911 that 'there was no intention of incorporating Tibet in China and previous treaties would be scrupulously observed'. He was warned that HMG would not tolerate any attempt to reduce Tibet to a client state of China which had independent treaty relations with Great Britain. It was the British who practically had reduced Tibet into a client state of China. Now the memorandum stressed the need for a written agreement between Britain, China and Tibet as a precondition for the recognition of the Chinese republic.[14]

China reacted to the memorandum with somewhat of a surprise and questioned the need for any new arrangement since the already negotiated treaties were working very well. China also reminded the British that it was they who had recognized the Chinese position in Tibet and had pledged not to intervene as long as the treaties were observed, and they were, in fact, being observed scrupulously. At this stage, China tried to further strengthen its position in Tibet by floating the concept of China being composed of five races—Chinese, Manchus, Mongols, Tibetans and Tartars who were joined in a democratic union and formed the territory of China.[15] While the Tibetans were not amused, the British perceived in this move, a threat to their north-eastern frontier.

Britain rejected the pretensions of China and was determined to implement its new policy of eliminating China from any role in Tibet. It decided to go ahead with its proposal for a conference with China and Tibet. That the border question would be part of the conference was not mentioned. The Secretary of State for India, Lord Crewe, calling China and Tibet as protagonists said on 28 July 1913, that unless something arose 'we shall be honest brokers, who will keep their eyes open with regard to those interests which I have described to your lordship'.[16]

In the tripartite Simla conference of 1914, China did participate, but as a reluctant party. Britain, however, successfully achieved its objective of pushing China out of Tibet. In the final document of the Convention, Article 9 was introduced along with a map with two lines—one red and one blue: the red line depicting the boundary between Tibet and India and the blue between China and Tibet. China objected to Article 9 and insisted on its removal since the borders were not discussed at the Conference. China was prepared to sign the Convention if Article 9 was removed. Since the British were not prepared to oblige China, the Chinese did not sign the Convention and even withdrew their initials which had been appended at the draft stage. The British minister John Jordan in a private letter to the Assistant Secretary of State in the Foreign Office, Sir Walter Langley, said he always worried about British commercial interest in China, and on 28 June 1914, before the Convention was signed said:

> [W]hether China signed or did not sign the Convention the future outlook seemed very unsatisfactory. If it signed, it would do so with a bad grace and with very little intention to observe it. If she refuses to sign, the position will be more acute and perhaps call for immediate action . . . Apart altogether from the effect such a step would have on our vast commercial and industrial interests in China.[17]

Given the Chinese reluctance to sign, the Secretary of State instructed Delhi that should China refuse to sign the convention, 'negotiations should definitely be terminated by Sir Henry'.[18]

Despite these instructions from London, McMahon found a way out to sign the convention along with Tibet without China appending its signatures. Consequently, after the convention had been signed, both the British and Tibetan representatives added a notation at the end depriving China of any of the privileges arising from this Convention. A joint communiqué to the effect was also issued by them.[19]

Following the Simla Convention, the British made several attempts to get China on board so that the relations between China and Tibet could be put on solid footing but to no avail. In 1921, Britain to induce China to sign the Convention, said that if China failed to sign, HMG would not feel unjustified 'in withholding any longer their recognition of the status of Tibet as an autonomous state under the suzerainty of China and intend dealing with Tibet, in future on this basis'.[20] Notwithstanding this, China continued to treat Tibet as under its jurisdiction by attempting to extend the jurisdiction of certain of its institutions over it unilaterally. For instance, Chinese cartographers 'persistently delineated Tibet as a province of China; China announced a proposal to open a branch of China's Central Bank in Tibet; a proposal to build a railway line into the heart of Tibet'; etc.[21]

For India, the most important outcome of the Simla Conference was the McMahon Line or the Red line marked on the map attached to the Convention, as the boundary between India and Tibet. The Tibetans having signed the Convention later demurred at the loss of Tawang, which now fell south of the new line. Since the British made no effort to occupy the new area, Tibet was happy to continue with its occupation. It even collected taxes and the local population continued to regard it as Tibetan territory.

The Simla Convention, 1914 was not published in the Aitchison's (an official collection of treaties and sanads relating to India and neighbouring countries complied by C.U. Aitchison), as was the rule, mainly because of the Chinese government's failure to ratify it, and nothing was done to give effect to it either. Many of the maps/atlases then published still showed the frontier of India along the administered border of Assam.[22]

Later, when it was decided to print the Simla Convention in Aitchison's compilation, there were deliberations to consider the McMahon Line as the boundary of India. The Assam governor, who was administratively responsible for the north-east frontier, in his letter No. 284-G.S. dated 7 May 1937 informed the Government of India that Tawang was undoubtedly Tibetan up to 1914 when it was ceded to India but that, though undoubtedly British it has been controlled by Tibet, and none of the inhabitants have any idea that they are not Tibetan subjects. He, therefore, expressed his apprehension that 'the continued exercise of jurisdiction by Tibet in

Tawang might enable China or, still worse, any other power which may in future be in a position to assert authority over Tibet, to claim prescriptive right over a part of the territory recognised as within India by the 1914 Convention'.[23]

To overcome any such eventuality in future, in a belated move, the Assam government was instructed to assert British control over Tawang either by actual tours, or by collecting revenue. The Assam government, however, felt it necessary that a more assertive course to affirm British authority be adopted, like collection of revenue, etc. A small expedition under Captain Lightfoot was finally sent to Tawang which was instructed that 'while there could be no possible doubt that the Indo–Tibetan boundary was definitely determined (by the McMahon Line), he was instructed to be scrupulously careful to give no impression that the matter can be reopened.'[24]

As for asserting British claim over Tawang, it was felt that Captain Lightfoot's presence in Tawang with an escort would itself be an assertion of British authority. Yet, he was cautioned that his 'conduct in all things should be such as may be calculated to cause least shock to Tibetan susceptibilities'.[25]

For whatever reasons, he was instructed to tell the locals that his mission was one of enquiry and not a final decision on the future of Tawang. It was a half-hearted approach. The Tibetan government however, lodged a protest with the Political Officer, Basil Gould, on the presence of Lightfoot in Tawang and asked for his withdrawal.[26]

Later in 1939, the acting Governor of Assam H.J. Twynam challenged the proposal to occupy Tawang, both on legal and political grounds and said, 'The fact that the Government of India had taken no step to affect to implement the McMahon Line from 1914 to 1938 must adversely affect its position both in equity and international law.'[27]

He, therefore, said since it was part of British policy to remain 'on good terms with Tibet' and an alternative should be considered before the government occupied 'an area, which has always been oriented towards Tibet ethnographically, politically and in religion' and which was under Tibetan administration. The alternative suggested was that the 'McMahon Line should be modified to run through Se la, a towering pass a few miles south of Tawang so that the monastery would be left in Tibet.'[28]

This decision that the British should allow Tawang to remain as Tibetan was approved by not only the Secretary of State for India, Leo Amery but also the British Foreign Secretary, Anthony Eden. Basil Gould, the Political Officer (Sikkim), on tour to Tibet was authorized to convey to Lhasa their decision that HMG would be 'willing to alter the frontier so as to run from the Se La not to the north of Tawang but to south of Tawang', which he conveyed to Lhasa while there. Copies of this memorandum were endorsed to the secretary to the Government of India in the External Affairs Department and the British Mission in Lhasa.[29]

However, no necessary amendments were carried out in the Simla Convention or the map attached to it until 1947 when the British demitted power in India. When India gained Independence in August 1947, though Tawang remained in Indian territory on the map, it was in fact under Tibetan occupation. Later in July 1948, the Government of India too, conveyed to Lhasa, that it would adjust the McMahon Line in the Tawang area in favour of Tibet.[30]

In early 1947, it was clear to the British in India that the time to pack up was not too far. Making a policy appraisal vis-à-vis Tibet, the British made a statement for the successor government and said on 8 April 1947:

[T]he conditions in which India's wellbeing be assured and the full evolution may be achieved for her inherent capacity to emerge, as a potent but benevolent force in world affairs—particularly in Asia—demand not merely the development of internal unity and strength but also the maintenance of friendly relations with her neighbours. To prejudice her relations with so important a power as China by aggressive support of unqualified Tibetan independence (for which, whatever may have been the situation earlier there has in the past year or two, been little sign of ardour in Lhasa), is therefore a policy with few attractions. It follows that while the Government of India are glad to recognise and wish to see Tibetan autonomy maintained, they are not prepared to do more than encourage this in a friendly manner and are certainly not disposed to take any initiative which might bring India into conflict with China on this issue. The attitude they propose to take may best be described as that of a benevolent spectator, ready at all times—should opportunity occur—to use their good offices to further a mutually satisfactory settlement between China and Tibet.[31]

However, about the McMahon Line which had been marked as the India–Tibet frontier in 1914 at Simla, it said:

[T]he Government of India stand by the McMahon Line and will not tolerate incursions into India . . . They would however, at all times be prepared to discuss in a friendly way with China and Tibet any rectification of the frontier that might be urged on reasonable ground by any of the parties to the *abortive* Simla Conference.[32]

There was a contradiction in the McMahon Line. In the Memorandum of 1944, it had been officially conveyed to Lhasa that it would be amended in favour of Lhasa. A reiteration of the McMahon Line, now as border, was qualified by a 'discussion for rectification' of the line and the conference of which it was a product was described as 'abortive'.[33] If the conference was abortive, then the fate of any decision taken also becomes uncertain.

An Independent India which inherited the rights and obligations of the British in Tibet treated the McMahon Line as its boundary even if Tawang (renamed North-East Frontier Agency by India) was in Tibetan occupation. Prime Minister of India Pandit Jawaharlal Nehru said in Parliament on 20 November 1950 that the McMahon Line, defined by the Simla Convention of 1914 'is our boundary and that is our boundary—map or no map'. He added, 'we stand by that boundary and we will not allow anybody to cross that boundary.'[34] This statement of the prime minister was unmindful of the fact that Tawang was in Tibetan occupation. It was also in the face of the prime minister's other statement on 30 December 1949 at the meeting of senior officers that 'China had never accepted the provisions of the 1914 Convention' which created doubts about the Indian boundary with Tibet.[35]

It is important to note that the McMahon Line was not a scientifically drawn line since McMahon had used a pen with a thick nib without conducting any surveys. Henry McMahon, who drew the line, later in 1935 delivering a lecture in London at the Royal Society for Encouragement of Art had said, 'For want of accurate local knowledge and absence of detailed surveys, rendered it impossible to define large portion of it [McMahon Line], except in a general term.'[36]

Although the line was drawn on the basis of then available information, McMahon himself had not ruled out the possibility of amending the boundary later, in the light of further information becoming available to either party.[37]

The British, as would be seen, in handling relations with Tibet and China, and between the countries as well, had followed dichotomous policies, which they left behind as their legacy. They were the most powerful political entity in South Asia and had enforced their will on the weak neighbouring native states in disregard to any established policy line. With the British leaving India, the iron hand had disappeared.

Interestingly, Kuomintang China, or the nationalist China which had come to power with the 1911 Chinese revolution now began asserting the rights that they earlier had in Tibet, which were on hold till the British ruled India. The Chinese vice foreign minister, George Yeh told the Indian Ambassador in Nanking, K.P.S. Menon, that it would like the 'abrogation or modification of unequal treaties' signed earlier with the British and that the commercial treaty under consideration would apply to Tibet as well.[38]

It's interesting that the British in their last days of empire had advised India that given the participation of a Tibetan delegation in a session of the Chinese National Assembly, if China and Tibet worked out some modus vivendi between them, India should neither object nor interfere.[39]

The Chinese had objected to Tibet's invitation at the Asian Relations Conference and also to the map at the conference showing Tibet outside China.[40]

As the British left India on 15 August 1947, Tibet assumed itself to be an independent country and wrote to Prime Minister Nehru on 16 October 1947 asking for a return of their territories which had been gradually included in India in the past. The territories claimed were extensive—Sikkim, Darjeeling, Bhutan, Ladakh, etc., 'on this side of the River Ganges . . . up to the boundary of Yarkhim'.[41] India, however, dismissed the Tibetan claims. Later, Nehru told Zhou Enlai, the Chinese Premier, that if Tibetan demands were accepted, India's boundary would literally be on the River Ganga and the Government of India could hardly countenance such a fantastic claim.[42]

Nehru continued to welcome communist China's victories in the civil war but also harboured reservations on China's impact on Tibet and India's north-eastern frontier and other regions where Tibetan culture, language and religion prevailed. As the civil war progressed and complete victory of the communists appeared certain, Nehru welcomed the victories disregarding former Ambassador to Nationalist China, K.M. Panikkar's apprehensions that new China would revive its historical claims on Sikkim, Nepal and Bhutan and even repudiate the McMahon Line.[43] The foreign secretary, K.S. Menon, too, was apprehensive about India's borders with Tibet, which were based on the Simla Agreement. He said:

> [I]t is true that we are not now in a position to uphold, by force or by diplomacy Tibetan independence; but it is no use blinking the fact that if we proceed to treat a Chinese invasion of Tibet 'an internal affair of China, we shall be executing a volte face and lending ourselves to the reproach that we have backed out of solemn engagements.[44]

Even Political Officer Hareshwar Dayal from Gangtok had warned, 'occupation or the domination of Tibet by a potentially hostile and possibly aggressive Communist power should be a threat to the security of India.'[45]

Nehru had ruled out the political officer's suggestion to hold Chumbi Valley and leverage it for Tibet. He had already on 9 July 1949 ruled out such an action.[46] His apprehension was if we were not in a position to give Tibet necessary support, this might in fact give the communists an excuse for its absorption.[47] Nehru's pussyfooting on Tibet kept the officials worried, particularly Hareshwar Dayal, who was located nearest the area which would be affected. In his letter, mincing no words, Dayal told New Delhi, 'communist domination of Tibet would cause nervousness and unrest among the border people along the whole of India's northern frontier from Ladakh to Assam and policing of that frontier which has hither to required negligible military effort and expenditure would assume immediate practical importance . . .'[48]

Not stopping at that, Dayal tried his best, though unsuccessfully, to convince Delhi that 'India's interest in Tibetan autonomy was essentially for its own security'.[49]

Just before the founding of the PRC, Tibet invited the wrath of the communist China by 'their reckless and suicidal step' of expelling the Chinese Amban from Lhasa.[50] The Chinese not only accused Tibet but also India as an 'accomplice' in his expulsion.

Until India recognized communist China, in China's perception, Nehru was a lackey of the British and Americans representing imperialist interests. China even found faults with the Indian foreign policy particularly toward its neighbours and referring to Bhutan, angrily commented:

> [S]uzerainty stands for the dark vassal system and protective system which is another name of foreign oppression, enslavement . . . the Nehru government has no legal right to announce its protectorate over Bhutan. The United Nations should examine this matter . . . Nehru and company are openly engineering a cleavage between different peoples in China undermining their unity and interfering in their internal affairs by declaring in the name of foreign country that Tibet has now recognised Chinese suzerainty.[51]

In another article in the *People's Daily*, Foreign Secretary, K.P.S. Menon saw irredentist tendencies which the 'Chinese government had always shown and which the new Chinese government may be expected to prosecute, whenever they get an opportunity'.[52] On 19 October 1949, Mao Tse-Tung in a message to the Communist Party of India said, 'Like free China, a free India will one day emerge in a socialist and people's democratic family; that day will end the imperialist reactionary era in the history of mankind.' Delhi was not unaware of China's suspicion that India was acting as a Trojan horse for the UK and the USA.[53]

In the seventeen-point agreement between China and Tibet signed in May 1951, Tibet was practically converted into a Chinese colony. China set about tightening its hold on Tibet. As a first step it looked into Tibet's contacts with other countries, which had become incongruous with its new status as part of China. It found that Tibet by virtue of Article 1 of the Nepal–Tibet Treaty of 1856 was paying an annual tribute of Rs 10,000 and it had already been paid up to 1952. When the tribute did not arrive in 1953, Kathmandu reminded Lhasa. The latter told Kathmandu to refer the matter to Beijing and that was the end of it.[54]

However, Tibet's contacts with India were too deep and all-embracing to be dismissed so easily. India had two permanent trade agencies at Gyantse and Yatung, and a seasonal one at Gartok. It ran hospitals, operated post and telegraph facilities, resthouses and guesthouses, and had a military escort stationed at Gyantse for the security of its establishments. It too had a representative office in Lhasa, but its status was not determined officially. As China occupied Tibet, Panikkar, the Indian Ambassador in Beijing, had warned Delhi that China could revive its old claims on Nepal, Bhutan and Sikkim. It was also apprehended both by Panikkar and Dayal in Gangtok that China might denounce the McMahon Line which India regarded its frontier with Tibet.

Nehru's discussions with Foreign Secretary K.P.S. Menon, Ambassador Panikkar and Political Officer Dayal had resulted in the PM acknowledging that Tibet's autonomy lacked international recognition and China's refusal to accept the 1914 Simla Convention were impediments for India to bat on Tibet's behalf. Nehru, therefore, issued instructions that nothing should be done to foster Chinese accusations on this count.[55] Friendship with China had become the cornerstone of Nehru's policy and he said, 'I am convinced of the importance of India–China friendship from the short- and long-term point of view.' He also insisted that India would stand by the

McMahon Line. Stating the logic of this policy, Nehru had said 'our present policy is primarily based on the avoidance of world war and secondly, the maintenance of honourable and peaceful relations with China'.[56]

Nehru was upbeat about China but wasn't sure of what China would do next in Tibet. Putting his faith in Chinese good sense he expected China to be benign toward Tibet. His dichotomous thinking made him believe that the balance of power was being disrupted in the vicinity of India. Communist China suddenly appeared to him to be different from the Kuomintang China, which had not created security problems. Nehru was doubtful about the Himalayas acting as a barrier.[57] As stated above, the status of India's representative's office in Lhasa was not officially recognized. He was supposed to be located in Gyantse and would visit Lhasa as and when required for official work. Over time, he had settled in Lhasa and the Tibetan government took an indulgent view and had acquiesced in India treating Gyantse as its official representative office in Lhasa.

It is worth pointing out again that when India attained Independence, the area called Tawang while shown on the map to be in India, was physically in Tibetan possession and India had in July 1948, like the British in 1944, conveyed to Lhasa that the McMahon Line would be adjusted in the Tawang area in favour of Tibet.[58] Communist China after occupying Tibet was negotiating with Tibet for an agreement ending its separate identity. Nehru balked and said 'our frontier itself may be challenged as it had been challenged by the previous Government'.[59] Yet he acknowledged that 'our policy towards China is of greater importance to us than our policy towards almost any other country'.[60]

India's statements that 'they never had nor now have any political or territorial ambitions in Tibet' and its desire to stabilize India–China border was not only welcomed in Beijing but were taken as an assurance that India would acquiesce China's takeover of Tibet without much fuss. China too had made it clear that it would not discuss Tibet with any other country since it was its internal problem. It left little space for India to intervene in matters related to Tibet.[61]

India finally realized the strategic importance of Tawang in the changed circumstances. As China–Tibet negotiations in Beijing were progressing, India feared that with the occupation of Tibet by China, the frontier of China would reach the plains of Assam, occupied Tawang in April 1951 setting aside Tibetan protests.[62]

In a show of friendship towards China, India without due diligence agreed to the Chinese suggestion to convert its representative office in Lhasa into a consulate and reciprocally allowed China to set up a consulate in Mumbai.[63] When the mission converted to a consulate, India's old relationship with Tibet became anachronistic.[64] Girija Shankar Bajpai, former Secretary General in the Ministry of External Affairs and the then Governor of Mumbai was worried at the very idea of a Chinese consulate in Mumbai. His concern was the impact that it would have on the large population of industrial workers of the city and 'the militant proletariat of communist persuasion'.[65]

Regarding the military escort stationed at Gyantse, Nehru had said 'there was no doubt that we will have to withdraw it, if it became necessary'.[66]

As India converted its representative office in Lhasa into a consulate, it came under the jurisdiction of the Indian Embassy in Beijing and ipso facto India accepted Chinese sovereignty over Tibet. Every Chinese action in Tibet hereafter became China's internal affairs and India lost the right to speak for Tibet. It too resulted in ending the status enjoyed by the political officer in Tibet, as a supervisory officer even when stationed in Gangtok. China now let it be known to the Indian officials in Lhasa that henceforth they could deal with the Tibetan officials only through the Chinese Foreign Bureau.[67]

On the question of Tibet, when Panikkar told Zhou on 13 February 1952 of India's desire for a fair settlement, Zhou avoiding a direct reply only assured him that he saw no difficulty 'in safeguarding economic and cultural interests of India in Tibet'.[68] Panikkar in his report to Delhi said he did not 'allude to the question of frontiers or relations with Bhutan, nor did Zhou raise it'.[69] On 11 July 1952, China had in its note to India described the situation left by the British in Tibet as a 'scare in the course of their aggression against China' and that the privileges that had 'arisen from the unequal treaties were no longer in existence'.[70] On 18 July, the director, Asia Department in the Chinese Foreign Office, reiterated that 'we want to make it clear that we do not recognise old British unequal treaties and wanted to set up relations between new India and new China in Tibet on a new basis'.[71]

Earlier on 11 February 1952 Panikkar in a conversation with the Chinese vice minister (foreign secretary) had said that India desired a settlement on Tibet satisfactory to both the countries in safeguarding their rights and interests.[72]

Worried about the so-called unequal treaties, China was never tired of repeating that they were no longer in existence. Zhou speaking to Panikkar on 15 June 1952 had presumed that India had no intention of claiming 'special rights' arising from unequal treaties and was prepared to negotiate a new permanent relationship safeguarding its legitimate interests and added that China did not propose to end abruptly 'the rights which were in existence like posts and telegraph, trade marts, etc., as this course would create a vacuum'.[73]

Panikkar had assured Zhou that India had already 'expressed willingness to negotiate a settlement on all points'. In view of Panikkar's assurance, Zhou suggested that as an immediate step, China wanted an agreement in principle about the nature of India's Lhasa mission and acceptance by both the sides that the technical questions relating to the withdrawal of army escort, taking over of posts and telegraphs etc., might be negotiated separately at a suitable time.[74] Panikkar explained to the prime minister that the 'question of boundary was not discussed and no allusion was made to any political problem in their conversation'. Nehru felt it odd that Zhou did not refer to the frontier question and stressed that 'we attach more importance to this than to other matters'. He insisted that India was also interested in the frontiers of Nepal, Bhutan and Sikkim.[75]

Pinning the responsibility for Zhou not raising the frontier question, Panikkar reminded the PM before his own departure for Beijing to take up his assignment, that Nehru had instructed him 'to avoid raising directly the question of frontiers as it might give them an opening and might indicate our own doubts'.[76]

Panikkar, in view of this, advised Nehru that 'we must stick to the position that the frontier had been defined and there was nothing for us to discuss. As such he felt 'it would be legitimate to presume that Zhou Enlai's silence on frontiers and not having even once alluded to Sikkim or Bhutan at any time even indirectly during conversation, would mean his acquiescence in, if not acceptance of our position'.[77] Confirming Panikkar's presumption of Chinese acceptance, Nehru in a reply on 18 June said 'in view of what you say, it will be desirable not to raise the question of our frontiers at this stage'.[78]

New Delhi, however, asked the Embassy to inform the Chinese Government that they had already been sensitized about the frontier which had been 'demarcated' along the McMahon Line and they had 'at no time objected or suggested any claim on (our) side of the McMahon Line.[79] The McMahon Line and Tibet had become synonymous for the Chinese and both were important to Beijing. Mao had already underlined the importance of Tibet to China when he said that 'although Tibet's population is small, its international position is extremely important and we must occupy it'.[80]

A note had been delivered to China on 2 August 1952 containing seven issues which needed settlement in Tibet. This note had excluded the question of frontiers.[81]

Panikkar, explaining to Bajpai, the Governor of Mumbai, the reason for excluding the frontier question, had said it was the prime minister's decision. Panikkar insisted that India's stand on the frontiers had been publicly and unequivocally stated and if China had any different opinion, it was for China to point it out. Pointing out that China was in 'effective occupation' of Tibet now for over a year and 'had not even alluded to the question of boundaries or given the impression that it would like that question to be reopened'. Panikkar further insisted the delay in this case operates to 'our advantage'. He believed that 'our reopening the issue would provide the Chinese with an opportunity either to accept the treaty which has been signed with Tibet or refusal of it with an offer to negotiate'. Panikkar did not envisage that China would accept the frontier as it existed, since every previous Chinese government had refused to accept it. And negotiating the boundary question afresh would not be 'advantageous to us'.[82] Unhappy, Bajpai persisted and stressed the need to make China accept the frontiers between 'our two countries unequivocally'. He advised that a note was formally presented to China detailing the Indian frontier with Tibet and added 'should the Chinese accept our position that would be in our interest and should they not accept, it would enable us to know where we stood in relation to China which might make us sad but leave us wiser'.[83]

In the meantime, the Chinese had no qualms in obstructing the day-to-day functioning of the trade agencies and the Lhasa Mission in whatever manner they thought fit and feasible. Strict restrictions were imposed on the free movement of Indian personnel. As opposed to the facilities enjoyed by the Chinese agencies in India, the Indian officers were afforded no occasion to move around or have any contact, even of a cultural nature, with Tibetans. The Indian Trade Agency at Gyantse, which had been washed away in floods in 1954, had not been granted permission for reconstruction for years. The Indian trade agencies also experienced a variety of small but irritating difficulties in their functioning in such matters as the hiring of transport and communication facilities. The two Indian wireless operators working for the Indian Representative Office were arrested and not released despite protracted correspondence. Even pilgrims were discouraged to proceed to Mount Kailash and the Mansarovar Lake.[84]

The matter came to a head when a fresh army detachment arrived in Tibet to relieve the earlier incumbents as per past practice, but the Chinese did not allow the turnaround to take place. China instead asked India to withdraw the military escort altogether since it had become incongruous with Tibet's new status as part of China, which was an independent and sovereign country. Faced with this unfortunate situation, the Ministry of External Affairs had sensitized Nehru of all the unsavoury happenings in Tibet and how the Indian establishments were being harassed. Reading through the note, while he decided to write to the Chinese premier for settlement about various issues bedevilling relations between the two countries, Nehru said, 'We undoubtedly have to withdraw our military escort. If the Chinese Government want us to remove our post and telegraph offices on the trade routes, we shall have to agree. For the present we need not raise the question of frontiers, but this will have to be brought up in a larger settlement.'[85]

Nehru was keen that nothing was done on the Indian side which might vitiate the atmosphere for the settlement of pending matters. A group of prominent Indians had decided to observe 'Tibet Day' by organizing meetings and adopt resolutions expressing sympathy for the people of Tibet in their 'temporary subjugation' and warning the people of India of the 'danger that lurks on the Indian borders' by the presence of the Chinese Army in Tibet. Nehru to avoid any complications with China asked Congressmen to stay away from this committee, since it would be an unfriendly act to China and was against the policy India was pursuing during these years.[86]

From Nehru's perspective, there were continuing global and regional tensions in 1953 despite Soviet leader Joseph Stalin's death, and the end of the Korean War had made it even more important for India to seek peace with China. But thanks to India's Neutral Nations Repatriation Commission (NNRC) role in Korea, Sino–Indian relations were not quite happy, as the Indian embassy in Beijing put it.[87]

The prime minister took up the matter with Chinese Premier Zhou on 1 September 1953 in a note in which he expressed his anxiety to 'come to a final settlement about pending matters so as to avoid any misunderstanding and friction at any time'. He referred to the note which had been delivered to Chinese Foreign Office on 2 August 1952 'about all pending matters which needed settlement'. Nehru expressed Indian willingness to discuss all pending matters and to modify certain practices and even to remove some of them, if they were considered affecting the dignity of China. The seven issues contained in the 2 August note were: (i) status of the Indian Mission in Lhasa; (ii) trade agencies at Gyantse and Yatung; (iii) the seasonal trade agency at Gartok; (iv) the right of Indians to trade in Tibet; (v) post and telegraph offices, (vi) military escort at Gyantse and (vii) pilgrimage. The question of frontiers stood excluded.[88]

Nehru had in his communication to Zhou suggested that all these matters were considered together, since piecemeal consideration of each problem would not lead to a satisfactory solution. He conceded that friction did crop up from time to time even on petty matters. Giving detailed instances of harassment of Indian establishments in Tibet, Nehru suggested discussions at the earliest in Delhi or Beijing on all such matters affecting relations between the two countries.[89]

Another note also drafted by Nehru on the lines of his note to Zhou was handed over to the Chinese Embassy in Delhi. This note too had reference of the note of 2 August 1952 detailing seven issues requiring settlement. This was in line with what the Chinese had told Ambassador Panikkar a few days earlier on 18 July 1952 that 'we want to make it clear that we do not recognize old British unequal treaties and wanted to set up relations between new India and new China in Tibet on a new basis.[90]

Regarding the army detachment which had already arrived to relieve the earlier one, the MEA told the Chinese Embassy that since the prime minister had already proposed discussions on all pending matters and a military escort was one of them, it would be desirable to wait for a reply from Premier Zhou. The MEA also noted that the PM had in his minutiae had said should the Chinese insist 'we shall undoubtedly have to withdraw our military escort' and similarly other facilities like post and telegraphs etc.[91] Joint Secretary in-charge of Chinese affairs in the MEA, T.N. Kaul, in his note to the foreign secretary advised withdrawal of troops straight away since 'our aim is to settle the bigger issues and we should not let smaller issues stand in the way and jeopardise the chance of a settlement of former'.[92] The foreign secretary after due consideration of the pros and cons of the Chinese stand said:

> [S]ince we have made some suggestion about a larger settlement and are convinced that this is the right way of handling this question, we should adhere to these suggestions and should act in accordance with them until a reply has been received to PM's message.[93]

Zhou in reply had attributed the present problems as 'vestiges' of the British aggression against China in the past, for which the Government of India was not responsible. He now suggested talks on these matters in December 1953, while making it clear that

Special rights which arose from unequal treaties between the British Government and the old Chinese Government were no longer in existence. Therefore, the relations between new China and the Government of India in the Tibetan region of China should be built up anew through negotiations.[94]

Nehru acknowledging Zhou's message said, 'I do not wish at this stage to go into the details of all pending matters which were mentioned in a note presented to your Excellencies' Government on the 2 August 1952 at Peking.'[95]

The most significant feature of Nehru's communications was overemphasis on the 2 August note which had listed seven issues and excluded the frontier question. This made it obvious to the Chinese that India, for whatever reason, did not want to discuss the frontier question.

Referring to Zhou's remarks about old treaties, Nehru told Ambassador Raghavan that Zhou's message raised 'some controversial points and there are a number of inaccuracies in it. However, I have not discussed these in my reply, as they are relatively matters of detail'.[96]

Having said that, the PM in a note to the secretary general and the foreign secretary, maintaining the earlier stance about frontiers, said, 'It is our well-declared policy that the [McMahon] Line is a settled one and not open to argument or discussion except perhaps with regard to minor tracts here and there which might be doubtful.'[97]

Nehru insisted Indian policy towards China was based on friendliness, coexistence and firmness with regard to any interference over India's basic right, but clarified 'the basic right is the preservation of frontier'. Nehru felt it 'exceedingly unlikely' that we would get back the territory which was the old trade route between Sinkiang and Kashmir and held by Pakistan.[98]

After the PM proposed discussions on Tibet, the Chinese had the very next month conducted high-level discussions with the Tibetan officials in Lhasa and examined records of the India–Tibet boundary to prepare for proposed discussions on the frontiers. The Consul General

A.K. Sen informed Delhi that the Chinese had told the Tibetans of their determination to repudiate the 1914 Simla Convention.[99]

As the groundwork for the discussions was being debated in the MEA, Panikkar, who after relinquishing his charge in Beijing had taken over as India's Ambassador in Cairo, volunteered a suggestion based on the policy he had pursued with the acquiescence of Nehru in Tibet. His suggestion was that during the forthcoming talks with China the frontier question should not be allowed to be opened. Should the Chinese insist on discussing the frontier question 'we must be prepared to break the negotiations'. He was confident that the Chinese were in 'no position to force the issue'. A major part of his letter was devoted to India's Bhutan policy where he advised that if China attempted to open diplomatic relations with Bhutan, it should be warned that 'any attempt on their part to open diplomatic relations with Bhutan will be considered by us as an unfriendly act.'[100] In another letter addressed to the foreign secretary, Panikkar, said in his judgement 'in the next three or four years China will not take any decisive step which can alienate us.'[101] If this was Panikkar's understanding of communist Chinese after his stay in Beijing for more than two years, one can regretfully say that his understanding was not only poor but disastrous and it put a question mark on Nehru's judgement of people around him since he went on entrusting him with more important and challenging jobs.

The Ministry of External Affairs, in working out a brief for the discussions in Beijing, recognized that the question of frontiers was 'obviously important'.[102] Yet, it was ruled out as an issue since the prime minister had taken the position both in Parliament and in public that there was no frontier question to discuss, and the frontier had been finally settled along the McMahon Line. Panikkar's letter had strengthened this position further. The brief prepared by the MEA accordingly did not propose discussions on the frontier question with China. In preparing the brief and in chalking out the strategy for the talk, the ministry went into some essential details. Since there were doubts about the McMahon Line, the ministry taking cognizance of the legal advice, recognized that since China had not ratified the Simla Convention, it could refuse to stand by it. Aksai Chin in the western sector and Tawang and Walong in the eastern sector were listed among the disputed areas. Surprisingly, while discussing frontiers, only the McMahon Line was being talked about. There were two other sectors that were ignored—the central sector bordering Punjab–Himachal and Uttar Pradesh, and the western (eastern) sector along the Aksai China–Ladakh border which was undefined in the Survey of India maps. But somehow, talking of frontiers, the emphasis remained on the Eastern Sector or the McMahon Line alone.[103]

As it happened, the new Chinese communist government in Article 55 of their 'Common Program' (which was their Constitution then) had already laid down that it 'shall examine the treaties and agreements concluded between the Kuomintang and foreign governments and shall recognise, abrogate, revise or re-negotiate them according to their respective contents'. It was the ministry's conclusion that this by itself did not imply that the new Chinese government would abrogate all the previous treaties unless expressly so done. India failed to realize that for China, the Simla Convention did not even exist since they had neither signed it nor ratified it. Unfortunately, the Government of India ignored this simple fact and went on relying on it for its claim on the McMahon Line.[104]

Delhi having decided not to discuss the border question remained extra cautious that no mention of frontiers was made even by any innocuous or incidental reference. Even a formulation that 'happily there are no territorial disputes between India and China' was ruled out for use by the Indian side out of fear it might provoke China to bring up the frontier question.[105] That the Chinese had already made it clear that the existing situation of the Sino–Indian frontier in Tibet was the vestiges of British aggression and 'no longer in existence', was sidetracked.[106] The brief prepared by the MEA finally suggested that should the Chinese raise the frontier issue, India should respond that 'the frontier is clearly defined' but minor changes could be considered only after China had accepted 'our present frontiers'.[107]

Ignoring all the negatives, the brief on balance felt 'it would seem best for us not to raise the question of frontiers ourselves unless the Chinese raise it and if they do so,

> [W]e should tell them firmly that there is nothing to discuss on the
> subject as our frontier is well established and clearly defined. On the
> possibility of China insisting on discussions, we should be prepared
> to break the negotiations, and walk out, as Panikkar had suggested.[108]

Other issues like functioning of trade agencies, India–Tibet trade etc.,
were not difficult questions since the prime minister had already said
that India would be ready to modify or give up altogether anything
which affected the dignity of China. The trade was not of much
significance and it was the Tibetans who were importing most of the
essential consumer goods from India. In comparison, India's imports
were confined to wool, Yak tails and borax.

Since China had two trade agencies in India against India's three
and if China were to demand another on a reciprocal basis, both
Gangtok and Leh were to be avoided due to their sensitive locations.

The delegation that the Chinese lined up for the negotiations
comprised Chang Han Fu, the Vice Minister of Foreign Affairs as
the leader, Director Asia Department, Chen Chia-Kang and an
assistant from the Chinese Foreign Bureau in Lhasa, Yang Kung-Shu.
Incidentally, the Chinese delegation comprised only Han Chinese
and no Tibetans, although all issues to be discussed related to Tibet
alone. It was not even clear to India whether the Dalai Lama was
aware of the impending talks on Tibet. It was on 27 January 1954
that Nehru asked the consulate in Lhasa to discreetly inform the
Dalai Lama, 'orally and very confidentially' that the talks on Tibet
were being conducted in Beijing and it was India's hope 'with the
agreement, we shall be able to continue our existing close relations
with Tibet.'[109] The trend of discussions in Beijing left no doubt
about China's determination to cut India off from Tibet altogether
and yet Nehru, unrealistically, hoped to continue the existing level of
relations with Lhasa.

On the Indian side, Ambassador Raghavan was asked to lead the
Indian delegation. Both T.N. Kaul, head of the eastern division and Dr
Gopalachari, deputy director, Historical Division of the MEA, were
deputed from Delhi to assist him. Dr Gopalachari was included for his
domain knowledge.

The negotiations opened in Beijing on 31 December 1953 at the residence of Premier Zhou Enlai who in his inaugural address took credit for starting talks in December itself 'as promised' and made a significant remark that:

> [T]he Chinese Government had already laid down the principles in 1949 [referring to Common Program] that all outstanding problems between China and other countries could be solved on the basis of mutual respect for territorial integrity, nonaggression and non-interference in internal affairs so as to enable peaceful coexistence.

He added that Prime Minister Nehru's government and the people of India feel the same way. On the basis of these principles, all outstanding questions between us which 'are ripe for settlement can be resolved smoothly'. He did acknowledge that there were bound to be problems between neighbours with a long common frontier, but on principles already mentioned by him 'all questions can be solved smoothly and speedily [and] we can show to the world that questions between Asian countries can be solved on a new basis and thus create a record'.[110]

Ambassador Raghavan who was the leader of the Indian delegation in his reply said: '[N]o doubt under Premier's guidance talks would be successful and satisfactory and *would settle all outstanding questions between the two countries in Tibet Region of China.*'

However, separately and informally, he hinted that 'outstanding issues between them were neither big nor difficult and capable of resolving speedily'.[111]

Zhou had made two significant remarks in his speech. By referring to the 'Common Program' he warned India that China did not take old treaties at their face value and only those 'outstanding issues, which were ripe for settlement' would be decided by the two delegations, notwithstanding India's expectation of settlement of all outstanding issues. There was no clarity on the Chinese side on the issues which were 'ripe for settlement' or for the Indian side, what was meant by 'all outstanding issues'. As far as India was concerned it had listed the 'seven outstanding issues' in its note of 2 August 1952, also referred by Nehru in his note of 1 September 1953 to Zhou.[112]

On 2 January 1954, at the first meeting between officials of the two sides, India, elaborating its agenda, confined itself to the same issues as already conveyed. As such for India, there was no other issue to discuss. The Chinese too had made India agree to their suggestion that during the course of negotiations neither side would issue any communiqué. The fact that China was discussing for the first time its historical relations with India, which held all the aces, implied there was substantial interest worldwide how the two countries would handle their negotiations, particularly China's behaviour. It may be recalled the US particularly had been watching developments in Tibet from the very beginning and had shown interest in helping India deal with China on the question of Tibet. India had a tough time keeping the US at bay. Now by making India agree in not issuing any communiqué during the negotiations, China found itself free to put India under pressure in submitting to its whims and fancies. The outside world and even the Indian pubic remained unaware of what was cooking in Beijing.

At India's request, the Chinese enumerated the principles, which Zhou had referred to in his inaugural speech would facilitate negotiations. They were:

1. Mutual respect for each other's territorial integrity and sovereignty;
2. Mutual non-aggression;
3. Mutual non-interferences in each other's internal affairs;
4. Equality and mutual benefit, and
5. Peaceful coexistence.[113]

It was emphasized that if these principles were adhered to, 'all pending questions that were ripe for settlement would be settled'.[114] The Five Principles of coexistence were unexceptional and were accepted (ratified) without debate or reservations. These principles became the template of India–China relations, which were included in the final agreement following the negotiations, and thereafter repeated ad nauseam in various statements. The Chinese can legitimately claim their authorship.

Soon India found China raising searching question about its trade agencies, their activities and facilities, including the number of Indian shops in Tibet. The cumulative effect of all this soon became evident when the trade agent at Gyantse requested both the political officer and the Ministry of External Affairs for action to ask the Chinese to 'conduct themselves with grace and friendliness' since the impact of negotiations together with Chinese propaganda was creating panic among local employees.[115]

India soon found China raising questions as if they were conducting an inquest in India's presence in Tibet. Normal discussions for any agreement are futuristic—how the relations would be conducted henceforth—of course, based on the past practices. But one party does not go into the intricacies of the relationship to tire out the other party. The Indian delegation was not prepared for the range of questions the Chinese raised, which not only kept the delegation on its toes all the time but also the Ministry of External Affairs in Delhi. The details asked by the Chinese were often hard to provide. The Chinese too, demanded their trade agencies at all sorts of places in India whether justified or not, apart from facilities which too were in excess of what they had made available to India or what was offered. For instance, China insisted that the Han Chinese nationals trading in Tibet should have the facility of visa and passport-free travel to India like ethnic Tibetans.

After more than a month of negotiations, nothing seemed finalized. The Indian delegation found its patience exhausted and complained to Chen Chia-Kang, Asia Director, that China had widened the scope of negotiations 'too far' and the Indian delegation was not authorized to discuss new points raised by the Chinese with the result that the viewpoints of the two delegations were too divergent. India said the delegation would probably have to go back to Delhi for fresh instructions. Chen, pretending to be taken by surprise, responded 'neither we nor you can show face to the world unless we have agreement on principle of equality and mutual benefit . . .' The Indian delegation responded:

[Y]our principles of equality should not be applied mathematically just as thought of Mao is not Marxism in abstraction, abstract sketch application to concrete conditions in China. We have come here to stabilize existing conditions with your agreement and without infringing China's sovereignty but you have raised new issues not based on existing facts. India cited as unreal their demand for trade agency at Almora and trade marts at places like Shillong, Dehradun, Simla etc., and permission for all Chinese nationals to enter India as traders.[116]

Taking the question of Han Chinese entering India without visa and passport, the Chinese insisted that if the Han Chinese residents in Tibet were not given the same facilities as the Tibetans, it would amount to discrimination between two classes of citizens of the same country. After much discussion, the relevant article was worded so as to not show any discrimination and yet accommodate the Hans. It referred to 'traders of both the countries known to be customarily and specifically engaged in trade between India and Tibet region of China'.

Whether China too was as accommodative as India, was soon put to test when India raised the question of trade between Tibet and Ladakh. There was traditionally trade between Ladakh and Tibet which had been disrupted in recent years. Kushak Bakula, the Venerable Lama of Ladakh had met Prime Minister Nehru when the negotiations for Tibet were about to begin and had requested the revival of the traditional biennial trade missions from Ladakh to Lhasa and continuance of the facilities for training of Ladakhi lamas in Tibetan monasteries. The prime minister had asked the Indian delegation to (consider) keep these questions in mind and make a general reference to the Ladakh trade with Tibet without going into the question of exchange of missions.[117]

As the question of Ladakh's trade with Tibet was raised, the use of two passes namely, Rodok and Rawang, which directly linked the two regions, also came up. The reaction of the Chinese took India by surprise for they were rather reluctant to enter into discussions on this question.[118] When pressed by India, the Chinese left India dumbfounded with their response. They suggested that in discussing the Ladakh trade, they did not want to get involved in the Kashmir question which was pending settlement between India and Pakistan. India pressed for it since it was the question of India's territorial integrity.

In view of the Chinese attitude, the question was allowed to rest for some time. When later India presented the draft of the agreement on 18 March, with both the passes included for trade between Ladakh and Tibet, Chinese reaction was no less sharp than before. Director Chen said, 'Rudok [Pass], impossible even if there was a deadlock'. He suggested an alternative route via Tashigong, which was outside the state and would not concede the direct route because China did not want to get involved in the India–Pakistan dispute.[119] Both the Indian delegation and Delhi were at the end of their tether, particularly when China threatened a deadlock. Yielding, Delhi changed track and asked the delegation 'if the Chinese continue to insist on their (Rudok and Rawang) exclusion, we shall have to agree. We must however, ensure that Ladakh's trade did not suffer by diversion to Tashigong route'. The MEA asked the ambassador to consider this 'carefully' and inform Delhi what he thought of it.[120] The ambassador in reply, sensing the ministry's thinking, quoted Chen to suggest if trade was diverted to Tashigong, it would not suffer. The ambassador, anxious to tide over the problem of Chinese obstinacy, added that the Chinese reluctance was 'perhaps due to there being military installations in that area'. It was a different matter the Chinese had never spoken of military installations; it was the ambassador's discovery.[121] On the same day, Delhi replied that since the Chinese were unwilling, the two passes were excluded.[122]

The ambassador's discovery of military installations and Delhi's instant acceptance was an attempt to cloak India's acquiescence before a determined China, even when the question of territorial integrity was involved! It did not worry Delhi, that despite its all-out efforts to woo China—taking up the cudgels on China's behalf in the UN Security Council—China was more sensitive to Pakistan's interests even when it was not present on the scene. Later when Kushak Bakula, a deputy minister in the Jammu and Kashmir government, wanted to go on a pilgrimage to Tibet, and China was approached to facilitate the visit, China while not welcoming categorically said Bakula was not welcome as a minister of J&K, he would be provided facilities as a VIP. Delhi had no reason to be disillusioned, since China at no time in the last three years, given it any indication of overt friendship. If India remained under the illusion of China's friendship, it was in fact India's misfortune. As far as China was concerned, theirs was a matter-of-fact relationship. If India had emotional ties toward China, it was India's problem.

It may be recalled that in 1950, when China first attacked Tibet, the Dalai Lama had asked for asylum, India had agreed and even conveyed as much should he decide to leave Tibet. Later in the face of the Chinese warning against asylum, Delhi had to hint to Lhasa that the Dalai Lama would better be served staying home to give guidance to his people at that difficult time.[123] Lhasa took the hint and the Dalai Lama decided to stay put.

In 1952, dissatisfied at India's resolution in the United Nations General Assembly on the repatriation of Korean prisoners of war, China had dubbed 'Nehru's resolution as parent of all evils'.[124] Nehru felt humiliated but found himself helpless; yet he said he did not want to lose China's friendship. China's disparaging remarks at the conduct of India's first general election, 1952, were ignored. In this background, the present conduct of China was not incongruous and India's acquiescence, equally in line with the past routine of bowing to Chinese diktats.

As stated above, the mandate of the Indian delegation was not to discuss the frontier question and the seven issues which India had presented to China for settlement in Tibet had, in fact, excluded the frontier question. Now when the negotiations in Beijing were underway, Delhi suddenly suggested to Ambassador Raghavan to ensure that the three passes—Qara Tagh, Lanak La and Domjor La—in the western sector were considered for inclusion in the agreement.[125] Raghavan pointed out to Delhi that since the three passes adjoined the disputed territory of Aksai Chin, asking for their inclusion would raise territorial questions.[126] Delhi forthwith replied 'we do not wish to raise Aksai Chin question and agree that three passes need not be specifically mentioned'.[127]

Once again, Aksai Chin as a disputed area, stared India in the face, but it was considered prudent to sweep it under the carpet instead of facing it squarely. Regarding other passes which were in the central sector—Lipuleh, Darma, Niti, Mana, Shipki La, Unta and Dhura—

these were determined to be border passes where entry was on the Indian side and exit on the Tibetan side. However, it was clarified that Kungri Bingri was not a border pass. Similarly, Demchok was not on the border, but on the right side of the Indus. The Demchok village was wholly within Indian territory.

The Ministry of External Affairs on 23 March 1954 sent two drafts—one for the preamble to the agreement—and the other for letters to be exchanged. The preamble contained the Five Principles of coexistence which the Chinese had at the very beginning enunciated and India had accepted unreservedly. The opening sentence of the draft restricted its mandate when it said it was for 'promoting and developing cultural, commercial and religious intercourse'. The reference to the frontier issue was conspicuous by its absence. The draft of letter dealt with the administrative measures for the functioning of the trade agencies, withdrawal of a military escort, transfer of assets of posts and telegraph, and rest houses and guest houses to China on reasonable compensation.[128]

Negotiations dragged on for three months with no end in sight. Delhi was getting exasperated at the delay in concluding the negotiations. In the meantime, the prime minister had said in Parliament that 'negotiations are likely to be completed "successfully" within a fortnight or so'. Foreign Secretary R.K. Nehru in conveying the PM's message said Delhi was anxious to finalize it 'as quickly as possible'. He asked Raghavan to report 'immediately how the negotiations are going and date by which they are likely to be completed'.[129] Reporting the progress in negotiations to the foreign secretary, Ambassador Raghavan attributed some of the delay to the health problems of some of the Chinese negotiators, thereby exonerating them and said it was not 'entirely due to Chinese'. Assuring that he was anxious to complete the negotiations at the earliest, particularly because of the possibility of Chang and Chen, the two Chinese negotiators, going to Geneva, Raghavan asked the foreign secretary to convey to the PM that 'Chinese negotiations, as with other delegations, always drag on like this'.[130]

In the next few days, while there were no delegation-level discussions, there were informal discussions on a one-to-one basis, which enabled some ground to be covered. But there was no dearth of sticking points.

As for instance, the Chinese were 'very definite that trade agents shall not enjoy immunity from search, arrest, detention and prosecution' as it was not considered necessary for the performance of their duties.[131] The Chinese were willing to give an informal understanding that they would enjoy these immunities but would not reduce them to writing. It meant that the trade agents would be at the mercy of the local officials without any formal protection, a tricky situation. Another was that the medical facilities maintained by the trade agencies would not be open to the local population. There were similar other hurdles which impinged upon the effectiveness of the agencies with the local population. The Chinese wanted to take over the post and telegraph and guesthouses by paying compensation but hinted at the possibility of their exchanging hands gratis. The vital question of immunities was dropped altogether, since Delhi was agreeable to it. But there was no end to the Chinese raising petty issues.[132] The ambassador now felt that there were too many residual and petty matters on which decisions were pending. On his suggestion, Delhi agreed to delegate to him the powers to take a view on those issues at his level, while ensuring India's fundamental interests were not compromised.[133] Some discussion also took place on the life of the agreement and its further renewal. India suggested tenure of twenty-five years while the Chinese wanted only five years. Alternately, the Chinese insisted on an eight-year-life which was agreed to by the Indian side, even if the delegation felt suspicious of Chinese motives.[134] It was agreed that there would be ratification of the agreement after signature. It was also agreed that all the three texts in Chinese, Hindi and English would be equally authentic. The importance to English text being authentic was done away with.[135]

Since there was no indication from Beijing that the signing of the agreement was anywhere in sight, Nehru was getting impatient. He underlined the urgency to Ambassador Raghavan of completing the negotiations in view of the political developments in Indo–China. Nehru felt if the agreement was signed and out of the way, it would have a 'salutary effect' but if it was postponed indefinitely, the effect would be contrary.[136] An upset prime minister told Raghavan that 'we cannot have our men sitting in Peking hoping for something to happen'.

His worry was that the delegation had already stayed there months too long. He was now prepared for suspending the negotiations to 'some distant date probably in Delhi for future resumption of talks'. At the same time, he was worried this would create an impression of 'failure which will not be good'.[137] And finally, he directed Raghavan to tell the Chinese that 'our men who have gone from Delhi will have to return even before Geneva Conference begins'.[138]

There was yet another climb down when Delhi agreed on Chinese insistence that there would be no restrictions on areas where 'Tibetans may trade' and Delhi was prepared to even assure them that it 'would give greater facilities to their traders on our side than will be available to the Indian traders in Tibet'.[139]

Before the draft containing six articles was finalized on 26 April, there were some more hitches which were stitched together. Finally, China insisted that before the agreement was finalized India make a public announcement that it would hand over post and telegraph installations without compensation. Otherwise, it was understood that all Indian assets would be transferred to China on payment of their depreciated cost. Raghavan in the face of this demand asked Delhi to authorize him to make this gesture in the spirit of friendship. In this context he referred to some file where the prime minister had agreed to this course of action, provided the agreement went through without difficulty. But the agreement instead of going through smoothly had to see many hiccups before it was finalized. Overcoming all the hurdles, Delhi at the end, made yet another gesture and agreed to the free transfer of telegraphic installations.[140] The 120-day-long negotiations culminated in the agreement which was signed on 29 April 1954 in Beijing by Ambassador Raghavan on the Indian side and by Chang Han-fu, Chinese Vice Foreign Minister on the Chinese side. There was an exchange of letters too, which became part of the agreement as per usual practice. The agreement contained, at India's insistence, though Chinese were initially reluctant, the Five Principles of Peaceful Coexistence in its preamble and the agreement came to be known as the Panchsheel Agreement.[141] Nehru, by the inclusion of the Five Principles, drew satisfaction that respect for territorial integrity would mean acceptance of Indian frontiers by China as they existed. It was for this reason, Nehru continued to believe that all the outstanding issues between India and China which included the borders were settled.[142] It was like clutching at straws after doggedly refusing to discuss the borders while giving up all the facilities and privileges voluntarily and unilaterally.

Glossing over the various hurdles and concessions that India had to make in the four-month-long discussions in Beijing, Nehru in making his statement in Parliament described the signing 'as a very important event'.[143] To pre-empt questions from members about the inordinate time taken to finalize the agreement, he said the delay was not due to any major conflict or difficulty, but because there were too many small matters that had to be discussed in detail and then settled. Taking shelter behind the Five Principles, which he had described as 'wholesome principles' and enunciated in the agreement, he said 'they indicated the policy that Government of India pursued in its relations with not only China but with other countries as well'. Though he himself had directed a 'no-discussion' on the frontiers and no discussion did take place, he however said, 'It is a matter of importance to us, as well as, I am sure, to China that these countries, which have now almost about 1,800 miles of frontier, should live on terms of peace and friendliness, respect each other's sovereignty and integrity and agree not to interfere with each other in any way and not to commit aggression on each other.'[144]

An inspired prime minister directed the Ministry of External Affairs to communicate the text of the agreement to all the Commonwealth countries, along with a note which should recall India's old connection with Tibet and a justification for the agreement 'in view of recent changes in Tibet' of course pointing out that 'petty difficulties were cropping up' from time to time.[145] He was so excited by the Five Principles that he asked Ambassador K.K. Chettur in Rangoon to commend them to the Burmese government in its relations with China.[146]

Regarding the border question, it remained a matter of perception whether only issues 'ripe for settlement' or 'all outstanding' were resolved, since neither side made any explicit statement. The prime minister in his judgement continued to believe that even if the frontier question was not discussed, it stood settled.

Nehru continued to believe that India gave up in Tibet what could not be retained but had achieved 'instead something that is very important, i.e., a friendly frontier and an implicit acceptance of that frontier.[147] This presumption was not based on any solid fact.

The opportunity to discuss and secure a clear and explicit recognition of India's border with Tibet during the negotiations was deliberately allowed to slip. Nehru's biographer Dr Gopal acting as an apologist blamed it on 'an ambassador who rationalized a shirking of unpleasantness' that 'the best defence of the frontier was a friendly neighbour'—a principle which indeed was sound, provided the frontier was a settled one. But Nehru had himself instructed that, 'the administration should be pushed right up to the borders and check-posts strung out along its entire length, priority should be given to the building of communications, the intelligence systems should be strengthened and the border areas developed economically and their inhabitants integrated to the national life of India.'[148]

Dr Gopal did not question why Nehru's instructions were not carried out, since neither any check-post was set up nor any other step, identified by him, taken.[149]

Nehru, notwithstanding his doubts about the finality of the frontier, recalled Mao's statement that India and China 'cannot afford to have war' and was satisfied that China's intentions toward India were peaceful.[150]

Nehru upset with the muted criticism of the agreement in Parliament in which some members had referred to these developments as the 'melancholy chapter of Tibet', disabused them and said:

Many things happen in the world which we do not like, and which we would wish were rather different but we do not go like Don Quixote with lance in hand against everything that we dislike, we put up with these things because we would be, without making any difference, merely getting into trouble.[151]

The people welcomed the agreement since the details of the negotiations and the climb down India had to make to get it finalized remained hidden. The press with its limited reach, depending on what the government dished out to them, remained enthusiastic. The *Amrita Bazar Patrika* gave it an enthusiastic welcome and editorially said, 'From the very beginning (Nehru) had ruled any discussion of India-China frontier, and in the resulting agreement he succeeded in getting approval of the McMahon Line.'[152]

The *Times of India* no wiser than the *Amrita Bazar Patrika*, too in its editorial on 1 May 1954 welcomed it and said 'the silence on the border question was welcome, in as much as, it is an acknowledgment of the existing boundary line . . . In any case the Indian government will stand by the McMahon Line and will not allow anyone to cross that boundary.'[153] It was the *Pioneer* which read the agreement between the lines and came to the conclusion that there was something amiss. It said, 'Nothing has been secured to shut out further penetration of Chinese communists into the regions bordering on China. India has yet to wake up to the reality of her north-eastern frontiers and to events which are likely to follow.'[154]

The *New York Times* called it as an Indian gift to China. Not too many people were aware, or could perceive, that India had given up every facility in return for nothing. If one were to look at the agreement in the background of Nehru's statement of 8 November 1950, what was given up was a policy decision and there was no regret about it. Nehru had already made up his mind to surrender the unilateral facilities the British had bequeathed to India while demitting power. In his perception, it was an imperialistic inheritance and their loss was not to be regretted.[155]

Nehru, upset by criticism of the agreement, blamed it on the critics who lacked awareness of the bigger picture. He accused people of talking vaguely without understanding the agreement and that we had given away more than we had gained. He insisted India gave up 'what in fact, we could not hold on and that in fact had in reality gone'.[156]

It was quite evident even from the preamble of the agreement that it related only to trade and intercourse between India and the Tibet region of China. Nehru, before the talks began in Beijing, had instructed the Indian delegation not to discuss the border question. They were indeed not discussed. Yet, he later insisted that the borders having not been discussed, were settled. This remained the blight of India's problem. Nehru failed to understand that well-defined, mutually agreed borders, are important for maintaining good relations among nations. They come into being as a result of agreements between stakeholders by adjustment of rival claims, interests, and ambitions at points where they adjoin.

The agreement was so crafted as if it was the first-ever agreement on Tibet, between India and China, and there were no contacts whatsoever between them ever before. It is normal practice when an agreement is signed to replace an old agreement that there is always a reference to the replaced agreement. China eminently succeeded in disinheriting the humiliating century without showing any concession in the bargain. The Indian strategy of presuming things on vital questions was flawed. India was fully aware of the weakness of its case, yet it remained in denial.

The unfortunate part was that the compromise was on fundamental issues like acquiescence on Chinese refusal to allow Ladakh direct access to Tibet since it was part of 'disputed' Kashmir and China would not like to get involved in the India–Pakistan dispute. China was sensitive to Pakistan's interest at a time when their bilateral contacts were minimal as compared to India's. So much for Chinese friendship!

Both T.N. Kaul and Gopalachari, on return from Beijing, submitted their reports to the ministry. Kaul in his report tried his best to justify the four months that it took to negotiate a simple agreement even when India had already decided to give up its privileges and advantages bequeathed by the British. His claim that it was the quickest international agreement negotiated by the Chinese government, past or present, is debatable. Sometimes negotiations do take a long time, even over a year, but in such cases the negotiations are conducted over many periodical sessions and not in one go, as it happened in this case.[157]

Kaul's report, otherwise too, suffered from questionable conclusions. His claim that the talks were cordial except for one or two points and the advantage of the prolonged negotiations was that China realized that 'meant business and would not be cowed down or exhausted into submission', did not stand scrutiny.[158] A perusal of the four-month proceedings tells a different story altogether. The list of compromises that India had to make was certainly not small and would not make an Indian comfortable or proud of the agreement. At times, even the prime minister felt impatient and frustrated at the never-ending negotiations but remained in denial.

Nehru did not accept Kaul's proposal for a non-aggression pact with China but accepted his suggestion to invite Chinese Premier Zhou to break his journey in Delhi while returning home from Geneva.

Nehru had read Kaul's report immediately on its submission but held over Gopalachari's report for study later. He took it with him to Mashobra (Simla Hills) where he went for a holiday. Its reading was a trigger for his orders that the 'undefined' boundary in the western sector in the Survey of India maps be defined by a definite line. The orders included withdrawal of old maps and printing of new ones with a definite line. He also instructed that the old maps were withdrawn and new maps distributed to the universities and embassies for display.[159]

The orders were complied with but without due diligence. That it could lead to serious consequences later did not apparently cross anyone's mind. It was an area between two independent countries, and in such cases the boundary is drawn in consultations with the other neighbour to avoid problems later.

While the new maps were indeed printed and issued, his earlier instructions that check-posts were set up all along the border remained ignored with no one held responsible.

After signing the agreement, India lost its contacts with Tibet and Tibetans and its ability even to speak for them or to them, became a casualty. The trigger for the negotiations was the difficulty that the Indian establishments in Tibet were facing. It was hoped that the agreement would enable them to function smoothly, unfortunately the problems of both Indian trade agencies and Indian traders multiplied manyfold instead. They struggled for survival in the face of the hostile local Chinese administration. If the note dated 26 October 1959[160] handed over to the Chinese government and another note dated 25 April 1960[161] that was handed over by the foreign secretary to the Chinese assistant foreign minister during Zhou's visit to India in April 1960 are any indications, the Indian establishments were smothered and finally had to be shut down.

The Indian initiative for the 1954 negotiations was Nehru's desire for good relations with China. He also wanted to give shape to his idea of Asian solidarity where both India and China would stand side by side as symbols of Asian solidarity. In the larger policy perspective, he had convinced himself that the future of Asia depended on the goodwill and cordial neighbourly relations among Asian nations. His convening of the Asian Relations Conference even before Indian Independence was a proof of his desire that Asia should get its lost primacy and glory back.

Fascinated by the Himalayas, Nehru saw in them a security shield in the north. On the flip side, this sense of security had a deleterious impact since he did not feel it necessary to take any defensive measures against any possible danger to Indian security from that direction and, therefore, looked upon China's occupation of Tibet benignly. Reciprocally, he expected China to be deferential toward India for its past sympathies, when it was being oppressed by the Europeans who had nibbled away its coastal areas and monopolized its geological wealth. Noble as his ideas were, his failure was in recognising that communist China had no place for sentiments or for past contacts. For China, the past was the 'century of humiliation', a bad dream to be forgotten as soon as possible.

The 1954 agreement resulted from Nehru's failure to understand the communist Chinese leaders, who were now occupying the throne in Beijing. His attitudes towards communists suffered from contradictions. His judgement of their characteristics remained dyed in Kuomintang colours, though he did not know them personally. In 1939, during his visit to China, he wanted to go to the communist areas to meet them but World War II intervened and he had to interrupt his programme and return home. He did not pick up the signals emanating from them that they were no friends to him or India. Unlike Nehru who had emotional attachment to China or the Chinese, they were a matter-of-fact people who drove a hard bargain where their interests were concerned.

Unfortunately, Nehru looked at China benignly and challenged those who looked at it differently. He did not look worried about China's shenanigans and remained unperturbed that in supporting China, he invited the odium of the western powers.

In making compromises, Nehru did not harbour doubts about China's intentions and still he said 'we have always to keep in mind the possibility of a change and not be taken unaware'.[162] Yet, he remained oblivious of those risks until it was too late.

In a world divided by the Cold War, Nehru sought to devise his own path, to live in peace and enlarge the region of peace. He held out his hand of friendship to countries emerging from colonialism to join him in the quest for peace. His idea of non-alignment gave him the option to stay out of the Cold War politics of superpowers. He insisted the success of Indian foreign policy should not be judged in the narrow sense of 'our own petty success or failure' but whether it 'involves the success or failure of the whole world'.[163] These parameters influenced him toward making China a partner in his campaign for peace. He was willing to sacrifice India's core interests even when China was not reciprocating or responding. That remained the bane of Nehru's China policy, of which the agreement on Tibet was only one example.

II

Indo–Soviet Treaty of Peace, Friendship and Cooperation, 1971[*]

On 9 August 1971, India signed a Treaty of Peace, Friendship and Cooperation with the Soviet Union, which was against its basic ethos of non-alignment.

India had zealously guarded itself against joining any military or political block in which the post-war world was divided. Prime Minister Jawaharlal Nehru had said as early as 4 December 1947 in the Constituent Assembly that 'we will not attach ourselves to any particular group'.[1] He elaborated it further while speaking at the Indian Council of World Affairs on 22 March 1949. Since then, India's policy of staying away from the Cold War politics of the superpowers had become the corner stone of India's foreign policy. Anxious for world peace, Nehru adopted policies which would ensure peace, as he asked Parliament 'not to measure the success or failure of his foreign policy whether it served India's interests or not as long as world peace was ensured'.[2]

---

[*] This chapter and Chapter 3 (The Simla Agreement: 1972) for a major part are based on the author's documentary study of *India–Pakistan Relations, 1947–2007* in ten volumes, published in 2012 by Geetika Publishers, New Delhi. The references from this compendium in the Notes section are indicated as 'Vol. No.' followed by the page number. It contains only official documents, both classified and unclassified. There are some documents in this chapter from another of the author's documentary study in five volumes: *India–China Relations: 1947–2000*, published by Geetika Publishers, New Delhi, in 2018. These have also been similarly indicated.

The major foreign policy issue which confronted India immediately after Independence was Kashmir. The UN Security Council in the post-war years was dominated by the United States. Preferring to go along with the United Kingdom opinion on South Asia, the US along with the UK and other western permanent members and even non-permanent members of the Security Council pitched the Council in favour of Pakistan on the Kashmir issue. Subsequently, the US co-opted Pakistan in various military alliances like SEATO (Southeast Asia Treaty Organization) and CENTO (Central Treaty Organization). The membership of these alliances helped Pakistan to arm itself with modern weaponry tilting the military balance in the subcontinent in its favour. India abhorred the politics of military alliances and rejected any proposal to join any of them. The Soviet Union was uncomfortable at the ganging up against India in the Security Council. It did see some merit in the Indian case on Kashmir and took an independent stand which favoured India somewhat. This brought India closer to the Soviet Union.

Prime Minister Nehru inclined towards socialism was attracted toward the Soviet Union's socialist agenda. The Soviet's own desire to enter into a treaty of friendship with India even in the fifties contributed to optimism in New Delhi for Moscow. It was another matter that New Delhi then found it inopportune to respond favourably to Moscow's overtures. Replying to Ambassador S. Radhakrishnan's letter conveying Moscow's approaches for a friendship treaty, Nehru had said that since the Kashmir issue was in the UN Security Council where the 'U.S. and others had formed a "solid phalanx" against us, we might go a little slow in taking further and obvious steps towards closer relations with the Soviet. He said for the present 'it would be a safer policy not to undertake any additional step which might make our relations with the Western powers worse'.[3]

Nehru's leanings toward socialism, abhorrence of the Western policy of military alliances and alienation due to the West's antipathy to non-alignment, facilitated a synergy between India and the Soviet Union. Apart from admiration for socialism, the Soviet Union's non-colonial past, made it attractive to Nehru. The visit of Soviet leaders, Nikita Khruschev and Nikolai Bulganin to India in 1955, proved a game-changer since they committed the Soviet Union on the Kashmir issue which had become critical for New Delhi. The Soviet veto in the UN Security Council saved India from a number of embarrassing situations.

As far as the Soviet Union was concerned, it saw India, lying on its southern flank, as a great strategic friend, if not an ally. The synergy so created, blossomed into great bonhomie in their relations through the Cold War years. The USSR became India's principal source of finance and technology for defence and civilian industries and also weaponry which continued until the dissolution of the Soviet Union. However, in 1962 at the time of the conflict with China, it was not the Soviet Union which had come to India's rescue but the western countries— the United States and United Kingdom. This, however, did not create any major long-term problem in relations with Moscow, which soon regained its old warmth thanks to the ideological differences that developed between Moscow and Beijing which fermented into political and territorial domains as well.

India had indeed received defence assistance from the United States in 1962 to meet the Chinese aggression, which was against non-alignment. Nehru, however, justified it on the context of extraordinary circumstances since, as he said, 'War had its own dynamics and momentum' and sometimes we have to do such things as obtaining arms aid from various countries, especially the west which normally we would have not done. But when one has to struggle for existence one has to do this kind of thing.[4]

Even after the war, Nehru did accept defence aid from the West but not before the United States had withdrawn its conditionalities, which it had sought to impose. Nehru remained firm in his belief that he had not forsaken his non-alignment.

In 1971, there was yet another such occasion when India faced a similar situation and found it necessary to make a compromise to meet an extraordinarily untoward situation that had been created in India's neighbourhood. Pakistan's domestic problem had spilled over into India and India could not escape getting involved. In the background of the revolt of the people of East Pakistan against its West Pakistani rulers, India faced a dilemma. Their troubles had a historical past in which India did not contribute in any manner, yet it had become its problem.

East Pakistan's troubles had their origin in the Lahore resolution of March 1940 which laid the foundations for Pakistan. The resolution moved by the Bengali leader Fazlul Huq had then declared, 'The areas in which the Muslims are numerically in the majority, as in the north-western and eastern zones of India should be grouped to constitute "Independent **States**" in which the constituent **units** shall be autonomous and **sovereign**.'[5]

The resolution was unambiguous on the creation of 'independent states' and not a single united Muslim state. Later speaking in Lahore, the Bengali nationalist leader who later was Pakistan's Prime Minister, Hussain Suhrawardy, had in 1946 called for 'each of the provinces of the Muslim majority areas to be accepted as a sovereign state and each province should be given the right to choose its future constitution or enter into a commonwealth with a neighbouring province or provinces'.[6] As late as April 1947, Khwaja Nazimuddin who later became both the prime minister and President of Pakistan had said, 'It is my considered opinion that an independent sovereign Bengal is in the best interest of its people.'[7] At the time of Partition in August 1947, a tenacious Suhrawardy along with the Hindu leaders of the Bengal Provincial Congress, had worked to keep Bengal a united 'country' and underlined the strength of Bengali nationalism. That the efforts of the Bengali leaders, both Hindus and Muslims, did not succeed was due to the opposition from the non-Bengali leaders of the Congress and the Muslim League from the other parts of India. In the north-western region, Muslims were divided among various provinces and despite having pride in their local identities, were a divided lot. The Bengalis, however, had some sort of synergy irrespective of their religion. That Bengali nationalism was vociferous and cohesive was an added attribute. The Muslims of Bengal professed Islam as a religion but otherwise were part of the larger Bengali nationalism. However, since the turn of the twentieth century, the Partition of Bengal and the formation of the Muslim League and its politics of Partition had created a sense of separatism among them as well. Nevertheless, they had reservations in joining the Muslims of the western provinces, who linguistically, culturally and even ethnically were different from them. Their only common factor was their religion.

In the Convention of Muslim Legislators in Delhi in April 1946, Abu Hasham, a member of the Bengal Provincial Muslim League had spoken in favour of a separate state for East Bengal, quoting the Lahore Resolution, but was overruled. Later at the meeting of the All-India Muslim League Council held in Delhi on 10 June 1947 to approve the Partition plan, Jinnah had manoeuvred the proceedings in a manner to negate any options except to accept a united Pakistan. Jinnah vetoed the suggestion that the members might be allowed to move a resolution for accepting or rejecting the Partition plan. He left the council in no doubt that the 'question before the House was whether it wanted to accept the partition plan as a whole and if the House was agreeable, a unanimous resolution, embodying the acceptance of the plan could be adopted by the Council'. His diktat held and the House agreed to a united Pakistan.[8]

Despite this manoeuvring, there were some voices from among the Bengali delegates who opposed the proposal for a united Pakistan. Professor Abdul Rahim from Bengal had strongly opposed the idea of a united Pakistan and said that the plan would ruin the Muslims of India, as a result of which there could never be any lasting peace in the country; that Muslims would not benefit by it and that the proposed division of Bengal and the Punjab will always give rise to mutual quarrels between the Hindus and Muslims. He noted that the income of West Bengal was three times that of East Bengal and wanted a 'total rejection of Pakistan'.[9]

Ironically, Abdul Hashim of the Bengal Provincial Muslim League who had opposed the Pakistan proposal even in 1946 and was even now expected to oppose it, was denied a chance to speak. He, however, made his point in a statement issued at the end and said that the League councillors in agreeing to a united Pakistan, had a three-fold fear complex: (i) a fear to oppose Jinnah; (ii) those who came from western zone were afraid that new avenues opened by the establishment of a new country might be closed to them if they opposed the top leadership, and (iii) even those who favoured rejection held back since it was a leap in the dark, which might lead to greater disaster.[10]

The Pakistan that finally came into being on 14 August 1947 was a geographic entity and not a nation. A nation evolves over a period of time on the basis of common history, cultural cohesion and much more. In this case, two peoples who had nothing in common between them, except their religion, were yoked together. The people in East Pakistan were socially, culturally, linguistically and ethnically integrated into the Bengali mainstream society and had doubts if a united Pakistan would be a cohesive society and country.

Religious fundamentalism which received buoyancy during the struggle for Pakistan, took over the narrative during Pakistan's early years of existence. But one cannot live by religion alone. The first shock was on the language question, since the official language of Pakistan was declared Urdu, which was the language of neither of the provinces in the whole of Pakistan.

When the first census was held in 1951, it was found that the population of East Bengal was forty-two million against the West's thirty-four. In the West, there was an ethnic cocktail of Punjabis, Sindhis, Pakhtoons and Baloch, speaking different languages, as well as the newly arrived migrants from India. Interestingly, there was little or no migration from south India which escaped the Partition divide. Unlike West Pakistan, both Hindus and Muslims in Bengal were a homogeneous linguistic group.

Legitimately, the national language of the new country should have been Bangla and its capital in Dhaka, East Pakistan. Pakistan as it emerged in 1947 was described by Salman Rushdie as 'that fantastic bird of a place, two wings without a body, sundered by the landmass of its greatest foe, joined by nothing but God'.[11]

The top leadership of the movement for the formation of Pakistan, principally M.A. Jinnah and Liaquat Ali Khan knew only Urdu among the vernacular languages of India and as such it found favour with them and Urdu became the official language of Pakistan. Jinnah, on his first and only visit to East Pakistan, had rejected the demand of the people there for Bangla as one of the two official languages of Pakistan, and thereby sowed the seeds of discontent at the very birth of Pakistan. It is important to note that though the people of the West spoke languages other than Urdu, they accepted Urdu readily since their languages used the same script as Urdu and as such they were not put to any particular disadvantage. In the East, Bangla used a different script altogether, which put them at a disadvantage. The language and the location of capital city of Pakistan decided the locus of power, which naturally became the western part.

As pointed out above, Jinnah during his visit to Dhaka in 1948 had ruled out any place for Bangla in the central administration. While speaking at the Dhaka University Convocation he had said:

> There can, however, be only one lingua franca, i.e. the language for inter-communication between the various provinces of the State, and that language should be Urdu and cannot be any other. The state language therefore, must be obviously Urdu, a language that has been nurtured by a hundred million Muslims of this subcontinent, a language understood throughout the length and breadth of Pakistan and above all, a language which, more than any other provincial language, embodies the best that is Islamic culture and Muslim tradition, and is nearest to the language used in other Islamic countries.[12]

Jinnah's stress was more on Islamic culture without realizing the value of people's culture. Giving importance to local culture was like provincialism to him which he believed could weaken Pakistan. He believed those who gave priority to local culture and traditions undermined the solidarity of Muslims. Referring to the language controversy in East Bengal he said, 'It is only one of the many subtle ways whereby the poison of provincialism is being sedulously injected into this province.'[13] Jinnah failed to perceive that the language was the basis of culture and a symbol of identity besides being a language of communication.

His successors did not try to heal the wounds created by Jinnah's fiat. To add fuel to the fire, Khwaja Nazimuddin, though a Bengali and the Prime Minister of Pakistan, in January 1952, justified Jinnah's decision on language in the interest of national unity. This proved disastrous and provoked a general strike in East Pakistan, creating a riotous situation with police firing killing many students. The language movement was the beginning of the end of a united Pakistan.[14] The declaration by Nazimuddin's successor Mohammad Ali Bogra, also a Bengali, giving Bangla the status of official language along with Urdu in May 1954, was too late and looked like appeasement. This happened after the Muslim League, which had spearheaded the Pakistan Movement, was punished in the provincial elections held only a couple of months earlier in March. It was the united front of the Awami League and the Krishak Sramik Party which won 223 seats out of 309. The Muslim League won only ten seats. The Muslim League's strategy to create a scare among the people that the future of the country was at stake proved counterproductive. For the people in the east, East Bengal was their country and not the western region, about which the Karachi administration was worried. The new government in Dhaka was now led by Fazlul Huq, who had ironically in 1940 moved the Pakistan resolution in Lahore. True to the resolution, he had told foreign correspondents that he favoured independence for East Pakistan in terms of the 1940 resolution which had called for 'sovereign and autonomous *states* in the northwest and the east' (emphasis added). For the central government was now headed by Choudhary Mohammad Ali, a Punjabi, this was not only unpatriotic but traitorous. This led the government in East Pakistan to be dismissed by Karachi and East Pakistan was placed under direct central rule.

The political leadership in the west captured power and the people in the east suffered many disadvantages. Of the four governor generals that assumed office until the 1958 coup of Ayub Khan, only one, Khwaja Nazimuddin, occupied this post as against three from West Pakistan—Jinnah, Ghulam Mohammad and General Iskander Mirza. But of the four prime ministers from the West, there were three from East. East Pakistan with an area of 14.9 per cent housed 52.6 per cent of the population, while West Pakistan with an area of 85.1 per cent had only to house the remaining 47.4 per cent of its population. Putting the two regions on par by the stratagem of 'One-Unit' scheme, the eastern unit with larger population was put at par with the lesser-populated western unit. This scheme was finally scrapped in July 1970 in the hope of containing the simmering discontent in East Bengal. This paradox extended all the way in all walks of life. By 1970, for instance, the share of the majority province in foreign service was only 16 per cent and in the army, 15 per cent.[15] Out of seventeen officers of the rank of generals in the army, there was only one from East Bengal. Among the 6000 army officers of all ranks, there were only 300 from East Bengal.[16] The national carrier, Pakistan International Airlines, had only 280 employees from the East against 7000 from the West.[17] The distance and the cost of travel between the two wings retarded the growth of national consciousness. The people of the two wings remained strangers to each other.

As pointed out, the discrimination against the eastern wing was glaring. The revenue distribution among the two units was not in proportion to their population. The total government expenditure in twenty years, between 1950–70 in Pakistan, was US$ 30.95 billion, out of which the East's share was only $9.45 billion or 30.45 per cent against the West's share of 21.49 billion or 69 per cent. Out of the total foreign assistance received by Pakistan, almost eighty per cent was spent in the West leaving a pittance for the East. By 1960, the per capita income of West was 32 per cent higher than the East. Although the growth rate in the East did improve in the 1960s, the growth rate in the West was still faster than in the East—6.2 per cent against 4.2 in the East.[18]

By the time General Ayub Khan had usurped the powers of the state in a coup in 1958, the Bengali opinion had become more hostile to West Pakistan than it had been in the early years. The military government now had made things worse since freedom of speech had been curtailed and it had become difficult for them to even air their grievances. Since the share of East Bengal in the armed forces was minuscule, under the military rule it was further affected adversely.

As the feeling of discrimination in the East grew, it was natural for a movement for autonomy to germinate and grow. The military regime found it difficult to deal with it. The 1969 Eleven-Point programme of the East Pakistan Students Action Committee was ahead of political parties since it demanded, besides democracy and autonomy, the scrapping of military alliances and an independent foreign policy like other newly-independent countries of Asia and Africa which had embraced non-alignment.

To neutralize the eastern wing's advantage in population, the Pakistan government found it handy to create anti-Hindu feelings in the East. The leadership in the western wing assessed that by creating insecurity among Hindus, they would migrate out of East Pakistan and that would help create parity or near parity in the population in the two wings. It was expected it would also reduce the bargaining power of East Pakistan in any future scheme of things based on population.

The 1965 war followed by the Tashkent Agreement had weakened Ayub Khan. The revolt of his foreign minister Zulfikar Ali Bhutto added to his woes. Several anti-Ayub rallies fomented feelings of dislike and he was compelled to resign, handing over power to another military dictator General Yahya Khan. Given Yahya Khan's easy lifestyle, the neglect of governance, the weakening of the government's hold on the day-to-day administration of the country was inevitable.

In the meantime, grievances of East Pakistan multiplied along with the language problem and finally became a trigger for popular revolt of the eastern wing against West Pakistan.

In 1948, the Language Agitation (Bhasha Andolan) had given birth to a new political party in the East, the Awami League, which articulated the problems of its people. Sheikh Mujibur Rahman disassociated from the Muslim League and joined the Awami League in 1949 as its joint secretary. In 1966, he had been elected President. The 1965 War made the people of the East Pakistan aware of their vulnerabilities as they found they were not adequately protected and felt the need for an independent security apparatus which could protect it from any attack from India. Later in 1966, at a conference in Lahore, Mujib representing the East Pakistan delegation had presented a six-point programme which finally became a charter of their demands.[19]

A major reason for the neglect of East Pakistan was the seat of power of the Pakistan Central government. Since the entire ruling class together with the bureaucracy, both civil and military, was located and confined to the West, they could not measure the depth of dissatisfaction of people located a thousand kilometres away. They treated the unrest simply as a law-and-order problem which was ascribed to the troublemaking and agitational nature of the Bengalis. They were dismissed as anti-Pakistani who had been affected by the anti-Pakistani propaganda of the people from across the other half of Bengal.

The first Constitution which was promulgated in March 1956 had to weather many hurdles, primarily created by the politically aggrieved Bengalis, before it achieved finality. A prolonged acrimoniously debated Constitution gave an equal number of seats—150—(to both) to each of the two regions. It was no solace to the politically conscious Bengali politicians, particularly of the Awami League persuasion, who saw in parity the denial of their rights as a democratic majority.

The politics of the East underwent a dramatic change in these years. Adversity brings even strangers together. All the political forces pooled their sinews forgetting their past animosities against each other in their battle against the Punjabi-dominated western wing. The Awami League's charismatic leader Sheikh Mujibur Rahman had by 1970, successfully motivated the common people under his umbrella, selling the six-point programme, (which is discussed later on,) as their Magna Carta. For the leadership of the West, it was nothing short of revolt against the established order. For once, the consolidation of political forces demonstrated the magic of numbers.

Sheikh Mujib's charisma and authority had ascended to a level that allowed him to pursue his Constitutional vision with faith in popular support. Already after his release from prison in the Agartala Conspiracy case he had been given the title of Bangabandhu (Friend of Bengal). He had declared that hereon, the eastern province of Pakistan would be called 'Bangladesh' instead of 'East Pakistan'.[20]

General Yahya Khan, who replaced Ayub Khan, was already facing trouble, created by Bhutto's agitation in the West, and did not measure up to another challenge coming from the East. In order to find a way out of the impasse, Yahya decided to hold the first-ever general elections in Pakistan in the hope that it would throw up a hung house, which the army would exploit to its own advantage. Nevertheless, it was a bold step since in Pakistan's existence of quarter of a century, no pan-Pakistan elections had ever been held and that too on the basis of adult franchise. It was a leap in the dark not only for the army but also for the entire nation.

The red rag for Yahya was the election manifesto of the Awami League. It included the six-point programme calling for a total overhaul of Pakistan's political and economic structure. The six points were:

1. There should be a federation of Pakistan on the basis of the Lahore Resolution which had called for the formation of Muslim majority sovereign **States** both in the West and the East;
2. The federal government should be limited to defence and foreign affairs;
3. There should be two separate currencies for each of the two wings;
4. The central government shall have no power to raise taxes; the expenditure for its functioning would be provided by the two wings from their budgets;
5. Foreign exchange earning of each wing should stay with each of them, and
6. A militia or paramilitary force for East Pakistan should be set up.

The six points sought to keep the two wings together territorially, but functionally semi-independent or autonomous. Mujib had then clarified that his six points were in the interest of East Pakistan but had inherent corresponding benefits for West Pakistanis as well as they were sure to derive equal benefits out of their implementation.[21]

West Pakistan, however, denounced it as a thinly veiled agenda for separation. That three of the six points directly *pointed* to economic issues and gave a clear signal that East Pakistan felt economically deprived. It was found that the foreign exchange earned from East Pakistan's export of jute was being usurped by the West Pakistani businessmen who had manoeuvred to set up shop in the eastern region replacing Hindu businessmen who had migrated out. It was found that six non-Bengali businessmen from the West had come to control 40 per cent of East Pakistan's manufacturing assets.

The signs of economic distress were everywhere in the East. Ayub Khan did recognize the urgency of undoing this unfair situation and his 1962 Constitution did call for the rectification of the situation but it finally did very little in that direction. As pointed out above, at no time did people in the East had reason to be happy with the policies constructed in the western wing. Their grievances only helped Mujib's stature grow higher and higher. Mujib's arrest in the infamous Agartala Conspiracy Case and release later, backfired for the regime in the west and raised his stature further among his people in the East. So his six-point programme assumed the character of a charter for freedom from West Pakistan.[22] He had become a political martyr and his support base already solid, went up substantially among the people. Between 1967 and 1969, there were continuous political disturbances in the eastern wing, particularly in Dhaka, and murmurs of serious trouble for Pakistan's future as a united country were being talked about freely. The American Consul General in Dhaka had reported his conversation with British Deputy High Commissioner, Roy Fox, to the US State Department. The conversation took place over a dinner engagement on 9 June 1969 and it was reported Roy Fox saw bleak future for East Pakistan. Fox had predicted that the martial law administration would 'be forced to hold elections which Sheikh Mujibur Rahman would win; East wing would break away from rest of Pakistan and Chicom (Chinese Communist) style communism would be ultimate winner'. Mujib would demand a large degree of provincial autonomy that would lead to the imposition of martial law. This, Fox predicted, would be followed by a general uprising that the Pakistan army would find difficult to control. How prophetic![23]

President Yahya Khan realizing that Mujib had emerged the undisputed leader who could speak for the entire eastern wing did not ignore him either. It was a different matter that he detested him. If there was a chance of lasting settlement then it would have to be with him, was his assessment. The only sticking point was his six-point agenda and it was not certain Mujib would make any compromise on any of those points. He was also worried that if Mujib did not moderate his agenda, it would undermine the central government, representing the Pakistan government internationally. The ray of hope was Mujib's assertion that his agenda was for autonomy and not separation.

The Legal Framework Order issued in March 1970, was based on preconditions which were acceptable to Mujib. He had told Yahya Khan that his six points were not 'the Quran or the Bible' and they were negotiable.[24] It was understood that the elected assembly would be charged with framing a new Constitution within 120 days of its formation and the new Constitution would set out the degree of provincial autonomy for the two wings. But a sting operation conducted by Pakistan Intelligence confirmed to Yahya that Mujib was, in fact, working for separation. Since the elections had already been announced, Yahya had no choice but to go ahead with them.[25]

It was sheer bad luck for both Yahya Khan and Pakistan that a few weeks before the elections scheduled for 7 December 1970, a terrible cyclone struck East Pakistan. It killed between 1,50,000 and 2,00,000 people and rendered another 1.5 to 2 million homeless. No leader from the west visited the east to assure the people of help in ameliorating their conditions or at least to empathize with the tragedy. The tardy manner of relief operations convinced the people of the east once again that their distant location from the centre of power had put them at a great disadvantage. The ensuing elections were seen as an opportunity to teach the leadership of the west a lesson. As the votes of elections were counted, the worst fears of the army and the leadership of the western political elite came true.

The Awami League had won the 160 seats it contested and along with seven of the indirectly elected women's seats, it notched up a total of 167 out 313 seats in the National Assembly, a clear majority. It gave the Awami League led by Mujibur Rahman a right to form a government for Pakistan. In the East Pakistan Assembly, the Awami League had won 288 elected and ten indirectly held women's seats, a total of 298 out of the total strength of 310—a clean sweep.

In the western part, the seats were split between various political parties. The Pakistan People's Party led by Zulfikar Ali Bhutto could win only eighty-one seats in the National Assembly. Its victories were mainly in the Punjab (sixty-two) and Sind (eighteen). It won just one seat in the North-West Frontier Province (NWFP) and nothing in Balochistan. It was a situation which the politicians from the western zone could hardly live with. No party from the west contested any seat in the east and neither did any party from the east, including the Awami League, contest seats in the west. It was a complete split between the two wings of the same country. It was a situation, which in Pakistan's short history, the leadership of Pakistan had not faced or even imagined. The political power which had always weighed-in in favour of the west, was now seen to be slipping into the hands of the east.

A jubilant Mujib, who had described the elections as a referendum on his programme, with newly gained confidence declared that no one could stop him from framing a six-point based Constitution. All the newly elected members from the east for the National Assembly took an oath jointly that 'we shall remain whole-heartedly faithful to the people's mandate on the six points'.[26]

Yahya Khan, appearing respectful to the mandate, travelled to Dhaka and before meeting Mujib, asked for a copy of the six-point programme, which left the Bengali politicians wondering at his casual approach. Had he not yet read the six-point programme of the Awami League, Mujib wondered, and whether Yahya would honour the electoral mandate, while the latter wondered whether Mujib would at all be amenable to any compromise.[27]

Mujib had indeed become more confident and averse to any compromise, which was a shock to Yahya Khan. A disappointed Yahya regretted that 'Mujib had let me down. Those who warned me against him were right, I was wrong in trusting him'.[28]

Yahya facing heavy odds in the east, flew back to Islamabad and consulted Bhutto and found him in an ambivalent mood, not wanting to commit himself one way or the other, keeping his cards close to his chest. Bhutto himself was in a quandary how to handle the peculiar situation which would leave him out in the cold. He insisted that no Constitution could be framed or a government formed at the centre without his party's cooperation/participation despite his party having won far less seats than the Awami League.[29]

Yahya apparently had decided to let Mujib form the government in the hope that some via media would be found to ensure the unity of Pakistan. He had even told the journalists that he had useful discussions with Mujib and significantly added 'when Mujib comes and takes over, I won't be there. It is going to be his government soon'. He once again reiterated that 'Mujib would be the future prime minister of the country.'[30]

That Yahya, at the behest of Bhutto conspired against Mujib, was exposed later in Lt Gen. A.A.K. Niazi's book, *The Betrayal of East Pakistan*. Niazi had commanded the Pakistan army in East Pakistan during the 1971 war and had to undergo the humiliation of surrendering to the Indian Army. He said Bhutto had refused to accept the role of an opposition leader and hatched the final plan for the dismemberment of Pakistan along with Yahya Khan at Larkana, Sind.[31] The controversy between Mujib, Bhutto and Yahya regarding the convening of the National Assembly made its own contribution in creating further confusion. Bhutto's intransigence was delaying the convening of the National Assembly. At a public meeting in Lahore, he threatened to boycott the Assembly and warned that any member elected from the west would not be allowed to attend it. Bhutto's speech betrayed his frustration since Mujib had given him no assurance of sharing power in the new government.

Gradually it was becoming clearer that if Mujib remained stuck to his six-point agenda then the only alternative was a military solution which, as it happened, became the final choice of Yahya Khan. On 26 March 1971, Yahya Khan in a radio broadcast dubbed Mujib and his party enemies of Pakistan and their actions treason, which would destroy Pakistan. He blamed the Awami League for creating a serious situation by its 'non-cooperation and disobedience movement'.[32] It was accused of insulting the Pakistan flag and defiling the photograph of the father of the nation, M.A. Jinnah. Yahya vowed not to let 'some power hungry, unpatriotic people to destroy and play with the destiny of 120 million people'. Yahya regretted the delay in taking action against Mujib while he searched for a compromise. He accused him of trying to run a parallel government.[33]

As Yahya was speaking, the army was fanning out in Dhaka; a reign of terror was let loose. East Pakistan was gripped in unrest and protest marches on the streets of Dhaka became a matter of routine. It had become perceptible to all that the central government was on the run, while the provincial government was in revolt.

New Delhi, next door, was watching the situation and studying the impact of those developments on India. It was cautious in extending support to Mujib even when he had sent a request through the Indian deputy high commissioner based in Dhaka. India was worried that Pakistan would act against India to divert attention from its internal troubles. It also aroused fears of a 'Greater Bengal' secessionist movement in the Indian states of West Bengal, Tripura and Assam. There was also the worry that a free Bangladesh would fall increasingly under communist influence with Maoists hijacking the movement, giving China another point of entry into the subcontinent.[34]

Prime Minister Indira Gandhi had another reason to be reluctant to intervene. She wanted 'Bangladesh' to first establish effective control in some areas and prove to the world through its own struggle that its people were with the movement for Bangladesh. Recognition from India of Bangladesh would only create the impression that India was trying to divide Pakistan, by setting up a puppet regime. She said, 'When the time comes, we will do it.'[35]

At this time, a somewhat daunting report from the Research and Analysis Wing (India's external intelligence agency) reported about the collusion between China and Pakistan and their antagonistic policy towards India, but it also said that since China was busy with the Sino–Soviet border dispute and the ideological conflict with the Soviet Union, it was unlikely that 'China would actively get involved militarily in an Indo–Pak conflict, should it happen'. The R&AW report, however, did not rule out the possibility of China adopting a threatening posture on the Sino–Indian border and even staging some border incidents to prevent the diversion of Indian troops assigned to meet the Chinese threat to the theatres of war with Pakistan. It also held out the possibility of China supplying arms to Pakistan in case of a war with India.[36]

Equally bad were the omens for India–Pakistan relations as the year 1971 opened. On 30 January, an Indian Airlines plane on a flight from Srinagar to Jammu was hijacked to Lahore. The passengers and the crew were returned and after some dillydallying, the aircraft was destroyed at Lahore airport. Pakistan's connivance was obvious since there was no official word of condemnation by the authorities for the incendiary action. Incensed, New Delhi convinced of Pakistan's official connivance, in a retaliatory response suspended all overflights of all Pakistani aircraft, both civil and military, over Indian airspace. This meant a long detour for flights between East and West Pakistan.[37]

In the meantime, the army oppression against the civilians in East Bengal had gathered momentum. On 27 March, Indira Gandhi, in a statement in the Lok Sabha sharing the agony of the people of East Bengal, expressed her concern over the developments there.[38] On 31 March, the Lok Sabha adopted a unanimous resolution expressing its 'profound conviction that the historic upsurge of 75 million people of East Bengal would triumph' and assured them that their struggle and sacrifices would receive the wholehearted sympathy and support of the people of India.[39]

As a first step, India decided to refer to East Pakistan as East Bengal and instructed its missions all over the world to henceforth use 'East Bengal', while referring to East Pakistan.[40]

As the repression of Pakistan army in East Bengal continued, the people started fleeing to India and soon as the cruelty of Pakistani army intensified, the exodus of people from East Bengal to India's neighbouring states increased to the level of an avalanche. It was found that the Pakistan army, which was entirely composed of West Pakistanis, was merciless in handling the revolt, created insecure conditions particularly for the minorities, read Hindus. The abduction of Bengali Hindu women by the Pakistani soldiers became a routine affair. It was yet not known to the Indian public that most of the people targeted were Hindus. It was feared that if this exodus continued and the identity of the victims became known, there was the danger of communal backlash in India and if that happened, India's agenda to put Pakistan in the dock would be derailed. India would then be left to handle communal violence in its own country and would suffer international opprobrium and left to defend itself to Pakistan's satisfaction. At the request of the central government not only media but also political parties including the RSS and Jan Sangh said to be Hindu organizations, acted responsibly in reporting the events in East Bengal. Seeing its plan failing, Pakistan accused New Delhi of sitting on judgement on its domestic situation and interfering in its internal affairs. It further accused India of launching a campaign of vilification and suggested India to treat the refugees, who had fled to India, as a humanitarian problem. But on its own, it made little effort to contain the atrocities. On the contrary, it resorted to greater repressive measures which led to ever-increasing numbers fleeing to India. As a neighbour, India was naturally receiving the flood of refugees while other countries whether in Asia or Europe though aware of the problem and tragedy through their own media and sympathetic to the refugees' plight, were not directly affected. Both the prime minister and the external affairs minister toured a number of countries, particularly in the west, to personally convey the tragic situation that also posed a real threat to peace and security in South Asia. To India's satisfaction, western media was not found lagging behind in documenting the tragedy. It was a different matter that western governments, particularly the US, wilfully ignored the genocide and even defended Pakistan.

As almost 10 million refugees crowded temporary camps set up for them in the Indian states around East Bengal, New Delhi found itself at the end of its tether. Bengali diplomats posted in Pakistani missions abroad started deserting their posts and sought asylum in the host countries.

At this time, the United States assured President Yahya Khan that it was 'in touch with the Government of India and have discussed the implications of the present situation, [and] have stressed the need for restraint'.[41] A couple of days later, Pakistan Ambassador Agha Hilaly accompanied by the Economic Advisor to Yahya Khan, met US President Richard Nixon and asked his help in restoring civil administration for which it was suggested,, that 'it would be necessary for the Indians to cease assisting insurgents' and added, 'Pakistan would welcome anything the US could do to influence the Indians in that direction'.[42]

Among the Asian countries, the Japanese government regarded the crisis not as an internal matter of Pakistan but as an international problem.[43] In Europe and the United States at the official level, there was little understanding of the tragedy or the financial burden India was carrying, in sheltering 10 million refugees.

There was another dimension to the problem. Pakistan, instead of taking any step to normalize or defuse the situation and prevent the exodus to India, was seen arming itself. The United States had been arming Pakistan since 1954 as a bulwark against the communist menace, of which China was a part. India felt outraged when in 1968 Washington had announced fresh supplies of arms to Islamabad. A worried India warned Washington that the fresh supply of arms 'would only encourage it in its policy of confrontation with India'.[44] Pakistan since 1954 had received defence supplies worth $2 billion. On 20 November 1970, both the British foreign secretary and defence secretary in their meeting at the State Department drew Washington's attention to the unsavoury development, but were left worried since the State Department justified supplying arms on various grounds, one of which was to prevent Pakistan getting supplies from USSR or China.[45] India's External Affairs Minister, Swaran Singh had confirmed in Parliament that France had not made any defence supplies to Pakistan since Pakistan's action began in East Bengal. The French had also confirmed that no supplies from previous contracts would be made.[46]

Media reports that the Soviet Union had supplied arms to Pakistan were denied by the EAM in the Lok Sabha. The Soviet attitude to India and Pakistan has to be seen in the context of the foreign secretary, T.N. Kaul's meeting with Russian Chairman Alexey Kosygin in May 1970, when he had assured Kaul that the future relations between India and the Soviet Union would become stronger, notwithstanding some misunderstandings that might have been created in the past. Kosygin had said:

> I can assure you that never again will there be any confusion which can cloud our relations with your great country. It is in the same light and against the same background that we will approach our talks with Yahya Khan. When he leaves our country he will be left in no doubt about our firm resolve to continue and strengthen our relations with India. We shall exert our influence with Yahya Khan and tell him that the establishment of good relations between India and Pakistan will not only be in his own interest but also in the interest of Pakistan.[47]

Kosygin even asked Kaul if he had any particular question which he wished Moscow should take up with Yahya Khan, 'in order to influence his mind and to improve relations or which are in the interest of India, please let me know' or to inform him later.[48]

The Soviet Union's geopolitical interest was to primarily limit Chinese influence in South Asia. Its calculation was that India possessed significant political, military and economic counterweight to China. Having decided to give priority to India, Moscow did not wish to disassociate itself, now that India was pitted against Pakistan with the possibility of China's collaboration. Even in 1965, Soviet intervention in Tashkent, while negotiating a peace settlement between India and Pakistan was essentially to deny any opportunity to China to meddle in South Asia. China's interest in South Asia was to ensure that India, independently or in combination with another county, was no threat to China's position in the region. The Chinese, therefore, worked to keep India politically unstable and supported India's main adversary in South Asia, Pakistan. The other dimension of Chinese policy was that instability and civil war in East Pakistan would radicalize the masses there and provide an opportunity for Maoist-oriented indigenous revolutionaries to step in.[49]

Initially, as the trouble began, Mujib had contacted the American ambassador in Dhaka who promised help but at a price. On 14 March 1971, the Indian Deputy High Commissioner in Dhaka, Sen Gupta reported to Delhi that 'U.S. Ambassador Farland during his talks with Mujib had agreed to ensure withdrawal of Pakistan army from East Pakistan on the condition of leasing Bay of Bengal islands for seven years'.[50]

While reporting the above, Sen Gupta also said Mujib was reluctant to agree to Farland's conditions but added if he did not get any help from any 'big Asian nation, particularly India', he might be forced to accept the American proposal ultimately. Sen Gupta strongly recommended 'if we can get gratitude of Bangladesh by showing slightest good gesture, our Naga and Mizo problems could be settled fully and Kashmir problem fifty percent'. Sen Gupta too had reported that two-and-a-half divisions of the Pakistan Army commanded by Lt Gen. Mitha Khan were being moved from Quetta to East Pakistan.[51]

That India was willing to help Mujib all along was evident from what Pakistan said, quoting the Indian spokesperson when its request for lifting a ban on overflights was not agreed to by India. Pakistan had attributed India's denial of its request to a statement of an Indian spokesperson on 8 March 1971 that 'it is obvious the people of East Pakistan would view any sudden ending of the ban with deep misgivings'.[52]

The situation in East Bengal was fast deteriorating but Yahya Khan under pressure from Zulfikar Ali Bhutto was seen dithering in taking the political process forward following the elections. In Delhi, Foreign Secretary T.N. Kaul, speaking to US Ambassador Kenneth Keating, asked if the US would be prepared to share the economic burden of looking after the refugees and warned of the possibility of pro-Chinese elements in East Bengal hijacking the movement.[53] In Washington, Ambassador L.K. Jha in his meeting with the Assistant Secretary of State for Near Eastern and South Asian Affairs, Joseph Sisco, impressed upon the need for Yahya Khan to be tough with Bhutto and not hijack the electoral verdict.[54]

But as the situation snowballed into a major crisis, New Delhi, did not want to appear fishing in troubled waters, but took care that the crisis in East Bengal was not allowed to lose its momentum. The protest marches overwhelmed Pakistan's military potential, thereby eroding its capacity to challenge the Indian army. India was attempting to foster a Pakistani Dien Bien Phu in East Bengal.

Meanwhile, the Afghan Ambassador in Moscow had brought to the notice of Ambassador D.P. Dhar a worrying possibility that Pakistan 'may engage itself in some diversionary activity in Kashmir—an activity which would involve India in a large-scale clash with the people there'. Ambassador Dhar thereupon strongly advised New Delhi to ensure steps against this possibility and prevent such a development which could expose Delhi to the countercharge of repression in Kashmir. He also advised that neither Sheikh Abdullah nor Afzal Beg, the Kashmiri leaders capable of creating trouble, be allowed to return to the Kashmir Valley. Were this to happen, he warned, it would take pressure off on Pakistan in East Bengal.[55]

While East Bengal was in revolt, the western region was not solidly behind Yahya either. Retired Major General Mian Ghulam Jilani, now a leader of the National Awami Party in the NWFP travelled to Kabul to meet the American ambassador. The ambassador did not think it diplomatically correct to meet a Pakistani politician in Kabul and authorized one of his senior officers for a meeting. Jilani told the American diplomat that the Punjabi-dominated West Pakistan leadership and the army find their hold slipping from East Pakistan. Calling West Pakistan, 'Punjabistan' he said it imposed its will by force on NWFP, Balochistan and Sind. He cautioned that Punjabi control would be fatal to western interests and 'will drive the Pushtun-Baluch-Sindhi confederation into radical arms'.[56]

Mrs Gandhi in her letter of 27 April 1971 to Kosygin expressed her hope that the USSR would use its power and prestige 'to convince the military rulers of Pakistan that the path they had chosen to cement their kinship with their Bengali citizens was unwise'. It apparently had an immediate effect, in that, Dhar on the basis of his conversations with the Russian foreign office officials reported to Delhi two days later that 'the Soviets while showing understanding had, by and large, agreed to share the political and financial burdens which the tragic events in East Bengal had cast on Delhi.' He had added that Moscow was convinced that the renewed Sino–Pakistan collusion was not superficial or limited to phrase-mongering but real in military terms. Drawing attention to the article in the *New Times* (a Soviet Publication), Ambassador Dhar added that 'the Soviet apprehensions that China was trying to encircle India was not a piece of rhetoric but a deep-seated belief that this was in fact so.'[57] The Soviets were fully aware of the happenings in East Pakistan through the reports of their diplomats posted there. On 22 March 1971, the Pakistani Ambassador in Moscow, Jamsheed Marker, was summoned to the foreign ministry and told of the serious developments in East Pakistan which had disturbed Moscow. Following this the Soviet Consul General in Karachi met Yahya Khan on 28 March and told him of the Soviet concerns on the breakdown of talks with Mujibur Rahman and expressed deep anxiety at the military measures that the Pakistan army had undertaken to tackle the situation there and asked for immediate measures for 'the cessation of bloodshed in

East Pakistan and for resumption of negotiations'. This gave Islamabad sleepless nights since it spoke of the fratricidal conflict in East Bengal and its negative impact on Moscow.[58]

Ambassador D.P. Dhar, while welcoming Soviet President Nikoly Podgorny's statement of 2 April, which Pakistani Ambassador Marker had described as 'admonitory', made an assessment of the Soviet position and said that Moscow had lost all hopes of bringing 'Pakistan round to a sensible position' and there was complete rupture between the two wings of Pakistan. It was assessed that the tenuous link between the two wings by naked military occupation was bound to wear off in due course. Ambassador Dhar agreed with the view that the Chinese would make empty threats. However, he felt the average Indian would feel that Pakistan had secured the help of both China and western countries.[59]

In a telegram on 29 April 1971, Ambassador Dhar informed Delhi of his discussions with Alexander Fomin, Head of the South Asia Department in the Soviet Foreign Office, and his doubts about Pakistan's offer of better relations with India. He took the opportunity to brief Fomin of the serious situation that had developed in East Bengal where Hindus were at the receiving end and the terror that the Pakistan army had unleashed was creating a combustible situation which could lead to 'massive retaliation' against the Muslims in India. Yahya Khan sensing the hostility of the Soviet leaders sent former Foreign Minister Arshad Hussain as his special envoy to Moscow to assuage Kosygin's worries. He was asked to assure Moscow that the reports emanating from New Delhi of the army's excesses were highly exaggerated, rather concocted, and only absolutely minimum force was being used where it was found necessary.[60] After Arshad had met Kosygin, Moscow shared this conversation with Ambassador Dhar assuring him that Arshad had left Kosygin 'unconvinced' of Islamabad's case. Going a step further, Moscow sent a copy of Yahya's letter to Kosygin and gist of the Kosygin–Arshad conversation to Mrs Gandhi. The PM was even asked if there was any message that she would like to send Islamabad, since Moscow intended to reply to Yahya's letter.[61]

The Pakistani case, which was articulated to Moscow by Arshad Hussain, was based on the following points:

i.   Pakistan questioned Mujib's mandate which was for autonomy and not for separation and hence he was responsible for the present disturbances;

ii. Pakistan would grant maximum autonomy to provinces under a provisional constitution;

iii. If the elected representatives accepted the provisional Constitution, the powers would be transferred to them;

iv. Arshad Hussain expressed a desire for better relations with India, and

v.   Yahya Khan had offered to pay compensation to India for the loss of the plane which was hijacked to Lahore in January 1971 and destroyed.[62]

Arshad Hussain tried to convince Kosygin that the situation in East Bengal had returned to normal as also on the India–East Pakistan border and the administration was now concentrating its energies on stabilizing the economy of the province. He assured Kosygin that the question of transfer of power to the civil administration in East Pakistan would be settled by the elected members of the National Assembly without holding fresh elections.[63] **But** Pakistan Ambassador Marker described Kosygin and Arshad Hussain's meeting as far from friendly. According to Marker, toward the end of June there were further exchanges between Yahya Khan and Kosygin and were examples of purposeful seriousness and a measure of polite understanding on Kosygin's part. From July onward, Soviet messages became increasingly hostile, and so did Pakistan's responses, resulting in a mutual hostility and deteriorating relations.[64]

In another meeting between Kosygin and Marker, the latter told Kosygin that his President intended to make a statement which would be conciliatory and defuse the tension. Kosygin warned if it failed in its objective, it could bring about a conflict.[65]

After Arshad Hussain left Moscow, Ambassador Dhar told Fomin that there was no let-up in the atrocities being committed by the Pakistan army and they were particularly targeting Hindus for butchery. He added that while India was doing its best not to allow this fact to be disclosed, the country and even 'rightist reactionary Hindu chauvinistic parties' like the Jana Sangh and the RSS had not allowed their balance to be disturbed, nevertheless the continued process of butchery of the Hindus had made the situation in the subcontinent highly explosive. And if this continues, he feared, it might lead to massive retaliation (against Muslims) in India. He also told Fomin about the desertions of East Pakistani diplomats posted in Pakistani missions abroad.[66]

Kosygin advised Marker to convey to his President that the Soviet Union was concerned about the developments in Pakistan and would like to see a 'peaceful solution between India and Pakistan'.[67] Not content with simply speaking with the ambassador, Kosygin sent a separate message to Yahya Khan referring to the refugee problem and hammering in the danger of interference by external forces. The Pakistani ambassador noticed a little lessening of the 'sound and fury' from Moscow, but could see a 'disquieting attitude of deep suspicion bordering on betrayal'.[68]

Mrs Gandhi in her letter of 27 April 1971 to Kosygin expressed the hope that the USSR would use its power and prestige 'to convince the military rulers of Pakistan that the path they had chosen to cement their kinship with their Bengali citizens was unwise'. It apparently had an immediate effect, in that, Dhar on the basis of his conversations with the Russian foreign office officials, reported to Delhi two days later, that 'the Soviets while showing understanding had by and large, agreed with her assessment'.[69]

Ambassador Dhar had already informed Principal Secretary to the Prime Minister, P.N. Haksar that the Soviets believe that the resistance in the east would not collapse and stressed that 'this resistance must not be allowed to collapse'. Like the Afghan ambassador he too advised caution against the possibility of Pakistan taking some diversionary activity in Kashmir, and wanted necessary steps taken to prevent it.[70]

In yet another letter, Ambassador Dhar told the foreign secretary of the possibility of the Soviets making a substantial contribution for relief operations for the refugees. He said the Soviet assessment was in conformity with the Indian assessment that the twain of East and West Pakistan were not likely to meet again. He asked Delhi to give him their various requirements for defence items in concrete terms for him to pursue with Moscow.[71]

Since the situation was getting out of control, Pakistan was worried and anxious to firm up support for any eventuality, particularly when it saw little sign of understanding from Moscow. The alternative of China appeared obvious. Already disappointed and resentful of Western countries supplying arms to India in its war with China in 1962, Pakistan had been drawing closer to China to snub its Western allies. That China was sensitive to Pakistan's concerns was not hidden from India. It may be recalled that during the India–China negotiations on the Tibet agreement in 1954, China's leaning towards Pakistan was clear as day, but India chose to ignore it and looked at China benignly, not only as a friend but as a brother (*Hindi-Chini bhai bhai syndrome*). Later, as Pakistan entered into anti-communist military alliances like CENTO and SEATO, China had readily accepted Pakistan's alibi that these alliances were not against China but India. Prime Minister Nehru while aware of these developments had ignored them in pursuit of Asian solidarity. That at the end he neither achieved Asian solidarity nor Chinese friendship, is a sordid but separate story of India–China relations.

As the situation in East Pakistan was taking an ugly turn, China thought it prudent to at least show Pakistan some intention of help. The *People's Daily* dubbing Indians 'reactionaries' and 'expansionist' and terming their interest 'preposterous', said it was in collaboration with the two superpowers and 'crudely interfering in Pakistan's internal affairs'.[72]

The following day, the Chinese premier Zhou Enlai while replying to Yahya Khan's message presented China as Pakistan's 'genuine friend' and assured him 'should the Indian expansionists dare launch aggression against Pakistan, the Chinese Government and people will, as always, firmly support Pakistan Government and people in their just struggle to safeguard state sovereignty and national independence'.[73] These were usual clichés which China used routinely in patronising third world countries and did not mean much, but were found to be adequate by Pakistan at this critical hour to scare New Delhi. If China had not entered the 1965 War, it was largely due to the United States' warning to the Chinese in Warsaw, (where there were regular contacts between the Americana and Chinese ambassadors) of the danger of going too far vis-à-vis India. Both Moscow and Washington were on the same page then.[74] Though the war was stopped by a UNSC resolution, the limelight was stolen by the USSSR by sponsoring talks between India and Pakistan at Tashkent. Moscow's main intention was to deprive China of an opportunity to fish in troubled waters.[75]

India was worried as it recalled several of China's statements in favour of Pakistan in recent years. It also recalled Bhutto's 17 July 1963 speech in the Pakistan National Assembly which had underlined the new phase in their relations. In another statement, Bhutto had insisted that while the India–China clash in 1962 was only a border conflict, India had used it to amass arms from the West, not against China, but Pakistan. Bhutto had then warned in the National Assembly that an attack on Pakistan would be an attack against the 'territorial integrity and security of the largest state in Asia'. He was cleverly using the Chinese Vice Premier Chen Yi's speech at the UAR (United Arab Republic, Egypt) National Day reception in Beijing to scare India.[76] These statements put together laid bare the Pakistan–China axis of hate.[77]

But to assuage the ruffled feelings of Americans and the British, Bhutto had given their ambassadors 'ringing assurances' that there was no secret agreement or understanding with China on defence matters, but added that China would support Pakistan in the event of an attack from India.[78] The United States was conscious of the perils of Pakistan getting too close to China and were doing their bit to prevent it and wanted India to contribute positively to end that trend, which was more in India's interest.[79] The State Department had already on 20 August 1963 warned its embassy in New Delhi that 'should Pakistan enter into an alliance with Chicoms (Communist Chinese) India would be flanked and the entire subcontinent endangered.'[80]

This was also the assessment of US National Security Advisor Henry Kissinger that China was unlikely to get involved in the India–Pakistan conflict since 'Chinese were cautious people'.[81] Kissinger's assessment at that time appeared somewhat motivated since he was making a clandestine visit to Beijing in the next few days through the good offices of Pakistan.

However, President Nixon reacting to Congress resolution not to aid Pakistan said, 'If we go along with Congress and cut off all assistance to Pakistan then we will lose what influence we have on the humanitarian problem,' and hence the need to 'keep some leverage in Pakistan'.[82] However, Shivshankar Menon, India's former National Security Advisor, said, 'If United States were not engaged in secretly negotiating an opening to China, it would not have backed Pakistan's crackdown to the hilt and may not have misled Yahya into overreacting thus encouraging a negotiated settlement with greater autonomy for East Pakistan, which was what the Awami League and others actually sought until late 1970.'[83]

In April 1971, Pakistan's foreign secretary, Sultan Khan, had visited Beijing and was somewhat disappointed since instead of assurance of Chinese intervention in case of a war with India, he was greeted with the sermon to improve relations with the people, take 'impressive' economic measures and 'commence political work' in East Bengal. Sultan Khan was further disappointed when he learnt that the advice had emanated from Mao himself.[84]

However, Islamabad did receive helpful signals from Washington. The US National Security Advisor, Henry Kissinger, on return to Washington from a covert visit to China had told the Indian Ambassador L.K. Jha that if war broke out and if China were involved on the Pakistan side, the US 'would be unable to help you (India) against China'. Kissinger also added for good measure, that he had been told by Zhou Enlai that 'Pakistan would not provoke war against India', because it was too weak but should India attack Pakistan, 'China would not sit idle'.[85] In November, Zhou had advised Bhutto, who had come calling along with his foreign secretary, Sultan Khan, not to provoke India in view of its own weakness. In order not to completely disappoint him, Zhou, as a sop, told him it would supply arms but not actually join in the war.[86]

The Chinese were giving out conflicting signals and keeping Pakistan hopeful and India guessing and yet not making any commitments.

Even before Bhutto's China visit, China had almost decided against any involvement in the India–Pakistan imbroglio and it hoped India too would not start the war. This conclusion was based on several assumptions, one of which was the unexpected initiative of the Chinese ambassador in Lagos (Nigeria) requesting a meeting with the Indian high commissioner, where he stressed the importance of friendly relations between their countries and hoped that the differences over the boundary could be resolved by negotiations. The Chinese ambassador refrained from mentioning any current issues between India and Pakistan in his conversation with his Indian counterpart.[87] However, the fact that the Chinese ambassador had taken the initiative in seeking a meeting without any provocation had its own significance. Possibly, the India–Soviet Treaty which already had been signed in August, had a sobering effect on Beijing. Notwithstanding these reports of China not actually entering the war, India remained worried about the China factor because of its past experience and its persistent hostile attitude towards India.

For some time, India had toyed with the idea of taking the issue to the United Nations. However, EAM Swaran Singh was wary of this option. He had told the heads of Indian Mission in western Europe in June 1971 that, 'I am fully convinced of the total ineffectiveness of UN organisations whether they are political, social or human rights. They talk and talk and do nothing.' India had come a long way from its faith in multilateral institutions since the fifties.[88]

The Indian Ambassador in Paris, D.N. Chatterjee, who among others was also consulted, strongly advised against the UN option pointing out that most of the third-world countries which dominate the UN General Assembly were themselves guilty of human rights violations in their own countries and would treat it as interference in the internal affairs of Pakistan. His fear was also that with the lapse of time, the core of the problem would be lost and Cold War politics would sweep it under the carpet. He reminded Delhi on the fate of the Kashmir issue in the UN.

This letter was addressed to the Joint Secretary (UN), but while forwarding its copy to Haksar, the PM's Principal Secretary, Ambassador Chatterjee had added a handwritten note and said:

India is regarded warily in the West because she is against the concept of imperialism and because she invented the 'Third World'. India is looked on with suspicion in the 'third world' because of her [subversive]sentiments for democracy, human rights etc. The Muslims world is wrathful because of our secularism. The communist countries regard India as insolent—and particularly dangerous—because we have rejected communism as the prime condition for progress.' He ended his letter sarcastically saying, 'We are, of course, on the side of God,' and warily asked, 'is God on our side?'[89]

External Affairs Minister Swaran Singh dismissed as ridiculous, Kissinger's charge at the behest of Pakistan, that India was preventing the return of refugees, but added the refugees would not go back under the same regime which had 'pushed them out'.[90]

Pakistan's Ministry of Foreign Affairs had advised its heads of mission abroad of Indian attempts to destabilize Pakistan and asked them to brief their host governments and the media about Indian shenanigans.[91]

At the UN, India successfully blocked Pakistan's move to get observers posted along the East–West Bengal border. Moscow had assured Delhi that should the matter come up before the security council, it would use its veto. Yahya Khan, in yet another letter to Kosygin, a copy of which was sent to the Indian prime minister by the Soviet ambassador, expressed confidence that he would be able to restore normalcy in East Bengal. He, however, added a caveat that it would depend on Indian cooperation since he blamed India for inflaming passions which were preventing the return of people who had fled to India. He requested Kosygin to use his influence with India to allow the restoration of normalcy in East Bengal.[92] It was, of course, Yahya's diversionary move which did not bear fruits.

Sheikh Mujibur Rahman had been taken to West Pakistan where he was put on trial. Prompted by Delhi, Moscow warned Yahya Khan 'if this were to happen, it would aggravate the situation seriously'.[93]

Besieged from all sides, Pakistan was encouraged by the 7 December 1957 statement of the US State Department that a threat to the territorial integrity or political independence of the member countries (of the

Baghdad Pact of which Pakistan was a member) would be viewed with utmost gravity and cautioned Moscow that the United States regarded that letter 'as in full force' and as applying to that situation in 1971.[94]

Yet again to help Pakistan, Kissinger told the Chinese Ambassador at the UN, Huang Hua that if China took measures to protect Pakistan, the US would oppose efforts by others to interfere with the Chinese.[95]

China, despite having failed Pakistan in 1965 on Kashmir, emerged Pakistan's most reliable option, but not quite. Pakistan's continued flaunting of Chinese relationship was essentially to intimidate India. To meet any possible challenge posed by the Pakistan–China nexus, India was anxious to keep China out of the current problem it faced in East Pakistan. The unfriendly attitude of the United States was an added worry. The only option appeared to be the Soviet Union. China's political relations with Moscow due to the ideological differences between them had gone downhill for many years. It was also found that the differences between them were not merely ideological but had seeped into political and territorial levels too. India was quite confident that Moscow would not let China take advantage of India's predicament. The security question could not be left to presumptions; rather it was felt necessary to have it sealed beforehand.

India, looking into various possibilities, was surprised to discover that Moscow itself had been anxious for a treaty with New Delhi since 1969, but it was India which had reservations lest it should hurt its non-aligned character. The Bangladesh developments were not on the horizon then, though the unholy nexus between Pakistan and China was in the making for quite some time. India had watched closely, the Sino–Soviet conflict widening from the ideological to political and finally to a territorial dispute, since China had laid claim to vast tracts of Soviet territories.

Moscow, worried about increasing Chinese bellicosity and a hostile United States, had in 1969 floated the concept of 'Asian Collective Security' to bring Asian nations together in a voluntary collective against China. India, in Soviet's calculations, would likely be the kingpin of that Asian Security concept as it had a score to settle with China since its defeat in 1962 and China's ever-increasing hostility against India. But India was still hesitant to move enthusiastically. Given the Soviet anxiety to isolate China, India's reluctance was on account of the damage the proposal for a treaty would cause to India's non-alignment policy which was the cornerstone of its foreign policy since Nehru's days. Yet, Moscow's proposal could not be rejected mindlessly and so Ambassador Dhar came to Delhi to consult with the Ministry of External Affairs. While in Delhi, Ambassador Dhar was informed by Romesh Bhandari, now the chargé d'affaires in Moscow, that the Soviets had said that a treaty would warn both Pakistan and China of the communality of interests of both the countries and it would, therefore, be a good insurance against any possible aggression by China or Pakistan singly or jointly. To push Delhi into action, it was added for good measure that Pakistan had been asking for such a treaty but the Soviets had yet not responded since it was their desire to enter into such a treaty with India first. Bhandari, giving a gist of his conversation to Ambassador Dhar, who was already in Delhi, said it was his impression that once the treaty was signed, there would be increased cooperation in different fields.[96] It was in this background that Ambassador Dhar met EAM Dinesh Singh on 2 April 1969 and gave him a gist of the Soviet assurance that they would come to India's assistance in case of any aggression from China or Pakistan. The added advantage expected from this treaty, according to Dhar, was a supply of more sophisticated weapons including bombers, which India needed badly besides the advantage of technology transfer. He strongly recommended the offer of a treaty be accepted. The minister while asking the foreign secretary to examine the treaty in consultation with the Ministry of Defence, suggested the prime minister should write a suitable letter to Chairman Kosygin.

Indira Gandhi in her letter to Kosygin on 30 August 1969 pointed out the dangers posed by China, to both the Soviet Union and India. While being positive to the proposal for a treaty she was keen that it should not appear to be an exercise in expediency but a declaration of high principles. India was well aware that it would have a global significance and attract worldwide attention, particularly because of its non-aligned policy. It was evident that even China's reaction would not be positive since it would find the treaty to be against it. To avoid prying eyes, it was suggested and Moscow was agreeable, that further negotiations for the treaty should take place in Moscow.

There were other reasons too for Mrs Gandhi to move cautiously on the treaty proposal in the then prevailing domestic political situation. Domestically, the right wing of the Congress party was arraigned against her, and she was worried about the embarrassment it would cause to her. Under the circumstances, the proposal for the treaty was put on the back burner. The Soviet Union too did not push India too hard, lest it should be put off.

The developments in Pakistan following Yahya's refusal to allow the political process to reach its logical conclusion after the Awami League's victory had created a combustible situation. Yahya's rejection of the six-point programme of the Awami League, the crackdown on the people in the east, the arrest of Mujibur Rahman, the reign of terror let loose by the West Pakistan army on the people of East Pakistan, had sucked India into the Pakistan-made conundrum. It was a situation not of New Delhi's making, but it could not run away from it.

At this time, there were two opinions in India, one led by strategic expert K. Subramaniam, who suggested 'a quick and full-fledged military campaign, a blitzkrieg'. The second opinion held by the PM, EAM and senior officials following the advice of the Chief of R&AW, R.N. Kao, was to 'follow an incremental and phased strategy'.[97]

Internationally, it was New Delhi's assessment notwithstanding the policy of non-alignment that things had gone too far and a dispassionate view had to be taken of the situation as it confronted India. The domestic political situation too had changed in favour of Mrs Gandhi after the March 1971 general elections and she was far more confident to face her political rivals weakened by an electoral defeat. Delhi decided to face the politico-military challenge of Pakistan head-on and decided to get rid of its past inhibitions and hesitations. Conscious of the Chinese challenge, however uncertain, two years after the proposal for a treaty was first made by Moscow, its revival now looked advantageous. To test if the Soviet interest in the treaty was still alive, in March 1971, Fomin, head of the Asia Department at the Soviet Foreign Office, was invited to a lunch engagement at the residence of Romesh Bhandari, a minister at the Indian Embassy. The ambassador broaching the subject asked Fomin about the 'Document', without reference to the past Soviet proposal for a treaty. As if waiting to be asked, the mere mention of 'Document' was enough to alert Fomin, who said that Moscow, sensing Indian sensitivities, had allowed the matter to hibernate all this time. He added if after the elections, the Indian government considered the time opportune and propitious enough for resuming stalled discussions on the 'Document', the Indian government would not find the Soviet government wanting in their desire to reciprocate fully. Fomin made an interesting observation:

> Mr Ambassador, did you wish to mention the 'Document' to know from me whether our position had in any way changed as a result of our talks with China, [and added] if that is so, our position with regard to the need and significance of concluding this arrangement with your country remains unaltered.[98]

Ambassador Dhar in his letter No. 220 AMB/71 dated 3 March 1971 reported the above conversation to New Delhi where upon the PM's principal secretary under instructions from the PM asked Dhar to seek an urgent meeting with Kosygin and brief him of the situation in East Bengal and enquire if there was any possibility of joint Soviet and American efforts to bring the conflict to an end and whether the Soviet Union would be prepared to share the burden of sustaining the struggle.[99] It appeared Delhi was still procrastinating on the question of treaty, since there was no mention of it in the letter.

As the situation in East Pakistan deteriorated further, Mrs Gandhi in her letter of 27 April to Kosygin listed the atrocities being committed by the Pakistan army in East Bengal and the stream of refugees coming to India straining its resources. She said Pakistan had augmented its strength in the east from one-and-a-half divisions to four, making it clear that Pakistan wished to use force to break the resistance of the people there. However, her letter failed yet again to make any mention of the need for a treaty. She had ended the letter with an earnest hope that the 'power and prestige of the USSR will be used in prevailing upon the military rulers of Pakistan to see that the path they have chosen to cement their kinship with East Pakistanis is unwise'.[100]

Ambassador Dhar reported back and said that in the past one week, he had several meetings in the Soviet Foreign Office, and a marathon meeting lasting four hours with Soviet Ambassador Pegov, who was in Moscow, and felt emboldened to 'draw some sense of assurance' that Moscow had given up on Pakistan and had aligned with the future of 'Bangla Desh' rather with the regime of doubtful durability. About the Pakistan–China collusion, he said that there were two views: (1) The Chinese threat was nothing more than an empty one, and (2) The Chinese were ready to intervene militarily. Dhar, however, preferred to go along with the first view. In the ambassador's view, if India were to sign the 'Document' it would be a counterblow to the Pakistani morale and 'they may succumb to the continuing pressure of the East Bengal situation'. Conversely, he believed it would 'immediately lift the morale of the average Indian sky-high'. While recommending this course of action, Dhar was conscious that there would be some anti-PM 'idle intellectuals' who would oppose it for the sake of opposing it. Finally, Dhar added that the Soviets might be unwilling to sign the 'Document' for fear of inviting 'a lot of abuse and calumny' against themselves from the Chinese.[101] On the same day, in another letter, this time to Principal Secretary to PM, Haksar, Ambassador Dhar reported Kosygin's positive attitude to the developments and expected the Soviets to announce a substantial contribution with a view to sharing India's burden for relief operations. He also reported that the Soviets were in agreement with the Indian assessment that East and West Pakistan were unlikely to meet and even Yahaya's envoy, Arshad Hussain, could not convince Moscow that the situation would be normalized. The Soviets were of the opinion that the struggle in East Bengal would be longer and that 'it will be self-deceptive to hope for its early termination'.[102]

New Delhi was keen on Soviet support but was anxious to avoid formal 'Documents', notwithstanding Soviet readiness. India without saying so, wanted Moscow to announce its support to India against China in a statement, instead of a formal treaty, but the Soviets were anxious for a formal document. The Soviet frustration with Delhi was writ large when Dhar met Defence Minister Marshal Grechko for his farewell call on 5 June 1971. Marshal was aware of the fast-deteriorating situation in East Bengal and India's vulnerabilities because of its failure to make any headway in its relations with China. He was eager that both India and USSR hasten the process of signing the 'Document'. One of the reasons for the USSR's urgency to sign it was, as pointed out above, its own ever-deteriorating relations with China and its strategic desire to encircle China. Grechko went to great lengths to try and hustle India into signing the 'Document'. What Dhar was seeking at this meeting was the supply of certain weapon systems, but the marshal sang a different tune altogether. He told Dhar not to worry about Pakistan, but take into account the unpredictable enemy from the north, and spoke of the tense situation that had developed on the eastern borders of the USSR where China had laid claim to 1.5 million km of Soviet territory encapsulating a population of eight million. He gave a detailed account of the Soviet army and air deployment which had made the Chinese 'aware of the superiority of the Soviet forces on the Eastern border and this had disowned their tail'. The Chinese knew of the Soviet mood and would not dare to play pranks with them. He added for Indian consumption:

[T]he Chinese were aware that India was relatively militarily weak. They could therefore, afford to be aggressive, even insolent and arrogant towards India. They had to be watched and India had to be careful.[103]

After a long sermon, the marshal said it would be of vital interest 'if our friendship was fixed in a treaty of mutual help of the kind recently concluded by the USSR with the United Arab Republic (Egypt). UAR. He went to the extent of telling the ambassador that the draft of the treaty had already been worked out and it had been shown to Defence Minister Swaran Singh when he had earlier visited Moscow. Reminding Dhar of the deployment of massive Soviet armed forces on the Soviet–China border, he delivered his final punchline:

Do you think that the massing of our troops in the western and northwestern borders of China does not help India directly in her defence against China? If the Chinese had not to contend against our forces, they would release their hordes for use against you [India]. We have to understand these problems in the military sense—in the operational sense.[104]

Dhar was duly impressed with the Soviet determination to help India. On the same day, he reported his conversation to Foreign Secretary T.N. Kaul and emphasized the all-pervasive Soviet interest in the 'Document', and said:

> [T]he mention of the 'Document' in various forms from Pegov to Grechko, from our Central Committee contact to a junior dignitary as Labochev in the Foreign Office makes it clear that in spite of developing crisis in our relation with Pakistan with the Chinese intervention as a distinct possibility, the Soviets would be prepared to accept the responsibilities and obligations which would devolve on them, as a result of such a commitment.[105]

The ambassador, fully convinced of the Soviet offer, tried to prevail upon New Delhi to give up its hesitation, if any, since it had been prevaricating for too long and accept the Soviet offer. He decided to make a forceful plea and said:

> Zaheedi (Iranian Prime Minister) shame-faced threat to us that Iran would come to Pakistan's assistance, the activities of the so-called consortium of some Islamic countries, the continuing threats from China, altogether make me wonder whether we are being wise in reacting in a lukewarm manner to the Soviet offer of unequivocal help to us. The pros and cons of this proposal and its present and ultimate utility can be judged in New Delhi in consultation with the Foreign Minister and other concerned authorities. It is however, important that we do have some sort of understanding of what we expect the Soviet Union to do for us in event of our country being involved in a conflict with Pakistan singly or along with her allies. I am not talking merely in terms of the political requirements of the

situation as it will develop as a consequence of a conflict of this type. In am more interested in the military aspect of the aid and assistance which we will need and which we are bound to seek.[106]

In the meantime, Washington on 3 June, had made an announcement of a fresh supply of arms to Pakistan. National Security Advisor Henry Kissinger in Delhi on his way to Pakistan for his clandestine visit to Beijing met Principal Secretary to the PM, Haksar, and insisted that the arms supplies were of marginal significance, and necessary to 'have some leverage with Yahya Khan'. To humour Haksar, Kissinger said:

I can only assure you that President Nixon and his closest advisers are anxious to make a fresh start. The President sincerely feels that in this whole region of south and southeast Asia, India is the only country which has all the potentialities of being not only a big power, but a power for peace and stability. Pakistan is only of a small regional significance and does not occupy any place in our global perspective.[107]

Kissinger appeared worried at the possibility of conflict between India and Pakistan and added that in that event, China would certainly react and this would lead India to rely on the Soviet Union which 'would cause complications for us in America'. After going through a lot of rigmarole about the US trying to hold talks with the Soviet Union on various international issues, he said as far as India was concerned there was no conflict of interest between the Soviet Union and the United States and both of them wanted a 'peaceful and stable India'. About China, Kissinger said he was anxious for an improvement of relations and wanted to move quickly in that direction and insisted that:

[I]f Chinese seek to dominate the areas outside their country, or, for instance, dominate India, we cannot connive at this. In this global view, Pakistan is only of regional significance.

But he did not disclose his real mission of working toward the opening of China.[108]

When Kissinger met Mrs Gandhi at his very personal request, she warned him that the situation in East Bengal did not brook any delay and left him in little doubt that it was not an India–Pakistan problem but between the two parts of Pakistan.[109]

President Nixon had in a personal letter to Mrs Gandhi expressed his concern at the situation in East Pakistan but hoped that 'Pakistan would take steps to defuse the situation' and insisted that the US must maintain a 'constructive' relationship with Pakistan so that 'we may retain some influence in working with them'.[110]

Mrs Gandhi, meanwhile, replying to President Nixon's letter of 1 July, sought to convey her frustration with the unhelpful attitude she found in Washington during her visit. She did not agree with Nixon's assessment that the situation in East Pakistan was returning to normal. She also rejected the suggestion that if UN observers were posted on the India–East Pakistan border, the problem of refugees would be solved. She conveyed her disappointment at the news of America making fresh defence supplies to Pakistan.[111] During her visit to London, Mrs Gandhi had found the British PM powerless against Nixon's obstinacy and the same situation confronted her in other European capitals as well.[112]

The unambiguous and forceful assessment which Ambassador Dhar made had an instant impact in New Delhi and it reacted quickly. Swaran Singh, who had in the meantime, returned to the external affairs ministry and was travelling to western Europe to exhort them to action, broke his journey in Moscow and found himself facing the Soviet Foreign Minister Gromyko, discussing the possibility of Chinese assistance to Pakistan in some details. Speaking to Gromyko, Swaran Singh said, 'I think China is the only country which has given all out, full and unequivocal support to the military regime in its military action in East Bengal,' which, in his opinion, had caused embarrassment to even pro-China elements like the Bhashani group which was ultra left. He then referred to the belligerent statements of Zhou Enlai pledging full support to Yahya Khan for the preservation of Pakistan's unity. Gromyko agreed that it was against the Bengali aspirations and said the extent of opposition to the Chinese was so virulent that anything Moscow supported, China opposed and vice versa.

Analysing China's position, Swaran Singh further said:

I have no direct information about these plans [of Pakistan–China collusion] but there is a good deal of circumstantial evidence which indicates a positive collusion between China and Pakistan.

He added, China had given substantial loans to Pakistan but had converted them into outright gifts later. He felt it was improbable that China's largess had no strings attached. He also pointed out to the frequent visits of Pakistani leaders to Beijing where they were received not only by Zhou but Mao also. He also pointed out to the ultimatum China had given in 1965 and referred to Bhutto's statement in the 1966 in Pakistan National Assembly.

Swaran Singh described as a misfortune, Pakistan's failure to be aware of the dangers which faced it ultimately, from its present friendship with Beijing. Confirming that there was no possibility of improvement in relations with China, he thanked Gromyko for the Soviet friendship and put it to him:

[A] situation may arise, which may demand the entry of Soviet Union into it in order to counter the difficulties which may be created by Chinese support to Pakistan. Perhaps, even now you will have to consider some appropriate steps by which Chinese support to Pakistan can be counter-balanced. This is the only way of eliminating the possibility of China and Pakistan pressuring India.

Gromyko clutching at EAM statement asked, 'What form this suggestion can assume . . . and what form Soviet assistance can take—that you wish us to pursue?'

Swaran Singh ducking the question said that he had just posed the problem and he was open for further discussions. Gromyko asked the EAM to recall the earlier proposal of 'signing some sort of a Document, some sort of a Treaty' and even when these discussions had reached an advanced stage, were suspended due to India's domestic problems. Gromyko, therefore, suggested he consult with his prime minister on the earlier proposal. Swaran Singh not wanting to postpone indefinitely the question of Soviet assistance, expressed his readiness to give his views straightaway and added that the PM had kept him informed of the earlier negotiations and suggested 'we can work on this Document and discuss it and arrive at a suitable agreement'. To avoid signing a formal document, Swaran Singh using the pretext of delay that negotiating a treaty might cause and asked if something could be thought of 'quickly'. There was desperation and contradiction in EAM's suggestion. Avoiding the treaty he said, 'If a situation develops unpredictably, we should not be found wanting or caught napping. There should be some understanding on that score.'

Gromyko, to avoid replying, said it needed to be 'studied very carefully; it deserves a lot of thinking' and wanted to know when India would be ready for a discussion on the treaty since earlier discussions on the draft were suspended because India wanted it. The EAM said while threads of the earlier discussions could be picked up, and India would accept the clause relating to the 'immediate consultations in the event of a certain unfortunate situation materialising suddenly', he stressed that negotiating the treaty would take time. He wanted to know in the interim period 'what could the Soviet Union do' to meet the unpredictable situation. Swaran Singh suggested a message be 'conveyed to the proper quarters' which may lead to the preservation of peace in this region and 'it may constitute one great single factor for averting the present threat to peace'. Again, clutching on to his statement Gromyko asked, 'in what way do you want us to make this statement? In what way should we formulate our attitude? You have to be more concrete.'

The EAM avoided a direct reply and said, 'There are various forms. There can be various ways.' Gromyko said as far as the proposed treaty was concerned it would need a further exchange of views 'in order to amend or alter the contents of the earlier draft'.

While the External Affairs Minister was avoiding the treaty and Gromyko perceived that if a statement, as suggested, was issued, India might lose interest in the treaty altogether, as had happened earlier.

At this point, Gromyko wanted to close the meeting, but the EAM asked for something 'more concrete'; the steps the Soviets 'contemplated to bring pressure on Pakistan and Yahya Khan.' He told Gromyko that he was unlikely to get a positive response from countries he was proposing to visit and therefore he wanted the Soviet views. He said as far as India was concerned, it was looking for steps which would 'immediately halt refugee influx; restore conditions of normalcy to bring peace and tranquillity to East Bengal'. He wanted to make it 'absolutely clear that under no circumstances shall we agree to a position where we have to accept these refugees permanently on our soil'.

Gromyko disappointed the EAM with his remarks that Moscow had not yet reached a stage of planning its action in more concrete terms since Moscow was planning to consult India for its suggestions which Moscow would take into account in planning its response. Perceiving little hope of getting any concrete result from Gromyko, the EAM now suggested an adjournment of the meeting which therefore remained inconclusive.

The next day, on 8 June, Swaran Singh had a longish meeting with Chairman Kosygin and gave him a briefing on the situation as prevailing in India, the tragic developments in East Pakistan, and the influx of refugees into India and the prime minister's determination not to allow their prolonged stay in India. To scare Kosygin, he said if no solution was found, he feared the danger of extremist elements favourable to China taking control of the movement which would be neither in the interest of India nor the USSR. Kosygin agreed with the assessment of the EAM and called Bhutto 'an accomplice agent of a vile tool of this ruthless dictatorship—a pathetic symbol of blind ambition'.

Kosygin, mulling the way the problem in East Pakistan could be settled, whether by 'establishment of an independent State or the founding of a democratic regime', was worried about Bangladesh's 'domestic jurisdiction'. He, however, advised the EAM that while maintaining a position of non-interference, 'we, at the same time, should take a resolute position against Yahya Khan regarding the question of refugees'. He suggested that the minister during his talks with leaders of other countries should maintain this position 'firmly'.

Swaran Singh felt that the Soviet reaction to the situation in East Pakistan was lukewarm. When Kosygin told the EAM that he would consult with his colleagues, Brezhnev, Podgorny and other members of the Politburo, and exchange views in greater detail, before drawing up a plan of action 'to bring about pressure by diplomatic and other means on the Government of Yahya Khan . . .', the EAM was disappointed, since Pakistan was not India's worry; it was China. To emphasize the Chinese factor, the EAM said:

> [I]n recent statements, China had pledged help to Pakistan and wanted Moscow to see the 'desirability of making a statement, at an appropriate stage, in order to counterbalance the effects of Chinese statements'. I do not suggest that such a statement should, in any way be specifically or otherwise directed against China. The statement could pledge support for the maintenance of the sovereignty and territorially integrity of India against any military adventure etc.

It was clear to Kosygin that Swaran Singh in asking for a statement was avoiding the need for a treaty. Both parties appeared to be involved in a war of wits. Not able to bring Moscow to play his googlies, Swaran Singh asked Kosygin for his assessment of the possibility of a China–Pakistan tie-up. Betraying his fears of China, Singh asked Kosygin about the possibility of China 'instigating Pakistan to start an adventure against India'. Kosygin, to Swaran Singh's frustration, said Moscow had not received any 'specific information in confirmation of that view'. However, to assuage the EAM's feelings he did not rule out the possibility of a provocation from China. Yet again, Kosygin to the EAM's disappointment said, 'Officially we have only been informed that China had supplied milk, dry milk to Pakistan,' but added, 'one cannot vouch against the possibility of China giving Pakistan a push to start an aggression.' He added, since India had more information, it should know better. Swaran Singh did not quote any definite intelligence about India's fears but repeated it was India's assessment that 'China would instigate Pakistan to harass and weaken India [and] they in that event would enter the conflict directly or keep us busy on the borders and tie up our troops'. In that event, 'we look up to you to take action which is capable of neutralising such a possibility.'

Kosygin as a palliative said, 'All I have said is all that we know. You know far better than we do.'

Swaran Singh, who personified patience, referred to the grave situation that existed in East Pakistan and expressed the hope that the Soviets would take appropriate action which would 'at once constitute a warning to those who want to disturb peace'. While thanking the Soviets for the help they had given in food etc., for the refugees, he said the prime minister had asked him to request him (Kosygin) to give his suggestions as to how India could effectively meet this grave situation. Kosygin referring to the EAM's earlier discussions with Gromyko said, 'He had just heard of a "Document", some sort of a statement or communiqué that you wish to issue at the conclusion of your talks with Gromyko,' and added, 'I would like to tell you that I agree fully with the draft [of the treaty] that your ambassador had earlier given us and also the manner in which the question of refugees had been posed in it.' Without showing any signs of frustration, Swaran Singh again drew Kosygin's attention to the 'belligerent statements recently issued by China pledging support to Pakistan' and asked Kosygin to consider the 'desirability of making a statement at an appropriate stage, in order to counterbalance the effects of Chinese statements'. Clarifying, he said he did not want any specific statement against China, but the USSR could 'pledge support for the maintenance of the sovereignty and territorial integrity of India against any military adventure etc'.

Not making any commitment about the statement, Kosygin only said that he would consult with his colleagues—Brezhnev, Podgorny, etc. He asked the EAM to continue his discussions with Gromyko on the Document/Treaty. Swaran Singh took the hint that Moscow would not bite, as the Soviets feared a statement would obviate the need for a formal treaty, and finally gave up and decided to hold another meeting with Gromyko and take the proposal for a treaty forward.

Interestingly, earlier to goad India into signing a treaty, Moscow had been highlighting the Chinese threat, and now suddenly to avoid issuing a statement, the USSR denied that they had any concrete information of a Chinese threat. They were worried that if a statement was issued, India would renege on the treaty, and so the Soviets suddenly found no merit in India's forebodings on China. It was insistent on a treaty for it wished to send a message to China, that it stood isolated in the context of its Sino–Soviet ideological and political dispute. Not wasting any more time, Swaran Singh came straight to the treaty and suggested that 'we should now pick up the threads of earlier discussions'. Gromyko assured him that it would act as a great lever of peace, which would be a deterrent both to China and Pakistan against embarking on a military adventure. When asked when India would be ready to resume the discussions, the EAM said that he intended to send a small team from New Delhi for this purpose. Gromyko expressed happiness at this.

An analysis of Swaran Singh's talks in Moscow would indicate that New Delhi had panicked on account of the possibility of a Chinese involvement on Pakistan's side in a war which appeared inevitable at that time. Its fear was China's involvement would mean a three-front war, against China on the Sino–Indian border, and against East and West Pakistan—the two fronts a thousand kilometres apart. India's resources would be stretched beyond its capabilities. Moscow taking full advantage of Indian trepidations made it finally negotiate a formal treaty, much against its wishes.

Before the Indian team went to Moscow, India looked at the earlier drafts of the treaty and finalized a fresh one, closer to the earlier draft and made it available to Moscow before the discussions took place there on 3 August 1971 between Soviet Foreign Minister Gromyko and D.P. Dhar, now Chairman of the Policy Planning Committee in the Ministry of External Affairs. Dhar was assisted by his successor, Ambassador Krishnarao Shelvankar.

Most of the changes in the Indian draft suggested by Gromyko were of an editorial nature and posed little problem in acceptance by the Indian side. However, when Gromyko suggested there should be indication of some economic activity like 'efforts to develop certain fields like fishing, merchant marine and rational utilisation of resources of the sea' in the draft, India was reluctant, since it was felt a 'reference to such economic activities would detract from the value of the Treaty' and so the Soviet side did not press the point.

India had proposed that the treaty be signed by the two foreign ministers, but the Soviets wanted it to be signed by the heads of government and suggested Mrs Gandhi visit Moscow to sign it. Finally, it was decided that it be signed by the two foreign ministers in New Delhi.

Dhar, during lunch, hosted by Gromyko in his honour, suggested that both countries should exchange information which would help them make an assessment of the overall strength and intentions of China and Pakistan, separately and jointly, while also making an appreciation of the attitude of the US in the context of the recent developments. Gromyko agreed provided Kosygin did.

The important issue that came up was the 'measures' that would be necessary to prevent 'Pakistan and her ebullient allies' who would feel tempted to unleash a war against India. Gromyko agreeing with Dhar said it had an important bearing on the obligations which flowed directly from the treaty. Dhar amplifying his point of view said that 'the threat of attack is absolutely apparent in the context of Sino–Pakistan behaviour towards India,' and added, there could be difference of opinion whether this 'threat of attack is absolutely imminent or is yet slightly remote'. Nevertheless, he said:

> [A]n obligation has been cast on the two parties to enter into consultations as to how such a threat should be removed. All the measures for this purpose, whether these are undertaken individually or in concert with each other or in alliance with likeminded countries, or from the forum of the United Nations, will have to be determined at least in broad outlines.

It was agreed that at the time of signing the treaty, a consensus on military, political and economic steps would become necessary in case 'an attack materialises as a reality, and the forms of consultation'. As such, Gromyko was advised to come prepared at the time of signing the treaty. Gromyko agreed and said he had no hesitation in admitting that these matters were important in themselves and had great relevance not only to the treaty but to the demands of the contemporary situation.[113]

Dhar had a separate meeting with Kosygin the next day when he pointed out that Yahya Khan was bellicose and his warmongering was matched in fervour and enthusiasm by China. He believed Pakistan's intransigence had been further strengthened by the help US had promised in return for Pakistan assisting Kissinger in his clandestine visit to Beijing. He, however, said if war was forced upon India, it was absolutely necessary to put our heads together to prevent it, and to take steps that adventure was not unleashed. This was our primary aim and it was one of the common endeavours of the USSR and India. Kosygin had earlier told Swaran Singh that many countries like Pakistan, China and the United States, would oppose the treaty, but he was confident that the people of those countries would welcome it. Kosygin said that Moscow had declined a request from Yahya Khan to receive a special messenger from him. Yahya had added while he was 'exercising patience, but patience had its limits'.

Before ending his long sermon, Kosygin sought to scare India, pointing out that Pakistan Intelligence and the United States knew the entire situation on India's borders, the deployment of Indian army and defence equipment etc., and emphasized 'to be careful' and yet again said:

> I would once again, particularly advise you to make a very careful assessment of what more you should do to ensure that a climate of absolute secrecy about all that happening on your borders is scrupulously maintained. Otherwise, you will face many difficulties and many dangers. Regarding the strength of the Indian army, he said it should be known in a manner that it was a warning to everyone and it should frighten your enemies.[114]

It must have left Dhar wondering about the advice and overemphasis of it.

As the discussions in Moscow ended, the next day, 6 August, the Soviet ambassador handed over a letter to Haksar, which was from Yahya Khan to Kosygin, in which Yahya had listed steps he had taken to defuse the situation in the east to facilitate the return of refugees. He blamed India for preventing the situation from normalizing and in the return of refugees. Yahya regretted that in the face of India's hostile statements, the return of refugees had been impeded. Blaming

India, Yahya had said Pakistan's peaceful intentions have failed to receive corresponding response from India and Pakistan had been subjected to 'intolerable provocations and Indian leaders had been threatening military action'. Yahya, at the end, requested Kosygin to use his 'considerable influence' in India to prevent India's interference in Pakistan's internal affairs and to remove the obstacles to the return of the refugees. Closing the letter, Yahya asked for Soviet's active mediation which would be 'a very important contribution for peace in the region'.[115]

The External Affairs Minister after touring several western countries had informed the Rajya Sabha that Pakistan was trying to convince them that the problem in East Pakistan was between Pakistan and India, while India insisted it was between West Pakistan and the people of 'Bangla Desh'. Taking note of Yahya Khan's reported statement that India was attempting to seize East Pakistan and his warning of war, Swaran Singh said that if on this pretext Pakistan attacked India, India was ready to defend itself.[116]

India's urgency was understandable. The problem in East Pakistan was getting complicated with each passing day. A report from Lt Governor of Tripura, A.L. Dias, was worrying Delhi. It had said 'the unequal struggle' in East Bengal was reaching the end of its first phase and the Pakistan army was 'ruthlessly' consolidating its position in the urban and semi-urban areas while restoring disrupted communication and fanning out in the countryside to establish itself along the border with India.[117]

As a final act, the Soviet Foreign Minister Gromyko visited Delhi and the Treaty of Peace, Friendship and Cooperation was signed on the 9 August 1971 in New Delhi. Informing the Parliament of the treaty on the same day, and describing it as a 'stabilizing factor in favour of peace and security in the region' External Affairs Minister insisted it was a 'credible assurance that in the event of an attack or threat thereof, the High Contracting Parties shall immediately enter into mutual consultations in order to remove such a threat and to take appropriate effective measures to ensure peace and the security of their countries'. This, he said, should 'act as a deterrent to any power that may have aggressive designs on our territorial integrity and sovereignty'. 'We shall not allow any other country or combination of countries to dominate us or to interfere in our internal affairs.' On the contrary, he said, 'We shall to our maximum ability help other countries to maintain their freedom from outside domination and their sovereignty.'[118]

The Soviet daily *Pravda* in its editorial said it effectively 'restrained' Pakistan and China from embarking on a course of military adventure against India and it would continue to act as a 'deterrent' against the hegemonistic goals of countries like China. At the end, Foreign Secretary T.N. Kaul's assessment was that Kissinger had, in fact, pushed India into the open arms of Moscow since in India's assessment, both the United States and China were seen backing Pakistan.[119]

The day after the treaty was signed, Gromyko, in a meeting with Mrs Gandhi continued to harp on Moscow's qualms over a Chinese intervention. He too told her the US was encouraging Pakistan through military supplies. He added that Soviet relations with China continued to be bad.[120] As a result of the treaty, last-minute assurance of the Indian Ambassador in Beijing, Brajesh Mishra, that China would not join the war to avoid any clash with the Soviet Union, was comforting to New Delhi.[121]

On 2 September 1971, China, after much contemplation, said it did not regard the treaty a friendly development and saw it as a sign of growing Soviet–Indian collaboration against itself.[122] The *People's Daily* on 6 December accused India of 'splitting activities' and blamed Moscow with supporting, encouraging and approving Indian aggression against Pakistan.[123]

A worried Pakistan sent its foreign secretary, Sultan Khan, to Moscow where he was given a stern warning against any kind of hostilities or use of arms, while insisting that they desired continued good relations.[124]

Around this time, the Shah of Iran tried to fix a meeting between Yahya and Mrs Gandhi which she turned down with 'an impertinent remark'.[125] Yahya again visited Tehran, ostensibly in a final attempt to arrange a summit meeting with Mrs Gandhi to avert war and asked the Shah to use 'every influence' to arrange such a meeting. But

American intelligence sources doubted this and it was believed that the visit was in fact to seek the Shah's assurance of Iranian support.[126] Disappointed, Yahya tried to muster support with Sri Lankan PM Sirimavo Bandaranaike and asked if she would help ease the situation. Since Bandaranaike was actively involved in international affairs as a leader of the non-aligned group, Pakistan expected to score more brownie points.[127]

The treaty with Moscow was not strictly a conventional military alliance, but it acted like one when the chips were down. It successfully kept both China and the United States from jumping into the fray, and consequently, the nuclear-powered US 7th Fleet sailed away quietly from the Bay of Bengal.

President Nixon explaining America's inability to help Pakistan, told Bhutto during his 1973 visit to Washington that:

> [W]e consider Pakistan to deserve our continued friendship regardless of India or the USSR. This is not just because we are pro-Pakistan, although I admire the guts and courage of the Pakistani people . . . It is in our interest that a nation not be overrun.

However, to convince Bhutto that the US did try to support Pakistan, Kissinger pointed out that United States had reminded Moscow of President J.F. Kennedy's letter to the USSR stating their commitment to members of the alliance. To console Bhutto, Kissinger told him of his feeling that 'Bangladesh would work to the long-range disadvantage of India itself' and pointed out to the 'Pakistani flags from time to time in Bangladesh'. Bhutto agreed and said India had 'burned its fingers in the furnace of Bengal'.[128] While staying out, the United States did encourage China to help Pakistan and Kissinger told Bhutto that he had asked the Chinese Ambassador at the UN, Huang Hua, that if China took measures to protect Pakistan, the US would oppose efforts of others to interfere with the Chinese.[129]

The covert operations intensified from August onward and finally escalated in October. The Mukti Bahini, which was composed of Bengali youth volunteers, received more support in terms of lethal weaponry and their attacks on the Pakistani army were proving impactful. Finally, the prime minister ordered a full-scale war on Pakistan on 4 December in retaliation to the bombing raids of the Pakistani air force in the western sector a day earlier. On 6 December, India finally and formally recognized the independence of Bangladesh.

When these developments were taking place, China was inducted to the UN and Mrs Gandhi magnanimously welcomed it.[130] Despite India's welcome, the Chinese Representative at the UN, Huang Hua, in one of his earliest statements in the Security Council poured venom against India. Speaking in the Security Council on 4 December 1971, he accused India of committing 'armed aggression' against East Pakistan and 'aggravating tension' in the Asian subcontinent. He debunked India's plea of refugees and said it could extend the 'refugee' issue to other refugees in India like Tibetans and groom the Dalai Lama for a 'counter-revolutionary rebellion'.[131] Speaking the next day, he rejected the suggestion for a ceasefire on both sides and insisted that India should withdraw its troops from East Pakistan first.[132] Yet again, speaking in the UN General Assembly, China reiterated its earlier position of calling India an 'outright aggressor' and repeated the possibility of India using the Tibetan refugees for aggression against China.[133]

Upset by China's 'harsh and ill-informed' allegations in the UN, Mrs Gandhi wrote to the Chinese premier to put the developments in the perspective of a revolt by the people of 'Bangladesh' and India's compulsions to go to the aid of 75 million people who had repudiated their allegiance to Pakistan. She appealed to him to use China's influence with Pakistan to make it acknowledge the will of the people of Bangladesh.[134]

On the day the Pakistan army in East Pakistan surrendered, China to hide its embarrassment issued a long statement accusing India of harbouring and cherishing the pipe dream of a Greater Indian Empire which would endanger not only Pakistan but also other countries in the region.[135]

While India successfully liberated Bangladesh without the Soviet Union entering the war, its support proved helpful in deterring China or other countries to come to Pakistan's aid and in the UN Security Council from being indicted by any of the permanent members particularly the United States, by use of their veto. The objective of the people of East Bengal to free themselves from the tyranny of the western region was achieved. It also enabled the 10 million Bangladeshi refugees camping in India to return home with honour and dignity. India won back the respect dented in 1962. New Delhi could heave a sigh of relief and bask in the restored national glory.

As the war ended, India found its inventory of arms and ammunition substantially depleted, which became a source of worry. There were enough reports that China had helped Pakistan to replenish its war losses and had even given additional supplies. India naturally could not sit back and watch helplessly.

Within a couple of months of the end of the war, an Indian delegation led by the old Moscow hand, D.P. Dhar, in his new avatar as Chairman of the Policy Planning Committee of the Ministry of External Affairs, along with the Chief of Army Staff General Sam Manekshaw, landed in Moscow with a shopping list. Kosygin told Dhar that there was no change in Moscow's relations with China and even the Soviet ambassador who had come to Moscow for consultations had not gone back to his post. He pointed to the malicious position that the Chinese had taken against the Soviet Union. Kosygin said after failing to help Pakistan during the war, China was now trying to strengthen its position opportunistically and finding ways and means to save face.[136]

Kosygin's tirade against China was only a preface for what was to come when Dhar and Manekshaw met Chief of General Staff Marshal Andrei Grechko. While India's priority was the possibility of a revanchist war from Pakistan, the marshal was not impressed. Without mincing words, he said India was overrating the threat from Pakistan. In his perception the threat came from China, which:

[H]ad stooped so low that they had not only repudiated the principle of socialism and fraternal internationalism but had now entered into open collusion with the U.S. imperialism not only against the Soviet Union and other socialist countries but against the whole of progressive humanity. China was the real danger and India would be well advised to constantly remind itself of this fact. She could ignore this fact only at her own peril.

Continuing, he said, 'History had cast the role of India and the Soviet Union into those of allies against this menace.' He said he saw the future clearly, where both countries should coordinate their strategies and 'plans and harmonise their defence organisations for meeting such an eventuality'. He suggested some sort of 'military alliance, a situation in which India would need Soviet Union and the Soviet Union would need India' to deal with the designs of China.[137]

India pointed out that there already was a treaty signed just last year, which was valid for the next twenty years and should be enough to meet any unforeseen eventuality. But it did not impress the marshal. Obviously, he was attempting to involve India in the larger Sino–Soviet ideological and political dispute with China. With India refusing to be entrapped in his conundrum, the marshal lost interest in India's shopping list. It was practically the demise of the treaty signed a year ago. Neither India nor the Soviet Union thereafter invoked or even mentioned the treaty. Looking back, it became clear why Moscow had insisted on a treaty in June 1971 when Swaran Singh was keen on only a statement from the Soviets which would have warned any third-party intervention in the event of a face-off between India and Pakistan. Moscow was aware that since 1947, India had studiously avoided entering into any military alliance or even an innocuous treaty. Even in 1962, at the time of India–China hostilities, western assistance was without any treaty or alliance. When India accepted arms from the United States to replenish the war losses and for the newly raised regiments, it was done only when the US had withdrawn its conditionalities. The Indo–Soviet treaty of 1971 was not a military alliance in the classical sense but an innocuous document. It was now that Moscow's anxiety and insistence on a treaty unfolded. It was not an entirely friendly gesture born out of worries for India's security. In fact, Moscow had calculated that if India deviated even once from its no-alliance/treaty policy, it would have no qualms of entering into another one, only a little more lethal!

III

The Simla Agreement, 1972[*]

The thirteen-day India–Pakistan war had ended with the surrender of Lt Gen. A.A.K. Niazi and the 93,000 Pakistani soldiers under his command in East Pakistan. The people of the newly liberated Bangladesh had declared themselves a free people and established themselves into a sovereign, independent country. The war had cut Pakistan to size metaphorically, geographically and even politically. What was left of Pakistan was less than half of the 1947-Partitioned country since it is the people who make a nation and not the landmass. Pakistani Ambassador Jamsheed Marker was closer to reality, when he said, 'To describe East Pakistan action as secession is an oxymoron, in terms of political science, for the reality was that the majority had "seceded" from the minority.'[1] He described the scene in the post-war period for Pakistan 'dubious' with Indo–Soviet predominance in the subcontinent 'overwhelming'.[2] History had come full circle with the emergence of Bangladesh.

The defeat of the Pakistan army shattered the myth of the Muslim-dominated Pakistan Army's invincibility. India had met the challenge of the United States and China, both politically and diplomatically, and emerged a top regional power in South Asia. By diplomatically engaging with the Soviet Union, western Europe and the United States and sensitizing them to the ongoing human tragedy in East Pakistan and

---

[*] This narrative is primarily based on the ten-volume study titled *India–Pakistan Relations* and *India–Bangladesh Relations* and referred to as *India–Pakistan* and *India–Bangladesh*, respectively, in the Notes section.

the spiralling refugee crisis in India, the Indian government succeeded in conveying to the world that India wanted a peaceful solution to the problem created by Pakistan's own misguided policies toward its own people. If war broke out, it was due to Pakistan's failure to treat its own citizens humanely and its army's atrocities on the civilian population of East Pakistan. India had declared that the refugees must go home with honour and dignity. The speed with which India reacted and conducted military operations indicated its resolve and willingness to use military power in pursuit of its national goals, but only as a last resort.[3] Mrs Gandhi not wedded to idealism, approached the problem in pursuit of her ultimate objective of defeating Pakistan and liberate Bangladesh ruthlessly. In conducting the pre-war diplomacy or even during the war itself, she displayed the mastery of realpolitik which was a tribute to her political leadership. Pakistan had been humbled by the loss of its export-generating and foreign-exchange-earning region, which impacted its economy later on.

As the war ended, the battered military regime of Gen. Yahya Khan felt relieved to hand over power to a civilian administration led by Zulfikar Ali Bhutto. Ironically, Bhutto was in fact, primarily responsible for the loss of East Pakistan. It was his intense pressure on Yahya Khan that had prevented the transfer of power to the Awami League under Mujibur Rahman after winning the majority in the National Assembly, and which finally ignited the spark that led the people of East Pakistan to revolt against the injustice perpetrated on them not only then, but since the creation of the country in 1947. Nevertheless, Yahya Khan did deserve kudos for holding the first-ever general elections in Pakistan based on adult suffrage. It is a different matter that he was motivated in holding the elections in the hope that it would result in a hung house giving enough scope to the army to manipulate the political scene.

Paradoxically, the wars of 1965 and 1971 happened under the army's watch. India was wary of another military regime. There was generally a feeling in India that it would be much easier to deal with a civilian administration even when it was headed by the much-maligned and much-hated Zulfikar Ali Bhutto. It has to be remembered that

Bhutto, as a foreign minister since 1963, had followed noxious policies in relation to India and had given a new twist to his country's foreign policy by introducing the China factor in South Asian politics.

As the war ended on 17 December 1971, both India and Pakistan were faced with the problem of overcoming the past and resuming snapped ties. The Pakistan Army had surrendered to the joint command of the Indian Army and the Mukti Bahini (representing the liberated country) and India was not free to act on its behalf. The new country had to make its own decisions.

Recognition of the new state of Bangladesh by a diminished Pakistan had become a major issue. Both India and Bangladesh insisted that unless Pakistan recognized the new regime, there was little chance of normalisation of ties between India and Pakistan, and Pakistan and Bangladesh. Pakistan was anxious to get its 93,000 prisoners of war released. Bangladesh refused to be a party to their release unless Pakistan recognized the new regime.

The legal status of Bangladesh, its recognition by various countries, admission to the United Nations and the future of 93,000 prisoners of war along with a peace settlement were now interlinked issues. Pakistan's first priority was to get the prisoners released. India's priority was to get Bangladesh recognized internationally particularly by Pakistan. Pakistan launched a major drive internationally to get its prisoners of war released without first recognising the new nation. The people of the new nation had suffered inhuman atrocities at the hands of the Pakistan Army which was guilty of human rights violations. The new nation also wanted some of the Pakistani prisoners, responsible for those crimes, to be tried for war crimes. Since every soldier could not be held responsible and tried for what had happened, only their commanders would be tried, and other prisoners treated humanely in accordance with the Geneva Convention.[4]

Pakistan had rounded up the Bengalis living in West Pakistan before the war and confined them to concentration camps as the war began. It now threatened reciprocally to try them for acting against the interest of the State, a trumped-up charge. Pakistan refused to recognize that they were in no way connected with the issues arising from the war, since they had taken no part in the war in any manner, and were living in the western region legally, as citizens of a United Pakistan.

The recognition of Bangladesh by other countries did not present much of a problem. India as well as Bhutan had recognized the new country and its government on 6 December 1971 itself. The Soviet Union recognized Bangladesh on 24 January 1972. To make Bangladesh feel a fully independent and sovereign country in every respect, the Indian Army which had entered the country to help its liberation, left by 15 March 1972. This enabled many countries to extend recognition to the new country. Practically, all west European countries recognized the new state in February 1972, while east Europeans countries recognized it earlier, with the Soviet, in January. The United States nod came in April 1972. In the meantime, India and Bangladesh on 19 March 1972 signed a twenty-five-year Treaty of Friendship, Cooperation and Peace.

When Bangladesh was admitted to the Commonwealth on 18 April 1972, Pakistan left it in protest. In the same month, Bangladesh was admitted to the Afro–Asian People's Solidarity Organisation. Next month, in May, it was admitted into other international organisations—the International Monetary Fund (IMF), the World Health Organisation (WHO) and the United Nations Conference on Trade and Development (UNTAD). Also, in 1972, it was admitted to the World Bank and the International Labour Organisation (ILO). Bangladesh was granted observer status after it applied to the UN for admission.

On the eve of the Islamic summit at Lahore in February 1974, Bhutto came under pressure from Islamic countries to recognize the breakaway country to enable it to participate in the summit. A seven-member delegation of Islamic countries went to Dhaka and persuaded the government to attend the conference on an assurance of Pakistan's formal recognition. On 22 February 1974, the inaugural day of the summit, Pakistan recognized Bangladesh and within a couple of hours, Bangladesh too extended recognition to Pakistan, which enabled Mujib to travel to Lahore and attend the summit.[5]

China, which had opposed Bangladesh's liberation, after Pakistan recognized the new country, did not oppose Dhaka's admission to the United Nations in September 1974 but dragged its feet on the recognition issue until after the coup and assassination of Mujibur Rahman in August 1975.

Bhutto, soon after taking over as President of Pakistan, had realized that unless relations with India were normalized his woes would not even begin to end. First, he tried to use the good offices of Colombo, which during the war had been helpful to Pakistan by allowing aircraft staging facilities while flying from West to East Pakistan. This was after India had banned Pakistan's overflights following the destruction of its civil aircraft which had been hijacked to Lahore. Bhutto was aware of the friendship Sirimavo Bandaranaike enjoyed with Mrs Gandhi and he used her to curry favour with the Indian PM.[6] Bhutto, as was his wont, could not help being too clever by half. He had sent a note to Mrs Gandhi through Sirimavo Bandaranaike which gave the impression that it was India which was having problems without the normalization of relations. (Bandaranaike passed on the note to Mrs Gandhi.) The first sentence in his message which he sent through Colombo read, 'both she and Mujibur Rahman are faced with situations which need to be resolved expeditiously.'

India not wishing to let him get away with this chicanery, asked Colombo subtly if there was any error in transmission of the message since it had not been possible 'to follow the meaning or significance of it'.

Colombo after checking with Islamabad replied that while there was no error in transmission, Pakistan now had asked to substitute the earlier first sentence with a new sentence which now read, 'she and I are faced with a situation which needs to be resolved expeditiously.'[7]

About this time India had given a note to the Swiss Embassy, looking after the interests of both India and Pakistan that 'India was ready to talk to Pakistan without any preconditions'.[8] Taken aback, Pakistan said if it did not hear to the contrary by 2 March, it would assume that its understanding on the issue was correct. The MEA decided not to reply thereby 'confirming correction of Pakistan's presumption'.[9]

A day earlier, Bhutto had shown his readiness for talks for 'genuine' peace and expressed his readiness to abjure confrontation, which, he claimed, had served Pakistan well in the past but was no longer valid.[10]

It appeared that Bhutto was unbelieving of India's generous offer and even asked the British Foreign Secretary, Alec Douglas-Home for help. In a message to Mrs Gandhi, Douglas-Home conveyed Bhutto's desire to make a fresh start by fixing an early meeting between them for a new agenda. He wanted Mrs Gandhi to invite Bhutto for talks, a request which the foreign secretary made on Bhutto's behalf.[11]

Finally, on 21 March, India gave a letter to the UN Secretary General and its members in the Security Council, expressing India's readiness for talks with Pakistan 'at any time, at any level, and without any preconditions'. A copy of this message was also given to the Swiss ambassador who passed it on to Pakistan's foreign secretary. The latter had described it as 'a very interesting message'.[12] Pakistan, still somewhat puzzled at India's generous initiative for talks without preconditions, sought reconfirmation from the Swiss.[13] The message without preconditions was a generous offer of one neighbour to another, to put Pakistan at ease.

There was hectic activity at several levels to enable the two countries to resolve their differences and allow for the return of normalcy. Pakistan's problem was twofold—normalisation of relations and the release of 93,000 prisoners—and a delinking of the two issues. It carried out intense lobbying internationally to build pressure on India. The difficulty was that India could not take a unilateral action, since Bangladesh would not agree to discuss their prisoners' release unless Pakistan had first recognized it. Pakistan too, was not open to Bangladesh's demand for a trial of any of its army personnel. Reciprocally, as pointed out above, Pakistan, as a bargaining chip, insisted that if any of its army personnel were put on trial, Pakistan would put the Bengali civilians who had been incarcerated in concentration camps in West Pakistan, on trial as well, charging them for acting against the state during the hostilities.

India faced pressure from many countries on the question of release of prisoners on humanitarian grounds. Replying to the Swiss ambassador's unfortunate remarks that the impression in western countries was that 'if India instead of Pakistan had its 93,000 prisoners in the other country, India's attitude would be different', the foreign secretary retorted 'after all, war is war; and asked how long it took for the German prisoners to return home after the end of World War II?' He insisted India had a genuine difficulty because of Bangladeshi sensitivities and their stake in decision-making.[14] Taking note that Pakistan would use propaganda against India, External Affairs Minister Swaran Singh had taken the precaution to inform some of the friendly countries of the hurdles in this regard.[15] The French interest in the restoration of peace was out of the ordinary. D.P. Dhar who had visited Paris explained to the French government the undesirability of the release of the equivalent of almost 'five Divisions of the Pakistan regular army who could be rearmed and deployed against us', unless durable peace was achieved. This apart, Pakistan's refusal to recognize Bangladesh created its own problems, since India could not act without the participation of Bangladesh. The French foreign minister, Maurice Schuman, even made a tentative offer of mediation, but Dhar adroitly ignored it. The Indian apprehension was the possibility of China joining Pakistan in acting against India at an opportune moment. But Schuman ruled out such a possibility as he said, 'China always talks loudly but acts prudently.' About Kashmir, the French suggested keeping it outside of the area of settlement.[16] Later, however, the French President Georges Pompidou had expressed his worry particularly on the question of the release of prisoners but Mrs Gandhi assured him that India would like to repatriate them as soon as possible. However, she added that 'neither our people nor our Parliament will understand the reasons for their return to a country un-reconciled to a durable peace with India.' She brought to his notice the problem of recognition in which Dhaka had an equal stake.[17] The Belgian foreign ministry too spoke to the Indian ambassador, and while it appreciated the position of Bangladesh in this context, Belgium stressed the greater responsibility of India as a 'detaining power'.[18] Replying to the concerns of the Sudanese President that until the prisoners' issue was resolved 'it will create many difficulties' the prime minister told him that while India would like to return them as soon as possible, the element of Bangladesh as an essential party to the decision on repatriation could not be ignored.[19]

Dhar had visited Moscow and in his meeting with Kosygin conveyed the prime minister's thanks to the Soviet leadership for their 'support and unfailing help extended during our difficulties'. Kosygin, noting little improvement in their relation with China, cautioned Dhar that the Chinese having failed to help Pakistan in the war, were now trying to strengthen their position in Islamabad 'in an opportunistic way'. Kosygin told Dhar that despite Bhutto's complicated statements, he (Bhutto) had come to realize that 'reunification with Bangladesh was no longer possible'. Kosygin cautioned Dhar that if the army held power in Pakistan, it would like to avenge its defeat, as otherwise it would not be popular with the people. Questioning Dhar on Kashmir, Kosygin asked him what India had decided about the future of Kashmir and further asked, 'have you or have you not decided to take that part of Kashmir forcibly?' Dhar innocently asked, 'which part' and Kosygin said, 'That part of 1.5 million population under Pakistani rule.' Kosygin then giving reason for his question said, 'You spoke of Kashmir as a bleeding wound, which causes trouble' and then added, 'the question is what has to be done to this bleeding wound' and added, 'should this wound be only bandaged now or has the time come for a surgical operation.' He believed India's response to this question would decide the future course of events.

Dhar had said:

We will do nothing to alter the present territorial status quo on the ceasefire line by force or any other means. There has not been, there is not and there shall not be any plans for this. I think the situation can be normalised by give and take. It is possible with suitable modifications of the Cease Fire Line, to convert it into an international boundary.

At this, Kosygin cautioned him that if India tried to change the status quo in Kashmir, then it was likely that the forces which want to support Pakistan to avenge its defeat would get an opportunity to do so. All this conversation was a warning to India not to disturb the status quo in Kashmir in negotiating peace. Dhar assured Kosygin, India would do nothing to disturb the prevailing status quo. Kosygin felt that the talks with Bhutto without the help of third parties would be useful.[20]

Dhar, after his talks in Paris and Moscow, came to the conclusion that the 'natural inclination is not to stir the Kashmir dispute too deeply lest it should foul the possibilities of an agreement which may be available otherwise on the remaining issues with Pakistan.'

For New Delhi's consumption, Dhar put it diplomatically that, 'I don't mean to say that I did not find full understanding for the first time of the need to resolving the Kashmir issue finally and satisfactorily but not in Kosygin's language, "by a bold surgical operation".'

There was new awareness in Dhar's assessment to New Delhi that the Indian case based on 'old archaic arguments the relevance of which you and I were doubtful even in 1948, would no longer wash' and therefore Indian 'presentation has to be fresh with a new look and it should bear the stamp of our new prestige and authority.'

Finally, Dhar said whenever he raised the Kashmir question: 'I could feel a yawn of boredom greeting me with an unexpressed pathetic question why raise an issue which is lying almost dead in the present state of dormancy?'[21]

Dhar was accompanied by Chief of Army Staff, General Manekshaw, during his visit to Moscow, so that the general could project the army's requirements for replenishment of the weaponry lost during the war and additional requirements for strengthening the army. These had become necessary because Pakistan with the help of China had not only replenished their war losses but added to its strength.

Kosygin had spooked Dhar on 'the malicious position of Chinese leaders against the Soviet Union' and added that the Chinese were unhappy about their failure to help Pakistan during the war and now were 'trying to strengthen their [Pakistan] position in an opportunistic way'.[22] That Kosygin's fears about China were motivated became clear when Dhar and Manekshaw met Defence Minister Marshal Grechko. As Manekshaw projected the defence requirements to the marshal, he like a true soldier and without mincing words or standing on formality trashed India's apprehensions about Pakistan and said the real danger was from China and suggested specifically a 'military alliance' between the Soviet Union and India. Addressing General Manekshaw, he said, 'India would need the Soviet Union and the

Soviet Union would need India and her support to deal with the designs of China.' He advised it was important, therefore, to talk in terms of realities of the situation rather than 'little phantoms like Pakistan'.

He delivered his lines like a dramatic performance:

> History has cast the role of allies on us against this menace. Both must get to defend them together against this menace and it would be wise for both the countries to coordinate their strategies and plans and harmonise their defence organisations for meeting such an eventuality.

Substantiating his argument, the marshal said Moscow had made it known 'unequivocally' to Beijing that any attempt on their part 'to disturb peace or encroach on Soviet territory would bring about a massive retaliation in which every weapon would be used for which it would take her long to recover'.

Answering General Manekshaw's request for arms, the marshal said bluntly, 'If we have an alliance, I shall earmark 50 Inter-continental Ballistic Missiles [ICBM] for your defence against China. I shall not locate them on your soil but on my own so that you do not run any risk.'

When Manekshaw persisted with his request, the marshal suggested that the PM request Soviet General Secretary Leonid Brezhnev and once cleared, he would 'not only give 150 tanks but 15,000 tanks'. Addressing Gen. Manekshaw again, the marshal said his talk was 'from a soldier to a soldier' and added 'history has cast the role of India and the Soviet Union into those of allies against this menace' and said, he saw the future very clearly; that they would have to defend themselves together.

Finally, he said: '[T]he time had come when India and the Soviet Union must enter into detailed understanding on how and in what manner Soviet and they should meet the Chinese threat whenever it materialises.'[23]

Dhar argued that the treaty, negotiated only a few months ago and valid for twenty years, was enough to bind them. But it fell on deaf ears. Both Dhar and General Manekshaw were disappointed at their

failure to receive any positive response to their shopping list. Marshal
Grechko was trying to bind India in the larger Sino–Soviet ideological
and political conundrum which Dhar was adroitly trying to avoid.[24]

Reporting on his discussions with the Soviet defence minister to
Haskar, the Principal Secretary to the PM, Dhar's letter underlined
Marshal Grechko assertion of a fresh treaty which sought to involve
the two countries in a 'program of cooperation, coordination and
even structural inter-relation of strategy, tactics between the Soviet
and Indian defence forces against a possible Chinese involvement in a
conflict with us or with the Soviet Union'.[25]

New Delhi was not only disappointed, but also worried, at the Soviet
refusal to their request for defence supplies, particularly when reports
of the Pakistan–China nexus and delivery of weapons to Pakistan from
China were multiplying. In view of this, the external affairs minister
decided to visit Moscow with the shopping list to impress upon the
Soviet leadership at the highest level to meet India's needs for fresh
defence supplies.[26]

But Soviet response was lukewarm, which prompted Haksar,
Kaul and Manekshaw to ponder over the worrying situation. While
Chinese intentions remained clothed in mystery, Gen. Manekshaw felt
both Pakistan and China could embark on a military course of action
around October/November that year. Haksar's view was irrespective
of their intentions, India should have the necessary military strength
which would be a deterrent to attack and that such a deterrent be built
while engaging in peace talks. The meeting noted the lack of response
from Moscow. They recommended the prime minister write to both
Kosygin and Brezhnev about it.[27] The prime minister considering the
importance of the matter wrote to Brezhnev the very next day. She
thanked him for sharing with her his conversation with Bhutto and also
conveyed her appreciation for the understanding that existed between
India and the Soviet Union on the problems of the subcontinent. She
gave some details of Bhutto's past trickeries and reckless actions which
had derailed all attempts at better relations between the two countries
and held him responsible for wrecking the Tashkent Agreement in
which the Soviets had a stake. Assuring him that India's objective
was not territorial gain or humiliating Pakistan, but the removal of

all causes of friction and hostility which had 'so unnecessarily marred our relations since independence'. She brought to Brezhnev's notice the shenanigans in which Pakistan indulged in the past under the influence of China and the United States. She also brought to his notice Pakistan's present efforts to arm itself for an adventurous course of action under the influence of its friends. Before reminding Brezhnev of India's request for defence supplies, as projected by the external affairs minister, she prudently brought to his notice Pakistani efforts to build up an increased military force which had put it virtually at par with India in this respect and said that 'I am prompted to remind you of some of our urgent needs about which my colleague, the Foreign Minister spoke to you and you were good enough to promise an early consideration of this matter, and I am awaiting your reply.'[28]

Separately, she asked Defence Minister Jagjivan Ram, if everything possible was being done 'to re-equip them [armed forces] satisfactorily and adequately to meet any threat or eventuality'.[29] The defence minister assured the prime minister that 'while defence services are on the alert, everything possible is being done within physical and financial constraints to equip them satisfactorily and adequately to meet any threat or eventuality in 1972–73'.[30]

While India remained apprehensive of Pakistan's arms build-up and its intentions with help from China and the United States, some countries were engaged in rescuing Pakistan from the adverse consequences of the war. The Soviet Ambassador in Dhaka told the Indian ambassador, S. Dutt, that the ambassadors of France, Denmark, West Germany and the high commissioner of the UK in Dhaka, had jointly spoken to him to convince him that any trial of the prisoners, as insisted by Dhaka, would 'take a serious turn and any possibility of understanding with President Bhutto would be ruled out'. They warned that world opinion also would be highly critical. Dutt, however, told the Soviet ambassador that the envoys had spoken to him too on the same lines. The Soviet ambassador felt that the ambassadors were anti-Soviet and anti-Indian and were putting obstacles to either India or the Soviet Union providing economic assistance to Dhaka. This was being done so that the United States could be asked to provide that assistance.[31]

Bhutto travelled through several Islamic and European capitals, and even Beijing, to canvass support on the prisoners' question and the political settlement with India. Pakistan also bought space in international newspapers and sent out delegations of the prisoners' wives to various western countries to evoke sympathy to their cause and build pressure on India for their release. Apart from prisoners, Bhutto was equally keen on a post-war settlement with India to normalize relations and restore snapped ties.

Receiving several requests on Bhutto's behalf for a meeting, Mrs Gandhi addressed a letter to him expressing her desire for working together for a durable peace. She reminded him of India's message to Pakistan and also to the UN secretary general for discussions between them without preconditions. She suggested a meeting between their appointed emissaries initially, to lay the groundwork, and asked for his reaction before nominating her emissaries.[32]

Bhutto while travelling through various countries wanted to visit Moscow to talk with the Soviet leaders, since he had surmised that his task would be easier if he could canvass Soviet support in his favour, given the friendly relations between Moscow and New Delhi. Though his visit to Moscow had been scheduled for the end of March, he wanted it earlier. It was rescheduled for 16 March 1972. A few days before Bhutto's arrival in Moscow, the Soviet ambassador in New Delhi called on D.P. Dhar, now Chairman of the Policy Planning Committee of the MEA, and former ambassador to Soviet Union. The Soviet ambassador had been instructed to find out from the prime minister 'if she had any wishes in the matter and if she would like the Soviet leaders to take any particular line or raise any particular question with Mr. Bhutto'. He also expressed his desire to meet Mrs Gandhi. On his request for meeting the prime minister, Chairman Dhar rebuffed him saying she had a hectic schedule. Dhar got the impression from his talks with the Soviet ambassador that Bhutto wanted to delink the issue of prisoners of war from the general peace settlement.[33]

Dhar, however, conveyed to the ambassador certain points, which in his perception, had the general approval of the PM and the foreign minister. The points he mentioned to the Soviet Ambassador were:

i.   Prisoners would be released as part of the overall settlement
     with the concurrence of Bangladesh government;

ii. India would insist on the 'settlement of Kashmir as an integral
     and irreducible content of a settlement by Pakistan';

iii. The prime minister would be prepared to forget the past and
     help Bhutto consolidate his position in Pakistan;

iv. To meet Pakistan's apprehensions that 'India was out to
     devour Pakistan and break it into pieces', India could give all
     the guarantees incorporated in a non-aggression treaty.

v.   If Pakistan were to give away 'purely theoretically in terms of
     settlement with us (on Kashmir), Pakistan would make up
     more from our friendship'.

In his note to the prime minister, Dhar suggested that she might
assure Pakistan that the agreement negotiated with it would not be one
between victor and vanquished, since such a settlement has, in history,
led to renewed and more violent conflicts.[34]

Wary of Bhutto, India had asked Kosygin whether it was safe to
negotiate for peace with Bhutto. Kosygin had felt that while it was
difficult to put too much faith on Bhutto's statements for peace, looking
at alternatives available in Pakistan and taking into account the situation
in which Bhutto found himself, he was the best bet. Kosygin however,
warned that if the army were to return to power, it would take revenge,
with the help of China and the US. He was convinced that without talks
there could be no solution to the problem, and it was desirable that some
confidence was reposed in Bhutto since he already had his back to the
wall. Dhar conveyed to Kosygin India's two reservations on the release
of prisoners: (i) recognition of Bangladesh, and (ii) risk involved in the
release of nearly a hundred thousand trained men capable of taking up
arms without seeing a faint glimmer of hope for peace.[35]

During his visit to Moscow, Bhutto met both Kosygin and
Brezhnev. Kosygin admonishing Bhutto said it was regrettable that
his advice to Yahya Khan to avoid using the army on the people was
ignored and Pakistan came to grief. He too had his reservations on
some of Bhutto's key appointments like that of Gen. Tikka Khan
as Chief of Army Staff. Bhutto said Moscow could be of help in

brokering peace. About his new credentials of a peacenik, Bhutto cited the release of Mujibur Rahman in the face of criticism by the army and without the handover of the prisoners. Bhutto said the delay in the release of prisoners was increasing his problems but he was convinced that India could not exploit the prisoners' problem indefinitely since international conventions and other realities would force India's hand. Bhutto, however, assured his interlocutor that he was now amiable for peace after overcoming intractable problems of the past and sought his advice. Bhutto felt the Soviet Union could make positive contributions. Describing the question of prisoners, a constant impediment, since Pakistan was already negotiating from a position of weakness, Bhutto added if India by prolonging the release of prisoners wished to impose a humiliating peace, Pakistan's position would only harden.[36]

Bhutto had been advised to be mindful of the United States and China when he met Brezhnev, since both had their own agenda and would exploit the situation. Brezhnev insisted that there was no solution yet for a settlement between India, Pakistan and Bangladesh and advised Bhutto to adopt a realistic policy. Waxing theatrical about the 'geographic range of his vision', Brezhnev said Moscow would like decisions that 'help in solutions and which would lay the foundation of a permanent peace in all the three countries'. Referring to the prisoners, Brezhnev said he fully appreciated Bhutto's problem and accepted his assurance that the repatriated prisoners would not be used for war, but added, essentially it was for India to decide. He expressed satisfaction that he (Bhutto) and Mrs Gandhi had agreed to meet. Brezhnev assured Bhutto that the Soviets would be prepared to contribute in all possible ways. He said the 'the treaty would mark a radical turn in developments, fostering peace between India and Pakistan and that such a step would require courage', which Brezhnev felt Bhutto always had. He was willing to lead India in a positive direction if he could be assured of Bhutto's positive attitude.

Referring to the recognition of Bangladesh by forty countries, Brezhnev said that 'history could not be reversed' and advised him to recognize the new nation. Bhutto pointing out that negotiating a treaty with India had always been difficult and in the past neither Jinnah, nor Liaquat Ali, nor their successors were able to do it, and expressed hope that with the Soviet help he would make a genuine search for a solution. On Kashmir, Bhutto insisted, relations were not conducive in a vacuum. In outlining his step-by-step approach, he suggested that 'an initial measure could be to change the name of the 'Ceasefire Line' to more accurately describe it as the 'Line of Control' (LoC). It was then that the phrase Line of Control entered in the lexicon of South Asian geopolitics. Bhutto requested Brezhnev that while speaking to Mrs Gandhi, his views and suggestions be treated as objective considerations and not conveyed as emanating from him. Brezhnev assured him, 'We will be very cautious in presenting them to Indira. Clumsy handling will spoil the best proposals.' At the end in an unforgettable bit of Bhuttoism, he said, 'If I fail, then I hope the Secretary General [Brezhnev] would send a wreath on my grave.'[37]

Bhutto assured Brezhnev he would recognize Bangladesh, but at a time of his choosing.[38]

Since Brezhnev had briefed Mrs Gandhi on the meeting with Bhutto, she wrote to him appreciating his advice to Bhutto over the importance of normalization of relations between India and Pakistan, as well as Pakistan and Bangladesh, and the emphasis he had laid on the 'perils of a gradual or piece-meal settlement and the need to strive for an overall settlement rather than some partial or secondary agreement'. However, her doubts about Bhutto's sincerity refused to go away. She said:

> [E]ven if he were now prepared to reaffirm his desire for peace in a new solemn treaty or pact, it would fail to provide us with an adequate guarantee of peace in the sub-continent, unless it was supported and supplemented by other agreements designed to eliminate the issues which have hither to served as pretext for Pakistan to keep alive tension and resort to armed conflict with India every few years.[39]

Mrs Gandhi assured Brezhnev that India had no desire to treat Pakistan as a vanquished power, nor did India have an appetite for territorial gains. She said India did not want to humiliate a people with whom it had close and intimate ties. But she still remained wary of Bhutto and said India could not ignore the influence that the United States and China might bring to bear in the shaping of Pakistan's policy and such influence might run counter to the interests of peace and stability in the subcontinent. She added that, 'For all these reasons I am convinced that any complacency on our part in India would be totally unjustified.'[40]

President Nixon in a summary of his talks in Beijing did not forget to boost a demoralized Bhutto and assured him of his sympathy and support and promised to help Pakistan with economic support.[41]

Following Bhutto's visit to Moscow, India took the initiative to assure Pakistan that peace and good neighbourliness were worthwhile objectives; whereas confrontation only diverted energies and resources from the war against poverty.[42]

After Bhutto's visit to Moscow, the India's emissary, D.P. Dhar— the man of all seasons, and Aziz Ahmed, Pakistan's Minister of State for Defence and Foreign Affairs, met in Rawalpindi and Murree from 26 to 29 April and drew up a five-point common agenda for the meeting of the leaders of the two countries toward a peace settlement.[43] On 29 April, another ten-point 'Agreed General Principles' document for submission to the summit was signed.[44] The two documents settled the modalities for the final summit between the two leaders for a durable peace in the subcontinent.[45]

Bhutto had agreed to these emissary talks reluctantly, since he was anxious for a meeting at the highest level.[46]

Once the dates for the summit were fixed, Bhutto sent his minister, Aziz Ahmed, to Moscow to brief the Soviets on Pakistan's possible stand during the talks. If Bhutto's own visit to Moscow earlier was to settle the broad parameters for peace, Aziz Ahmed's visit was to brief Moscow on specific issues. Bhutto had by now crystalized his ideas on the future relationship with India and Bangladesh. Mr Fomin, Head of the Asia department in the Soviet foreign office told the new Indian Ambassador, Shelvankar, that Aziz Ahmed in briefing the Soviet leaders only repeated what was discussed between the India–Pakistan emissaries in Murree in preparation for the summit and had nothing new to state. However, he had assured that Bhutto would work for lasting peace and would carefully avoid any harsh or unfriendly remarks. Pakistan expected that India would release some of the prisoners, if not all, before the start of the summit to create a friendly atmosphere. Aziz gave the impression that Bhutto during his visit to Muslim countries, had tried to impress upon them to defer recognizing Bangladesh until Pakistan had decided on the question. Fomin was at pains to emphasize to Shelvankar that everything the Soviets said was in line with their understanding of the Indian position.[47]

Aziz Ahmed had requested Kosygin to convey to Delhi that:

> We want to live in peace with India. We wish also the restoration of peace and normal conditions in Bangladesh. This is the paramount goal. The President is ready to discuss with Mrs. Gandhi any problem which she would like to touch at the forthcoming meeting, including the question of a peace settlement. We think, it will be unrealistic to consider that all the problems, including that of Kashmir, which could not be settled for 25 years, can be resolved during the five-day meeting. If all the issues are not settled at one meeting, the leaders of our countries could meet again.

The message appeared somewhat arrogantly worded when it said Pakistan would not agree

> [T]o such a settlement which would be dictated by India or would be connected with the renunciation by the President of main principle of basic national interest. The settlement should be an honourable, honest and just one for both the parties. Otherwise, there will be no settlement and that would have disastrous effect.[48]

The moot point which emerged from the above discussions was that apart from the prisoners, the question on which the success or failure of the conference would depend was Kashmir. Aziz Ahmad had told the Soviets that, 'it would be unrealistic that all problems, including Kashmir which could not be settled for 25 years, can be solved during one five-day meeting. If all the issues are not settled at one meeting, the leaders of our countries could meet once again.' Ahmad produced the impression, in the words of the Soviets that 'Bhutto is ready to achieve ultimately in principle an agreement on this matter in Simla on the condition that such agreement would remain strictly secret for some time until the President paves the way in Pakistan for making this agreement public'.

What Aziz Ahmad said about Kashmir remained the Pakistani stand throughout the negotiations and the final settlement rested on this question alone.

Moscow sent a complete resume of discussions with Aziz Ahmad to Prime Minister Gandhi in a memorandum.[49]

On the day the memorandum was delivered, the prime minister had already left for Simla, and it was handed over to the external affairs minister. The memorandum indicated that the Soviets had used all their efforts to 'prompt' Bhutto to take the course of the speediest normalisation toward reaching a final political settlement taking into account the present realities. Aziz Ahmad assured that Pakistan wanted to live in peace with India and wished for 'restoration of peace and normal conditions in Bangladesh'. The Soviets claimed to have supported the Indian position on the necessity of a final settlement on a mutually acceptable basis.

Swaran Singh after reading the memorandum assured Ambassador Pegov that if 'Bhutto was ready to work for conversion of ceasefire line into a permanent boundary, then the summit would succeed in creating the atmosphere of peace and in reversing the military confrontation between India and Pakistan'. The EAM told Pegov that while India would accept the ceasefire line into a permanent international border, it would be the final position and not the starting point of negotiations 'on which Pakistan can again raise objections'. What Swaran Singh failed to read was that Pakistan would indeed accept the ceasefire line as a final settlement not now, but later, and without putting it down on paper.

The EAM's final word to Ambassador Pegov was 'our unfortunate experience of the past is that Pakistan spokesmen speak with different voices in Moscow, Beijing, Washington and India . . . We will judge (them) carefully what Bhutto (had to) says'.[50]

The stage was set for the inauguration of the summit between the two heads of state of India and Pakistan in Simla, the capital of the State of Himachal Pradesh, which used to be the summer capital of British India, and the venue of another controversial conference in history, the Simla Conference, 1914.

A careful study of the pre-conference developments and discussions at various levels left one with the impression that the terms of the conference were set by the defeated party. Bhutto kept his chin up refusing to be humiliated despite the defeat in the war which had cut the Pakistan of 1947 into two halves. In fact, it was India which gave the impression of being the most anxious party for a peace settlement, to Pakistan's relief.

India was not only relieved but was enthused at the message from Moscow that Bhutto was prepared for a settlement on Kashmir on the ceasefire line, which was what India wanted since 1948. It may be recalled that in October 1948, Nehru in his meeting with the British Prime Minister Clement Attlee, Foreign Secretary Ernest Bevin and Pakistan's first PM, Liaquat Ali Khan, on the sidelines of the Commonwealth Prime Ministers' Conference in London, had offered Pakistan that they retain what they had grabbed and end the fighting.[51]

Nehru, however, maintained that this offer was made as his personal suggestion. But even a personal suggestion made by a prime minister to another prime minister in the presence of Atlee and Bevin carried an official status. Interestingly, Nehru in his telegram from Paris to Sardar Vallabhai Patel on 30 October 1948 made no mention of this offer, even when he mentioned his talks with Liaquat on Kashmir.[52] Neither did this offer figure in the report on his foreign tours to the Cabinet a month later. Liaquat Ali Khan on return from London said in a radio broadcast that he had made it clear to the Indian prime minister that 'the only just solution of this problem was to admit the right of the people of Kashmir to express their free opinion about the question of accession to Pakistan or India'.[53]

It is noteworthy that this offer to settle the Kashmir issue on the ceasefire line with some additional territory, was repeatedly made to the Pakistani leaders, by Nehru and his successors, but it was Pakistan which always rejected such an offer.

Nehru, to start with, had some fascinating ideas about the future of Kashmir. Upset with the manner in which the UN Security

Council was dealing with it, he had made a policy appraisal which he described to V.K. Krishna Menon in London, as 'one or two minor variations'. However, his 'minor variations' were, in fact, fundamental. Describing them to Menon he said, 'One is the possibility of Kashmir being considered more or less independent and guaranteed by India, Pakistan and possibly the U.N. The other is the possibility of some kind of partition.'[54]

Rejecting the ceasefire-line solution in view of Pakistan's history, and the possibility of its acceptance now, enthused India. India's optimism was anchored on the fact that once the Kashmir problem was out of the way, all other problems would sort themselves out. Kashmir remained the force majeure for the last twenty-five years for Pakistan and governed all issues of significance between the two countries, whether trade and commerce, or scientific and cultural cooperation. India's trade with landlocked Afghanistan suffered on account of Pakistan's refusal to provide transit facilities for Indian trade with Afghanistan. India, therefore, looked to Simla with great expectations as did Moscow.

India's hopes were short-lived. Even before the talks could begin, signals from Rawalpindi suggested things were not going to be smooth. India was not encouraged by Bhutto's message of 27 June to his people on the eve of his departure for Simla. His message conceded that the past twenty-five years were 'an era of confrontation' and the result was that the people remained the 'poorest, the most under-fed, illiterate, and disease-ridden'. He was honest to admit that for almost three decades while the two countries quarrelled, the world 'watched us with cynical amusement'. These were home truths which needed to be told to a demoralized nation for a compromise to be worked out with India, since they had been fed on a diet of anti-India rhetoric since the birth of Pakistan. Bhutto described 'dialogue' as the 'civilized way' forward. India wasn't enthusiastic about his reference to Kashmir as he interpreted India's insistence on a final settlement on the state as a covert desire to acquire more territory, inferring India had already grabbed Hyderabad, Junagarh and Manavadar. Insisting that the right of 'self-determination' was a 'birthright' of the people of Jammu and Kashmir, he sought to remind Mrs Gandhi that it was 'not only enshrined in the UN resolutions but also acknowledged by the prime minister of India Jawaharlal Nehru, her father'.

India understood this was necessary as a palliative for a demoralized Pakistan. Soviet optimism was hedged by Pakistani reservations on Kashmir that its immediate solution did not look positive but was certainly possible later. Bhutto had warned India that there would be no peace 'at the expense of Pakistan's sovereignty'. He added that the talk of war trials and ill-treatment of non-Bengali federalists can in no way contribute to peace in future. He insisted that for achieving durable peace the 'consequences of the last war must be eliminated, prisoners and civilian internees must be returned and withdrawal of armed forces must be arranged forthwith'. His subtle message had been earlier conveyed to the Soviets, that since the search for peace was long and arduous, neither could all the past differences be settled in one go, nor 'the leaf of history be torn off in one week of talks'. The progress could only be achieved, he cautioned India, step-by-step and talking directly rather than through intermediaries. In expressing his desire for peace, Bhutto warned 'not at any price' neither at the expense of principles nor honour. At the end, addressing his people, he said, with their blessings he would 'cross the broken bridges and reach the mountain top'. Setting the terms for the conference, and giving the example of the Treaty of Versailles, which was imposed on Germany after the First World War, he cautioned that a one-sided settlement cannot lead to durable peace, but instability and war.[55]

His message was addressed to multiple constituencies—his own people, India and the international community. It was a cautious message yet had vivacities of egotism and conceit. Finally, it must be admitted that a representative of a defeated nation through guile, craft and dexterity sought to set the parameters and tone for the conference.

Prime Minister Gandhi welcomed his speech, particularly his statement of forgetting the past and looking forward to the future.[56]

While summarizing the main points of Bhutto's speech for Mrs Gandhi, her Principal Secretary, P.N. Haksar, stressed that Bhutto's tone suggested a deep desire for peace and new beginnings. He told Mrs Gandhi that to sell the detente, she would need to convince both the Indian people and Parliament that Bhutto, who was unpopular in India, was now an 'entirely different person'. Haksar suggested she make Bhutto aware of the intensity of feelings in Bangladesh which was 'very extremely sensitive' to the question of the Joint Command. Bangladesh had insisted that they be a necessary party to the settlement of the question of not merely the prisoners, but also of the repatriation of civil internees. He suggested that the PM tell Bhutto of the need to get over the 'terrible legacy of the past' and the need to enunciate new broad features for a future relationship. Lastly, he stressed the need to set the principle of bilateralism in settling existing differences or any new differences that might arise in future.[57]

The Secretary to the PM, P.N. Dhar, felt the speech was 'not too disappointing', rather 'sounded reasonable' particularly when addressed to the home audience. He wished to convey a message of hope to keep their morale high. About Kashmir, Dhar said, 'We (should) show our willingness to abandon our rights to Pakistan-occupied Kashmir and some further territorial adjustments without disadvantage to Pakistan.'[58]

On the eve of the conference, the French were empathetic to Bhutto once again. President Pompidou spoke to Ambassador Chatterjee who summed up the French position and said they asked for: (i) magnanimity, (ii) release of prisoners, (iii) Kashmir to be dealt with in second phase, and (iv) recognition of Bangladesh by Pakistan. After the ambassador explained India's position on Kashmir in detail, Pompidou still felt 'how Bhutto could at one stroke recognize Bangladesh and also renounce claims on Kashmir since he was not strong enough for this'. Pompidou felt that after the release of prisoners and a modicum of normalisation of relations, Bhutto's attitude may be different. The ambassador disagreed and cited India's bitter experience of the last twenty-five years with Pakistan on Kashmir.[59]

Prime Minister Gandhi in an interview with Pakistani journalists made it clear that in the resolution of India–Pakistan issues, a third country (Bangladesh) was now also involved and India could not interfere in Pakistan's relations with it. She advised that sooner Pakistan 'patched up or come to some agreement with Bangladesh, the easier it would be to deal with all other questions'. Since Mujibur

Rahman would not talk with Pakistan unless first recognized, it was for Pakistan to decide. Bangladesh being a sovereign nation had to decide for itself and India could not intercede.[60]

The plenary of the conference was brief. Mrs Gandhi in her remarks welcomed Bhutto's desire to forget the past and the need for a fresh look at the problems. Bhutto's speech, referred to many changes that had come about in the world, and stressed the need for peace and assured India that Pakistan would work toward it. Despite many past prejudices, he wanted to turn the corner for a new beginning. He said he wanted 'to begin with this assurance to you [Mrs Gandhi] and your delegation and to the people of India that we would forget the past bitterness and hostilities and will strive to attain peace with honour'.[61] 'Peace with honour' was the underlying message he wanted to convey.

The discussions between the officials of the two countries following the plenary could not agree on the release of prisoners. On the Indian side, the discussions were led by the Chairman of the Policy Planning Committee of the MEA, D.P. Dhar, and on the Pakistan side by Aziz Ahmed, Minister of State for Defence and Foreign Affairs. The latter's remarks were unfortunate. He said if India wanted to keep the prisoners indefinitely, Pakistan would not mind and added it would not be conducive to durable peace. He conceded that it would present certain difficulties for the President but he would cope. His bizarre argument was that the army was traditionally recruited from the Punjab where the people were used to their 'menfolk going to war and dying by the thousands' and also their families were 'not seriously agitated over the continued detention of the Prisoners in India'. He regretted Mujibur Rahman's absence at the meeting, that would have made it tripartite, to sort out the prisoners' issue. Replying, Chairman Dhar said he had even indicated at the emissary-level talks in Rawalpindi that a settlement would be subject to: (i) conclusion of a peace settlement, and (ii) India's commitment to Bangladesh on the question of prisoners. He added his formulation was clear that 'Pakistan should agree to consult and associate Bangladesh'. Dhar warned that Pakistan's failure to accept it or provide an alternative formulation acceptable to India could jeopardize not only this question but the entire understanding arrived at earlier in Rawalpindi in April. He said recognition of Bangladesh by Pakistan would 'be very helpful in resolving not only the question of prisoners, but also other issues of a sub-continental character'.

Aziz Ahmed's frustration was apparent in his response that the Pakistan delegation could not return home with a peace settlement alone. The repatriation of prisoners and the withdrawal of forces in the western sector was necessary and 'there would be little merit in continuing discussions'. Pakistan was told to face reality. Summing up the discussions, Chairman Dhar said it was possible to: (i) perceive a broad, viable perspective of peace which could be followed by normalization of relations, (ii) vacate occupied territories and (iii) repatriate prisoners of war, and the only hurdle in reaching such a peace settlement was the lack of Pakistan's agreement to the association of Mujibur Rahman on the question of repatriation of prisoner.[62]

A joint statement issued at the end of the first day's deliberations quoted Mrs Gandhi hopeful that the talks between the two countries 'would mark a new beginning'. The statement added that the official talks were held for two hours in a 'cordial and constructive atmosphere'. The statement noted that Prime Minister Indira Gandhi and President Bhutto also met separately in a restricted session. No details of their discussions were given out.[63]

On the next day, 29 June, there were two sessions when Aziz Ahmad recalled his earlier statement that the peace accord should be 'compact, simple and in accordance with common international usage, and secondly that it should contain an effective machinery for peaceful settlement of disputes'. Aziz said that the agreement should be such as the President could sell it to the people of Pakistan. He pointed to the joint declaration between the United States and the USSR and said he wanted to follow the formulations contained therein. India said it was hardly any basis for them to follow. Responding to Pakistan's suggestion for a self-executing machinery, Dhar pointed out that 'self-executing machinery or similar expressions were product of past suspicions and mistrust' and suggested a bilateral dispute resolution mechanism. Aziz disagreed and suggested an international method of dispute resolution 'like arbitration, mediation, judicial settlement etc.', but Dhar insisted on the bilateral approach. Haksar said he was not OK to be influenced by the 'echoes of the past' and that Pakistan must accept new ideas and new approaches. He was clear that each country had its own compulsions and it was for each country to manage those compulsions. He insisted that 'we cannot permit our individual internal compulsions to affect the settlement in favour of either party'. Responding to the Indian draft treaty Aziz said it was worse than even the Tashkent Declaration and again insisted on a self-executing mechanism. In this context, he pointed to the Bagge Award and Kutch Tribunals which succeeded in settling border disputes.

Kashmir came up for discussion on 30 June, when Aziz Ahmad said Pakistan could not possibly consider any solution as long as there was no progress on the question of the repatriation of prisoners and troop withdrawal from areas occupied in the western part. He insisted that Pakistan ardently desired peace and added he could not however enter into discussions on Kashmir. The leaders of the two countries might wish to make a reference to this issue in a separate communiqué 'although substantive negotiations would have to await a more propitious juncture, say six months or a year. The question of timing was important'. Aziz Ahmad asked why it was essential to settle the Kashmir question 'today', 'especially when Pakistan did not enjoy equality in negotiations' and suggested 'future summits could tackle this question'. India rejecting the concept of self-determination for integral parts of a country, wanted a settlement on Kashmir to avoid future conflicts. Aziz, however, insisted since the right of self-determination for Kashmiris was conferred on by the United Nations and initially agreed upon by India. He disagreed to the repeated queries from Principal Secretary Haksar on flexibility in this position.[64] The draft agreement proposed by Pakistan, however, mentioned a 'respect for the ceasefire line in Jammu and Kashmir supervised by the UN Military Observers Group in India and Pakistan'.[65] This essentially meant no way forward on Kashmir.

On 1 July, India had submitted its revised draft agreement in which Pakistan wanted two provisions added, namely, (a) calling for withdrawal of all forces from each other's territories and a 'position which fully respects the ceasefire line in J&K (supervised by the UN military observers' group) and, (b) repatriation of all prisoners and civilian internees in each other's custody in conformity with the Geneva Convention, 1949.[66]

The two documents became the basis on which discussions in the full-delegation meeting took place on 1 July. India wanted to establish the practice of bilateralism and included in the documents a provision that all disputes between the two nations 'shall be resolved bilaterally by peaceful means'. The Pakistanis again made two reservations, (i) on Kashmir where Pakistan insisted on status quo, and (ii) repatriation of all prisoners and civilian internees.

Bhutto in his comments ruled out the proposal for a no-war declaration which he said 'conjures up a sense of capitulation'. Responding to Bhutto's demand for repatriation and withdrawal of prisoners and internees, Foreign Secretary Kaul ruling them out, said this could happen only after durable peace had been established. Mrs Gandhi said both the Pakistani proposals with regard to Kashmir and release of prisoners were not acceptable since the people in India expected a solution to this long-drawn problem. Bhutto maintained if India continued to hold on to prisoners, a resolution on Kashmir would become more difficult. Bhutto also maintained that if Bangladesh insisted on a trial for war crimes, it would be a point of no return. If there was a trial for prisoners, there would also be trial for Bengalis in Pakistan. The PM also said if Pakistan were to recognize Bangladesh, then there was the possibility of Bangladesh softening its stance and it was essentially a question between the two countries—Pakistan and Bangladesh. Pakistan continued to insist that any concession on these sensitive issues would give the impression that the agreement had been arrived at under duress and would not pass muster in the national assembly. Being conscious of the pressure on the issue of Kashmir he tried to wriggle out suggesting, 'in the foreseeable future an agreement will emerge. It will evolve into a settlement. Let there be a line of peace, let people come and go. Let us not fight over it.'[67]

Essentially, Bhutto all along, wanted to maintain status quo in Kashmir. When during the course of the conference, Foreign Secretary T.N. Kaul spoke to Bhutto with Mrs Gandhi's permission and reminded him that at Tashkent, as foreign minister, he had himself said that 'Kashmir was the basic cause of all our differences; why he was now hesitant even to make any mention of it?' Bhutto replied and said he 'remembered Tashkent' and admitted to what Kaul said but added, 'he did not represent a defeated country at Tashkent as he did at Simla'. He went on to add that 'the people of Pakistan would think he had given in to pressure if he accepted any mention of Kashmir now. Bhutto said, 'Insha Allah, in due course, we shall settle it finally, bilaterally and peacefully without prejudice to the recognised position of either side.'[68]

What he told Kaul informally and what he said at the conference table had a futuristic element in it. External Affairs Minister Swaran Singh cautioned him against going back to the UN resolutions which would not solve the problem and argued in favour of a break from the past. Mrs Gandhi again assured Bhutto that India had no intention of keeping the prisoners indefinitely, but pointed out that they had surrendered to the joint command of India and Bangladesh and Pakistan had to talk to Bangladesh as well and it would not work unless Pakistan recognized it.[69]

The meeting at the summit level was deadlocked. The Pakistani delegation had almost packed up to go home. The Indian camp was disappointed too, for they had laboured hard for a final settlement. Bhutto himself was in a dilemma since it was his mechations that led to the loss of half of Pakistan. His nation was demoralized, economy in shambles, 93,000 Pakistani soldiers held as prisoners of war, and a chunk of his territory in the western region under Indian occupation. He could hardly afford to go home empty-handed. His frustration was best described by his daughter, Benazir, who was in Simla with him. She had confided in her Indian Liaison Officer, Miss Veena Datta (later Mrs Veena Sikri) a foreign service officer, the 'depressed and frustrated mood' of her father. Describing her lunch with him on 1 July, she told Veena: 'Mr Bhutto refused to eat anything and was lost in thoughts throughout the meal.' Continuing, Benazir said, 'Suddenly he pushed away his chair,' and told her that the 'summit talks were so badly deadlocked and were heading for a failure'; and was about to leave the room, but at the door he turned back and said, 'There seems to be just one ray of hope.'[70] His ray of hope made him plead with

Mrs Gandhi for a last-minute meeting on one-to-one basis, which she magnanimously agreed to.

The circumstances of the meeting were best described by a foreign service officer K.N. Bakshi present at the dinner that night. Suddenly both Mrs Gandhi and Bhutto got up and left the room midway through their dinner. According to Bakshi, 'A meeting had taken place between them on second July where no one else was present.' At the meeting, there was nothing new in what Bhutto told the prime minister, but he conveyed it to her with an even greater passion than he demonstrated in public.

According to Bakshi in every turn of phrase, every gesture and expression, he emphasized that he wanted peace with India. He said he was fully convinced that conflict cannot resolve anything, that the future lies only in cooperation and that they have a historic duty to write a new chapter in their bilateral relations. He played up his relatively short (and short-lived) democratic credentials and emphasized he had just been elected President and he had enemies all round him—in the armed forces, in the establishment and in the political opposition. They would kill him if he was seen to have capitulated. Responding to Mrs Gandhi's suggestion that the existing ceasefire line provided the best solution to the Kashmir problem, Bhutto agreed but said this could not go into an agreement since he would be thrown out by his people though added he would prepare his people for this solution in the long run. However, in the meantime reposed faith on soft borders and creating trust and friendship.

Bakshi said this was the understanding Bhutto reconfirmed on Mrs Gandhi insistence. Bhutto promised to recognize Bangladesh to enable the prisoners to go home. According to Bakshi, the agreement was signed in the early hours of 3 July, though it bore the date 2 July 1972.[71]

Bhutto was desperate to have something positive to show his people. The understanding so arrived at between India and Pakistan was verbal so that it would pass muster with the National Assembly and the people.

Though there was a choice for a secret agreement, Mrs Gandhi in the interest of transparency chose an open agreement. Regarding

Kashmir, it may be recalled that the Soviet memorandum which Pegov had handed over on the eve of the talks, was fresh on her mind. It had cautioned that Bhutto was prepared to accept the ceasefire line as an international border, not now, but in due course. This too, Bhutto had said at the full delegation-level meeting on 1 July that 'in the foreseeable future an agreement will emerge'. This essentially was the burden of what he had said to Mrs Gandhi in their one-to-one conversation. Keen to give peace another chance, Mrs Gandhi apparently accepted the verbal understanding and signed the agreement which enabled Bhutto to return home as he had promised 'with firm conviction that we can embark on a new era of peace' and set the foundation of a durable peace'.[72] In his separate message, Bhutto assured prisoners and internees that their essentially human problem would be resolved before long and the agreement 'should lead to their early return home before long'.[73]

What was agreed verbally between the two leaders has since remained a mystery since there is no authentic record of the conversation. Essentially, it was what Bhutto had said at the conference on 1 July which he repeated perhaps, a little more elaborately and passionately to Mrs Gandhi later on. As soon as she emerged from the meeting, Mrs Gandhi briefed her Principal Secretary P.N. Haksar and his secretary P.N. Dhar. But as it happened, neither of them made any official record of what was told to them as standard procedure. Since officers get transferred over time, it is the recorded conversations or remarks that remain testimony to the past. To that extent, both were remiss in not recording what was told to them. Perhaps it was, in their judgement, too insignificant a matter to be recorded since it was essentially what Bhutto had already said at the conference table.

However, another officer, J.N. Dixit, in his book *Anatomy of a Flawed Inheritance* has claimed that he was present with Haksar when 'Mrs Gandhi briefed us on what transpired'. According to Dixit, 'Mrs. Gandhi told Bhutto that she was sympathetic to his concerns and that she would hate to appear to be dictating terms to a defeated adversary . . .' Dixit said, Mrs Gandhi elaborated the merits of the Indian proposal that neither country should gain or lose territory and no transfer of population from one side to the other be made and the Kashmiris as an ethnic community are left undivided on the Indian side. The Line of Control was, therefore, an ethnic and linguistic frontier, being the limit of political influence of Sheikh Abdullah and his National Conference Party. Bhutto was reported to have responded in this context that 'he had come to the conclusion that the Indian proposal was the only feasible one' but to be implemented step by step later and not to be written in any document and she agreed it should not be recorded and implemented gradually.[74] Whatever Dixit wrote in 1995 had little archival value. Dixit claimed that he was standing with Haksar. The briefing was for Haksar who was the senior-most bureaucrat and Mrs Gandhi's Principal Secretary. Dixit, at best, could have overheard Mrs Gandhi speak, which was also unlikely, since matters like this between the PM and her senior-most officer would be spoken discreetly. The briefing was not for Dixit as he was a middle-level officer at that stage in his career.

On 7 August, in her letter to Sri Lankan Prime Minister Mrs Bandaranaike about Kashmir Mrs Gandhi said:

> On the Indian side, we felt that durable peace was not possible without a settlement of the Kashmir question. The President assured me that he would like to do this and seemed to accept what he himself called a 'line of peace' on the border. However, he did not wish to make this public at present.[75]

This is the most authentic version of her talk with Bhutto. Obviously, Bhutto gave no particular undertaking. He had said this even during the full delegation level meeting on 1 July.

A few days later, in another letter to Bhutto, she referred to a statement of the spokesperson of the Pakistan Foreign Office on Kashmir, and told Bhutto that it 'appeared to us to be at variance with our understanding of the nature and character of the line of control'.[76] This reference was about the demarcation of the Line of Control which was at odds with her own understanding on the final solution to the Kashmir question. Indeed, there was some controversy about the Line of Control and there was some correspondence about it as well. But in any correspondence between the Governments of India and Pakistan or between Mrs Gandhi and Bhutto, until 1977 when both were in power, there was no reference to any understanding on Kashmir's final solution. The absence of a proof of the understanding arrived at between them was acutely felt when Pakistan, after Bhutto had been executed, completely denied any knowledge and challenged India to produce the note if it had it. It is true that the understanding was indeed verbal. Nothing prevented Haksar or his colleague P.N. Dhar, to record the briefing they got for future official reference and posterity, which is common practice. A note then recorded, would have unimpeachable archival value.

P.N. Dhar, secretary to the prime minister, later in 1995 in an article in the *Times of India* of 4 April 1995 and reprinted in the *Journal of Peace Studies* of March/June 1995 issue, confirmed two important points: (i) that the understanding was verbal and not written and (ii) that she did brief him along with Haksar. He, of course, gave no reason why either of them failed to record what was told to them. They were senior officers and should have known the archival value of such a note for record and posterity.[77]

In accepting Bhutto's verbal assurance against her better judgement, Mrs Gandhi made an erroneous assessment that a chastened Bhutto was a different person and would stand by it. Dhar's article left one with the impression that Bhutto did mean to implement the assurance. As Dhar said, 'Pakistan People's party [PPP] presumably in implementing Bhutto's assurance established its branch in Pakistan Occupied Kashmir (POK) in 1974 and offered the POK to become the fifth province of Pakistan.' Bhutto also introduced many administrative changes in Gilgit and Baltistan for their eventual integration with the rest of the country, but no further steps were taken for their eventual merger. Dhar's article, written after more than two decades of the conversation, cannot carry much conviction or credibility. The article, at best, reflects his desire to cover his failure in recording the conversation then and there. However, Foreign Secretary T.N. Kaul, who was an active participant in the drama that was enacted in Simla, said in his book there was neither a verbal understanding nor any secret understanding. Kaul insisted 'it was an open agreement openly arrived at'. Later, even Pakistan maintained that according to their understanding, there was no secret agreement, or for that matter any agreement, which Bhutto made to Mrs Gandhi in their one-to-one meeting. But reading between the lines, and from Dhar's article and other pieces of information, one gets the impression that there was definitely some understanding if not a formal agreement, as is normally understood, which enabled the formal agreement to be signed on the following morning (which was verbal). Simply put it was that Bhutto would accept the LoC as a permanent border between India and Pakistan. Similarly, the note by Miss Veena Dutta does leave one with the impression that there was some understanding.

That the Simla agreement did not solve the problems was self-evident and also confirmed by the foreign secretary, while briefing heads of foreign diplomatic missions in New Delhi, two days later. It was not even expected, since it was known and even accepted from the beginning that the problems lingering for the past 25 years would not be resolved in a week's discussions. About Kashmir, the foreign secretary said that henceforth the two countries would respect the line emerging on 17 December 1971 and not the old ceasefire line of 1949, of course, without prejudice to their recognized positions.[78]

Pakistan President Bhutto had a tough time in the National Assembly in the debate on the ratification of the agreement. Allegations of surrender and duress were made. But in his lengthy speech he successfully warded off all criticism and had the agreement ratified. Listing the compulsions under which he was operating in India, he had said:

India had all the cards in her hands, and India is not a generous negotiator. They had Pakistan's territory. They had East Pakistan separated from Pakistan. They had 93,000 prisoners of war. They had the threat of war trials and so they were sitting pretty.

Claiming that he had 'upheld Pakistan's dignity, sovereignty and self-respect under tiring and difficult circumstances' he asked rhetorically, 'what did Pakistan have as a bargaining chip? Riots, labour troubles and all sorts of internal dissentions?' He made it clear that he kept his pledge of not compromising on principles or the right to self-determination for the people of Jammu and Kashmir. He insisted that as promised, he also did not discuss Bangladesh with India. He claimed that he had redeemed national honour in signing the agreement. About the prisoners Bhutto said, if he had compromised on Kashmir, and settled it, the prisoners would have been released. He blamed the Russians for the stalemate.[79]

In India, Prime Minister Indira Gandhi intervening in the debate in the Lok Sabha on the Simla Agreement trashed all criticism made against it and described it as 'the beginning though a small beginning, but a good beginning'.[80] External Affairs Minister Swaran Singh in his speech too, described it only as a first step, a beginning in the process of establishing peace, friendship and cooperation based on the principle of equality of sovereign nations and 'not in the spirit of a victor dictating his terms to the vanquished'.[81]

Notwithstanding the lack of resolution of the Kashmir question, the Simla conference did make way for subsequent conferences that triggered recognition of Bangladesh, release of prisoners, return of occupied territories in the western sector, exchange of internees and normalisation of relations between the two countries. The conference itself remained a testimony to the desire of the two countries to find a peaceful approach to the India–Pakistan problems. The agreement was projected by Radio Pakistan as a 'first step toward durable peace (and) a good beginning for reducing tension between the two countries'. In its effusive and demonstrative welcome, Radio Pakistan said it opened a 'new upsurge of mutual trust' and sought to replace 'mistrust and suspicion with justice and good neighbourliness'. It was described as based on the policy of give-and-take without Pakistan having relinquishing its principles. The broadcast was meant to give direction to public opinion and influencers within and outside the country. The Pakistani commentators, however, took special pains to highlight that Pakistan did not have to yield an inch of its territory in West Pakistan. Apparently, they were happy to get rid of the Bengalis since there was no regret over the loss of East Pakistan. As a sign of euphoria, it was contrasted with the failure of the Arabs to get their lands occupied by Israel in 1967 vacated, notwithstanding the support of the superpowers and the United Nations. For home consumption, the emphasis remained on the fact that India had accepted Pakistan as a party to the Kashmir dispute without specifically nullifying the UNSC resolutions. Finally, Pakistan rightly gloated that even if it lost the war, it won peace.

For a year after Simla, Bhutto remained engaged in getting his prisoners released and did not raise any contentious issues. However, soon after the agreement on prisoners' repatriation was signed in August 1973, and they returned home, Bhutto went back to his old ways. On 7 November 1973, Bhutto addressing a public meeting at Rawalkot said that he could assure the Kashmiris that they could count on his support at every stage of their liberation struggle. At another meeting, he said, 'If the people of Kashmir are prepared t sacrifice, the Kashmir problem would be resolved,' and added, 'we should be prepared for everything and every sacrifice.' The Ministry of External Affairs reminded Pakistan in an aide memoire that 'such statements by the highest authority in Pakistan could cause apprehensions among the people and the Government of India regarding Pakistan's intentions to implement the Simla Agreement'.[82] When there was no signs of Pakistan stopping such exhortations, Swaran Singh, the EAM, drew the attention of Aziz Ahmed to the statements of Bhutto reminding him that they ran contrary to the spirit of the Simla Agreement.[83] Aziz Ahmed replied that India's conclusions were based on certain excerpts taken out of context from Bhutto's speeches but when they were read as a whole, these were fully justified.[84] However, the EAM while replying to the debate on the international situation in the Rajya Sabha in 1973 and taking note of Aziz Ahmed clarification, insisted that Pakistan should fulfil its assurances given in the agreement.[85] Swaran Singh again felt constrained to draw Aziz Ahmed's attention to another Bhutto speech at Rawalpindi which was violative of the Simla Agreement.[86] Aziz Ahmed again had the same old excuse that India had read the speech out of context.[87]

Strangely enough, Mrs Gandhi's letter of 30 March 1974 to Bhutto regarding recognition of Bangladesh was silent on Bhutto's indiscreet pronouncements on Kashmir in violation of an undertaking given by him to her personally. If only she had reprimanded him for violating his personal commitment to her made on 2 July 1972, the world would have known that there was something more to the text of the agreement. After this letter, Mrs Gandhi wrote four more letters to Bhutto (on 22 May 1974, 20 March 1975, 11 April 1976 and 31 December 1976). In none of these letters did she even remotely refer to his verbal commitment of 2 July 1972. After Bhutto was executed, Pakistan cast strong doubts on any such understanding. Pakistan maintained that it had found nothing in their archives and asked India to produce any evidence it had in support of their contention. With that the Simla saga got buried forever and India–Pakistan relations returned to the pre-1971 days and old disputes continued to dominate their relations. The new Advisor on Foreign Affairs, Agha Shahi, continuing with the earlier Pakistani stance said on 7 December 1978 that the dispute on Kashmir should be resolved in accordance with the UN resolutions accepting the right of self-determination.[88]

What were Mrs Gandhi's compulsions in accepting a verbal understanding on such a vital question? Her intervention in the debate in the Lok Sabha on the Simla Agreement gave some clues. She was concerned if there was no agreement, things would go out of hand and the positions on both sides would harden, resulting in a stalemate for a long time to come. She wanted to bury the past and move toward a new future. She perhaps wanted to turn the face of Pakistan away from the past bitterness and hatred to the new direction of peace and understanding. She was apparently worried that any agreement to which Pakistan did not voluntarily subscribe would be an imposed one and could give birth to revanchist feelings among the Pakistani public which would not be good in the long run, as it happened in Europe after the First World War.[89] At the end Bhutto, the 'dramatist' had carried the day at Simla.

It may be added in parenthesis that soon after P.N. Dhar's article was published in 1995, as indicated above, the Pakistan Foreign Office spokesperson rejected any suggestion that there was any secret or even verbal understanding at Simla. The Pakistan Foreign Office pointed to an assertion by Mrs Gandhi in the *Indian Express* of 24 April 1978 that any talk of a secret understanding was 'absolutely ridiculous'.[90]

In 1995, Pakistan PM Benazir Bhutto, Zulfikar Ali's daughter, who was present in Simla, denied any knowledge of the verbal agreement, though she was regularly briefed by her father. It was a diplomatic denial. Pakistan Ambassador in Moscow Jamsheed Marker however said:

> In my opinion, knowing Bhutto, it is just possible that he smooth talked her with some kind of assurances, but if so, and again knowing Bhutto, he made quite sure that they did not find their way into the written record. In the final analysis, what has been achieved is a general understanding that the Simla Agreement stands up on par with the United Nations Resolutions for the purpose of settling the Indo–Pakistan dispute over Kashmir.[91]

Mrs Gandhi was driven in not pressing for a final solution on Kashmir due to the Soviet advice against it and given the support they had extended in 1971. But as far as Pakistan was concerned, it allowed the pot to boil. It had become necessary for the PM to accept Bhutto's word, otherwise the relationship would be uncertain, as happened after the Agra Summit later.

Pakistan was right in its assessment of the Simla Agreement that it lost the war but won peace. In Moscow, the Pakistani Ambassador Jamsheed Marker saw the Simla Agreement as a 'diplomatic triumph of Bhutto'. He said to describe it a 'success' would be a 'weak word' and added:

> [S]tarting from a position of greatest possible disadvantage and weakness, Bhutto had a few cards to play except his own intellectual brilliance and innate diplomatic skill. Yet, he managed to extricate his prisoners of war and recover lost territories without conceding anything of substance to the triumphant and dominating Indians… What cannot be ignored, however, are the skill and finesse that characterised Bhutto's performance at Simla and the substantive results that he achieved despite all odds.[92]

The euphoria generated at Simla was short-lived. With little to bind it to an understanding on Kashmir, Pakistan returned to its old ways. The subcontinent to this day continues to live with same baleful consequences of 1971. Pakistan's realization that it could not take J&K by conventional war led to its pursuit of nuclear weapons and other asymmetric means to slake its desire for revenge on India for breaking up Pakistan.[93] The return of the military regime within a few years brought back the acrimony of the earlier years. Pakistan reneged on bilateralism and had no qualms in raising the Kashmir issue at the international fora, as and when it considered necessary, despite India's protests. It ruled out an armed clash with India in the future concluding that it was a losing proposition. Pakistan found it cheaper and safer to wage a proxy war and promoted cross-border terrorism and financed militancy in the border areas of India utilizing the perceived grievances of some linguistic and religious minorities to promote disaffection against the central government and the country.

Explaining his oft-repeated slogan of a 'hundred-year war' Bhutto had said, it was a 'metaphysical concept'. It meant a small nation would never surrender its rights till eternity. As long as it exists, Pakistan would fight for its right and that appears to be its living credo. To boost the morale of his people, he talked of 1962 and 1965 and said Pakistan had lost those opportunities blaming them on Ayub Khan, and said:

> Could not we in 1962 confront India and take Kashmir. But at that time the Field Marshal was hiding in Hunza and we were searching for him. In1965 also, had it not been for failings, weaknesses and corruption, we could have gone on to Delhi.[94]

All this he said within a dozen days of kowtowing for a settlement. At the end, India was left wondering at its own wisdom.

Was the emergence of Bangladesh as an independent country conducive to peace? Unfortunately, the emergence of the new nation was not accompanied by a new administrative set-up. East Pakistan's bureaucracy became Bangladesh's bureaucracy except for suspected collaborators of the old regime. The bureaucracy, which for quarter of a century had adopted an antagonistic and aggressive position against India, could hardly revise its stance on problems carried over from earlier days. Bengali officers repatriated from Pakistan to Dhaka joined the bureaucratic machinery and worsened the situation. The Bangladeshis perceived north Indians to be synonymous with West Pakistanis—people who had bossed over them and treated them with disdain. Bengali military officers who had been repatriated had an anti-Indian orientation built into their psyche over the last twenty-five years which helped in the creation of armed forces which was not prepared to see the Indian Army in any other mould. The protection granted to the Pakistani prisoners of war (PoWs) was seen in the ethnic mould. The assassination of Mujibur Rahman in a coup only exacerbated the situation and the anti-Indian narrative returned with a vengeance. By the end of 1972, Bangladesh politics had become fractious. There was antagonism between the regular forces and the police and former freedom fighters. Senior political leaders like Maulana Bhashani became openly critical of Mujib's politics and methods of governance. It was felt that Mujib had lost touch with the sentiments of his party. It had, therefore, become necessary for Mujib to adopt an anti-Indian stance to create credibility with Bangladesh's internal and external forces. By the end of 1972 it had become clear that Mujib was getting isolated from political forces within the party which distanced him with India. This finally culminated in the tragedy of his assassination in August 1975.[95]

The first flush of victory and the emergence of Bangladesh made India believe that its stand against the two-nation theory was vindicated. But the old narrative returned to haunt India. India was disappointed when the old issues of the Pakistan days returned to sour India–Bangladesh relations. India expected that the old issues of the Pakistan days would get resolved in a new climate of friendship and goodwill prevailing in abundance at the beginning of 1972. Unfortunately, the issues like the Farakka Barrage and the sharing of waters of common rivers, exchange of enclaves, and transit facilities to India's northeast which had stood suspended since the 1965 war, became major issues of conflict. As pointed out in the previous chapter, soon after Bangladesh's liberation, Henry Kissinger perceived that 'Bangladesh would work to the long-range disadvantage of India itself' and pointed out to the 'Pakistani flags from time to time in Bangladesh'. Bhutto had agreed saying India had 'burned its fingers in the furnace of Bengal'.[96]

The identity of the new country separated from Pakistan was in question especially due to the dilution of its Muslim identity during the 1971 struggle against West Pakistan. Unfortunately, soon after getting rid of West Pakistan, Bangladesh returned to the Bengali Muslim identity to be the determinant instead of its earlier secular Bengali culture, albeit short-lived.

If Pakistan had Kashmir to confront India, Bangladesh found Farakka the flagship of its crusade against India as New Delhi watched helplessly at the unfortunate turn of events. The All India Congress Committee in its resolution adopted at the Gauhati session in November 1976 regretted that Bangladesh had adopted the path of confrontation.

Half a century later, and after many ups and downs, relations with Bangladesh have returned to a friendlier phase, while the relations with the rump Pakistan continue to suffer from the malevolence of old days. For Pakistan, the Kashmir issue is as alive today as three-quarters of a century ago, despite India's surgical strike on 5 August 2019. The world at large has subscribed to India's solution. Pakistan can only draw satisfaction and solace from the fiction of the continued presence of Kashmir on the agenda of the UN Security Council.

IV

India–Sri Lanka Accord, 1987[*]

On 29 July 1987, India and Sri Lanka signed an accord whereby India pledged to help Sri Lanka in resolving its ethnic problem between the Sinhalese and the Tamils. The Tamils who inhabited the north and east provinces had their problem run *pari passu* with the history of the island since Independence in February 1948. The conflict was born out of the uneven balance between the two ethnic communities— the majority Sinhalese 74 per cent against the 12.6 per cent minority Tamils. Minorities which are diffused across the country present little problem but not when they are concentrated in one distinct area. In Sri Lanka, the Tamil minority was by and large confined to the north and east provinces. While the north (Jaffna) was wholly Tamil, in the east though the Tamils were in majority on Independence, a substantial Sinhalese population relocated there from other parts of the island as part of the government's colonization policy. This reduced the Tamils to a minority. The majority Sinhalese spoke Sinhala; the Tamils spoke Tamil and had a distinct culture. Both the communities had migrated from India way back in history but lived in separate areas with little interaction between them. This failed to create the bonds that go to the making of a nation.

There is another Tamil group, known as plantation Tamils or Estate Tamils, who were brought from India as indentured labour by the British

[*] Much of the narration in this chapter is based on documents from the author's five-volume compilation of official documents both classified and unclassified published in 2001 titled *India–Sri Lanka Relations and Sri Lanka's Ethnic Conflict 1947–2000* (Geetika Publishers, New Delhi. Five Volumes).

in the nineteenth century to work on tea and coffee plantations. They faced a different kind of problem for citizenship. On independence, Sri Lanka introduced citizenship laws which denied citizenship to a large number of plantation Indians even though they were living on the island for over a century. It caused serious concern in New Delhi, but finally, the bulk of them were taken back in India and the remaining were given their citizenship rights in Sri Lanka. They are housed in the Central Highlands away from the areas of ethnic Tamil habitation. The only thing common between them and the Jaffna Tamils is their religion and language. They are not part of the ethnic problem that the Lankan Tamils faced.

On the eve of independence, the British had given the island a Constitution based on the democratic principle of majority which formed the basis for the island's polity. The Tamils even then had shown a lack of confidence in getting a fair deal from the Sinhala community. In a memorandum to the then British Prime Minister, Clement Attlee, they had expressed their fears and said, 'The proposed constitution sets up only an irremovable communal oligarchy in perpetual power and paves the way for an immutable succession of Sinhalese Buddhist Prime Ministers.'[1]

To their disappointment nothing came of it. The amendment proposed by the father of Tamil nationalism S.J.V. Chelvanayakam, to the motion of thanks for the governor general's address in the House of Representatives on 26 November 1947, shortly before independence, had asked, 'Why Tamils should not have the right to secede from the rest of the country if they so desire to do so?' It was not an auspicious beginning.

The two communities not only lived in isolation from each other, their educational backgrounds also added to the problem. The Tamils were then comparatively better educated and were professionals and historically occupied most of positions in the central government in Colombo during the British rule, which were disproportionate to their numbers. The Sinhalese were agriculturalists, comparatively less educated, and were not professionals and much less represented in the services. The differences of religion further accentuated the problem. The Tamils are Hindus, the Sinhalese follow Buddhism. Tamils, ignoring the imbalance of 12.6 per cent versus 74 per cent in population, not only aspired but insisted on parity with the majority community. Tragically, the Sinhalese, too ignored the recommendations of the Official Language Commission in 1951 that both the Sinhala and Tamil be declared the official languages of the island.

On independence, the two north and east provinces, housed two million Tamils who occupied one-third of the surface area, leaving two-thirds for the 18 million Sinhalese. The 12.6 per cent Tamils were 92 per cent of the population of the north province (Jaffna) alone, and 68 per cent of the east province. The two provinces occupy three-fifths of the island's coastline. The influential and obscurantist Buddhist clergy in their self-proclaimed role of defenders of the faith against the imaginary threats of the holy trinity—the country, the community and religion—opposed any concession or compromise with the Tamils on any issue whatsoever.

The economic contraction and limited employment opportunities further generated antagonism.[2] In the early, post-independence period, an attempt was made by Prime Minister D.S. Senanayake to forge a measure of unity between the two communities. The enactment of the citizenship laws of 1948 and 1949 though impacted only the Estate Tamils, gave enough cause for worry to the ethnic Tamils who formed the Tamil Nationalist Federal Party in 1949 with its three-point agenda: (i) an autonomous region for the indigenous Tamils, comprising the north and east provinces in a federal set-up with the rest of the country; (ii) parity of status for Tamils with the Sinhala language, and (iii) citizenship rights for the Estate Tamils.[3]

The ambitious S.W.R.D. Bandaranaike, an enlightened cosmopolitan, liberal, Oxford-educated gentleman and a prominent member of the United National Party (UNP), in 1952 decided to defect from the party to form a separate political outfit the Sri Lanka Freedom Party (SLFP). His main agenda then, was to declare Sinhala the only official language of the country if he won the 1956 elections, which he did. It was the beginning of the conflict in the island. Ironically, in 1944, J.R. Jayewardene had proposed to replace English by Sinhala language and Bandaranaike had then opposed the suggestion and insisted that English should be replaced by both Sinhala and Tamil languages. It is unfortunate that the same Bandaranaike in pursuit of power threw prudence to the winds! Was it so simple? Many of the steps that were taken in response to the 'Sinhala Only' policy of Bandaranaike had become unavoidable. By 1955–56, Prime Minister Sir John Kotelawala's policies had built so much resentment amongst the Sinhalese that demands from extremists had become inevitable— major concessions to Buddhism and Sinhala language and culture— which Bandaranaike's policies fulfilled. Changes in foreign and defence policies, establishing diplomatic ties with the communist nations, the adoption of non-alignment policy and the closure of British bases had instilled in the people a new identity and a sense of direction. As his most perceptive Tamil critic after his assassination said, 'Under his rule the Ceylonese began to understand that they were first-class Asians, not third-class synthetic Europeans.'[4]

It was then that the Tamil members of Parliament formed themselves into a Tamil United Front and vowed to struggle for the creation of a Tamil State which 'will offer to federate with the Sinhalese State on terms of complete equality if acceptable to both the nations or elect to remain independent'. The Tamils, however, refused to accept that the language of the 74 per cent could be the national language of the country alone!

In a counter move, the Tamil Federal Party, at its convention at Trincomalee in August 1956, called for the formation of a Tamil linguistic state calling the present legislation as the most iniquitous and worst piece of legislation perpetrated on the Tamils in the last 300 or more years.[5] To soften the Tamil opposition, Bandaranaike signed a pact with the nationalist Tamil leader, Chelvanayakam, promising to create Tamil regional councils with devolution of substantial powers and for the use of Tamil in the north and east provinces.[6] Even when the National Convention of the Federal Party had approved the pact, it was considered 'an interim adjustment', the ultimate objective being the achievement of a Tamil linguistic state within the federal union.[7]

The pact met with strong opposition from the Sinhalese, principally the powerful Buddhist clergy. Under pressure,

Bandaranaike decided to annul it. He used the Federal Party's satyagraha (civil disobedience movement), against the government's decision to introduce number plates with 'Siri' markings for government vehicles, to annul it. The Federal Party declared that they had to fight back for survival or to be 'ever content to remain as a subject race'.[8] The statement made by Bandaranaike in Parliament on 4 July 1958 was another setback for the Tamils, since he had said that 'the parity of status for the Tamil and Sinhala could not be a solution of Ceylon's language problem' (since) such 'a solution would lead the country to chaos'.[9] To placate the Tamils, on 18 August 1958, the Parliament adopted a bill for 'reasonable use of Tamil language' providing for its use as a medium of instruction in schools for admissions, examinations, public services, correspondence with the central government and for administrative purposes etc., which by all accounts was a reasonable step but was rejected by the Tamils. This attitude of the Tamils made a solution to the problem difficult over time and their problems only peaked.

After the assassination of Bandaranaike in 1959, his wife Sirimavo Bandaranaike took over and during her first tenure from 1960–65, the Sinhala language was enforced with greater vigour alienating the Tamils further, particularly when the Parliament adopted a legislation requiring courts to give their judgments mandatorily in Sinhala.[10] The Tamils remained indignant. They were particularly outraged that while provisions for the use of the Tamil language could be amended by ordinary legislation, amendments to the use of Sinhala required Constitutional amendment.[11]

Paradoxically, the Indian High Commissioner, Y.D. Gundevia (1957–60) did not see or even perceive that the Tamils had any problem at all, when he said:

Till now, the little island had been a picture of a harmonious, well integrated, multi-racial society, with its about three million Hindus, one million Christians and seven million Buddhists. No one asked how or why the Tamils, who formed only thirty percent of the population were holding more than forty percent of the jobs in government offices.[12]

If the Bandaranaike–Chelvanayakam Pact in 1957 did not work, the Senanayake–Chelvanayakam Pact in March 1965 too, failed to yield any positive result because of the pressure from Buddhist monks. The continued Tamil disgruntlement and frustration with the majority disdain to their grievances led to the strengthening of a Tamil consciousness that transformed into sub-nationalism and finally to Tamil nationalism. The Sinhala chauvinist leadership instead of advancing the idea of a monolithic unitary sovereignty to build the Sri Lankan nation, succeeded by its policy of 'Sinhala only', in creating not one, but two nations within one state.

It was not only High Commissioner Y.D. Gundevia in Colombo alone who did not perceive that the Tamils had any grievance or problem with the regime. New Delhi too remained unaware. By all accounts, New Delhi enjoyed excellent relations with Colombo. In December 1960, Sri Lankan Prime Minister, Sirimavo Bandaranaike, was on an official visit to Delhi and Prime Minister Nehru described her visit as a 'pilgrimage', and had said while

> [W]e have had the privilege of welcoming many distinguished guests here, but I can say with perfect honesty and truth that, you, madam, are particularly welcome and your visit here has given us very special pleasure for a variety of reasons.[13]

During the entire visit, the Tamil problem was not mentioned. After Nehru's death, his daughter Indira Gandhi, as prime minister, also enjoyed excellent relations with Sri Lanka, and Sirimavo personally. Indira had given Colombo satisfaction on the question of Estate Tamils by taking large numbers back in India, (which her father had refused); on maritime boundary negotiation and had also conceded Colombo's claim on the island of Kachhathivu. On 6 May 1976, External Affairs Minister Y.B. Chavan had told the Lok Sabha that there were 'no outstanding problems between the two countries'.[14]

After Indian intervention in East Pakistan and the creation of Bangladesh in 1971, the Tamils in Sri Lanka were somewhat encouraged that India could be expected to lend its support in their favour. The Indian government had initially regarded the Tamil problem as Sri Lanka's internal problem which it should resolve with its citizens. India was loath to interfere in the internal affairs of a small and friendly neighbour. No one was convinced that a parallel existed between the situation that led to the Indian intervention in East Pakistan and the situation in Sri Lanka. It is worth noting that Mrs Bandaranaike had emerged as a leading light of the non-aligned movement enjoying prestige disproportionate to her country's size and resources and this could hardly be ignored by Mrs Gandhi.

If India was not enthusiastic in promising support to Lankan Tamils, it was also aware that in Tamil Nadu itself there were secessionist sentiments not too long ago. It was feared that any support to a Tamil irredentist movement in Sri Lanka could revive old ambitions of Indian Tamils for a pan-Tamil state. So when Tamil leader, S.J.V. Chelvanayakam visited India in 1972, he did not find New Delhi enthusiastic.

The Tamil national movement continued more or less peacefully for an honourable place in the island's political landscape and even joined the Sinhala parties in coalition governments whenever there was a hung house. But their perceptions remained unchanged. In 1976, to give a new impetus to the Tamil national movement in Sri Lanka, the Tamil United Front emerged in its new avatar as the Tamil United Liberation Front (TULF). By just adding 'Liberation' to its name, it put the government on notice that they were entering a new phase in their struggle against the Sinhala State. They realized that the earlier policy of sharing power as a junior partner in a coalition with the Sinhala parties had created the impression among the majority community that Tamil aspirations were being catered to with the crumbs.

The 1976 Tamils' Vaddukoddai Convention was a landmark event in the Tamil struggle for an honourable place under the sun. The resolution adopted at this convention emphasized the differentiations made between the two communities historically and called upon the TULF to formulate 'a plan of action and launch without undue delay the struggle for winning freedom of the Tamil nation'. It was a Tamil war cry.[15]

The tragedy surrounding the fourth Tamil International Conference in Jaffna was enough to break the camel's back. The repression with which the people attending the conference were treated and the burning of the Jaffna library housing priceless and timeless collections of Tamil literature was seen as a challenge to Tamil nationalism. There was no looking back thereafter.[16]

After the death of the charismatic Tamil leader Chelvanayakam in 1977, a youth organisation known as the Liberation Tigers of the Tamil Eelam (LTTE) declared itself his heir referring to Chelvanayakam as 'Thantai Selva'.[17] The Tamils felt that their grievances were being ignored and they took to violent methods to make the Sinhala State take notice. The LTTE had no qualms about using violence as a tool, to give vent to its anger at the 'iniquitous regime'. About this time, more youth militant organisations sprung up. Some of them were the People's Liberation Organisation of the Tamil Eelam (PLOTE), Eelam Revolutionary Organisation of the Students (EROS), the Tamil Eelam Liberation Organisation (TELO), the Eelam People's Revolutionary Liberation Front (EPRLF) and the Eelam National Democratic Liberation Front (ENDLF). Each one of them had 'Liberation' as a signature in their name. Instead of pooling their resources together they operated independently without a coordinated plan of action. In most cases, they were rivals and were engaged in murderous attacks with each. Assassination and bomb blasts became routine events in the life of Tamil youth in the north. Though the Government of India had as yet not committed itself to the Tamil cause, in Tamil Nadu there was plenty of sympathy for them. These groups could cross the narrow Palk Strait and find a safe haven with ease, melt into the local population and enjoy immunity from the Sri Lankan police and laws whenever under heat in Jaffna.

The 'Tigers' in the Liberation Tigers of Tamil Eelam, the most lethal of them all, was the emblem of the Chola Kingdom, symbolic of a powerful nationalist ideology.[18] Its leader Velupillai Prabhakaran consecrated his struggle with the blood of the Tamil Mayor of Jaffna, Alfred Duriappah on 27 July 1975 by murdering him. It was the first assassination of a Tamil by a Tamil in the country. To tide over its financial problems in the early days, the LTTE indulged in bank robberies and such like actions. Henceforth, the LTTE became the cutting edge of the Tamil national movement. Initially, the LTTE worked with other Tamil militant organisations, but became an independent body after it had eliminated all its rivals.

In an interview to journalist Anita Pratap of the Calcutta weekly, *Sunday Magazine,* LTTE leader, Prabhakaran described how he was impacted by the ethnic problem as a school boy. He said he had grown up hearing tragic stories of Tamils who had suffered grievously at the hands of the Sinhala security forces. His experience in terrorist activities for twelve years had 'convinced him beyond doubt' that the path he had chosen was the correct one, since 'armed struggle is the only way out for emancipation of our oppressed people'. He told Anita Pratap that he had even established contacts with foreign militant organisations like Al Fatah and received arms and training.[19]

By the adoption of violence as an instrument for redressal of its grievances and the killing of innocent Sinhalese civilians and later even dissident Tamils, LTTE wrecked its moral superiority, but that did not bother Prabhakaran.

In November 1978, the political committee of the LTTE had issued a document called, 'The Struggle for Tamil Eelam and the Liberation Tigers' which articulated the need for its birth, its relevance and its role in the future. Mincing no words, it provided the ideological raison d'être for the type of activities in which it henceforth engaged itself.[20]

Anti-Tamil riots in August 1977, in which many Indian Tamils too suffered, roused New Delhi somewhat. A protest was lodged with Colombo and Prime Minister Morarji Desai sent a personal message to Lanka prime minister, J. Jayewardene, expressing his hope for the early return of normalcy. However, the Tamil Nadu legislative assembly with M.G. Ramachandran as chief minister did not feel bound by diplomatic niceties and unanimously passed a resolution expressing its 'rude shock' at the happenings in the island. It urged New Delhi to pressure Sri Lanka to stop 'violence and atrocities which the Tamils in Sri Lanka are subjected to'.[21]

These riots, however, did not dent the bilateral relations since there was perfect bonhomie in evidence during Jayewardene's visit to New Delhi in October 1978. His visit was free of any contentious issues. President Sanjiva Reddy in his banquet speech referred to 1977 as 'special' and said, 'It was then that the people in both the countries showed the innate strength of their commitment to freedom.' Jayewardene in his reply speech referred to the arrest of his son that year when the SLFP government under Sirimavo Bandaranaike was in power in Colombo. He had said, 'I will not go into recent history, but there are many parallels that can be drawn between the events that took place in your country during the last two years and the events that took place in our country during the same period.'[22] He was referring to the Emergency which Mrs Gandhi had declared in India and the events in his country which led to the arrest of his son. In February 1979, Prime Minister Morarji Desai visited Sri Lanka. Whether in their banquet speeches or in Morarji's speech in the Lankan Parliament or in the joint statement, the letter 'T'(amil) did not find mention.[23] Mrs Gandhi, now out of power, lamented that the Indian government was going out of its way to be friendly with the Lankan government.[24] She was peeved that she had become the butt of Jayewardene's jibes and an avoidable witticism, even though his target was Sirimavo. His remarks had received wide publicity in India which upset Indira Gandhi. She had a long memory and when she returned to power in January 1980, his remarks still rankled. In any case, she 'never liked Jayewardene and she was right in her instinct', was the assessment of Chinmaya Gharekhan, a senior Foreign Service Officer in the prime minister's office.[25]

There was again racial violence in 1981 which India described as Sri Lanka's internal matter.[26] Mrs Gandhi on returning to power had started helping the Tamils, perhaps piqued about Jayewardene's remarks in Delhi. In March 1983, the Indian fortnightly *India Today* carried a story, 'Training Camps for Tamils in India'. The Sri Lankan Parliament discussed it and the Colombo media carried reports based on the story described it as exposing India and its leaders. The Lankan prime minister said it was for New Delhi to take note of it and take remedial action. Adding, he said, Colombo had tolerated this 'nonsense' but India could not bully Sri Lanka. The debate in the Sri Lanka Parliament was charged and emotions ran high.[27] India's denial had little credibility, as it indeed was deeply involved in this sordid exercise. B.G. Deshmukh, the cabinet secretary, later noted in his book, that the Sri Lankan affair also created and nurtured a cult of violence in Tamil Nadu. He wrote:

> The Central Government conducted training camps for Sri Lankan militants and liberally equipped them with arms. The State Government gave them all help and full freedom not only of movement but also of collecting money for arms. In fact, M.G. Ramachandran, the Chief Minister openly gave a donation for this purpose. The militants defiantly imported arms from outside which resulted in their free availability throughout Tamil Nadu.[28]

Meanwhile, Sri Lanka adopted a new Constitution which sought to give the Tamils greater protection of the Supreme Court against any infringement of their rights. It did not, however, convince the Tamils. On the contrary, it provided further fuel to Tamil militancy which had taken up arms in their struggle against the state. Under the new Constitution, Jayewardene had declared himself President and Ranasinghe Premadasa had taken over as prime minister. The President was now determined to eliminate the militants since he felt it was no longer possible to hold discussions with them. He even said that unless terrorists were eliminated even the political arm of the Tamils, the moderate Tamil United Liberation Front was unable to function for fear.[29]

The LTTE, in a relentless struggle to project itself as the sole representative of the Tamils, successfully discredited or destroyed almost all other rival militant groups, emerging as the sole entity without which a solution to Sri Lanka's ethnic problem was impossible. It succeeded in gaining international recognition and organized itself as a state within the state by controlling territory in the north, providing civil and criminal justice, collecting taxes in the areas under its control. The Sri Lankan Tamils respected Prabhakaran as much as they dreaded him. The Tigers had in their armoury a potent weapon which enabled them to mystify everybody—the cyanide capsule—to be used if captured by the police. It was a curious blend of obscurantism, absolute nihilism and revolutionary commitment. It resulted in the marginalization of moderate Tamil forces represented by the TULF. Prabhakaran had issued an obiter dictum preventing Tamils extending any sort of cooperation to the government. LTTE too set up an office in London, and submitted a memorandum to the Non-Aligned conference in India in March 1983.

1983 was the most tragic year in the history of the ethnic conflict—Prabhakaran had returned to Jaffna from Tamil Nadu. In January, a UNP worker was killed in Vavuniya, in February a police inspector, in March an army vehicle was ambushed and in April three UNP candidates for the local body elections were shot dead in Jaffna and police stations attacked. But it was the ambush of thirteen Sinhalese soldiers which provoked large-scale violence against the Tamils. During the ten days of violence, life and property of Tamils, including Indian Tamils living in Colombo, came under attack. The killings appeared to be organized, the rioters seeking out Tamil homes with lists in their possession.[30] The next day, *The Times* reported that army personnel actively encouraged looting and killings. The *Illustrated Weekly*, *India Today* reported that the attacks were well organized.[31] While the government estimate put the number of dead at 350, the Tamils estimate of the dead was 2000. The number of refugees in camps in Colombo was between 8000 and 10,000. *India Today* on 31 August 1983 reported that the most dangerous misconceptions were that all Indians were Tamils and all Tamils were terrorists. There was a sense of being overwhelmed by Sinhala chauvinism and fingers were pointed to a larger communist conspiracy and a Naxal plot which inferred India's involvement in its expansionist ambitions. However, the president also knew that the most dangerous tendencies were stirred up by the elements within his own rank. He had to face the unpalatable fact that hardliners within his government had encouraged punitive acts against the Tamils to intimidate them.[32]

Yet, President Jayewardene in an interview with the correspondent of the *Daily Telegraph* of London had said that there 'are no areas of negotiations as long as the terrorists are active'. He remained pugnacious and truculent in his interview.[33]

Jayewardene was not unaware of the problem, but populism and competitive Sinhala politics cramped him from taking steps to ameliorate Tamil grievances.

While the need of the hour was applying balm on Tamil wounds, the government adopted the sixth amendment, calling up all members of Parliament to disown separatism and take an oath to that effect. Unable to take such an oath, sixteen Tamil members of Parliament, resigned from their seats. Their departure from Parliament created a vacuum which was filled in by Prabhakaran and other members of the LTTE for whom it was a bonanza since his ranks suddenly swelled. It created a wave of sympathy toward the cause of self-determination among Tamils expatriates. The riots of 1983 had a homogenizing influence. With social dislocation in normal boundaries, the governing interaction between the rich and the poor changed. Being Tamil acquired a virtually emblematic significance.[34] The refusal of the Tamil members of Parliament to take an oath against separatism was not a politically correct step and it confirmed to the Sinhalese their irredentist intentions.

A prominent member of the Cabinet, Lalith Athulathmudali, distanced the government from the riots and described the violence, in which officials of the Indian High Commission were also attacked, as an 'anti-government move than communal violence'. He blamed an unseen hand behind this move which wanted to disrupt the cordial relations existing between India and Sri Lanka.[35]

President Jayewardene, in his televised broadcast to the nation on 22 August, after a hiatus of three weeks, blamed the violence on the Tamils, for advocating separation and reiterated that in future too, he would not hold talks with such people.[36] Moderate TULF was proscribed and it shifted its base to Tamil Nadu in India. Upset, New Delhi summoned the Sri Lankan high commissioner to express its concerns and distress. The high commissioner asked whether the concern was of the Government of India or the Tamil Nadu government. He was told that the concern came from the highest level of the Government of India. Assuming this to be an interference in its internal affairs, an angry Colombo told Delhi that it had desisted from making any adverse comments on similar events in India out of concern for neighbourly relations. Now it was Delhi's turn to be worried about Colombo's reaction. Colombo had inferred to India's handling of Sikh militancy in Punjab. Stung, the spokesperson of the MEA rejected the charge of interference and said India valued its ties with Colombo. A couple of days later, in the course of her press conference in Chennai, Mrs Gandhi sought to assure Colombo that India was 'against any secessionist movement in any sovereign country, and did not condone terrorism either'. That she was under pressure from Tamil Nadu was evident when she said, 'I am aware of the great concern of the people of Tamil Nadu at recent developments regarding the Tamil population in Sri Lanka.'[37] The Tamil Nadu factor was apparent in the statement of the External Affairs Minister (EAM), Narasimha Rao, in the Lok Sabha on 27 July 1983. His statement did not differentiate between Sri Lankan and Indian Tamils and the members were not satisfied with Rao's statement. As the Rajya Sabha was debating the issue, the prime minister telephoned President Jayewardene to express her 'grave concern' on behalf of Parliament, the people of India in general and the people of Tamil Nadu in particular, and suggested Rao visit Colombo. Jayewardene agreed. This was a positive development in that Lanka conceded India's locus standi in the current developments.

During his visit, Rao conveyed Mrs Gandhi's readiness to assist Lanka in whatever way Colombo wished in the prevailing situation.[38] The underlying message was that the distinction between the two Tamils was only semantic. Colombo did accept Rao's visit but was quite miffed at India's undue concerns at the events in Sri Lanka. According to leaks in the press, while preparing to receive Rao, Jayewardene asked his ministers to 'ascertain from their guest how India had solved its communal problem when the extremists had asked for a separation'. An irked Sri Lanka Prime Minister Ranasinghe Premadasa later said in Parliament that 'India should not play hide and seek with us. India should invade us openly and we are prepared to lay down our lives to defend our country'.[39]

A correspondent of the United Press International (UPI), based in Colombo who had circulated the news that Colombo had asked for military help from the US, the UK, Pakistan and even Bangladesh, was expelled from Colombo for circulating fake news. But it did scare New

Delhi for once, and Mrs Gandhi telephoned Jayewardene to assure him that India meant no harm to Sri Lanka. India, as a precautionary measure, even checked with the countries concerned about the authenticity of the report and was relieved that no such request had been made by Colombo. New Delhi made clear to those countries that it would not tolerate any such military intervention by any outside power, thus establishing the doctrine of regional security in which India had a dominant role.[40]

Mrs Gandhi once again underlined the doctrine of regional security when speaking in the Lok Sabha on 5 August, 1983 stressing that India neither wanted to interfere in Sri Lanka nor posed any threat to it, but warned that any extraneous involvement would complicate matters for both the countries. Colombo felt uneasy since the message from New Delhi was not only loud and clear but ominous too. A government spokesman in Colombo said that these rumours appeared to be aimed at destroying the close ties of friendship that existed between the two countries.[41]

Violence continued unabated in Sri Lanka. India's expression of concern on behalf of the Tamils had made Lankan Tamils more assertive and uncompromising too. Colombo now realized that under domestic pressure, New Delhi could not stay uninterested. To propitiate New Delhi, Jayewardene sent his brother H.W. Jayewardene to New Delhi as his special envoy. Mrs Gandhi made use of his visit to assure him that India posed no threat to the territorial integrity and sovereignty of Sri Lanka, but candidly said that 'because of historical, cultural and such other close ties between the peoples of the two countries, particularly between the Tamil community of Sri Lanka and us, India cannot remain unaffected by such events'.[42] Implicitly, Colombo once again conceded India's locus standi in the matter.

Before the arrival of the president's brother H.W. Jayewardene, there was a 70-minute strategy session at Principal Secretary Dr P.C. Alexander's room. The prominent participants were: G. Parthasarthi, the interlocutor; K.S. Bajpai, Secretary in the MEA; Thomas Abraham, Joint Secretary and a couple of other officers of the MEA. At the very beginning, Alexander posed the question: 'whether we were clear in our mind that we did not favour Eelam, a separate Tamil state?' There was general agreement on this point that 'an independent Tamil state would have profound implications for us and could lead to secession of the south'. That was the conclusive argument.[43] In other words, India would not support Tamil separatism lest it should encourage a pan-Tamil movement. It may be recalled in the initial stages of the Bangladesh struggle, India had a similar apprehension that an independent East Bengal might give birth to the movement for a greater Bengal. But the tempo of developments in East Bengal did not permit New Delhi to remain unconcerned.

Foreign Secretary Maharaj Krishna Rasgotra, anxious to evolve India's own Munroe Doctrine was willing to help the Eelam Tigers get their independent state.[44] Nevertheless, Rasgotra remained worried about Sri Lanka and believed that 'it was bound to break up into two at some stage'. Chinmaya Gharekhan, then Joint Secretary in the PMO, believed that Rasgotra was not bothered about this aspect too much. Rasgotra said our politicians in the south and the Opposition could not care less about the embarrassment they were creating for the government by their selfish and shortsighted demands.[45]

The assurances of territorial integrity, by and large, were enough to create some confidence in Sri Lanka. The President accepted India's good offices and thereafter, G. Parthasarathi visited Colombo as the prime minister's special envoy, in August 1983. His mandate was to discuss any scheme or proposal which was not injurious to Lanka's territorial integrity. His efforts resulted in some measures which were contained in a document called 'Annexure-C'. It suggested devolution of powers at the regional and district level to neutralize the disadvantages imposed on the Tamils by the 'Sinhala only' policy. The annexure did not mention the merger of the north and east provinces, which Parthasarathi had initially proposed, and his mission ended in failure.[46]

It was no secret that the Parthasarathi Mission was not acceptable to some of the members of the Lankan Cabinet. One minister, who openly criticized it, was dismissed by a peeved President.[47]

The President made proposals for a possible solution to the ethnic problem at the All-Party Conference in January 1984.[48] In three subsequent meetings, the President further elaborated on them but without any positive reaction from the hard-core elements among the Tamils.

New Delhi was caught in a big dilemma. Pledged to the territorial integrity of Lanka, it was unable to support any demand for a separate Tamil State and the Tamils were not prepared to settle for anything less. The prime minister's problem was the manner in which the Tamil problem snowballed and created an emotional upsurge in Tamil Nadu in favour of Sri Lankan Tamils.

However, External Affairs Minister Narasimha Rao privately believed the Jaffna Tamils regarded themselves superior to the Indian Tamils, let alone Indian Tamils (Estate Tamils) in Sri Lanka. Rao insisted that he knew for a fact that 'our Tamils do not care at all for Sri Lankan Tamils; in fact, they hate one another, but they are using the situation solely for political purposes; without giving the slightest thought to broader implications'. Gharekhan, however, wished that 'Rao would express his views to the Prime Minister and others'.[49]

Prabhakaran had reservations on India's involvement in training the militant groups in India, since initially his rival organisations like the TELO, EROS and the PLOTE were being trained. He was then in Jaffna and feared it would undermine the supremacy of his LTTE. The LTTE considered itself a home-grown group, built brick-by-brick by its own efforts.[50]

Unlike others who saw the LTTE as a militant organisation trying to force a solution by means of coercion, the LTTE had different ideas about itself. Prabhakaran said:

> [W]e wish to state clearly and emphatically that we are not a group of armed adventurists roaming in the jungles with romantic illusions, nor are we a band of terrorists or vandals who kill and destroy at random for anarchist reasons…on the contrary we are revolutionaries committed to revolutionary political practice…we are the armed vanguard of the struggling masses, the freedom fighters of the oppressed.[51]

India's excessive interest in Colombo's ethnic problem revived latent historic Sinhalese memories of the Chola rulers plundering and ravaging the Sinhala kingdom in the eleventh century. Indian intervention in the Bangladesh crisis too raised Sinhalese fears that it would be the next target of a hegemonic India. India's increasing support to the Tamils and militant organisations and running and/or allowing them to run training camps added to Lanka's fears. It is ironic that India failed to use its friendly relations both with S.W.R.D. Bandaranaike and his wife Sirimavo, who were primarily responsible for anti-Tamil policies, when both Nehru and his daughter had an opportunity to intercede without being misunderstood. This in spite of the fact that in 1971 India had extended military assistance to Mrs Bandaranaike to crush a Janatha Vimukthi Peramuna (JVP) insurrection in the south of the island. JVP had in its ranks among Buddhist monks and a large body of disgruntled unemployed youth. It had inherited a Marxist ideology and emulated Che Guevera. However, India's concern then was to avoid involvement in the internal affairs of its neighbours.

On 11 March 1984, Prabhakaran lamented that the Parliamentary system not only failed the Tamils but also 'aggravated' their plight. He insisted that the LTTE's struggle was for independence.[52]

Colombo remained quite articulate in peddling Tamil demands as secessionist in the international fora. On 24 September 1984, Foreign Minister A.C.S. Hameed, speaking at the United Nations, said that no government had tried harder to resolve this problem by accommodating the minority Tamil community. He referred to the dissatisfaction of the majority community for being too accommodative toward the Tamils. He touted the dissatisfaction of both the communities with the government as proof of handling the problem in a balanced and impartial manner. Drawing a red line, he said, 'Under no circumstances can we or will we accept the division of the country.'[53]

The Tamils, particularly the militant variety, had built up a major network of support through the Tamil diaspora. After the 1983 anti-Tamil riots, a large number of Tamil youth, who had lived a hard life in Lanka, migrated to the West and carried with them Tamil grievances in the councils of the world and international media. They became a major source of funds for the Eelam movement, spearheaded by the LTTE. With time, the diaspora became more uncompromising on the Eelam question than the Tamils in Sri Lanka. Unmindful of the consequences, the Tamil diaspora continued to be the powerhouse of the LTTE.

India's espousal of Tamil cause had already created misunderstandings with Sri Lanka. India now found some other contentious issues in the island: lease of the Trincomalee Oil Tank Farm, Voice of America broadcasting facilities in the island, military assistance received from Israel and other agencies, apart from the West and South Africa. India providing arms and training facilities to the Tamils on its soil was not expected to contribute to the climate of confidence between the two neighbouring countries. Prime Minister Ranasinghe Premadasa was never tired of using ill-tempered language against the Indian top leadership while demanding the expulsion of the Tamil militants operating from Indian soil. He often alluded to the situation in the Punjab to justify Colombo's actions against the Tamils militants.

In October 1984, Prime Minister Indira Gandhi was assassinated. Her son Rajiv Gandhi, who until 1980 was a pilot with Indian Airlines and had kept aloof from Indian politics, succeeded her. He had to reluctantly join the hurly burly of Indian politics in February 1981 on the tragic death of his younger brother, Sanjay, in June 1980, besides pressure from his mother. His experience, therefore, in politics was limited before he became the prime minister. Natwar Singh, who was his foreign minister, said later that Rajiv lacked experience and was not familiar with the history of the ethnic problem in Sri Lanka. In handling the ethnic problem, Natwar 'got the impression that Jayewardene was getting the better of Rajiv Gandhi'.[54] It was natural for Rajiv to fall back on his advisers. The selection of J.N. Dixit, a hawk, as Indian High Commissioner in Colombo, was not the best choice. In his book *Assignment Colombo,* Dixit wrote that he always felt that 'India need not have indulged in the mendacity of denying India's support to the Tamil militants'.[55] It was no wonder then that the advice that emanated from the high commissioner was highly pugnacious and belligerent.

Jayewardene, who had come to Delhi to attend the funeral of Mrs Gandhi, made unfortunate remarks which hurt Rajiv Gandhi. He drew a parallel between the event that followed her assassination and events following the assassination of thirteen Sinhalese soldiers in July 1983 resulting in anti-Tamil riots. He was referring to the anti-Sikh riots that followed Indira Gandhi's assassination. An upset Rajiv Gandhi disabused him of his perception and stressed the two situations were 'not comparable'. Mincing no words, Gandhi curtly told Jayewardene that he was greatly 'distressed' at the comparison. He candidly told Jayewardene that 'because of long historical, cultural and personal ties between the peoples of Sri Lanka and India, developments in Sri Lanka must unavoidably affect us, especially in our state of Tamil Nadu, where 65 million Tamils live'. But he also assured Jayewardene that the

> [E]thnic problem in your country is for you to resolve. We have not interfered and we do not wish to interfere in any way. I should like to reaffirm my government's unflinching support for Sri Lanka's unity and integrity. We do not encourage or favour separatism and are firmly opposed to all forms of violence and terrorism.[56]

A month later, Gandhi expressed his concern at the rapidly escalating violence in the northern and eastern provinces which left many Tamils dead, including Tamils of Indian origin. He accused the island's security forces of indulging in indiscriminate violence.[57] The Lankan Foreign Minister A.C.S. Hameed expressed surprise and regret at Gandhi's statement. He said he (Gandhi) had failed to take note of the escalation of terrorist violence, which necessitated counter action from the security forces. Regarding attacks on fishermen in the Palk Strait, he said Indian fishermen had no right to fish in Lankan waters but had regularly violated its waters and gave figures of such violations in recent years showing a rising trend.[58]

In June 1985, Jayewardene visited New Delhi when it was agreed that India's good offices would be used to find a solution to Lanka's ethnic problem. Jayewardene had promised to declare amnesty for Tamil militants provided they surrendered their arms unconditionally.[59]

Colombo welcomed Rajiv Gandhi's statement that India 'will not support terrorist acts conducted against Sri Lanka from Indian territory'.[60]

Making a fresh beginning, the prime minister organized a ceasefire between the Lanka government and all the Tamil groups and arranged talks between them at Thimphu, Bhutan. The talks failed because of the conditions put jointly by the Tamils including the LTTE, which were:

i.   Recognition of Tamils as a distinct nationality;
ii. Acceptance of demand for a Tamil homeland and its territorial integrity, and
iii. Right of self-determination for the Tamils.[61]

These conditions were anathema to Colombo and even against the Indian commitment to finding a solution within Sri Lanka's Constitution. The Sri Lanka Government, however, welcomed Rajiv Gandhi's repeated statement that 'he opposed independence for the Tamils and any solution should fall within the Lankan Constitution'.[62] The TULF, however, blamed the failure of the Thimphu talks on Colombo failing to meet its demands.[63]

With the advantage of hindsight, Dixit, on the failure of the Thimphu talks said, 'It had become obvious that neither side was animated by positive attitudes or motivations to achieve a practical and durable solution, which was India's objective.'[64]

Embittered, Foreign Secretary Romesh Bhandari, expressed similar sentiments and said his efforts were being 'frustrated by the dilatory tactics of the Sri Lankan Government and the Tamil leaders'.[65] Dixit claimed that India tried to persuade the Tamils to give up their demand for break-up of Sri Lanka and the Eelam.[66] But the Tamils were not prepared for that.

Jayewardene, finding his efforts getting nowhere, claimed he was a friend of the Nehru family, and invoking his past contacts with the family, pleaded with Rajiv Gandhi for his cooperation in preventing terrorists from using the Palk Strait for their entry and exit to and from south India which would help in restoring normalcy in the island.[67]

More than anything else, it was the militants' activities that continued to muddy the waters of the Palk Strait. Jayewardene again brought to Rajiv Gandhi's notice reports of 'regular movement of weapons, explosives and manpower from south India to Sri Lanka' and asked him for increased vigilance by the Indian coastguard and navy.

There was a sting in the letter. The President's son and daughter-in-law when visiting India had met Gandhi and had brought to his notice the activities of R&AW, which he said he found 'difficult to believe'.[68]

Pakistan President Zia-ul-Haq could not resist the temptation to pour oil on burning fire. Following his visit to Colombo, he offered Lanka arms and ammunition plus a grant of Rs 5 million as well as training facilities for the Lankan army, as suggested by the Lankan authorities.[69]

The two countries now appeared to indulge in a polemical conversation, in which the problem of Indian fishermen appeared prominently. On 15 March, India's External Affairs Minister, Bali Ram Bhagat in a statement, reiterated his commitment to a political solution within the framework of the island's unity, but said the escalation in violence in Sri Lanka had resulted in a refugee problem in India.[70] Foreign Secretary Romesh Bhandari's visit to Colombo was yet another opportunity to reemphasize India's commitment to Sri Lanka's territorial unity and sovereignty.[71] Making a statement in the Lok Sabha, the prime minister referred to his meeting with an all-party delegation from Tamil Nadu led by Chief Minister (M.G. Ramachandran) who reported a continued influx of refugees and a disruption in the activities of Indian fishermen in the Palk Strait. Gandhi expressed his concern and said he was in touch with Colombo and promised to convey his distress to the Lankan President and the need for a political solution 'acceptable to all parties concerned'.[72] A couple of weeks later, Prime Minister Gandhi emphasized the problem of Tamil refugees and the need for them to go back home.[73] But the concern that India had failed to persuade the Tamils to tone down their activities was absent in his statement. He now put the ball completely in Colombo's court saying, 'if successive governments in Colombo since independence had shown the necessary vision and spirit of accommodation, I am confident that your country would have been spared the agonies it is facing today.' He assured the President that he was acutely conscious of the dangers of terrorism for obvious reasons, and assured him that India 'does not and will not support' terrorism from the Indian territory.[74]

But a spate of critical statements in the Indian Parliament made Jayewardene ask for a meeting with Rajiv Gandhi, who though sceptical of the suggestion, finally met him between 1–3 June 1985. Both agreed on the need to take the agreed steps for a 'political settlement which would be acceptable to all concerned, within the framework of the unity and integrity of Sri Lanka'. Jayewardene also promised general amnesty for the Tamils provided they surrendered their arms unconditionally.[75] When Foreign Secretary Bhandari visited Colombo, he was again made aware of Colombo's oft repeated pre-condition for talks; the 'suspension' of terrorist activities for 'meaningful' discussions leading to a political settlement.[76] There was no dearth of statements from either side reiterating the need for a political settlement to unify the island, but the situation on the ground showed little improvement. President Jayewardene once again told Prime Minister Gandhi that there was a regular movement of weapons, explosives and manpower from south India to Lanka and the need for greater vigil on the movement of Tamils in the Palk Strait.[77] Rajiv Gandhi, for the umpteenth time, reiterated that India was for a solution entirely within the Constitution of Sri Lanka and any help required would be provided.[78] About terrorism, he told the Sri Lankan TV channel Rupavahini that India had paid a heavy price for terrorism and would do everything to end it.[79] In the face of Tamil intransigence, India failed to carry out its oft repeated commitment to end terrorism without feeling embarrassed. India also failed to accept that it had little leverage with the Lankan Tamils, and that they were a law unto themselves with the support of the Tamil Nadu government and its people. In fact, Tamil Nadu was not having an easy time with the Lankan Tamils in the state. With their number touching 1 lakh, they had put a severe burden on the resources of the state besides creating numerous social and law and order problems for the administration.

Gandhi sounded naïve when he said that 'if violence in Lanka was to stop there must be an agreement between the Tamil militants and the Sri Lanka Government'. He conceded that Colombo had given a 'working paper' for discussions and the Tamils had not given any paper on their position. When asked if he was convinced Colombo was sincere in their talks, Gandhi ducked the question and said that 'he could answer the question if the other side also was talking'. Once again it was clear that if there were no talks it was because of Tamil intransigence and New Delhi's lack of leverage to make them behave.[80]

As military operations stepped up in Jaffna, Gandhi told news agency, Press Trust of India, that 'it is one thing to deal with terrorists but it is quite another to victimize large segment of the population only because they happened to belong to a particular ethnic group'.[81] It has to be remembered that in a civil strife of the type raging in Sri Lanka, it was not possible to differentiate between the partisan and the innocent. If innocent civilians suffered, it was collateral damage.

India could not have been unaware that Colombo strongly believed India's mediatory role was biased in the favour of the Tamils. The Tamils on the other hand, taking note of over a lakh of their people in India as refugees, were conscious that it was the Bangla refugees which were the tipping point for India's involvement in the Bangladesh crisis. They expected that their refugees would also spur New Delhi into a Bangladesh-type involvement and to that extent were unperturbed at Colombo's strong-arm measures against them. This prompted more people to seek refuge in Tamil Nadu. Jayewardene was getting disillusioned with India's attitude of assuring Colombo of its unity yet not wielding influence with the Tamils to accept a compromise solution.

To justify its position, TULF drew Prime Minister Gandhi's attention to the difference in the situations in India and Sri Lanka. They pointed out that in India there was no single linguistic group which could dominate any other linguistic group(s), whereas in Sri Lanka the 74 per cent Sinhalese posed a different type of problem altogether for the minority Tamils. Pointing to the Punjab accord negotiated by Gandhi with the Sikhs, TULF pointed out it had the provision for redrawing state boundaries and if Colombo was genuine in its intentions, it could adopt the same principle and merge 'traditionally Tamil-speaking areas in the Northern and Eastern Provinces' into a single unit.[82]

The militants, particularly the LTTE, were indulging in violence on a greater scale than before, inviting greater repression from the government which according to an MEA statement included 'indiscriminate aerial bombing and strafing of Jaffna peninsula'.[83] EAM Bali Ram Bhagat speaking on an adjournment motion in the Lok Sabha expressed his 'grave concern' at the happenings in Jaffna.[84]

The Sri Lankan government responding to the statement of the EAM in Parliament on 26 February 1986 expressed regrets and said while it had accused Colombo of genocide of the Tamils, it had failed to make any comment on the killings of the Sinhalese and Muslims at the hands of the Tamils militants. On fixing a timeframe for legislative actions, Colombo said it needed consensual acceptance of such resolutions by the entire polity. It added that a timeframe could not be conceived 'unless such timeframe was also applied to the interdiction and removal of Indian based terrorists against Sri Lanka'.[85]

The MEA spokesperson expressed grave concern on the large-scale military operations and insisted that there could be no military solution to the ethnic problem.[86] According to media reports, the statement of the spokesperson was drafted by EAM P. Shiv Shankar and issued after it was approved by the prime minister, who had just then returned from his African tour. In view of the current situation, the EAM even cancelled his proposed tour to Brazil to the G-77 ministerial meeting.[87]

Jayewardene's frustrations were apparent in his interview with Radio Australia during his visit to Canberra. He had said India's role was vital because 'it is helping the terrorists'. To India's mortification, Jayewardene, replying to a question, called Pakistan 'a better friend' while accusing India of employing double standards. He pointed to India's Sikh problem and what Rajiv Gandhi was doing in Punjab.[88]

Colombo's slogan was a military solution to a military problem since 'one cannot preach nonviolence to those who come with the gun'. He made this statement when Indian minster P. Chidambaram was in Colombo holding talks on the package offered by the Lankan government.[89]

The ethnic problem had by this time undergone a sea change. The moderate TULF had been pushed to the margins and the LTTE was calling the shots. The Palk Strait had become an artery for those wanting to use Tamil Nadu as a sanctuary and support base for their activities in Jaffna. The LTTE were now using the Indian fishermen and their boats for their illegal activities both to ferry men and material in and out of Jaffna. The role of Indian fishermen had become indispensable for Tamils either out of commitment or for greed or under threat from the militants. They were now involved in activities other than fishing and ran into trouble with the Sri Lanka navy, which was responsible to stop the illegal activities of Indian fishermen. This became another friction point between India and Sri Lanka.[90]

New Delhi, while acting as mediator, indulged the militants as they had become a law unto themselves. There was no one even in Tamil Nadu, who could wield some moderating influence on them. The *Washington Post* on 12 May 1986 had said the terrorist movement in Sri Lanka would die if India cracked down on illegal Tamil activities and stopped the flow of weapons across the Palk Strait. The weekly intelligence report compiled by the Mid-Atlantic Research Associates quoted Indian sources to claim that the 'domestic political factor' constrained the prime minister from any such action which could 'increase his unpopularity' in Tamil Nadu. A report from Colombo in The *New York Times* on 11 May had described the days ahead as dangerous for Sri Lanka, considered a model of democracy and development in the third world. The report also said there had been a series of violent incidents among the guerrilla groups where Tamils died at the hands of fellow Tamils.[91]

In an interview with the American magazine, *Newsweek,* Prabhakaran insisted Indian support was humanitarian and that he expected India to support Eelam in due course. He wanted the American people to support his movement since they were facing genocide.[92]

High Commissioner Dixit tried to browbeat Jayewardene, threatening that if the military operations in Jaffna were not stopped, India's offer of its good offices would stand jeopardized. Jayewardene snapped back with a loud and sound message that military operations would not stop without militants stopping their terrorist acts. Colombo appeared chagrined at Indian pressure while failing to apply corresponding pressure on the Tamils to cease their acts of violence.[93] A day earlier, Prime Minister Gandhi on return from his African tour, had said that Colombo 'under the guise of fighting terrorism' was shedding all pretence of striving for a political settlement.[94]

More worrying for Delhi were the reports of internecine wars among the militant groups which cut the ground not only from under the TULF's feet but India's too, thereby undermining the moderating role of India. At least 175 Tamils were killed by fellow Tamils. Out of this struggle, the Liberation Tigers of the Tamil Eelam (LTTE) emerged the strongest and the only organisation able to carry on the Tamil fight for their rights. They were best trained, fully armed and well organized. There was a general feeling that ascendency of the Tigers would make the prospects of future talks for a negotiated settlement more difficult. Since most of the groups had their headquarters in Madras (Chennai) the internecine clashes among the rival groups in the city, mirroring the Jaffna attacks, rocked Chennai. The Central Telegraph Office in the city and an Air Lanka airliner parked at Chennai airport became the targets of bomb attacks. The American weeklies, *Time* and *Newsweek* reported that Tamil Eelamists were bent on wrecking India-sponsored peace efforts. In the face of these adverse developments, reports were rife that Lanka had approached friendly nations for arms. Already, Pakistan had trained 1,600 Sri Lankan armed personnel, while Israeli advisors had provided training in intelligence gathering techniques. And Western commandos trained the security forces in advance counter-insurgency measures.[95]

To end the crisis, on 4 May 1986, Colombo submitted final proposals based on territorial and Constitutional unity, while detailing the devolution of powers to the provincial councils. It kept the door open for further consultations to arrive at a final settlement.[96]

Describing terrorism as a cowardly attempt to instil terror in the minds of the people, Jayewardene showed his party, the UNP, the dichotomy of India pushing Britain and the US to extradite Sikh militants, and Britain asking the US to extradite IRA extremists.[97]

The LTTE not satisfied with anything less than the Eelam, intended to declare unilateral independence. It was anyway in virtual control of the Jaffna peninsula where the government's writ had ceased to run. It ran the civil administration of the province and the government feared the LTTE would unilaterally declare independence. The question of UDI came up in the Lanka Parliament and the Minister of National Security, Lalith Athulathmudali, said the path the terrorists had taken had reduced the government's options but assured the members that the government was taking appropriate action, like the 'temporary suspension of fuel supplies' to Jaffna. It was expected that lack of fuel would disrupt the terrorists' plans, since they couldn't operate without fuel. Describing it a temporary measure, he accused the Indian press of being jingoistic, calling it 'use of military option'.[98] Two days later, intervening in a debate in Parliament, Athulathmudali said, 'Whatever steps we are compelled to take…does not mean one bit a diminution of our commitment to a political resolution of this problem.' He pointed out the nature and quality of the threat from the terrorists to justify the action that had been taken in Jaffna.[99] Speaking in Parliament on 19 February 1987, Jayewardene had recalled the discussions in Bangalore at the time of the SAARC conference and thereafter, when an agreement was arrived at in the form of a working paper. He showed his willingness to work on that basis.[100] On 9 February, Dixit handed over a paper from Rajiv Gandhi to Jayewardene, which curtly told him that India could not resume its efforts for a settlement 'as long as the current military operations against the Tamil civilians continue' along with a blockade affecting civilians with the possibility of violence increasing. Colombo in an equally curt reply said on 13 February that Sri Lanka would not carry out any further military operations and also withdraw the blockade when the terrorists ceased their violent acts and stopped interfering with the running of the civil administration of the Jaffna province. With this statement, the president gave comprehensive details of the framework paper.[101]

While there was no dearth of statements from New Delhi in support of Tamil aspirations, Minister Natwar Singh added yet another, when he told the Lok Sabha on 11 November 1986 that 'only a negotiated political settlement can resolve the ethnic crisis in a manner, which would ensure that the Tamils obtained their legitimate rights within the framework of the unity and integrity of this neighbouring country'.[102] But there was no clarification on the nature and extent of Tamils aspirations and legitimate rights within the framework of the unity of the island. Its vagueness created confusion in the minds of Lankans. Since the Tamil struggle had been hijacked by the LTTE and its only aspiration was Eelam, New Delhi while appearing not to support it, could not openly oppose either, for fear of Tamil alienation.

Meanwhile, the SAARC summit in Bangalore created an embarrassment for New Delhi. President Jayewardene was frustrated with India and in his speech, a copy of which India had managed to obtain before delivery, it was found the President intended to indict New Delhi. On India's intervention, he promised to delete the relevant anti-Indian portions.[103]

But in delivering his speech he gave details of the growth of terrorism in the island and described it a 'direct challenge to the elected government of the island and the rule of law'. Elaborating on the various steps that had been taken to arrive at a political settlement, including that in consultation with India, he avoided the temptation of directly indicting India, though it was clear who the villain of the piece was.[104] Though the Indian prime minister ignored his speech, the damage was done. Natwar Singh found talking to Prabhakaran, who was in Bangalore, 'an exhaustive experience' and warned him if he did not behave, 'there could come a time when he would have to face the combined might of the Indian and Sri Lankan armies'.

Prabhakaran's response to Natwar's scarcely veiled threat was, 'I shall never give up Eelam even if I am to die for it.'[105]

Prabhakaran got a shot in the arm when two Indian ministers, P. Chidambaram and Natwar Singh, came to Chennai and met him at the Tamil Nadu chief minister's office. CM M.G. Ramachandran gave him Rs 40 million in cash.[106]

India did try to clip Prabhakaran's wings by confiscating his communication equipment, but it had to be returned due to the sympathy wave he evoked in Tamil Nadu where he went on a hunger strike in protest. An irked India found itself helpless. Sensing the Indian mood, Prabhakaran shifted his base back to Jaffna to ensure independence of action.

In the midst of these developments, High Commissioner Dixit conveyed to President Jayewardene that P. Chidambaram and Natwar Singh would visit Colombo to carry forward discussions on Colombo's proposals. Dixit said India's emphasis and approach regarding the ethnic problem was to 'evolve a package of proposals which will be fully responsive to basic Tamil aspirations that would remove the genuine historical apprehensions of Sri Lankan Tamils. At the same time, Dixit assured the President that 'such a package does not erode Sri Lanka's unity and integrity'.[107]

The principal proposals that emerged from the meeting between the Indian ministers and President Jayewardene on 19 December 1986 were: reorganization of the eastern province, institutional links between the eastern and northern provinces and a merging to take place later and the creation of a new office of vice president to be occupied by a Tamil.[108]

Before the 19 December proposals could achieve any concrete results, the atmosphere had become vitiated on account of Colombo's tendentious press campaign and large-scale violence in the wake of military action by the Sri Lankan security forces. Following this, the Lankan Parliament decided that there would be no merger of the two provinces in question.[109] These developments led Rajiv Gandhi to address a top-secret message to Jayewardene conveying his distress over military operations in Jaffna describing them a 'dangerous political signal' which would make 'it difficult for India to persuade militants to resume political negotiations in the current circumstances'.[110]

Colombo had already resorted to the measure which prevented even essential supplies reaching Jaffna. Jayewardene had announced that 'this time, the fight is a fight to the finish'.[111]

Sri Lanka justified its actions against the Tamil militants in Jaffna since it had become necessary to regain control of the province which had come under the effective control of the LTTE and it was they who were running the civil administration to the exclusion of the island administration.

Responding to criticism of the government handling of terrorism, Athulathmudali told Parliament that the criticism ignored the nature and quality of the threat from the terrorists. He pointed out that they had foreign bases, foreign sources of supply and a large body of people sympathetic to them which made the task difficult.[112] On 23 April, the ruling UNP had adopted a resolution asking the President to order security forces to 'annihilate terrorism and terrorists' dubbing them 'murderers'.[113]

In the face of these developments, India thought it prudent to tell the Tamils to act responsibly. The ministers of external affairs, home and the minister of state for internal security flew to Chennai and in a joint meeting with the Tamil Nadu CM advised the Tamils to take India's counsel seriously. Unfortunately, the advice proved in vain. The Indian statement said that Tamils were advised not to hinder the current consultations with Colombo and allow the negotiations to reach a fruitful conclusion. According to a report in the *The Hindu*, foreign secretary A.P. Venkateshwaran had told the Tamils that they should not expect India to support their demand for Eelam and that India would work for an equitable political settlement.[114] All appeals/advice, as in the past, had little impact on the Tamils.

India was upset with the militants for calling the TULF president Amirthalingam 'a traitor'. The TULF was a moderate body and India had kept it in the vanguard in its negotiations with Colombo, since it was convinced that some settlement was possible only when TULF was at the helm of affairs on the behalf of the Tamils.[115] Therefore, calling its president a 'traitor' was unacceptable for India. However, Sri Lanka was in a conciliatory frame of mind and was prepared to be accommodative. It agreed to certain concessions, which involved amendment of the Constitution like an amendment to the provincial council bill, concurrent and provincial lists, as well as a detailed memorandum on law and order, apart from land and land settlement and education portfolios. In short, it was a comprehensive set of proposals made since August 1985.[116] But Colombo backtracked after media quoting official sources said that the Indian ministers had imposed a solution on the country. The Indian high commission decried the propaganda as motivated.

Following Prabhakaran's return to Jaffna in January 1987, the violence there had escalated.[117] Cabinet Secretary Deshmukh was critical of the state of affairs in Delhi. He said, 'The Prime Minister had taken upon himself to involve in the day-to-day developments instead of the Ministry of External Affairs.' He lamented that the external affairs minister had got marginalized because of being changed frequently— between 1985 and 1989 there were five—and 'he [Gandhi] thought it was enough to keep them informed only when absolutely necessary'.[118]

The Colombo-based *Weekend* had carried a story that the LTTE had set-up their own administration bypassing Colombo, would declare UDI. Athulathmudali, the minister of national security, listed the steps being taken to thwart their move, one of which was suspension of fuel supplies to Jaffna. However, Colombo remained distrustful of India's reaction. Taking a dig at India and chastizing it, Athulathmudali said that those who preached a peaceful approach to the problem seemed to forget that the pressure must be on the terrorists and not on the Sri Lankans. He made it clear that Colombo was not going to accept UDI or any other form of it. Making a reference to the embargo on fuel, he was upset that it had aroused feelings across the Palk Strait as if Lanka was going to do something terrible. The government blamed the situation on the LTTE's intransigence and India's failure to prevail upon the militants to give up violence. The ban on fuel supplies was justified to derail the LTTE's civil administration. Colombo repeated the support LTTE enjoyed from foreign sources, foreign bases, foreign supplies and from across the Palk Strait for the prevailing situation. Colombo was stating the obvious. If the ethnic violence refused to abate or end, the Tamils for their uncompromising attitude, and India for failing to persuade them to a compromise, must share responsibility.[119]

As the Lankan offensive at the beginning of January 1987 gathered momentum, it met fierce resistance from the LTTE. The Lankan security forces killed hundreds of Tamils. LTTE was hardly behind in this killing spree. But the balance for once, appeared to be in favour of Colombo. This was a direct confrontation between the Lankan army and the LTTE for the first time. The army realized that unless the LTTE was defeated militarily or weakened, there was little hope of a negotiated settlement.[120]

India realized its limitations but unable to forsake the Tamils midstream, went on pressurising Colombo asking for military operations to stop and fuel supplies to resume. In order to hit the LTTE hard, Colombo's military action escalated further. The north province, Jaffna, was placed under a thirty-six-hour curfew, train services were suspended and with no prospect of fuel supplies resuming, India realized the situation was critical. Colombo did indicate its readiness to stop its operations, rather warned that it was predicated on the 'clear understanding that all further discussions to be held or solutions to be evolved shall be within the framework of independence, territorial integrity and unity of Sri Lanka'. High Commissioner Dixit responded that India was unable to resume its good offices unless military action was suspended.[121]

It was a strange situation where an ambassador accredited with the Government of Sri Lanka was threatening his host government to surrender to an organization, which in its eyes was a terrorist body. Such language is usually used by ambassadors when the two countries are at war. Sri Lanka was a neighbour and still a friendly country at that.

On 12 February 1987, Rajiv Gandhi in a top-secret message conveyed to President Jayewardene his 'distress' at the military operations and termed them a 'dangerous political signal'.[122] Intervening in the debate on the President's address in the Lok Sabha on 3 March and in the Rajya Sabha on 4 March, the prime minister lamented that the steps taken by Colombo had caused him 'great pain' and regretted that it had become difficult to continue the process of negotiations.[123]

On 14 March, Rajiv Gandhi sent senior Congress leader Dinesh Singh to Colombo as his special emissary.[124]

When Lok Sabha discussed the Lanka question again on 18 March, members did not hesitate to use unparliamentary language against President Jayewardene which had to be expunged. But the government did not agree with the demand of the members to internationalize the Tamil issue.[125] On 6 March, the TULF president in a letter to the prime minister mentioned the plight of the Tamils in view of the military operations and claimed that since June/July 1983 more than 11,000 Tamil civilians—men, women and children—had been 'mercilessly massacred'. The letter, while thanking the prime minister for whatever steps he had already taken to protect the Tamils, now requested 'further steps' like provision of 'food and fuel' supplies and raising the plight of the Tamils in international fora.[126] After Dinesh Singh met Jayewardene in Colombo, Gandhi sent another confidential message to President Jayewardene through R&AW's channels to the Lankan Director General (Intelligence and

Security), and thanked Jayewardene for receiving Dinesh Singh and promising to end the blockade in favour of a political settlement.[127] An official statement in Colombo, after the cabinet meeting on 17 March, announced concessions ostensibly at the request of political parties, on the sale of kerosene, engine oil and firewood and rationing of petrol and diesel 'in a way that would not assist the terrorists'.[128] However, TULF remained indifferent, informed the prime minister that military operations were continuing and Tamils in considerable numbers had been killed, and property including places of worship had been destroyed. On fuel supplies, the TULF said that despite the announcement of the lifting of the embargo, people continue to be 'deprived of fuel and the situation remains unchanged'.[129] The atmosphere was suddenly vitiated after an attack by the LTTE against civilians in Trincomalee. New Delhi, aware of the identity of both the perpetrators (Tamils and LTTE) and the victims (Sinhalese), remained hesitant to identity either of them and merely spoke of the 'ghastly massacre of 100 Sri Lankan citizens, mostly civilians and belonging to all the prominent communities of Sri Lanka...'. India sought to absolve the LTTE. New Delhi's refusal to name the culprits only encouraged the LTTE in its insidious activities which was a negative signal to Colombo and the Sinhalese people in general of India's partisan approach.[130] Sri Lankan Prime Minister Premadasa, known for his acerbic tongue against India, recalled his advice to Mrs Indira Gandhi not to encourage the terrorists by providing them sanctuary and training facilities in India. He wanted India to be proactive and take action instead of wringing its hands in sorrow.[131] The escalation of violence in the island and New Delhi's description of it as 'aerial attacks and other military measures taken by the Sri Lankan Government' resulted in large-scale civilian casualties. India regretted Premadasa's statement which 'foreclosed the political option'.[132] To soothen Delhi's frayed nerves Jayewardene sent a top-secret message to the Indian prime minister conceding that there was resumption of military operations, but assured him that these would be completed in a few days. He appealed that while he appreciated his (Gandhi's) difficulties, India should also appreciate Sri Lanka's difficulties. Suggesting that the reports of military operations were exaggerated, he added that the LTTE needed to be made aware that it was not invincible and a 'battered LTTE may be little more receptive to talks'.[133]

The Rajya Sabha had a lengthy debate on 8 May where members spoke of the plight of the Tamils and the Minister of State for External Affairs, Natwar Singh, while assuring them said that the government was fully aware of the developments on a day-to-day basis and kept the situation under watch. He conceded India had not been encouraged by the attitude of Colombo since their actions were aggravating the situation in a way that was making the lives of the citizens of Sri Lanka, 'who are Tamils, a painful existence, which this House condemns, this country condemns and the Human Right Agencies are condemning and we are trying our best'.[134]

During May 1987, the Indian Parliament spent countless hours discussing two points: (i) concern at the denial of basic rights to Tamils, and (ii) enlarging the area of its concern, it accused Lanka of endangering the security environment by its activities around the Trincomalee Tank Farm by involving Israel and even Pakistani intelligence agencies.[135] The prime minister addressed the Congress Parliamentary Party and ruled out the use of a military option, but there was exasperation in dealing with Colombo.[136]

In order to reoccupy Jaffna, Colombo on 26 May, unleashed the combined strength of its armed forces with directions to raise Jaffna to the ground. The area was placed under a twenty-four-hour curfew. On 27 May, inaugurating the headquarters of the Bank of Ceylon in Colombo, the President minced no words and declared that he had ordered the security forces to fight until Jaffna was liberated.[137] New Delhi was deeply concerned. After high-level discussions in Delhi, the high commissioner was instructed to convey the prime minister's message to Jayewardene that the 'current military operations and violence of an unprecedented nature had completely changed the basis of our understanding of the island's ethnic problem'. An oblique warning was put out that if the 'genocide' did not stop, India may be compelled to review its policies towards Sri Lanka.[138] Appalled, External Affairs Minister Narayan Dutt Tiwari told Parliament that 4000 Tamils had been killed in these operations.[139]

Several acts of terrorism, including bomb blasts which led to hundreds of casualties, worsened the situation further. The worst was the bomb blast at Colombo's bus terminal which killed 107 people and injured 300.[140] Obviously, it was an act by the LTTE, but New Delhi remained unmindful of it.

On 28 May, worried about loss of Tamil lives in military operations Gandhi said, 'The horrific loss of innocent lives of this magnitude in cold blood by the army of their own country could not promote a solution.' He accused Colombo of choosing the military option and warned 'from the rubble and ashes there can only arise a total alienation of an entire people, a more determined militancy and more extreme options. The time to desist from military occupation of Jaffna is now, later may be too late'.[141] When India's apprehensions were brought to Jayewardene's notice, the enraged President dismissed them with the remarks, 'India can go to hell.'[142]

Attempting to salvage the remnants of its failed policy, Delhi flexed its muscles and asked High Commissioner Dixit to make it clear to Colombo that it would not let down the Tamils at this hour of crisis and warned that India would have no alternative but to provide the Tamils necessary logistic support, a euphemism for military support. The underlying message was loud and clear that India would not allow the military subjugation of Jaffna nor allow the Tamils to be brought to their knees. Relations between two neighbouring countries reached almost breaking point with the risk of a military confrontation affecting the peace and security of the entire region.[143]

On 1 June, to convey that India meant business, Colombo was informed that as a humanitarian act, India would send relief supplies to Jaffna since the city had already 'suffered a 5-month-old economic blockade and was victim of military assault, killing thousands by sustained strafing'. India intended to send relief supplies, including fuel and other essentials like rice etc., to Jaffna by boats on 3 June, accompanied by Indian Red Cross personnel. Colombo was asked for an urgent concurrence (not permission).[144] Colombo in a hard-hitting reply the same day, rejected Indian allegations of a shortage of supplies but conceded the situation had indeed become acute. Blaming India, it said if the situation had become difficult it was due to the patronage that the separatists enjoyed from Tamil Nadu, 'a constituent of the Republic of India', thereby tacitly holding New Delhi complicit in Tamil terrorism. Colombo showed willingness to receive supplies 'purely in the interest of good neighbourly relations' but suggested the modalities be worked out between the representatives of the two governments.[145] Upset by the Lankan response, the same day, Rajiv Gandhi, in a personal top-secret message, interpreted Colombo's message as a 'willingness to receive supplies' and decided to send aid on 3 June by 'civilian craft'.[146] Another message on the same day was delivered by Dixit to the Lankan Foreign Minister Hameed asking him to authorize the Lankan high commissioner in New Delhi to nominate a Lankan representative 'to join the international media to inspect the relief goods before despatch'.[147] Hameed replied that there was no situation 'calling for outside assistance'. He warned that 'any unilateral action will be considered a violation of the independence, sovereignty and territorial integrity of Sri Lanka'.[148] Simultaneously, on 2 June, Jayewardene in a confidential message to Gandhi accused the LTTE of having massacred 'many innocent Sri Lankans' and reminding Gandhi that they both had condemned acts of violence and were against terrorism, as such, asked him 'why are we, who are both opposed to terrorism, and suffer from it, quarrelling about the supply and distribution of aid which we are agreed can be used to help those who need it'.[149]

Gandhi ignored Jayewardene's reply and bent upon carrying out his diktat informed him that twenty fishing vessels would leave Rameswaram for Jaffna as proposed.[150]

Taken aback at the message, Jayewardene instantaneously replied that Colombo would be willing to receive supplies if they were received by his government and distributed by the Lankan Red Cross. Alternatively, he proposed that an Indian representative be asked to coordinate the supplies with Lankan authorities. He warned, 'any other method of delivery will be seen as serious breach of our territorial integrity' and feared otherwise an impression would go around among the people that India was providing relief to the LTTE. Jayewardene again insisted that there was no shortage of supplies in Jaffna, and added that even fuel rationing had since been lifted.[151] Dixit conveyed the message to Delhi and said that the president was prevailed upon by his Prime Minister, Premadasa, known for his anti-India views, in refusing supplies.[152]

India refused to accept Colombo's reasonable proposal and briefed the envoys of various countries stationed in New Delhi of the offer of humanitarian assistance and the efforts made by India to get Colombo to cooperate. Meanwhile, Colombo warned the fishermen at Rameswaram that the boats that approached the Lankan waters would be sunk. Delhi regretted Colombo's threat to boatmen and asked High Commissioner Dixit to convey to Colombo its decision to go ahead with its plan to deliver relief supplies without delay.[153] Lankan Prime Minister Ranasinghe Premadasa told Parliament of the Indian message which he said 'was not in accordance with the normal traditions' and referred to the Punjab agitation by the Sikhs and asked if Sri Lanka were to send supplies like this to them it would create unimaginable confusion.[154] On the same day, 2 June, Dixit delivered yet another message to Colombo reiterating India's decision to send supplies because of the 'prolonged suffering and agony of the people of Jaffna'.[155] On 3 June, an MEA spokesperson confirmed that nineteen boats loaded with supplies, and a vessel carrying Indian and foreign journalists, had left Rameswaram. The Indian spokesperson also later reported that Lanka did not allow the supplies to be unloaded and said India was 'deeply distressed' that 'on one pretext or another the supplies were blocked'. Before the flotilla decided to return, the 'negotiations' between the Lankan and Indian officials had deteriorated into a war of nerves.[156]

The *New York Times* on 2 June reported that India's move to send a convoy of ships to northern Sri Lanka was the 'first overt attempt by India to undercut Sri Lankan sovereignty and intervene directly in Colombo's four-year-old battle against Tamils seeking a separate nation state'. *Time* magazine's Delhi-based correspondent Steven Wiseman reported that since 1971, when India 'invaded' East Pakistan and helped it to become Bangladesh, New Delhi had not intervened directly in a neighbouring country's domestic affairs. The report said India's action was 'certain to cause concern in Pakistan and other countries distrustful of India's motives'.[157] A spokesperson of the Chinese Foreign Ministry expressing his concern at the developments, said on 3 June, 'Sri Lankans should settle their own internal affairs and no other country should interfere.'[158]

The crunch came the next day on 4 June when the MEA spokesperson announced that 'consequent to the refusal of Sri Lanka Government to allow relief supplies to Jaffna by boats, the supplies would be air-dropped by the aircraft of the Indian Air Force' because of the condition of the civilian population of the Jaffna peninsula which had 'serious implications for peace and security of the area'.[159]

Before taking this step, the issue was discussed at the meeting of the Cabinet Committee on Political Affairs (CCPA), where the option of airdropping supplies was considered. It was understood by the committee that airdropping might not be 'an act of war against Sri Lanka', but it would clearly mean 'violating its sovereignty'. Natwar Singh was upset that Colombo had not even been informed. His objection was that Sri Lanka was 'an independent sovereign nation and a member of the United Nations, the NAM and the Commonwealth, besides it was India's close and friendly neighbour'. Natwar expressed his worry that the matter might come up in the UN Security Council, particularly when Colombo was at this time, a (non-permanent) member of the council and if the matter came up, other members would sympathize with Sri Lanka. Thereupon, India's Permanent Representative at the UN, Gharekhan was instructed to make all efforts to prevent the matter coming up in the Security Council.[160] The views of Minister for Internal Security P. Chidambaram and Intelligence Bureau Chief M.K. Narayanan, both Tamils, prevailed. They said, 'If we did not send supplies and Jaffna fell to Sri Lankan forces, the Tamil population in Tamil Nadu would rise in revolt.' New Delhi was driven by Tamil Nadu in dealing with Colombo, and once again yielded in fear of the state, instead of calling off its bluff. Rajiv Gandhi accepted the CCPA's recommendations and IAF planes escorted by fighter planes were to airdrop supplies over Jaffna.[161]

Just as the aircraft were ready to airlift the supplies, Sri Lanka's high commissioner was summoned to the Ministry of External Affairs at about 2 p.m. He was informed that the aircraft would take off any time around 3 p.m. and that he should inform Colombo of India's decision. By the time the conversation ended it was 2.55 p.m.[162]

The gap of 55 minutes indicated that before the high commissioner decided to convey the information to Colombo there were acrimonious exchanges and he would have questioned India's right to airdrop supplies violating his country's airspace. There was no time for the Lankan high commissioner to return to his office and inform Colombo, so he used the MEA's telephone to alert his foreign minister of India's decision of airdropping relief supplies as the planes were readying to take off. Foreign Minister Hameed described it a 'naked violation of Sri Lanka's independence and an unwarranted assault on its sovereignty and territorial integrity'. The IAF, meanwhile, completed its task.

Sri Lanka's decision to block supplies by fishing boats had affronted New Delhi, the 'regional superpower', Dixit explained to Lankan Deputy Foreign Minister Tyron Fernando at a social meet. Dixit said, 'Lanka had humiliated India by sending the fishing boats back which had affected India's credibility with its own citizens in Tamil Nadu and the country's standing as a mediator who could not safeguard the interests of Sri Lanka Tamils.' Dixit told Fernando being credible in the eyes of Sri Lankan Tamils was necessary 'as otherwise the ramifications would be a break-up of Sri Lanka'. Dixit ended his diatribe on a highly caustic note suggesting if India instead of airdropping supplies, exercised the option of breaking the blockade by military action, it would 'have had much more serious implications for Sri Lanka and India–Sri Lanka relations'.[163] It was nothing less than a big and more powerful country browbeating a small and helpless country. This experience left an adverse long-term impact not only on Sri Lanka but on other neighbours of India as well.

The official reaction in Sri Lanka, the Buddhist clergy, the public and the media was that of fury. Sri Lankan Foreign Minister Hameed in two press conferences on 10 and 12 June condemned the Indian action. It was speculated that Colombo may approach the UN Security Council. Sri Lanka's ruling UNP's Parliamentary Group put out a statement that it recognized Colombo did not have the wherewithal to confront India but recalled that Colombo during the 1967 drought and famine in India had sent 18,000 tonnes of rice, though it was importing the commodity for its own needs. The statement ended with a jibe that Sri Lanka was following the tenets and teachings of Buddha and Gandhi, 'though their teachings are not respected any longer by the Indian and Tamil Nadu governments'.[164]

Expressing the travails of a small nation, Foreign Minister Hameed bemoaned, 'Sri Lanka had no military or other means of preventing this outrage.' The Sri Lanka media called it 'raw and naked violation of Sri Lanka's independence and sovereignty'. On 9 June, an estimated 8000 Sinhalese including 300 Buddhist monks staged a demonstration in front of the high commissioner's residence. The high commissioner was handed a memorandum by Monk Venerable Gnanissara which acknowledged India as the land which gave Sri Lanka its religion. The incident too had caused bad blood between Jayewardene and Gandhi. The angry President called the airdropping, a personal affront and accused India of flexing its muscles. Jayewardene retorted that 'Sir Lanka and Sinhalese too want peace with the Tamils, but not the kind of peace that comes riding on the India Air Force Planes'.[165]

Other countries were not empathetic to India's position either. Nepal, a small country, mulled the issue for a couple of days and on 7 June expressed 'grave concern' and condemned it as 'a violation of Sri Lanka's territorial integrity'. A foreign ministry spokesperson in Kathmandu said Nepal deplored the Indian intervention and would always condemn such violations of sovereignty. He claimed that Nepal had made contacts with other countries in the region, to try to find a solution acceptable to both India and Sri Lanka, which he indicated could be the appointment of a regional figure, acceptable to both the sides, who would suggest a course of action that met their legitimate interests.[166] The issue figured at the briefing at the UN Secretariat too, following Colombo's protest.[167] Responding to what was called a 'mild' statement by UN Secretary General Javier de Cuellar, a correspondent of the Associated Press in Pakistan, Iftikar Ali, asked the secretary general's spokesperson whether the UN Chief was not worried about protecting the territorial integrity and sovereignty of 'a small defenceless country like Sri Lanka' and in a supplementary question asked what steps the secretary general 'will take to prevent a recurrence of such incidents'. Although most delegates expressed the view that the matter should rest for the moment, the strongest support for a security council meeting came from Muslim countries. Both Libya and Bangladesh voiced strong statements in favour of a council meeting. Bangladesh said 'as a matter of principle, Bangladesh does not view with favour violation of the territorial integrity including air space of one state by the other'.[168] It was another matter that Bangladesh itself had emerged an independent country by India's intervention over a decade ago.

The airdropping of supplies made Colombo realize the limits of defiance of a regional power much bigger in size and resources than itself and the need to make peace with that reality. As a first step toward acknowledging that reality, Colombo entered into a formal agreement with Delhi for receiving additional humanitarian supplies for distribution in the north, thereby removing the immediate irritant that had led to the airdropping.

The initial enthusiasm of Tamil militants about Indian involvement in the Lankan conundrum gradually started eroding as they perceived India had its own agenda. India's repeated assurances to Colombo of India's respect for its territorial integrity and sovereignty ran counter to the Tamils' agenda for a separate homeland, or Eelam. Delhi too felt frustrated about its failure to goad the Tamils to accept the solution offered by Colombo which it considered fair. India often found itself compromised and its image dented internationally. The India–Sri Lanka relations had become hostage to the LTTE's wishes.

Colombo's military campaign in the north and its roll back under Delhi's pressure gave food for thought to Sri Lanka. Recent happenings convinced Colombo that no political solution of the Tamil problem was realistically possible without India, despite Delhi's lack of adequate leverage with the Tamils in general, and militants, in particular. This had relegated the India-backed moderate TULF out of reckoning. Colombo found dealing with Delhi advantageous to the extent that if a solution was found, it would be India's responsibility to sell it to the Tamils. Colombo also concluded that since Delhi had repeatedly pledged itself to preserving and respecting Sri Lanka's sovereignty and territorial integrity, it would not prescribe a solution which would be incompatible with the island's Constitution. That

India itself was facing a similar separatist problem in the Punjab was an added insurance.

Foreign Minister Hameed had told Colombo newspaper *Sunday Times* that the problem could not be solved without India's participation because it was an internal issue with external dimensions.[169] Just when Colombo appeared ready to concede space to India in settling its domestic problem, Rajiv Gandhi's interview with *India Today* magazine blaming Sri Lanka for using the negotiations to buy time for a military solution, vitiated the atmosphere. These remarks coming from the prime minister when Sri Lanka was still smarting from the humiliation of a violation of its airspace, stung Colombo, and it did not want it to go unchallenged. Sri Lanka summoned the Indian high commissioner to the foreign office and lodged a strong protest and released a statement describing Gandhi's remarks as 'incorrect and without foundation'.[170]

Despite irritants, there were straws that could be clutched. Below the turbulent Indo–Sri Lanka waters, there were softer currents capable of promoting a dialogue for a peaceful settlement. Rajiv Gandhi gave the first indication of it on 29 June 1987 while speaking at the luncheon of the Indian Association of Foreign Affairs Correspondents in New Delhi. He said, 'India was awaiting indication from Colombo for a new initiative on the resumption of a dialogue on finding a negotiated settlement of the ethnic conflict,' and added significantly that 'the ball is now in Sri Lanka's court' and the government was in touch with both Colombo and militants. The implications of this were more than clear. India gave enough indications that any settlement worked out between New Delhi and Colombo would be acceptable to the Tamils not excluding LTTE. It was stated that India would use all its resources to ensure that the Tamils did not spoil the party, at least this time around.[171] The assurance that any settlement arrived at between India and Sri Lanka would be acceptable to the LTTE was given without discussing the broad outlines of the proposed settlement with it.

Sri Lanka, as a first step, at the advice of Rajiv Gandhi, gave up its plans to hold elections to the various local bodies and sixteen Parliament seats which Tamils members had vacated earlier. Following the return of Dixit from Delhi after consultations, Hardeep Singh Puri, the first secretary in the high commission, who had been sent to Jaffna

secretly to talk to the LTTE, returned with the distinct impression that
the Tamil body was somewhat chastened and not completely averse
to a negotiated settlement. It is significant that the high commission
had officially denied the report of Puri's Jaffna visit.[172] The Colombo-
based daily the *Sun* stood by its report of the visit after India's denial.
A few days later, the *Financial Times* of London in a despatch from
Colombo reported the 'confidential parlays' between the two countries
to end the ethnic conflict. It said, 'The proposals go further than any
previous solution towards meeting the Tamil demands, which are
largely supported by India.' The paper claimed that these proposals
were drawn up while Prime Minister Premadasa, who was averse to
any compromise, was away in Japan on an official visit. There was
opposition from some cabinet ministers too, besides the Opposition
leader, Bandaranaike, and the public generally. It was feared too
much was being given away which would result in a 'worsening of
the conflict'. The main Opposition feared the proposed merger of
the north and east provinces, would result in Tamil dominance. The
Financial Times claimed that all the Tamil leaders, even those in exile
in Madras, had responded positively.[173] The heart of the understanding
was that Colombo had in principle agreed to the merger of the two
Tamil provinces of north and east to create the substance of a Tamil
homeland. To enable President Jayewardene to sell the settlement to
the Sinhalese, it would be sugar-coated with a proviso that the future
of the merged provinces would be decided through a referendum after
one year in the east province alone. Since the Tamils did not enjoy
full majority in the east, the settlement left the possibility of a status
quo ante. The east province had a Tamil majority on independence,
but in the last couple of decades, the Tamils had been reduced to a
minority by the government's policy of resettlement of Sinhalese there
and also the exodus of Tamils abroad. Therefore, a referendum a year
later would restore the status quo ante, a ploy which was not accepted
by the Tamils who accused India of bad faith.

On 17 July, the high commissioner met President Jayewardene in
the presence of the cabinet ministers. It was enough of an indication
that something was cooking and the Colombo media went to town

with reports of a settlement. The Indian high commission, worried that the premature disclosure could be injurious to the efforts underway, categorically denied the reports.[174]

Athulathmudali, the minister for national security, explained to the worried executive committee of the ruling UNP on 27 July that the domestic problem had developed into an international one, particularly 'with the involvement of India' and asked members to accept the reality of Indian involvement, whether they liked it or not, and explained the obligations which India had agreed to assume under the settlement.[175]

When the outlines of the proposed settlement were given to the TULF, it was unhappy and pointed out several reservations, the principal one being 'referendum' after merger of the two provinces, on the plea that 'the peace sought to be achieved would be shattered and there will be conflict and turmoil again'.[176]

Sri Lankan Prime Minister Premadasa on return from his Japan tour was livid at the proposed agreement and called for a referendum on the proposed settlement. He was convinced that 'LTTE would not accept what had been offered'.[177]

In Delhi, the going was not easy either. Opposition leaders expressed their disappointment since the LTTE had 'reservations on this accord'. They were assured that efforts were continuing to make it fall in line. However, on 27 July, two days before the agreement was to be signed, the details of which were still under wraps, Prabhakaran finally rejected the proposed accord describing it as 'an act of betrayal' and threatened that he would continue with his armed struggle. His basic reservation to the accord was the provision for Tamils to surrender arms. In a strongly worded statement, he blamed Rajiv Gandhi for betraying the Tamil trust, and said being unaware of the details of the accord, the LTTE had walked into a trap. He went to the extent of saying the LTTE may have to face the Indian army.[178]

It was now decided to get Prabhakaran to Delhi to try to overcome his resistance. Hardeep Puri was again flown to Jaffna to persuade the elusive Prabhakaran who had several questions and reservations about coming to Delhi. Puri was able to prevail and got him to

Delhi. The prime minister met him and listened to his objections. A conciliatory statement was issued on behalf of Prabhakaran after the meeting, claiming that the prime minister 'listened to our concerns with keen interest and utmost sincerity' and described the discussions inconclusive since there was a hint of their resumption on his return to Colombo after signing the agreement.[179] That the press release was issued by the LTTE only a day after the meeting indicated it was issued under some pressure.

Prabhakaran's own discussions at various levels created more doubts for him. He had strong reservations on disarming his cadres and surrendering weapons. He could perceive that India was bent on going ahead with the agreement, which he thought would be the death knell of the LTTE, and the sacrifices his men had made for Eelam would go waste. Perceiving that he might not be allowed to return to Jaffna, he gave his tacit approval to the proposed agreement and returned to Jaffna in an Indian Air Force helicopter. There, he reneged on all he had agreed to in Delhi.[180] Dixit said that though he was not present at the talks between Rajiv Gandhi and Prabhakaran, the latter 'demanded three to five crores of rupees' to enable him to look after his cadres while awaiting their resettlement.

Gandhi agreed to pay Rs 3–4 crore (Rs 30–40 million), which according to Dixit were channelled through the concerned agencies of the Government of India.[181] As later events proved, the LTTE was made to appear conciliatory in its approach, as Prabhakaran had no choice left in the five-star prison of the Ashoka Hotel in New Delhi.

The LTTE was not alone in refusing the draft agreement. The moderate TULF leaders too were far from satisfied. A day before the agreement was scheduled to be signed the TULF was shown the draft for the first time at a meeting at the ministry of external affairs in South Block. The copies of the agreement which were given to the TULF to study were taken back even before the meeting ended. Their request for a takeaway copy was refused. They were not even asked for their views or comments when it was evident that they had strong reservations, particularly on the referendum only in the east province after the two provinces had been merged. It was obvious to TULF that New Delhi was determined to go ahead oblivious of their views. The TULF did not go public with its disapproval since it wished to avoid an open defiance of the Government of India. Nevertheless, it was upset that the entire exercise in Delhi was aimed at getting its consent after the agreement had in fact been finalized and there had been no consultations to improve upon it to give the Tamils some satisfaction.[182] The TULF was now anxious to put on record its opposition. In a letter to Gandhi, it conveyed its misgivings to the agreement and warned that if it was implemented, 'the peace sought to be achieved will be shattered and there will be conflict and turmoil again'.[183]

The Indian officials in New Delhi who were euphoric initially, were shell-shocked at not only the LTTE's rejection of the agreement but the TULF's as well. An official spokesperson of the MEA expressed the government's deep disappointment with the LTTE's response but hoped that it would fall in line, while assuring it that government would make every effort to meet the legitimate aspirations of the Sri Lankan Tamils. But Prabhakaran had told the Press Trust of India that the accord would remain 'only on paper' since it had ignored Tamil aspirations. Describing Rajiv Gandhi's decision on the accord as 'disappointing and shocking' Prabhakaran said, it amounted to a 'stab in the back of the Tamils'. He categorically declared he would not adhere to the truce and would not lay down arms, which was the core of the accord, until the Sri Lankan army had dismantled their military camps in Jaffna and moved to the barracks. He insisted that he was tricked into coming to Delhi.[184]

Director (IB), M.K. Narayanan, was sceptical of LTTE's acceptance of the agreement, but the R&AW chief, A.K. Verma was confident that he could manage Prabhakaran since it was R&AW which was the channel of communications between South Block and LTTE and was manoeuvring things with the LTTE for New Delhi. Rajiv Gandhi also consulted the Army Chief General K. Sundarji, who in his usual flamboyant style assured the prime minister that should LTTE renege, 'the Army will finish it within a week or ten days'.[185] It was perhaps his style of functioning, since in 1984 at the time of military action in the Golden Temple, he had behaved similarly to the embarrassment of Prime Minister Indira Gandhi.

The prime minister was personally guiding the Indian policy toward Colombo. Days before the accord was signed, External Affairs Minister Narayan Dutt Tiwari was relieved of his portfolio and the prime minister himself took charge of the ministry. Incidentally, in the five-year tenure of Rajiv Gandhi, there were five ministers who headed the external affairs ministry. At the last minute, Rajiv Gandhi somehow decided to consult the erudite and sagacious Narasimha Rao, former External Affairs Minister, then holding charge of the Ministry of human resource development and asked Dixit to show him the draft of the accord. The draft was shown, but Rao's comments were not taken into account. Rao had made three perceptive comments: (i) don't rush into the agreement; (ii) consider the wisdom of being the direct signatories to the agreement (the idea was that it should be signed by the Tamils and India could be a guarantor) and (iii) assess carefully whether the Tamils and Colombo had a genuine desire for such an accord or was it a tactical move for an interim period.[186] It was incisive and logical advice from an old warhorse, but as events showed, prudence had little value for the flamboyant lot at the South Block.

Since the contents of the agreement were not made public until it was signed, there was little debate or discussion in public or in Parliament of either country. Dixit said if it had been done 'it would never have come about'.[187]

The agreement was built on the back of the people who were affected by it and for whom it was being negotiated. This was a situation where nothing seemed to work since practicality was missing. No effort was made to overcome Tamil reservations. The prime minister remained firm on his decision to go ahead and fly to Colombo as planned to sign the accord. Dixit had confirmed to President Jayewardene that there was no change in Gandhi's travel plans to Colombo to sign the agreement. Jayewardene having failed to subdue the Tamils enjoying Indian backing, saw in the agreement a glimmer of hope. He welcomed the proposition of ending the curse of terrorism and separatism if India helped. It was a clever move on Jayewardene's part, even if it meant making a temporary compromise with the country's sovereignty since it would end the scourge of terrorism while ensuring the unity and territorial integrity of the island, particularly when India had taken the responsibility to implement the agreement as well.

It was the time when public protests in Colombo against the accord were at their peak and the President feared that he would be ousted by Prime Minister Premadasa. Rajiv Gandhi extending full support against any possible upset ordered Indian naval ships with 'crack' units of the Indian army positioned at the Colombo port, ready to intervene should the President come under direct threat. Though nothing of the sort happened, large-scale protests and riots continued in the city which was under curfew when the prime minister arrived.[188] But India was worried about the Rajiv Gandhi's security in Colombo when the whole city stood in opposition to the agreement. Soon the disturbances had spread practically to the whole of the island except the north. It was suggested that the prime minister postpone his visit by a few weeks. The opposition to the accord in Colombo was so strong that no cabinet minister was prepared to be the minister-in-waiting for Gandhi, a customary requirement.

'The Accord to establish peace and normalcy in Sri Lanka' was signed in Colombo on 29 July 1987. To invest the accord with necessary importance and prestige, it was signed by Rajiv Gandhi and Jayewardene personally.

Altogether it was an iniquitous accord. Colombo was made to sign it under compulsion with a much bigger and powerful country in its neighbourhood. It described Sri Lanka as a 'multiethnic and a multi-lingual plural society'. The two Tamil provinces, north and east, recognized as 'areas of historical habitation' of Sri Lankan Tamils were to be merged. The Tamils' claim to the two provinces as their exclusive homeland was diluted with the provision of a referendum after a year, casting doubts on the permanence of the merger. The merger was seen as a ploy to lull the Tamils into complacency. India undertook to disarm the Tamil militants in the island and provide military assistance to prevent terrorism that was prejudicial to the unity and integrity of the island. India undertook to disarm the militants by their surrender of arms. Separately, a provision for the induction of an Indian Peace

Keeping Force (IPKF) to disarm them should they fail to surrender arms, was made. The accord went beyond the immediate issue of Tamil concerns in accepting what India perceived to be its security concerns—use of the Trincomalee Tank Farm, future of the Voice of America broadcasting station, presence of foreign military advisors etc. Most of these obligations were one-sided, which were thrust upon Colombo. The Tamils for whom it was negotiated remained dissatisfied and rejected the accord. The Sinhalese too remained dissatisfied at being goaded by a 'regional bully' into accepting conditions perceived to be undermining their country's sovereignty. Gandhi's statement on Sri Lankan TV on the day the accord was signed convinced no one when he described it as 'representing the unity of hearts which guaranteed the unity of a nation'. Jayewardene, however, remained optimistic that the end of terrorism would promote investments and tourism and lead to prosperity of the country.[189]

The main provision of the agreement—merger of the two provinces —was deceptive since Jayewardene while speaking at the joint press conference with Gandhi, within his hearing had said that he would personally campaign and canvass against the merger of the provinces at the time of referendum. His commitment was only tactical. Gandhi not reacting acquiesced to what Jayewardene had said. Rajiv Gandhi's description of the accord as a 'short, straightforward looking and practical document which working together as brothers would build a harmonious and prosperous Sri Lanka' convinced nobody.[190] In a separate interaction with Indian journalists travelling with him on the way back to India, he was miffed at a question that the agreement would reduce Sri Lanka to the status of Bhutan or establish a parallel between the IPKF and Soviet troops in Afghanistan.[191]

The prime minister had put his own prestige at stake and could not go back on it. After taking over the reins of government, it was his first major foreign policy initiative and it was felt that its success would catapult him in the big league for solving a problem festering since the independence of Sri Lanka in 1948. He was looking for a place in history and his officials were bending backward that he was not denied that place. Did history give him that place?

It was the lack of political experience of the prime minister that was at work. As a pilot with Indian Airlines, he had shown little or no interest in politics, despite his mother being the prime minister and living in the same household along with his politically active younger brother, Sanjay. It was the death of Sanjay in June 1980 that catapulted him into politics and he joined the Congress party as its general secretary, an office he held until the assassination of his mother, Indira, on 31 October 1984, when he took over as prime minister. During his days as general secretary there was nothing of any significance that he handled which could catapult him in the front row of politicians. His first test came soon after he was sworn in.

In para 6 of the annexure of the accord, it was stated that 'an Indian peace keeping force may be invited by the President to guarantee and enforce cessation of hostilities, if so required'. Quite to the contrary, as the main agreement was being signed by the two leaders, their foreign secretaries were simultaneously dotting the 'i's and crossing the t's of another letter inviting the Indian Peace Keeping Force 'to bring about the cessation of hostilities'. In their statements to TV journalists and at a press conference, neither of the two leaders gave any inkling that such a confidential agreement had been signed. Replying to a question whether there was any proposal to send an Indian peace keeping force, Gandhi ducked the question and said that 'it depends on what they ask for'. The fact was that the Lankan foreign secretary had already 'asked appropriate military assistance to ensure the surrender of arms' and in addition dispatched 'with immediate effect of some naval vessel' to stabilize the situation and 'to preserve the unity, stability and integrity of Sri Lanka'. It was not until the next day, 30 July, while making a statement in the Indian Parliament about the agreement that the prime minister disclosed the landing of the IPKF in Jaffna that day.[192]

The accord, like the fable of the blind men and the elephant, meant different things to different people. Rajiv Gandhi was ecstatic that he had achieved for the Tamils much more than they had asked for and the Indian bureaucracy patted itself for securing justice for the Tamils and security for India. Jayewardene was relieved that he had successfully cut Indian support from under the feet of the LTTE. Prabhakaran was livid. The Sri Lankan army felt relieved that they no longer had to face the dreaded Tigers. For the Buddhist clergy, it was a blow to Sinhalese pride and to the average Sinhalese it was a nightmarish throwback into history with the large-scale presence of the Indian army, their historic foe. To the JVP it was a cause célèbre which gave a new lease of life to their flagging anti-India agenda. For the ruling UNP, it was a dubious achievement, and for the Opposition SLFP, a petard to hang their opponent, the UNP.

Gandhi was elated as he told the Parliament on return from Colombo, that he had returned from a 'momentous' visit.[193] His excitement was again at display, when a few days later on 2 August, while receiving the Palestinian Liberation Organization leader, Yasser Arafat, at the airport, he described the accord as 'an agreement of the century'.

The proof of people's resentment was yet again on display while inspecting the Guard of Honour presented by the Lankan marines at the time of Rajiv's departure, when he was attacked by one of the ratings with the butt of his rifle. He saved himself by ducking the attack. It was the first signal of strong disapproval of the accord which Gandhi experienced. On 28 July, a day before the accord was signed, Anura Bandaranaike, leader of the Opposition in the Sri Lanka Parliament wrote to Gandhi recording not only his own disapproval, but also the Cabinet's and the country's as a whole. Colombo was torn by serious rioting and curfew had been imposed in the city until Gandhi left.[194]

On 29 July, as the accord was signed, Jayewardene in an interview to N. Ram of *The Hindu* conceded the opposition to the agreement but added 'he did not want to overestimate them either'.[195] Speaking at a public meeting in Chennai on 2 August, Rajiv Gandhi assured Chennai that it would usher in 'peace and tranquillity' and secure justice for the Tamils, and 'provide autonomy approximately like that of an Indian State'.[196] Jayewardene in a brief address to his nation in deciding to end the war and violence recalled the example of Emperor Ashoka who had given up war as an instrument of state policy.[197]

Natwar Singh, minister of state for external affairs, in replying to the debate in Parliament said the agreement had been 'welcomed from

Peking to Peru and Washington to Moscow' and touted it as a great achievement. Repeating he said, 'If I may say so, it has been welcomed from Moscow to Washington via Calcutta.'[198] Sycophancy at its worst!

Since 1983, when India first got involved in Lanka's ethnic problem it had insisted that it was only providing its good offices to facilitate a solution. By signing the accord, it became a party on behalf of the Tamils who were not only kept out of the negotiations but had opposed it vehemently. To that extent they were not committed to the accord. Delhi failed to realize that ever since it got involved in the ethnic problem, the Tamil intransigence had increased considerably. They hoped that India's weight would browbeat Colombo into offering a package that would create a Tamil state, if not sovereign, at least one bordering on sovereignty. The events leading to the birth of Bangladesh were fresh in their mind, which encouraged them in this thinking.

The accord was signed after the ethnic conflict had already exacted a very high price. The democratic spirit of the island's Constitution was its first casualty. The country had now virtually turned into an authoritarian state with draconian powers, courtesy the Prevention of Terrorism Act. Civil liberties stood either abridged or subverted. The island was dotted with army and police check-posts. The capital city, Colombo, was like an armed camp. Some 600 Sinhala civilians had been killed and between 500 and 600 uniformed soldiers dead. And several times that number of Tamils had been killed and over 1.5 lakh rendered homeless, living in Tamil Nadu as refugees. A permanent cleavage had permeated into an already divided society with little hope of being united. The defence was accounting for 19 per cent of the budget on the eve of the accord as against 4 per cent in 1976. Tourism, the largest forex spinner, had been crippled. The commodity prices in the world market stood depressed, thus affecting the economy severely. In this social, economic and political quagmire, the accord failed to bring the much-needed relief for the poor masses, who in any case were bearing the brunt of the conflict. The biggest gain for Sri Lanka was that India, which had stood by the Tamils, had been neutralized and won over to the Sinhalese side for the future.

Delhi signed the accord convinced that Tamils were not capable of withstanding the pressure of the Sinhala state, and whatever help was rendered would placate not only Sri Lankan Tamils but Tamils in Tamil Nadu too. In fact, the accord alienated both the Tamils. New Delhi suffered from misconceptions and misperceptions and felt convinced that having contributed to training, arming and financing the militants it had gained enough leverage to arm-twist them. However, the contrary happened. The failure of the Thimphu talks was one of the most glaring examples of the Tamils' disregard of Indian advice. Most Indian attempts to promote a settlement were sabotaged by the LTTE which indulged in unprovoked violence. The blame for the stubbornness of the LTTE or the Tamils, generally lay at India's door due to its overzealous canvassing on their behalf without any corresponding leverage over them. The Tamils and particularly those with the LTTE, encouraged by the heightened expectations aroused by Delhi, came to believe that a little more pressure would make Delhi fully and deeply involved and once its prestige was at stake, Eelam would not be too far. The Bangladesh experience guided them all the way. Now, the accord came as a deathblow to their dream of Eelam.

The LTTE, in Chief Minister M.G. Ramachandran, had not only a patron but also a financer. His support was so fundamental that he continued to provide finances to the LTTE even after the IPKF had launched operations against the LTTE.[199] As luck would have it for the LTTE, soon after the accord was signed, Ramachandran passed away on 24 December 1987.

The uphill task began when an attempt was made to implement the agreement. Prabhakaran, who had made good his return to Jaffna, against New Delhi's fond hope that he would stand by the accord, reneged. He continued to perceive it as a death warrant for him and his cadres. If his 4 August speech, which he made immediately on return to Jaffna from Delhi, was anything to go by, it was clear that his fears were titanic. He was worried the 'monster of Sinhala racism will devour this agreement' and pledged 'to continue his fight for the objective of Tamil Eelam'.[200] On the issue of disarming his cadres, Prabhakaran insisted the political structure of the Tamil state be established first. Nevertheless, the LTTE did make a pretence of surrendering arms even if they were obsolete. This token surrender was enough for President Jayewardene to claim that the LTTE had taken to the democratic way of life. Raising hopes for the future he said, 'The terrorists had agreed, in future to act democratically under the laws of Sri Lanka.'

Internationally, the world acclaimed the agreement and gave Gandhi a shot in the arm and enabled Natwar Singh to claim the international community's adulation for the prime minister. It also enabled him to declare that the implementation of the accord had been 'remarkable by any standards' and more than most people had expected. However, when the accord came up for discussion in the Lok Sabha, lack of national consensus stood out in bold relief. The opposition remained sceptical, since the government had brushed aside Tamil reservations. Natwar Singh described the lack of progress in the surrender of arms by the LTTE as an 'acceptable flexibility' and added that efforts were being made to minimize the differences among the Tamils. Concluding he said:

> If this problem had to be resolved, if an end had to be found to this ethnic problem, if the security environment had to be prevented from getting worse, if the refugees had to go back, if the prisoners had to be released, and if the events that had darkened the life and menaced the future had to be terminated, then something like this agreement had to be produced.

To humour the LTTE, Natwar Singh said that this agreement was made possible 'to some extent by the sacrifices made by the LTTE' and the government was in constant touch with Prabhakaran and had endeavoured to allay his fears regarding his own security and that of his cadres.[201]

The LTTE while surrendering unserviceable arms had clandestinely tucked away most of the serviceable ones. Prabhakaran remained more than convinced that he could not dismantle the 'security' apparatus which he had built over the years which everyone had been forced to sit up and take notice. If Prabhakaran ever had any intention of giving up arms, the terror unleashed by another equally determined rival guerrilla outfit, the People's Liberation Organisation of Tamil Eelam (PLOTE) in its last bid for supremacy, convinced him that he could not depend on anyone else but himself. And for that he must not only stay fully armed but further strengthen himself and his cadres.

In a momentous turn of events, the Indian Peace Keeping Force sent to enforce the accord, ended up fighting the Tamil Tigers, as the LTTE cadres were known. It was an unfortunate showdown between a regional military power and the perceived forces of indigenous mass-nationalism, howsoever misguided. In retrospect, it soon became apparent, rather painfully, that the accord and its consequent military intervention miserably failed to achieve its twin objectives of asserting India's hegemonic position in South Asia and defusing violence in Sri Lanka. India's intervention which endured precariously for almost two-and-a-half years left 1,155 Indian defence personnel dead. What was appalling was that the LTTE became the bête noire of the IPKF and the ethnic conflict between Sri Lanka and its Tamil population turned into an Indo–LTTE war if not an Indo–Tamil war. As the IPKF operations expanded, most of the Tamils, both Sri Lankan and Indian, combatant or otherwise, decried the agreement. The LTTE not only turned its guns on the IPKF but also targeted any Tamil who dared to cooperate with the Indian army.

As early as 20 September 1987, the spokesperson of the MEA accused the LTTE of engineering large-scale violence in which 100 Tamils were killed in the north and east provinces. On 24 September, yet again, the spokesperson accused the LTTE of instigating the Tamils in the northern town of Mannar to picket an IPKF camp compelling the army to respond with stronger measures. India, however, continued with its efforts to persuade the LTTE's top leadership to enter into the mainstream of the island's political life and stay within the parameters of the India–Sri Lanka accord.[202]

Even when High Commissioner Dixit personally went to meet Prabhakaran in Palaly not only to allay his fears, but also to offer him a prime position in the northeast administration, Prabhakaran was not propitiated.[203] Prabhakaran insisted on 'my way or highway'. The interim administrative arrangement worked out between Dixit and Prabhakaran failed to take off again because of Prabhakaran's dictatorial attitude on the appointment of the head of the interim administration. There was no dearth of crises which gave Prabhakaran excuses to sabotage the implementation of the accord.[204]

The crisis over the arrest of sixteen LTTE cadres for trying to smuggle arms and their subsequent suicide, spelt disaster and gave Prabhakaran yet another opportunity to renege from any commitment. On 28 September 1987, two months after the signing of the accord, Lanka's Minister of National Security, Lalith Athulathmudali, said in an interview that the 'island's peace accord was like a steeplechase that was faltering at the second fence...'[205]

Prabhakaran not only refused to arrive at a settlement, but also felt free to indulge in violence and had now killed 100 men, women and children, which according to the MEA was another 'attempt to prevent the implementation of the accord'. This happened within 48 hours of the Sri Lankan presidential secretariat's communiqué that the LTTE had formally assured the Indian high commissioner that it would fully cooperate in the implementation of the accord.[206] Continuing with its killing spree, on 6 October, LTTE killed half-a-dozen Indian soldiers, which led the IPKF to initiate 'Operation Pawan' against the LTTE. This practically marked the collapse of the accord and put the IPKF and the LTTE on a collision course. The LTTE did feel the heat of 'Operation Pawan' which demonstrated to Prabhakaran the will of the IPKF to act against the LTTE. It was a shock to Prabhakaran. Desperate, he now approached the Tamil Nadu leaders for a halt to the IPKF's military operations indicating willingness to talk, which the MEA described as a manoeuvre to generate sympathy. The high commission told the media that the IPKF had overrun the LTTE stronghold of Chunnakam near Jaffna town. India tried to be patient with him but it was he who fired the first shot at the IPKF at Jaffna and provoked it to undertake 'Operation Pawan'.[207]

Sri Lankan Minister Gamini Dissanayake, representing President Jayewardene at the Commonwealth Heads of Government Meeting in the Canadian city of Vancouver, met the Indian prime minister and described to him the LTTE's failure to surrender arms as 'unfortunate'. Gandhi reassured him of 'the ability of the IPKF to deliver what was expected of it'.[208]

'Operation Pawan' invited the odium of the Tamil Nadu politicians. The DMK leader in the Rajya Sabha on 6 November accused the IPKF of 'butchering Tamils' and asked for a ceasefire. Some even blamed the Centre for 'their foolishness', given the manner in which India had got bogged down in Sri Lanka. Emotion in the House ran so high that the speaker had to intervene repeatedly to expunge the members' remarks. The prime minister bemoaned that Prabhakaran had reneged from his promise to support the accord. Listing the dangers inherent in his attitude, the PM said:

> The LTTE's repudiation of the agreement, their attacks on Sinhalese and Muslims in the East and their murder of Sri Lankan soldiers threatened to produce a Sinhala backlash that would have destroyed the agreement and produced a cycle of violence worse than any the island had so far seen. The victims were mainly Tamils, especially in the South and Central Highlands.[209]

Unabated violence created fissures between India and Lanka. A disappointed Jayewardene blamed India for its failure to implement the accord, which 'should have been accomplished by the middle of August'. The ruling UNP recapitulated for the benefit of Delhi the three tasks that had remained unaccomplished: (i) a complete disarming of the LTTE; (ii) elections in the north and east, and (iii) cessation of hostilities in the north and east. To put India on the defensive, Minister Gamini Jayasuriya in the Sri Lankan Parliament listed steps taken by Colombo for the implementation of the accord and lamented that by drawing away its troops to the barracks, 'over 200 Sinhalese and 150 Tamils and even Muslims ended as cannon fodder to the adventurist terrorists—and all this under the protection of the 10,000 Indian Peace Keeping Force'.[210]

When the Rajya Sabha discussed the accord on 6 November for the umpteenth time, the Tamil members, as in the past, were unsparing in their scathing attack of the government's Lanka policy. They described the events in Lanka as the 'butchering' of all Tamils by the 'so called Indian Peace Keeping Force'. DMK leader Murasoli Maran in opening the debate indicted the IPKF and said:

It is shocking to the whole mankind, shocking not only to the Tamils in Tamil Nadu but also to the Tamils living all over India and Indians living all over the world and it is something, unheard of, something not ever thought of, something un-Indian, something brutal, something uncivilised which is going on there in Sri Lanka and it is being perpetrated by our own, our very respected armed forces.[211]

DMK member V. Gopalsamy in his devastating criticism used unparliamentary language and his remarks were not allowed to go on record. The AIADMK member Aladi Aruna was no less critical when he said he stood for the accord but 'not at gun point'. The representatives of the other parties who participated in the debate had no good words for the accord and were equally critical. However, the ruling Congress remained convinced that the agreement was the only panacea to resolve the ethnic conflict.[212]

Prime Minister Gandhi, as the author of the accord, re-emphasized its merits which he said had been acclaimed internationally. In his statement in the Lok Sabha on the 'Situation in Sri Lanka', he continued to feel assured that it would meet Tamil aspirations and maintain the unity and integrity of Sri Lanka and restore peace and security. He, however, regretted that the LTTE was deliberately wrecking the agreement when India had got the LTTE everything it wanted, disregarding the cost to its credibility with other militant groups. Elaborating Gandhi said:

We overlooked the LTTE's vicious propaganda even before the outbreak of hostilities, not just against the agreement but also against India and the IPKF. In the Interim Administrative Council, they were given a clear majority of seven out of 12 members including the Chairman of their choice. Other Tamil militant groups were excluded at Prabhakaran's insistence. While the GOI has accommodated every concern of the LTTE, the LTTE have not honoured any of their commitments.[213]

Gandhi did not realize the one essential pre-requisite was the acceptance of the accord by the Tamils before signatures. Had the advice of Narasimha Rao been taken that it should be signed by the Tamils, India would have perhaps avoided the ignominy it had to face now.

Prabhakaran in a signed and lengthy statement accused the IPKF of engaging in a full-scale war against the LTTE and assuming the role of a repressive army eliminating both the Tamil freedom fighters and innocent civilians. He indicted India for mounting a 'massive propaganda war to rationalise and legitimise its [IPKF's] actions' and to discredit the LTTE in the 'eyes of Indians and world public opinion'.[214]

Prabhakaran's wailing compelled Delhi to offer him another opportunity to come clean on the surrender of arms but to no avail. He continued to insist that he had surrendered 'most of his arms', a claim Delhi was loath to accept.[215]

Failing to make Prabhakaran behave, Delhi made an unsuccessful bid to wean away his cadres by offering them carrots in abundance, in return for their surrender. Delhi offered them not only security and protection, but a liberal monetary offer and facilities for resettlement in the future if they bid goodbye to the LTTE. To India's embarrassment, the cadres who were committed to their cause did not find the Indian carrots palatable.[216]

On 27 December 1987, Gandhi, while unveiling the statue of Satyamurthy, a freedom fighter, to mark his birth centenary at Pudukkottai (Tamil Nadu) claimed that the agreement had 'achieved much more than had been achieved before' and that all Tamil groups except 'one of the militant groups' had accepted it and held the LTTE responsible for killing most of the 'militant Tamils and many hundred, thousands of innocent Tamils'.[217] Sri Lankan frustration was even greater since they had compromised their sovereignty in entering into the accord, and they started doubting their wisdom in signing it. Colombo naturally directed its indignation at the IPKF. Sri Lankan Foreign Minister Hameed lamented in Parliament that the IPKF which had come in the country neither for 'active combat', nor 'to be engaged in in-fighting' had failed to perform the basic task envisaged in the agreement of July 1987, viz., 'to conduct the peace-keeping operations (and) recover the arms and ammunition from the terrorists'.[218]

Notwithstanding the problems in implementing the accord, relations between the top leadership of the two countries remained cordial. To mark the relationship, India felt happy to invite Jayewardene to be the chief guest at the Republic Day celebrations in January 1988. This was India's way to convey the message of friendship and create an amicable climate. Jayewardene was quite generous in giving his approval to several measures that Gandhi had proposed in implementing the accord. These included the announcement of the merger of the north and east provinces and appointment of a governor for the merged province; elections to the provincial councils; association of the Election Commission of India with the preparation and scrutiny of the voters' lists; non-exclusion of militant leaders in the election process and amnesty to Tamil militants.[219]

At the state banquet in Delhi for the visiting President, the Indian President served the peace accord in good measure as an antidote to all the problems of Sri Lanka. Jayewardene in reply carefully skirted any reference to the six-month-old peace accord since he was conscious that back home it had further polarized an already polarized society. However, in an interview with N. Ram of *The Hindu*, he expressed his satisfaction with the discussions in New Delhi.[220]

The President was embarrassed when on return home, the leader of the Opposition, Sirimavo, asked him whether his visit had indeed brought peace. Jayewardene's own optimism with the accord was reflected in his opening address to the Parliament's new session, when he thanked India for sparing the Sri Lankan army units from duty in the north and enabling their redeployment in the south to control the Janatha Vimukthi Peramuna (JVP) violence. The JVP's opposition to the accord was an ideological aversion of India. One of its theoretical explanations was Indian expansion in Sri Lanka. It described the Estate Tamils as the fifth column of Indian imperialism. The accord gave the JVP an additional momentum to wage a war against the government. The President, however, remained hopeful that with the IPKF's help, it would be possible to bring violence under control.[221]

Disconcerting reports about the contacts being made between the Sri Lankan government and the LTTE worried High Commissioner Dixit, who in a statement decried such attempts that undermined the peace accord.[222] Gandhi continued to extoll the virtues of the accord. While speaking in Parliament on 2 March, he claimed it had secured justice for the Tamils and ensured the unity and integrity of Sri Lanka. For India, he said that 'it secured our security interests, and secured non-alignment in the region'. Gandhi was interrupted by a Tamil member who told him 'innocent Tamils were being killed there'. Gandhi however retorted that the 'very task of the IPKF is to protect the innocent Tamils'.[223] A couple of days later, Jayewardene in a top-secret message dispatched through R&AW channels recounted to Gandhi the activities of the LTTE which he said were disturbing the demographic balance in the East Province.[224]

Prabhakaran, in trying to build his bridges with Gandhi, in his letter pledged to work the agreement but had no qualms to accuse Delhi which he said was 'persistently rejecting [his] urgent and sincere plea for peace'. He claimed his concern was based on 'the legitimate fears of the chauvinistic attitude' of Colombo.[225] Minister Natwar Singh making a statement in the Rajya Sabha however said that there was 'no clear signal' from the LTTE that they want to sit down and discuss peace.[226] The Tamil political parties in India supported Prabhakaran's demand and asked New Delhi to resume negotiations with him.[227] Unable to get any succour from Delhi, LTTE charged India with splitting the Tamil movement for 'securing its diplomatic ends'. Not sparing the R&AW either, he charged it acting independent of Delhi and even at the behest of the US's Central Intelligence Agency (CIA).[228]

Failure to disarm LTTE, the key element of the accord, remained the sticking point in Sri Lanka and a great embarrassment to Rajiv Gandhi personally. There were elements in Sri Lanka who felt that Colombo had given away too much in the agreement and still more in the letters exchanged along with the signing of the agreement. Their grouse was somewhat justified since India had shoved too many unequal obligations on Colombo, without assuming any corresponding obligations. To deflect the charge, India hinted that it would not be averse to consider a treaty with Sri Lanka on reciprocal basis and on the lines of the Indo–Soviet Treaty of Peace, Friendship and Cooperation, 1971. It was recalled that the question of such a treaty was discussed when Jayewardene had visited Delhi in November 1987 and later again when he was in Delhi for Republic Day as chief guest. Gandhi too confirmed that the MEA officials were looking into its possibility.[229] Sirimavo Bandaranaike was alarmed at these reports and questioned the very need for a new treaty since the policy of non-alignment left little scope for a document of that nature.[230] Colombo was in a fix. It feared that the proposed treaty could get mired in another controversy in the face of non-implementation of the already signed accord. The first priority was to make the accord work somehow, otherwise it would lead to another acrimonious debate. In view of these fears, the question of a new treaty was allowed to hibernate.

But it resurrected itself suddenly when Prime Minister Ranasinghe Premadasa in answering a question from a Lankan journalist, who had travelled with him to Hong Kong, had asked him whether the India–Sri Lanka Accord had undermined the country's independence. Answering, Premadasa had said, 'I think an accord of this nature between two sovereign states should be reciprocal.' He promised to work to bring about the reciprocity by signing a friendship treaty on the lines of the Indo–Soviet friendship treaty. He hoped that once that happened, a lot of misunderstanding would be cleared 'both nationally and internationally'.[231]

Reacting, the Indian high commissioner told *The Hindu* that India was well aware of Premadasa's preference, and was quite willing to discuss such a proposal.[232] Later, when Premadasa took over as the President, the two countries did exchange drafts of such a treaty.[233] Yet, somehow the treaty did not materialize.

As the accord came under stress, the Indian media too became critical and questioned its relevance. Perniciously critical views were expressed about Gandhi's motivation in signing the agreement. It was said it was an attempt to divert attention from the Bofors guns scandal, which had tarnished his image. There was also the accusation that Gandhi had paid a personal bribe to Prabhakaran to persuade him to endorse the agreement. These pressures resulted in Rajiv Gandhi following a two-track policy—continuing with military operations while trying to remain in touch with the LTTE to tame it.[234] That a payment was indeed made to LTTE was also referred to by the Sri Lanka Freedom party in its statement of 8 August 1988 describing it a 'shameful deal'.[235] New Delhi was upset with Dixit for disclosing the payment,[236] but Athulathmudali denied any knowledge of the payment.[237] LTTE once again had asked for Rs 150 crore for the rehabilitation of LTTE cadres and LTTE-related institutions.[238] Colombo got wind of it and in a confidential note asked New Delhi to channel the money through the Sri Lankan government.[239]

At the end of one year, on 23 July 1988, Rajiv Gandhi was disappointed at the LTTE's response to the surrender of arms and to join mainstream politics. On the other hand, LTTE yet again described the accord as one which 'aids and abets Sinhala–Buddhist chauvinism'.[240] As the events unfolded, the LTTE–Sinhala war morphed into an India–LTTE war. The Sri Lankan army sitting in the barracks watched India's discomfort with glee. Some jingoistic Sinhalese politicians even made snide remarks that Jayewardene had inveigled the Indian prime minister by his Machiavellian methods to fight the Tamils. The unhappy, moderate Tamils were subjected to contradictory pulls generated by the IPKF and the LTTE due to the emerging military confrontation.[241] India was not surprised that the LTTE was defying it. The LTTE had in the past, several times, done this but India remained helpless and went on pressuring Colombo for concessions to appease the LTTE.

As the confrontation between the LTTE and the IPKF gathered momentum, the IPKF came once again under attack from the Indian Tamil Parliamentarians and Tamil political parties in Tamil Nadu, accusing the IPKF for killing the Tamils in the island. The North East Provincial Council (NEPC) even when constituted failed to deliver. The IPKF occupied nearly one-third of Lankan territory and two-thirds of its coastal area and the media too played its role in creating an alienation among the people, particularly when the Lankan army had exited the Tamil areas for the barracks. The local administration too was paralysed. It was well known that the northeast was out of the pale of Colombo's administration.

The LTTE facing all round criticism as the villain of the piece decided to hit back. In two statements made on 9 July and 26 October 1988, it had described the accord 'a dead letter' accusing New Delhi of desperate efforts to implement it by 'unleashing all-out-war against the liberation movements'. Analysing the causes of the failure of the accord, Anton Balasingham, an ideologue of the LTTE, repeated the charge that it was due to an imposed agreement arrived at disregarding the 'wishes, aspirations, fears and hopes of the people of the island particularly the Tamils'.[242]

If earlier the Sinhalese alone were critical of the IPKF, as the conflict deepened, to India's embarrassment, the Jaffna Tamils too became critical of the IPKF, accusing it of many human rights violations and making capital out of Tamil misery and misfortunes. In October 1988, fifty faculty members of the Jaffna University, in a statement, accused India of arming the militants from 1983 and marginalizing the people. It said though India was the common patron of all militants, divisions and antagonism among them had grown at a rapid pace, culminating in the annihilation of the Tamils.[243]

As expected, Prime Minister Ranasinghe Premadasa was elected President in December 1988 to replace Jayewardene as his term was coming to an end. With his election, the discourse between India and Lanka changed altogether—from the implementation of the accord—to the withdrawal of the IPKF. Premadasa was a staunch opponent of the accord. It would be recalled the agreement in July 1987 was signed in the teeth of his opposition. He did not even attend the signing ceremony and remained aloof. His election manifesto had pointedly called for the withdrawal of the IPKF. The writing on the wall was now clear and India did not fail to read it.

Apprehending the possibility of change, Gandhi, as early as October 1988, had expressed his confidence that the accord would not be disturbed even if there was a change in the Lankan administration.[244] Premadasa's election made High Commissioner Dixit rush to New Delhi where he gave the prime minister his assessment of the emerging political situation in the island.[245] To pre-empt any move on the withdrawal of the IPKF, Dixit on return to Colombo informed the new President that in addition to the two battalions of the IPKF already withdrawn, another two would leave the island soon. He added India would be prepared to consider the revision of the accord on the principles of mutual benefit and reciprocity.[246]

Notwithstanding the friendly and conciliatory noises made by Delhi, the noises emanating from Colombo were too shrill for Delhi's comfort. If earlier Colombo was friendly and India had only LTTE to contend with, now the situation in Colombo had changed altogether and India felt besieged.

The manner in which Perumal, the newly elected chief minister of the newly merged Northeast Provincial Council, functioned left much to be desired. After taking over as the chief minister, he had visited New Delhi, held consultations with the prime minister and the Tamil Nadu leaders, which did not give comfort to the new regime in Colombo. Delhi did nothing to disabuse him of his indiscretions. If there was noticeable increase in the estrangement between the Lankan and Indian leaders since the election of the new president, it was not unexpected.

The LTTE saw in this an opportunity to snipe at Delhi. It projected India as interfering in Sri Lankan internal affairs to promote its own strategic interest, while the Tamil cause suffered. Prabhakaran in his letter of 7 February 1989 approached the UN Human Rights Commission in Geneva, challenging India's bona fide and held it responsible for 'continuous occupation and repression' (in the north) under the cover of peacekeeping operations. He sought to convey to the world that the 'Tamil people were deeply disillusioned and disappointed with Indian policy and have lost all trust in India accusing Delhi of having aggressive and hegemonic designs in the region.'[247] Mounting pressure, the LTTE on 21 March 1989 accused the IPKF for the massacre of 300 civilians and in an orgy of violence, it killed fifty-seven IPKF personnel and wounded sixty, capturing thirty-two, besides killing eleven Sri Lankan soldiers. A press release issued by the LTTE's Political Committee branded IPKF as an 'occupation army' engaged in the killing of the Tamils and reminded President Premadasa that he had 'unwittingly' failed to realize that the IPKF was the enemy of Sri Lanka.[248]

The LTTE fusillade fitted into its strategy to get rid of the IPKF. Both Colombo and the LTTE felt if they were to come to the negotiating table, then the rationale for the IPKF's presence would vanish. On 13 April, the new foreign minister, Ranjan Wijeratne, to the embarrassment of India, sought to reach out to the LTTE for talks with the government. He said, 'We are pleased to invite the leadership of the LTTE to have talks with the government.' In a dirty dig at India, Wijeratne added, 'When a nation is wrecked by internal conflict, only outsiders will reap the benefits.' Reacting to the LTTE's positive response, Colombo asked it to nominate its accredited representatives to facilitate dialogue anywhere in Sri Lanka.[249] When the LTTE agreed to talk, it was the secretary to the President who acknowledged the LTTE message and remarked that 'the President appreciated it'.[250]

The Colombo press reacted cautiously. The *island* and the *Sun* provided a rough indication of the public mood when they advised circumspection in falling into the LTTE trap. Political circles too remained cautious. The question hotly debated was what the two sides, with so much dividing them, could negotiate and whether any agreement was possible at all since successive governments in Colombo in the past had been constrained by the forces of Sinhala nationalism and chauvinism from making any concessions to the Tamils. Sinhalese nationalism had become more radical and militant over the years especially after the formation of the JVP, and Premadasa had very little leeway to accommodate the militants. Nevertheless, the LTTE and the government unified over the withdrawal of the IPKF, outwitting Delhi.[251]

The LTTE sought to wield a double-edged sword which would help it avenge its humiliation at the hands of the IPKF. Without the LTTE support, the northeast administration would collapse and the LTTE would fill the vacuum. In the process, the LTTE was taking advantage of the call for the IPKF's de-induction and if it happened it would take credit for something which was imminent and would allow it to have the last word. In the end, India which tried to humble it would itself stand humbled. India did lose face, in that the July 1987 accord seemed aborted practically after the sacrifices of hundreds of Indian soldiers. Sri Lanka, which had invited the IPKF, had turned hostile. In India, the Tamil constituency was no less hostile and neither was Parliament placated. To add insult to injury, the LTTE declared it would not observe ceasefire until the IPKF had left.[252]

Tragically, the initiative was now with the LTTE. The MEA reacting to the proposal for talks between the LTTE and Colombo, and caught in the most unenviable situation, conceded that talks were always good and India would support any move which would lead to peace. Barely hiding his embarrassment, the MEA spokesperson reacting to a question said, 'If the talks are held, they would come within the framework of the India–Sri Lanka agreement.' The determined journalist, out to embarrass the spokesperson again, asked whether Delhi was consulted while Colombo offered to hold talks with the LTTE. The spokesperson clearly discomforted said the Indian mission in Colombo was in daily contact with both the parties at various levels and while India was involved in the process, it would 'study the offer and its acceptance and ascertain its veracity'.[253] It was clear to everyone that the LTTE had taken the driver's seat and was pressing the accelerator too, and India was desperately trying to keep its toe on the brake. Colombo had in fact become the advocate of the LTTE. Foreign Minister Wijeratne denied reports that the LTTE had any preconditions for the talks. To propitiate Delhi, Premadasa had a fifty-five-minute-long conversation with the new high commissioner, Lakhan Lal Mehrotra, who had replaced Dixit. As Mehrotra presented his letter of credence to the President, the President stressed the need to remove any misinformation between India and Sri Lanka since it was a greater problem than misunderstandings. Premadasa hoped Prime Minister Gandhi would visit Colombo 'to see for himself the vast fund of goodwill that existed for India among the people'.[254]

There was no end to India's tribulations. The *Sunday Observer* from Colombo on 16 April sought to blame the IPKF for the massacre of Muslims in the east province on the basis of a briefing given by Foreign Minister Wijeratne who had just then ended his tour there. Wijeratne too had made a similar statement on local TV. Though the high commission rejected the allegation, the newspaper stood by its story.[255]

In the midst of all-round attacks, Indian Foreign Secretary S.K. Singh made a dash to Colombo and delivered a message from the prime minister to President Premadasa. A press note issued by the high commission at the end of Singh's visit said that 'the visit represented the continuing dialogue between the governments of the two friendly neighbours on matters of mutual interest', which included a review of the implementation of the India–Sri Lanka accord.[256] Ironically, the press release had no reference to the withdrawal of the IPKF even though the prime minister had on 25 April told a high-level meeting of army commanders in New Delhi of India's intention to withdraw the IPKF 'as soon as possible'. He had also added for good measure that though the IPKF had 'done the nation proud...we should consider handing over its control to the elected government in the northeast province, so that they could protect themselves against any de-stabilisation that arises'.[257] The reference to the handing over of the IPKF-held territory to the northeast government was unfortunate since the IPKF was operating on the basis of the agreement with the central government of the island and not on behalf of any provincial administration. It was an admission that India had lost confidence in Colombo.

India had to suffer more humiliation when Wijeratne justified the decision to airlift the LTTE representatives from the jungles of the north to Colombo for talks with the government. He said it was to ensure that they were not 'inconvenienced'.[258] The LTTE had become a VIP organisation for Colombo. Wijeratne poured more salt on India's wounds, clarifying that any settlement with the LTTE would not be within the framework of the India–Sri Lanka agreement but within the laws of the island since they were talking to their own 'countrymen'. Referring to the message which Indian foreign secretary had delivered to the President from Rajiv Gandhi, Wijeratne clarified that Gandhi wanted to be kept informed of the developments. Condescendingly, Wijeratne sought to assure India 'nothing will be held back [and] there are no secrets'.[259]

As the talks between government and the LTTE progressed, there were a series of communiqués issued by the President's office on the talks. The LTTE, with the tacit connivance of the government, used those communiqués to indict the IPKF. The government too, in its communiqués, used the LTTE's charges against the IPKF. It quoted the LTTE to describe the IPKF as an occupation army, which had brought 'untold hardship and suffering to the people', holding it responsible for the massacre of 5000 Tamils.[260]

Pitted against heavy odds, the Indian high commission, next day, valiantly tried to ward off 'unwarranted charges' against the IPKF, which had not taken into account the enormous difficulties of the job that was entrusted to it. The high commission regretted that the Presidential communiqués were being allowed for propaganda by the LTTE.[261]

The negotiations between the LTTE and the government were made to appear heading toward an understanding which would allow them 'to seek a negotiated political settlement'. Encouraged, the LTTE refused to relent on its propaganda barrage against the IPKF. In its press release of 20 May, the LTTE accused the IPKF of 'military repression and terror against the Tamils in the occupied northeast region of the island'.[262] The IPKF now came under attack from Amnesty International which accused it of committing atrocities, a charge India called biased, and strongly denied.[263] In the midst of these developments, Principal Secretary to the Prime Minister, B.G. Deshmukh, visited Colombo and handed over a letter to the President from the prime minister. He too entered into discussions on the question of withdrawal of the IPKF and the devolution package. However, at the end, these discussions were described as 'exploratory'.[264]

Nothing seemed to be going right for the IPKF. A senior Indian Police Service Officer, D.R. Karthikeyan was asked to spend a fortnight in the area of IPKF operations in the northeast and give a report on the ground situation. His report unfortunately gave little comfort to Delhi. His findings were that the LTTE was 'popular' with the people and 'also controlled the area'. His assessment of Perumal, the chief minister of the northeast province, was that though loyal to India, he 'lacked both popularity and strength on the ground'. About the IPKF, his assessment was that its morale was 'low' and senior officers did not even know 'why the IPKF was there and why the Indian armed forces should be fighting a war against the people of Indian origin and killing them and getting killed by them'. He strongly recommended talking to the LTTE or otherwise 'withdraw the forces immediately'.[265] Even the new high commissioner, Mehrotra, found that the LTTE challenge was not a cakewalk for the IPKF 'on a terrain that was LTTE's home ground and where it was not without popular support'.[266]

What Premadasa told the Parliamentary group of his ruling UNP gave the LTTE the respectability it did not deserve. He said because of the government talks with the LTTE, it had joined the mainstream of Lanka's politics.[267]

In the general elections held in October 1989 in India, the ruling Congress party, led by Rajiv Gandhi lost badly. It won less than 50 per cent of the seats it had won in 1984. It was evident that the people who gave him an unprecedented mandate in 1984 were greatly disappointed by his policies in the last five-year period. His initiative to sign accords as panacea for the problems of the day could not be implemented, and like the Sri Lanka accord did not bring him any credit. He had signed some other accords on domestic problems which could not be implemented either and remained on paper alone. The Bofors scandal too contributed in his defeat. Since no party had won a majority on its own, a coalition government under Vishwanath Pratap Singh, as prime minister, and Inder Kumar Gujral, as external affairs minister, was formed. Lakhan Lal Mehrotra had already replaced Dixit in Colombo as India's high commissioner. Both the government in Colombo and the LTTE tried to build bridges with the new set-up in Delhi. Premadasa in his message of felicitation to the new prime minister welcomed his desire to improve relations between the two countries, which had 'come under strain in recent times'.[268] Lankan Foreign Minister, Rajan Wijeratne, visited New Delhi soon after the government had been sworn in, where the question of de-induction of the IPKF was discussed. The possibility of finalising a friendship treaty which had been earlier under discussion, but lying dormant, was considered too.[269] However, a member of the Colombo delegation giving indication of the talks in Delhi said it 'did not produce the sort of unqualified commitment for the withdrawal of the IPKF' which Colombo had expected.[270] Wijeratne's briefing on his Delhi visit recalled the understanding with Rajiv Gandhi that 'the IPKF would be moved out of this country by 31 December'. The LTTE too appeared anxious to take advantage of the new regime in Delhi. In a conciliatory move, Anton Balasingham, the second most important

LTTE leader sought to blame its past estrangement with Delhi on the bureaucracy. It was hoped that the 'new administration would ensure that the new people will understand and accommodate' the LTTE's point of view. It too blamed Rajiv Gandhi's foreign policy particularly on 'certain crucial provisions of the India–Sri Lanka accord and the manner in which it was implemented'. Reassuring India, Balasingham said the LTTE 'would not go against the cordial relationship between India and Sri Lanka' and asked Delhi not to interfere militarily in the ethnic problem of the island and suggested it adopt a fresh policy.[271]

Past developments had convinced New Delhi that the ethnic problem had no easy solution. The disenchantment of Sri Lanka with the presence of the IPKF too, had become more cacophonous than before. Delhi was unhappy that the IPKF was being asked to pack up without accomplishing its task. It still refused to believe that the manner in which the accord was drawn up on the back of Tamil disfavour and signed against their wishes was highly flawed. The voices for the withdrawal of the IPKF had become sardonic and derisive. New Delhi had not bargained for such an eventuality nor was it prepared to accept it either. If earlier it was India which had its way and airlifted supplies to Jaffna against the wishes of Colombo, it was now Lanka's turn to avenge its humiliation by making India feel helpless and withdraw.

At the time when the accord was signed in July 1987 and the IPKF was deployed, the time frame for its deployment or return was not on anyone's mind. It was expected that the surrender would not take time, particularly when Prabhakaran had supposedly agreed to its implementation. It was not clarified nor was it understood that the IPKF deployment was essentially to enable the LTTE surrender its arms honourably, since surrender to the Sri Lankan army would appear like a surrender of the vanquished to the victorious. It was intended to guarantee to the doubting Jayewardene that India meant business. But the manner in which it happened vitiated the whole atmosphere and what was intended in good faith seemed insincere.

Rajeev Gandhi was stumped, when in November 1987, the BBC, perhaps for the first time, had asked him if there was any timeline for the IPKF withdrawal. Caught off guard, he said 'this was really up to President Jayewardene'. Discounting any danger of being bogged down, he had said, 'This should be a short, sharp exercise and our boys should be back soon.'[272]

General Harkirat Singh, the General Officer Commanding 54th Infantry Division of the IPKF made an indiscreet statement that it would 'not go from Sri Lanka until Tamils are satisfied and their aspirations are met'. He had also said that the IPKF took orders from nobody except from the Government of India. This created a storm in the Lankan Parliament. To cool tempers, Colombo referred to Gandhi's statement made to the Egyptian newspaper *Al Gomhouria* and said the IPKF was in Sri Lanka to assist Colombo and must operate under the command of the Sri Lankan President and leave when ordered to do so by him.[273]

During Jayewardene's visit to India on Republic Day, 1988, the MEA had declined a question on the return of the IPKF. On 16 March 1988, Minister Natwar Singh had in answer to a question told the Lok Sabha that the IPKF had gone to Lanka at the invitation of Colombo and the question of its duration 'will have to be decided in that context and there was no question of its stay there permanently'.[274] Two days later, Natwar Singh repeated this position in the Rajya Sabha.[275] High Commissioner Dixit had however told the Colombo paper *Lankadeepa* that it would return as soon as its task under the agreement was complete.[276] The vagueness in Indian responses created uncertainty for Colombo and doubts were raised about its withdrawal anytime soon. The pressure started building up since the IPKF operations did not appear to be making any headway either in disarming the LTTE or in controlling the violence.

In the background of Defence Minister K.C. Pant's visit to Colombo on 13 May 1988, Lankan minister Dissanayake had said he would discuss with the President 'the time frame for the withdrawal of the IPKF'.[277] However, New Delhi clarified that the defence minister's visit was for further discussions on the implementation of the India–Sri Lanka Accord which was an indication that withdrawal of the IPKF was not on Pant's agenda and the IPKF's strength would be based on operational requirements and the role it was required to play.[278] As a pressure tactic, the Lankan home minister, K.W. Devanayagam, in his letter to Pant, paid tribute to the IPKF performing a difficult task but listed its failures too, which, he said, had even made the functioning of the local administration impossible. There were enough hints that the IPKF had become a liability and it was time for it to leave.[279] To Pant's embarrassment, the LTTE's indictment of the IPKF was even harsher. It accused the IPKF of killing civilians and 'brutally raping' women while trying to teach 'democracy to Tamil nation' and spending millions of rupees 'to bomb and burn Tamil areas' crushing the Tamil liberation struggle, in the hope that it could implement the accord, which it described 'a charter of servility for the Tamil, by destroying the LTTE and its leaders'.[280]

The joint statement issued at the end of Defence Minister Pant's visit made no reference to the de-induction or even partial withdrawal of the IPKF.[281] Within days of Pant's visit, New Delhi announced that 'a contingent of the IPKF, not required operationally, had left for India'.[282] The Lankan Parliament was informed accordingly, on the same day.[283]

As 1988 drew to a close, and the current term of President Jayewardene was coming to an end, in an interview to the BBC, he made a balanced statement leaving it to the new President to decide on the IPKF's withdrawal 'either immediately or in a phased manner provided that he was satisfied that the Sri Lankan forces could meet the present situation'.[284]

Given the past position of Premadasa on the signing of the accord or its operation, his call for de-induction of the IPKF was not unexpected but inevitable.

Prime Minister Gandhi, who had staked his reputation on the implementation of the accord was caught in the crossfire between Premadasa and Prabhakaran and found the going tough. Six months into office and in a surprise move, that too on the holy occasion of the pinnacle unveiling ceremony at Chittavivekashramaya Temple in Battaramulla, Premadasa called upon India to withdraw its troops from the island by the end of next month, 'July 1989', since the presence of foreign forces in an independent country was 'a slur on its self-respect' and 'it devalued its freedom'. He questioned the rationale for presence of the IPKF now that there were talks between the government and the LTTE for restoration of peace on the island. To put more pressure on India, the President said Sri Lanka could not host the next SAARC summit with self-respect with foreign troops on its soil.[285]

Not allowing the grass to grow under his feet, Premadasa the very next day repeated his demand for de-induction by the end of July because of his election pledge and the withdrawal would enable Colombo host the SAARC summit. To further pressurise Delhi, he said he was deputing his foreign secretary to the Indian capital to complete the formality of consultations. He reminded Gandhi that Colombo had submitted 'several proposals' for the friendship treaty which he expected would further strengthen relations between them.[286] Caught by surprise, the MEA reminded Colombo that India had already initiated the process of de-induction depending on certain parameters and its message had puzzled Delhi. Talking to N. Ram of *The Hindu*, Premadasa justified his demand because of threats from the JVP and his commitment to the electorates.[287]

This set in motion a chain of letters/messages between the two leaders. In a span of a month-and-a-half ten such letters/messages were exchanged. In the acrimonious correspondence each tried to outwit the other. Gandhi's insistence that the withdrawal and implementation of the agreement must go together, did not echo in Colombo.[288]

As a measure of additional pressure, the Parliamentary group of the ruling UNP adopted a resolution reinforcing its president's demand for the IPKF's withdrawal. Before the resolution was adopted, there was concern that peace might suffer if the IPKF withdrew. Premadasa did not subscribe to this fear asking the doubting Thomases whether there was desired peace during the IPKF presence over two years and what harm would come if they left.[289] In the Lankan Parliament, Foreign Minister Wijeratne said, 'We would ensure that they were withdrawn and we would also strive determinedly for the "demerger" of the North and the East provinces at the earliest opportunity.'[290]

Following the President's demand for withdrawal, Wijeratne had visited Delhi and it was agreed that 'consultations will continue' to create the conditions 'as envisaged in the Indo–Sri Lanka Accord to facilitate IPKF withdrawal'.[291] Two days later, leader of the Opposition Anura Bandaranaike raised the question of withdrawal of the IPKF in the Lankan Parliament.[292] Foreign Minister Wijeratne in his statement tried to further pressurise India, repeating what Premadasa had said earlier, that 'having a foreign force in an independent country is a slur on its self-respect, devaluing the freedom of the country'.[293]

Premadasa asked the people to desist from any action which would prolong the need for the IPKF to stay longer since he believed it had not only failed to restore peace but its failure had also resulted in 'peace being disturbed in other parts of the country'.[294]

Refusing to be hustled, Delhi replied to Premadasa's 2 June letter on 20 June reminding him that the IPKF went to his country at a time when 'the situation seemed headed inexorably towards the breakup of Sri Lanka' and it was at a heavy cost that the IPKF prevented it. Regarding its withdrawal, he insisted, that both the countries needed to jointly draw up a mutually agreed schedule, for the full implementation of the India–Sri Lanka Agreement and complete withdrawal of the IPKF.[295] High Commissioner Mehrotra drew the attention of Foreign Minister Wijeratne to the fact that his President had not shown the courtesy of taking the prime minister into confidence before asking for the withdrawal of the IPKF by a particular date.[296]

On 26 June, President Premadasa warned that after 29 July, the IPKF 'would have to be confined to the barracks'.[297]

The obstinate President refused to back down and on 28 June asked the Indian prime minister to stop all IPKF operations against the LTTE since it had 'announced complete cessation of hostilities against the government' and had agreed to settle all the problems through negotiations.[298] Two days later, he followed it up with a detailed letter reminding Gandhi that the IPKF had come to Sri Lanka at the request of its President and now at his request must withdraw.[299]

Responding to reports from Colombo that the LTTE had agreed for cessation of hostilities and expressed its desire to find a political solution to the ethnic problem, the MEA spokesperson asked Colombo if the LTTE would resume the process of laying down arms and give up their demand for Eelam in favour of the unity of Sri Lanka.[300] This provoked Wijeratne to tell Prime Minister Rajiv Gandhi rather insolently 'to stop poking his nose in Sri Lanka'.[301] Prabhakaran taking advantage of the situation butted in and told the prime minister, that the LTTE had stopped its hostilities and described its decision to enter into peace talks with the government as an 'outstanding historic achievement' and therefore the conditions to facilitate the IPKF's withdrawal had been created.[302] In the face of the hostile position taken by the President, India could only regret Colombo's precipitate and unilateral call for the withdrawal of the IPKF. Rajiv Gandhi found himself at his wits end and decided to ask Cabinet Secretary B.G. Deshmukh to try to cool the tempers in Colombo.[303] But Deshmukh was rebuffed by Premadasa who accused India of not being loyal to the accord since there were certain Tamil groups campaigning for Eelam from its (India's) territory. Finally, Premadasa threatened that if the IPKF was not withdrawn immediately, he would be prepared to go to any length to achieve it and 'would not care if the Indo–Sri Lanka Accord was abrogated by the Parliament and relations with India ruptured'.[304] Taking the wind out of the President's sails, Deshmukh told him that it would pose no threat to India and that he could go ahead, even if he declared the IPKF 'an occupation force'.[305]

Prime Minister Gandhi was briefed by Deshmukh and the high commissioner about their assessment of the situation which included the threat of the president to abrogate the accord and rupture relations. JVP too had threatened the assassination of the entire Indian community in Sri Lanka and the staff of the high commission, which had been branded as imperialist. The prime minister regretted the President's confrontational attitude and felt it desirable to avoid any provocation. He, however, suggested that should the Sri Lankan army come out of barracks and act menacingly against the IPKF, it would act in self-defence. He too emphasized the need to impress on the Sri Lankan army, government and the people, of the disastrous consequences of pushing the two 'very friendly armies into a hostile confrontation'. The prime minister, worried about the security of Indians, had instructed that 'plans be kept ready to rescue the Indian community' in such a contingency while families of the staff of the Indian high commission and Indian banks in Sri Lanka should be withdrawn straight away.

The general security situation had come to such a pass that an additional security force to defend the Indian high commission against any mass demonstration or assault was ordered. Further, it was decided that if need arose, to help out its personnel, 'air and sea' rescue operations were to be undertaken.[306]

On 28 July 1989, it was announced in Colombo that the Sri Lankan foreign minister would visit New Delhi to discuss the time schedule for the 'withdrawal of the remaining IPKF contingent in Sri Lanka'.[307] On the same day, the MEA spokesperson in New Delhi announced that the withdrawal would commence from 29 July 1989.[308]

In the meantime, the Lankan government had formed a peace committee of all political parties and ethnic groups to settle differences apart from a Security Coordination Group. Keeping in view the efforts of Colombo to forge peace among various communities, it was agreed between the two foreign ministers to complete de-induction by 31 December 1989.[309] Colombo media quoted unnamed sources in New Delhi to qualify that a complete withdrawal would depend on whether the Tamils get assurance about their safety.[310]

On 30 November, Wijeratne told journalists that the IPKF had withdrawn from Batticaloa and it had returned to normalcy with the deployment of the Lankan police and army. He still estimated there were 30,000 Indian troops in Sri Lanka. He also appealed to LTTE not to create any problems.

New Delhi denied that the new government of V.P. Singh had ordered a speeder withdrawal of Indian troops from Sri Lanka. An Indian defence ministry statement clarified that the prime minister had ordered withdrawal from four northeast districts from 7 December.[311] The Lankan foreign minister during another visit to India in December failed to pressurise New Delhi into any firm commitment on the complete withdrawal of the IPKF.[312]

A distraught and frustrated Wijeratne refused to meet the high commissioner and asked him to write to him instead. The LTTE taking advantage of the situation reiterated that once the IPKF had left and the illegal army in the northeast had been disbanded, there would be no need for the LTTE to bear arms and it would convert itself into a political party.[313] In yet another visit to New Delhi, Wijeratne was promised final withdrawal by 31 March 1990.[314] Unhappy, Wijeratne told the Colombo press of his frustration at the failure of India to abide by the 31 December date.[315]

Worried about the safety of Tamils, New Delhi told Colombo that it would 'take a very serious view' should their safety be compromised after the de-induction of the IPKF.[316] Wijeratne, however, held the IPKF responsible 'for creating conditions which endangered the safety and security of the Tamils'.[317] A day earlier, Stanley Dominic, the leader of the LTTE's political wing threatened to attack the IPKF if it did not move out by March.[318]

The protracted correspondence between New Delhi and Colombo was a dialogue of the deaf. Both batted from their perspectives which were miles apart. Finally, the IPKF left on 24 March 1990. To bid it farewell, the defence minister of Sri Lanka and its three service chiefs were present at Trincomalee. High Commissioner Mehrotra in his farewell message reminded Sri Lankans that IPKF did not forced itself on Sri Lanka, but 'it was in a moment of such grave crisis that Sri Lankan Head of State, in his sovereignty, had decided to invite the Indian Peace Keeping Force'. Paying tribute to the IPKF he said:

> History will record your achievements in golden print and the memories of those of the IPKF who have laid down their lives to preserve the unity and territorial integrity of a friendly neighbour will last in our hearts for ever. A proud and grateful nation awaits your arrival back on Indian shores.[319]

The IPKF exited Sri Lanka paying a heavy price. Its task remained unfulfilled. Its image was tarnished and battered, and its reputation sullied. In human terms it paid a heavy price—the total number of all ranks killed was 1155 out of which fifty-five were officers; wounded numbered 2854. The IPKF killed 2592, wounded 1159 and captured 1185, overwhelmingly Tamils. It was the end of the story of Tamils killing Tamils, while the Sinhalese watched with some glee and sorrow since they saw the economy of their country destroyed and their national pride in a shambles.

Velupillai Prabhakaran, the bête noire of the IPKF in a statement on 1 April 1990, described the departure of the IPKF as a 'historic turning point' and said:

> [W]e have successfully foiled the Indian military intervention. Now the Indian occupation forces have completely withdrawn from our homeland. The termination of the Indian intervention is a grand victory of our struggle . . . For more than two years we fought a ruthless war shedding our blood against a formidable military force, against a mighty power in Asia . . .[320]

But the LTTE did not wish to shut the door completely on India. To keep a window open for the future, it sought to assure New Delhi that it was not antagonistic either toward the Government of India or the people of India, but it was hurt at the 'misguided policies' of the earlier regime, which compelled it to oppose them.[321]

After the IPKF finally left Sri Lanka, Gandhi, now out of power, spoke about the compulsions which motivated him to go in for the IPKF route. In an interview to the Kolkata-based magazine, *Sunday* (19 August 1990) he said, 'I would like to point out that the IPKF in Sri Lanka was not fighting for Tamils against the Sinhalese. It was not fighting the Sinhalese against the Tamils. It was fighting for the unity and integrity of Sri Lanka.'

But did it resonate with the people or the government in Colombo? It was a fight between the two factions of people of the same country and third-party intervention was uncalled for. It is unfortunate that he still regretted the decision of the IPKF's departure. He had blamed it on the new government's 'keenness on distancing themselves from the previous regime's carefully considered policies than in making a real assessment of the damage that would be caused to both countries and their inter-relationship by any deviation from these policies'.[322]

Jayewardene had his own reason to regret the IPKF withdrawal which he felt would create a vacuum that he feared would be filled up by the LTTE.[323]

And thus closed an unfortunate chapter in Indo–Sri Lanka relations. Whatever its rationale, an interventionist policy proved disastrous and detrimental to India's long-term interest. India itself was facing a similar problem of separatism in its border state of Punjab where some separatists armed and financed by neighbouring Pakistan were operating against India's territorial integrity. There were differences whether it was a political problem or one of security. None however, disputed India's right to deal with the problem in a manner which in New Delhi's assessment was appropriate. New Delhi had every reason to accuse Pakistan of cross-border terrorism and taking undue advantage of a minority community's presumed grievances, providing them sanctuary, finance and training, supplying arms and allowing the use of Pakistan's territory to mount attacks across the international border into India.

The problem Sri Lanka faced was not too different from the one faced by India. Essentially, it was a minority problem. Their initial demand for parity of their language with Sinhala and then escalating it to a merger of the north and east provinces to create a united Tamil province had created doubts in Colombo given the Tamils' demand for a homeland and then, Eelam or independence.

The de-induction of the IPKF finally closed the unfortunate chapter which had begun with the signing of the Indo–Sri Lanka Accord on 29 July 1987. After almost three years of IPKF operations, the Tamil problem continues to linger till this day. It is now on the back burner, because of the defeat of the LTTE and the elimination of Prabhakaran himself at the hands of the Sri Lankan army. Tragically, his innocent minor son too was killed by the Sri Lankan army. New Delhi became a tool in Tamil hands, since it was they, particularly Prabhakaran, who charted the course of events and New Delhi was helpless to make them see reason. Even the TULF, a moderate Tamil organization, was marginalized because Prabhakaran overpowered it by bumping off any one who tried a different path than that chartered by him. His approach was egoistic to their language and culture. New Delhi failed to realize that Prabhakaran and his LTTE members were fascists who subscribed to the idea of ethnic superiority of Tamils. Using violence as its creed, the LTTE cadres were equally motivated, and they lived in military-style discipline even conquering the fear of death.

The Tamils being a minority by numbers suffered from a persecution mania even before the independence of the island. This aspect was looked into by the Soulbury Commission which in its report in 1945 before the island's independence, concluded that there was no substantial indication of a general policy of discrimination on the part of the government of Ceylon and that the minorities were exaggerating the precariousness of their situation.[324]

Indeed, in any badly skewed population ratio there are occasions when prejudices creep in and certain steps get taken by the majority community to the disadvantage of the minority community, it causes grievances. In Sri Lanka, the Parliamentary forum and other peaceful means were not closed to them. They held the balance between the two Sinhala political parties, the UNP and the SLFP. Whenever the elections returned a hung house, and there were indeed such occasions, Tamil support was sought and they were part of coalition governments. That they failed to use these opportunities to their advantage speaks of their lack of strategic thinking.

At no time since its involvement in Sri Lanka, did India assess the Tamils' willingness to adjust or arrive at compromises on their demands. But with India backing their demands, it made them intransigent and hopeful that they would finally get them their homeland or Eelam as in the case of Bangladesh. While militants like the LTTE revolted, the moderates rejected any compromise solution offered by Colombo and New Delhi failed to rebuke them for their stubbornness. Their behaviour in Thimphu stands out an as example of their obstinacy and uncompromising attitude.

One has simply to recall what Indira Gandhi had said when the Soviet Union had intervened in Afghanistan that, 'no country is justified in entering another country'. Once again, she had stated that '…any situation arising out of the use of force in international relations and intervention or interference in the internal affairs of a sovereign state is inadmissible'. On 15 December 1980 after the visit of Soviet leader Leonid Brezhnev, Mrs Gandhi had said in Parliament that, 'we have expressed our opinion on all forms of outside interference'.[325] Standing on a high pedestal and pontificating to others, both Mrs Gandhi and her son, Rajiv, crossed the Lakshman Rekha which is fundamental to relations between nations and against the basic principle of international relations. India's intervention put it at a disadvantage in the eyes of the international community particularly among its neighbours. The outcome of this policy has been injurious to India's long-term interests. Tragically, Rajiv Gandhi had to pay with his life for his Sri Lanka policy, first aligning with Prabhakaran and then leaving him in the lurch. If he was not spared, neither was Premadasa, who made use of Prabhakaran to get the IPKF out of the island. The LTTE was a monster which devoured both. At the end, the Tamils lost their bargaining power and India its moral authority to intervene on their behalf.

If today India's neighbours cosy up with China, it is thanks to the overbearing and chauvinistic policies of New Delhi in the past. What an Indian scholar said in an article in the *Economic and Political Weekly* bears testimony to it.

> Sri Lanka uses China to balance India's dominance in the Indian Ocean region by supporting in 21st century 'Maritime Silk Road Strategy', thereby increasing its diplomatic negotiating leverage. Chinese scholars view India as a dominant power and hence view any South Asian nation that cultivates a relationship with China as a tool to offset New Delhi's influence in the region. Consequently, China seizes every chance when Sri Lanka and other nations in the neighbourhood seek to balance India.[326]

India's policy was denial of the reality of post-war politics that it is the people who become sovereign and it is their will which prevails in deciding their nation's policies in the world today. The mighty American army could not subdue the will of the Vietnamese people, nor could the other superpower, the Soviet Union, break the will of the Afghans. India is surrounded with small countries, which are not contiguous among themselves and must deal with each other only through India, and hence the need to cater to their sensitivities becomes paramount.

The Sinhalese people were against the accord and India was fully aware of it and yet it chose to ram itself against a reluctant people— both Tamils and Sinhalese—and suffered the avoidable ignominy. The accord was an attempt to reconcile the irreconcilable aspirations of two citizens of the same country and if it failed in its application, it surprised no one, except perhaps its author. Later, on 1 December 2022, launching the book *Geopolitics of Technology* edited by Ashley Tellis and others, Tellis had asked External Affairs Minister S. Jaishankar about India's experience in projecting its military power outside India. Jaishankar had pointed to the IPKF experience and added it was a 'very, very difficult, troubling and counterproductive' experience and India should not allow itself again to be 'sucked in endless and open-ended commitments'.

V

India–United States Civil Nuclear Energy Agreement, 2008[*]

On 10 October 2008, the Government of India and the US Government signed an agreement on Civil Nuclear Energy Cooperation covering nuclear reactors and aspects of the associated nuclear fuel cycle, including enrichment and reprocessing. It contained a full reflection of the key understandings of the 18 July 2005 and March 2006 joint statements and India's separation plan. The agreement sought to enable the creation of a strategic reserve of nuclear fuel to guard against any disruption of supply over the lifetime of India's reactors. The agreement provided that all aspects of the nuclear programme would remain unhindered. It also provided for multi-layered consultations.

The agreement had overcome the disabilities created in the background of the Cold War particularly since India's peaceful nuclear explosion in 1974 and its refusal to sign the Nuclear Non-Proliferation Treaty (NPT). The prevailing regime was set by the nuclear states, who also happened to be the five permanent members of the UN Security Council—the US, the Soviet Union, the United Kingdom, France and China. All of them had tested their nuclear weapons before 1 January 1967 as ordained by the NPT and signed on 12 June 1968, which came

---

[*] Between 2002 and 2013, the author has published an annual series titled *India's Foreign Relations* for the Ministry of External Affairs, which was a compendium of all documents bearing on India's foreign relations in a particular year irrespective of the ministry/department which originated the document. In the current essay, these are referred to as 'IFR'.

into force on 5 March 1970. Since the Indian test happened in 1974, and it had not signed the NPT, India was treated like a pariah by the self-proclaimed high priests of non-proliferation. An esoteric subject, it turned out to be a 'problem' between India and the US for many years. The US had adopted legislation which sought to contain and restrain India's ambitions to develop a nuclear energy programme even if for its economic development. The NPT through its framework, the International Atomic Energy Agency (IAEA) through safeguards and the Nuclear Suppliers' Group (NSG) through its trade regulations, created barriers for India's access to nuclear technology. The restrictive regime was further enlarged by the technology control and restraint regimes established thereafter, like the Missile Technology Control Regime, Australia Group, Wassenaar Arrangement, etc.[1] The US had taken an unfriendly attitude on Kashmir but India had taken it in its stride.

India's defeat at the hands of China in 1962 and China's nuclear test in 1964 had set India thinking of its security afresh. New Delhi which was an ardent supporter of disarmament and had asked for the abolition of all nuclear weapons in the early years of its independence was forced to give up its old policy in this respect. It then considered the pros and cons of going nuclear, but found its cost too prohibitive. It canvassed with the nuclear powers to see if they would give a collective guarantee against nuclear blackmail to non-nuclear states. The top leadership of the MEA—External Affairs Minister M.C. Chagla, Foreign Secretary C.S. Jha and Principal Secretary to the Prime Minister L.K. Jha, separately visited Moscow, Washington, London and Paris but at the end were disappointed since none of them would subscribe to a statement which, in legal terms would amount to taking on indefinite and unlimited liabilities beyond the UN Charter. It was then that India had started thinking of an independent nuclear programme.[2]

India conducted its first peaceful nuclear test in 1974 which attracted severe sanctions from the US. Unmindful of them, New Delhi continued to develop nuclear energy which culminated in a weaponized nuclear test in 1998. Pakistan not to be left behind and for parity with India conducted its test a couple of weeks later to the mortification of the US since its policy of preventing the proliferation for nuclear weapons had gone for a six. Washington mainly held India responsible for this profane development and enforced still stricter sanctions. India justified that its test was necessary for its security against China.[3]

Be as it may, its weaponized nuclear test gave notice to the world, that India had unambiguously, unapologetically and irrevocably become a nuclear armed power. US President Bill Clinton rejected India's security justification and said that, 'It is not necessary to manifest national greatness by doing this.' Clinton's perception that the tests were more a vanity affair than a 'cold national calculation of its security needs' was seen in New Delhi as 'insulting' and ill-informed. The *New York Times* editorially undermined the tests when it said on 13 May 1998 that 'beyond minor border disputes, China had no hostile design on India'.[4]

Upset by the United States' reaction to India's nuclear test, Jaswant Singh, who held various portfolios under PM Atal Bihari Vajpayee's NDA-I government, such as finance, external affairs and defence, lamented in the US journal, *Foreign Affairs*, against nuclear apartheid. He made a case for India's nuclear test and said India suffered because of the policies of the nuclear powers. He pointed out that after the end of the Cold War, little had been done to 'ameliorate India's security concerns'. The rise of China and continued strains with both China and Pakistan had made the 1980s and 1990s 'a greatly troubling period for India'. Jaswant Singh regretted the extension of the NPT in 1995 'indefinitely and un-conditionally' and their perpetuation in the hands of five countries busily modernizing their own nuclear arsenal. He insisted that India was a nuclear weapon state without anyone granting it that status. India's 'weapons are of self-defence, to ensure that India is not subjected to nuclear coercion'.[5] India while conducting the tests had vowed not to be the first to use its nuclear weapons.

In view of India's nuclear test, any chance of the US relaxing restrictions now met with hostile reception. Both the arms control organizations as well as non-proliferation high priests were outraged. The countries which were against giving India any access to nuclear technology argued that if India got nuclear fuel supplies from others, it would help it to free its domestic fuel for weapons while using the imported supplies for domestic use.

To India's advantage, another dimension emerged which changed the strategic scenario altogether. The heydays of US–China relations appeared to be coming to an end. Washington, looking at the future appeared keen not only to roll back its cooperation with China, but looked for a counterweight in Asia. India suggested itself. As a big country it had made sufficient progress since the days of 1962 to emerge a strong power in Asia rivalling China. It was, therefore, perceived by many experts that Washington in loosening technology control in favour of India would try to trap India into an anti-China framework. The interests of both appeared to converge. Ashley Tellis, an expert in Security and South Asian affairs, and former Special Assistant to the US Ambassador in India, Robert Blackwill, had argued that continuation of the earlier policy of keeping India at bay would have worked against the US's long-term interests.[6]

At the beginning of the new millennium, some changes in the US posturing toward India were perceptible. Perhaps 9/11 had made Washington see India's logic on terrorism more clearly. In the changed scenario, the contributions of the Indian diaspora too played an important part in the US thinking toward India. The economic liberalisation of the nineties had become attractive to American business and by the turn of the millennium 33 per cent of the cumulative foreign investments in India were from there. Interestingly, while Washington was trying to turn a new page, the Indian public continued to suffer from past prejudices, which took time to change. With all these developments, at the political level, the US was still holding on.

Washington, under President Clinton, after imposing sanctions had made its relaxation conditional on: (i) sign the Comprehensive Nuclear-Test-Ban Treaty (CTBT), (ii) establish a fissile material cutoff regime, (iii) restrain its strategic missile capability, (iv) establish stricter export controls, and finally (v) a solution of the Kashmir issue.[7]

The genesis of the new policy of the US is to be found in the article that Condoleezza Rice, Senior Fellow at the Hoover Institution and Professor of Political Science at Stanford University and future NSA and Secretary of State to President George Bush, wrote for the American journal *Foreign Affairs* under the title, 'Promoting the National Interest'. A committed Republican, Rice pointed out the alternatives for the US foreign policy under a Republican administration since she felt there were various drawbacks in the policy under the Democratic President, Bill Clinton. Making a concrete suggestion she pointed out the need to pay closer attention to India's role in world affairs. She decried America's 'strong tendency conceptually to connect India with Pakistan and to think only Kashmir or the nuclear competition between the two states'. She said India was 'an element in China's calculations' but not in Washington's. She insisted, it should 'be in America's too'. While conceding 'India was not a great power yet' she asserted 'it has the potential to emerge as one'.[8] Later, Rice in her book, *No Higher Honour*, recalled that the idea for a change in policy toward South Asia matured while campaigning for President George W. Bush's election. The change had become necessary she said, since the US was 'fed up with trying constantly to defuse the situation between India and Pakistan' for terror attacks, which she said 'came from Pakistani elements'. She saw Pakistan as a 'troubled state, riddled with extremism in its mosques, its madrassas, and unfortunately, in its security services'.[9]

It was about this time that a 635-page monograph by Ashley Tellis, written for the Rand Corporation appeared. It supported Condoleezza Rice's thesis. Sumit Ganguly, Professor at Texas University, in his review article in *Foreign Affairs* found the American policy running counter to much of the prevailing wisdom about non-proliferation. Tellis had argued forcefully that the US should pursue a differential rather than a universal non-proliferation policy, one that explicitly takes into account the particular security concerns of India and adopt a more nuanced non-proliferation agenda towards India. Sanctions originally devised to coerce India on nuclear issues had outlived their usefulness.[10] This was also Ambassador Blackwill's conclusion in 2002. He had argued that while

[E]xercises, visits and exchanges are key to build joint military capacities for future interoperability, India also naturally, views defence sales as a way to gauge the potential for substantive future bilateral military cooperation. In that regard, I am pleased to report that the past political disconnect that hamstrung American defence sales to India are fading away.[11]

While sanctions had a baneful effect on the Indian economy, they also alienated a significant section of the Indian strategic community in the US. It did, at the same time, help India to develop a self-reliant capacity in critical military technologies.

With the collapse of the Soviet Union, the country that had stood by India in war and peace, ceased to exist. India's Cold War policy posture of non-alignment too lost its relevance. India now saw the US as the kingpin of the unipolar world. Overcoming the hang-ups and hesitations of the past, New Delhi departed from Nehru's much-admired policy of non-alignment, the positivity of which however, remained shrouded in mystery. Any departure from it was considered irreverent by the successive governments which were headed either by Nehru's progeny or other Congressmen or with Congress support which found it difficult to depart from his policies. The Indian people too had become prisoners of past narrative and were not ready for a change.

If one looks at the India–US relations in the broader context after the collapse of the Soviet Union, it was Bush Senior, who started thinking of relations with India. A beginning was made when he met with Indian Prime Minister Narasimha Rao on 31 January 1992 in New York on the side lines of the UN summit. They discussed ways and means to make a fresh beginning, overcoming the past. In their discussions, nuclear cooperation did come up for consideration as the starting point. This was at the root of all the strains in their relations when the US had slapped restrictions on cooperation with India for testing a nuclear device in 1974. There were some further discussions from time to time but not much progress was achieved.[12]

Emerging India was seen as a 'global economic power, based largely on the creativity of its people'. The US was so overwhelmed with the contributions of the Indian diaspora, that an impressed President felt it necessary to seek a 'broad and deep relationship with India, which he saw as a natural fit for the US strategic interests'.[13]

Before Rice's article in *Foreign Affairs*, some influential Republicans who were Bush's foreign policy advisors and included such luminaries as Philip David Zelikow, Nicholas Burns and Ambassador Blackwill, cumulatively called 'Vulcans' were determined to change the terms of the US–India engagement. They sought to find ways to connect directly with New Delhi's political elite and adopted a different approach from the past called 'de-hyphenation', i.e., to delink India from Pakistan in the formulation of policies toward South Asia.[14] Blackwill, as already pointed out, as the US Ambassador in New Delhi (July 2001–July 2003) in Bush's first term, was a protagonist of better India–US relations.

The Bush administration, however, continued to apply restrictions on the high-leveraged military technologies for fear of undermining the regional military balance with Pakistan.[15] The developments in Afghanistan in the wake of 9/11 had made Pakistan once again a valuable ally of the US. Bush was not prepared to give up on Pakistan, since it was a longstanding relationship, which remained crucial to peace in the region.[16] India was unhappy that Bush had given Pakistan the status of a 'major NATO Ally' in his first term.[17]

However, the need for a change had otherwise become pressing, since the liberalization of the Indian economy in the nineties by Prime Minister Narasimha Rao. Prime Minister Atal Bihari Vajpayee too had grasped the need for liberalization and had given a strong dose of reforms to the economy. India in its reformist mood acutely felt the absence of high technology, which had become a scare commodity because of the restrictive policies of the US which held their monopoly. Therefore, when lights flickered in Washington, India did not miss them. In 2001, in a breakthrough meeting between Prime Minister Vajpayee and President Bush in New York, several areas of cooperation were identified, one of which was stimulating high-technology commerce, toward realizing the goal of transforming India–US relations. A year later, the two countries agreed to stimulate 'bilateral high technology commerce' towards achieving the goal of 'transforming India–US relations'.[18]

Notwithstanding India's refusal to contribute to the America's Iraq operations, US Defence Secretary, Donald Rumsfeld while looking for effective allies to meet the challenge America faced in Asia, zeroed in on India. India had the second largest army in the world with experience of fighting insurgencies in various terrains and was perceived a valuable asset as an ally.

As the US moved towards dismantling its old policy and tested Indian waters, it found the government in New Delhi, receptive to the changes which Washington had envisaged. To start with, the sticking point remained high-technology trade including the 'dual use' items. America, however, needed India and it agreed to provide that satisfaction against diversion to third parties of dual use technologies.[19]

Foreign Secretary Kanwal Sibal on a visit to Washington, yet again, reiterated India's assurance when he said:

> Government of India's commitment to non-proliferation has been unwavering and its record impeccable...as our scientific and technological capabilities in the private sector have grown, we have further strengthened our controls in export of nuclear and missile related materials and technological as a national security imperative.[20]

Philip Zelikow, counsellor at the State Department and otherwise a scholar of some repute, in consultation with Dr Rice had drawn up the National Security Strategy document in 2002. He noted differences with India on its nuclear and missile programme as well as on the pace of India's economic reforms. He argued there was a common strategic interest between the two countries. He said, 'Today we start with a view of India as growing world power with which we have common strategic interests.' He advocated a growing partnership with India which would enable the US to address and shape a dynamic future.[21] The memo that Zelikow drew for President Bush laid down the road map for bringing India into the nuclear regime. The President who had already been thinking on these lines, heartily endorsed it.[22] The pace, however, remained somewhat sluggish and there were hesitations on the part of the US. In July 2002, in Bush's first term, National Security Advisor Brajesh Mishra's initiative for nuclear cooperation with the US was ignored by US Secretary of State Colin Powell, even when Mishra offered to place a number of nuclear reactors under international safeguards.[23]

In 2002 and 2003, there was a frequent exchange of high-powered visits between the two countries and several forums sprung up to discuss the varied issues connected with the new policy. The media was obsessed with terrorism and Pakistan could not sense the all-important changes which were in the making. There was no public discussion on these important issues being considered between the two countries either.

A series of dialogues on the nuclear issue, following India's nuclear test, between Foreign Minister Jaswant Singh and US Deputy Secretary of State, Strobe Talbott, had helped bring some understanding between India and the US. India was seen warming towards Washington after the standoff on India's nuclear test had died down. Prime Minister Vajpayee's visit to Washington in February 2003 was utilized to affirm the commitment to qualitatively transform India–US relations and to discuss ways to stimulate bilateral high-technology commerce as a step toward enhancing the new relationship between them.[24]

On 13 January 2004, Prime Minister Vajpayee in Delhi and President Bush in Washington, simultaneously made statements on 'Next Step in Strategic Partnership'. They expressed their agreement to expand cooperation in three specific areas—civil nuclear activities, civilian space programme and high-technology trade, besides expanding dialogue on missile defence. It was stated that the cooperation in these fields would deepen the ties 'through reciprocal steps that will build on each other'.[25] The completion of NSSP-I was expected to increase further cooperation between US companies and India's civilian space programme by eliminating delays and uncertainty in processing requirements. This phase was completed in 2004.

2004 turned out to be an important year in many ways. It was the beginning of the second term of President Bush when he started in right earnest to devote attention to relations with India. It was also in 2004 after the general elections in India, that another coalition government, this time led by the Congress party under Prime Minister Dr Manmohan Singh took over the administration in New Delhi. One of the coalition partners in the new government was the Left group with fifty-nine seats which had ideological reservations on closer relations with the US. The former Foreign Service Officer, Natwar Singh, emerged as the new external affairs minister. Another former IFS officer and former Foreign Secretary J.N. Dixit replaced Brajesh Mishra as the national security advisor. The new Foreign

Secretary was Shyam Saran and the new Ambassador in Washington, Ronen Sen.

In September 2004, it was announced in Washington that with the conclusion of the first phase of the 'Next Step in Strategic Partnership' (NSSP), the US had been able to make modifications in its export licencing policies that would permit certain exports to power plants in safeguarded nuclear facilities. They were declared fully 'consistent with the U.S. government's non-proliferation laws, obligations and objectives'.[26] This presaged a change in the perception of the US on the necessity of nuclear energy and that it was no longer as hazardous as before and could fulfil the energy needs of tomorrow. In April 2005, the White House came out with a new energy policy: 'nuclear power can provide for tomorrow's needs since technology had made it safe, cleaner and more efficient'. It was made known that the President would encourage new nuclear power plants and eliminate the delay in the nuclear plant licensing process by modifying the existing laws.[27]

Reducing dependence of countries on hydrocarbon became the keyword of Bush's energy policy.

While discussing a cap on India's nuclear weapons programme, the US concluded that while not aiding India's nuclear weapons programme it would ensure that international cooperation with India was adequately safeguarded. Its principal motivation for agreeing to change the global nuclear rules in favour of India was a strategic one—to transform relations with India amidst a changing global balance of power.[28]

As the first phase of NSSP got completed, Foreign Secretary Shyam Saran frankly told the Americans that its implementation should not be seen as a 'reward' of some kind of good behaviour on New Delhi's part, rather it should be seen as an expression of a relationship based on a commonality of interests and concern between two democracies in the area of nuclear non-proliferation and extension of growing defence cooperation.[29]

Natwar Singh had visited Washington to represent the Government of India at the funeral service of former President Ronald Reagan. He used the opportunity to assure Washington that in view of national consensus on foreign policy, the new government would continue with the earlier policy.[30]

Those were early days of the coalition government and Natwar Singh, perhaps had not taken into account the Left's allergy towards the US, of which the prime minister was cognizant. Within the Congress party itself, there were strong left-leaning elements which had ideological antipathy toward the US. A former chairman of the Atomic Energy Regulatory Board, A. Gopalakrishnan was sceptical of any cooperation with the US, particularly after the experience of Tarapur, where it had withheld fuel supplies after 1974. A confident Gopalakrishnan felt that 'India's main interest in imports of reactors was because of the potential for attracting foreign capital investment into our nuclear sector and not necessarily for any superior technology inflow'. Yet, he believed that in the area of fuel supplies, India would need American cooperation in getting international supply of enriched uranium.[31] Apart from Gopalakrishnan, there were other nuclear scientists, who were naysayers. But the prime minister personally was in favour of relations with the US which was a source of high technology, essential for India's rapid economic growth.[32] But political compulsions were far more important for the prime minister than a warm relationship with Washington since he knew the Left parties were unlikely to extend support for it in Parliament, which was critical with the fifty-nine seats that they held. He wanted to tread cautiously.

Apart from the Left's reservations, Prime Minister Singh was not unaware that even some of his advisors were split on deeper relations with the US. Thirty years of US efforts to cap, freeze and roll back India's nuclear programme, had scared Indian atomic scientists, engineers and diplomats, who had encountered American hostility all along. The past experience deterred them from accepting the change. It was argued that even if the present administration was helpful, there was no guarantee future administrations would be equally conducive.[33] However, 'it was clear across the Indian political spectrum that the economic transformation of India required at least a working relationship with the global hegemon, the United States, whose orders prevailed globally'.[34] Despite trepidations, Prime Minister

Manmohan Singh did not balk at shaking hands with the US when he met President Bush in New York in September 2004. They were able to refigure their relations as a partnership between 'two equals'.[35] The prime minister's speech at the 'Council on Foreign Relations' was a reiteration of India's assurance to the US of its 'responsible record' against proliferation when he himself expressed his concern 'at the unrestrained proliferation of nuclear and missile technology'. He claimed the NSSP to which India and the US had committed their countries, would raise their cooperation in these areas to higher levels.[36] The NSSP agreement enabled the Bush administration to give clearance for a classified technical presentation of the Patriot Advanced Capability (PAC)-2 anti-ballistic missile system to India in February 2005 in response to a request made in 2002.[37]

The PM warmly congratulated President Bush on his re-election for the second term, assuring him that India would stand by the US 'in strengthening international peace and stability'. Having said that, Dr Singh expected a new road map, that would be an integral element in their broader relationship that would enable them 'to moving ahead expeditiously through the NSSP'.[38] In Bush's second term, Condoleezza Rice, who was national security adviser in his first term, was elevated as Secretary of State which was a trigger for the policy change towards India.

On 7 November, Prime Minister Manmohan Singh speaking to journalists accompanying him on board his flight to The Hague to attend the India–EU summit once again stressed the importance of the US to India's economic development and said, 'We are living in a world of unequal powers . . . we have to use the available international system to promote our interests and engage the US,' which played 'a very important role in world economy and the world political system.'[39]

US Defence Secretary Rumsfeld on a visit to India in December 2004 told the prime minister that President Bush had 'impressed upon his senior colleagues the importance of improving relations with India'.[40] And then came calling Condoleezza Rice, the elevated Secretary of State. Her discussions in New Delhi gave her an inkling into the hidden potential of the relationship. It was her first visit abroad after assuming charge of the new portfolio, which underlined the importance that she attached to relations with New Delhi. As already stated, she was the one who had first recognized the importance of India in US's strategic policy in Asia, which looked set to unfold now.

The prime minister underlined to Rice the importance of energy and need for dialogue between their countries 'covering all aspects, including various traditional and non-traditional sources of energy'. Later in a media briefing, the MEA spokesperson clarified that energy cooperation included nuclear energy.[41]

Rice's trip was unique in that she put forth an unprecedented framework for cooperation, 'something that took even the Indian government by surprise'. While many in India were focused on the future of US–Pakistan ties, Rice transformed the terms of the debate completely, by revealing that the Bush administration was willing to consider civilian nuclear energy cooperation with India.[42] She had promised a presidential visit, and most important, publicly declared the end of 'hyphenation' when she told the *India Today* magazine that 'the Bush administration no longer saw the need to always speak of India and Pakistan in the same sentence'.[43] End of 'hyphenation' was her point of conviction. Even in 2000 when suggesting a new-look policy towards South Asia, Rice had suggested a de-hyphenation between India and Pakistan. The visit essentially was her recognition of India's importance as a factor contributing positivity to the stability and prosperity of Asia.[44]

Shortly before Rice's visit, India's Nuclear Chief Anil Kakodkar publicly made a 'momentous' announcement that India's largest 540 MWe Tarapur-IV had gone critical despite the technology denial regime imposed by the US. Former Chairman of the Nuclear Power Corporation, S.K. Jain, who was also member of the Atomic Energy Commission, proudly referred to the occasion as a maturing of India's nuclear technology regime.[45] Though India had indeed developed nuclear technology, Rice's visit put the spotlight on its critical role in expediting economic development, an area where India was deficient. In 2008, the Atomic Energy Commission had said that the current installed capacity was 6.78 GW and it was expected to go up to 63 GW by 2032.

However, the nuclear disaster in Japan stressed the need for reconsideration. But Prime Minister Manmohan Singh was quick to assure the nation that India's nuclear hub was safe with the added assurance from the nuclear establishment that it would undertake a technical review of safety systems.[46]

At this point, the prime minister was somewhat surprised to receive a call from President Bush explaining his decision to supply F-16 aircraft to Pakistan. It was a significant and one-of-a-kind gesture since such courtesy had never been extended to India in the past. The PM expressed his disappointment, but there was no persistent campaign in the Indian Parliament or media against the F-16s as in the past.[47] The State Department spokesperson insisted that the supply of weapons to Pakistan would not affect the overall balance of power in South Asia. India, while not satisfied, acknowledged that their relations 'were never better'. Clarifying the change in his personal stance towards the US, K. Natwar Singh told the BBC 'that was old Natwar and this is new Natwar'.[48]

By now there were enough straws in the wind to convince one that the PM had decided to join hands with the United States for faster economic growth and better political relations. India Inc. too favoured closer relations because they could see fresh business opportunities opening up in this relationship. A survey in 2007, by the US-based PEW Research Center confirmed that India's middle classes were more pro-US than those in most other countries. As many as 71 per cent had a favourable opinion of the US, the highest proportion among the sixteen countries surveyed, compared with 54 per cent three years ago.[49]

In 2005, EAM Natwar Singh during his visit to Washington found the President appreciating the talent of the Indian people, and to his pleasant surprise, Bush determined 'to use the next four years of his second term to further strengthen their relations to take them to a much higher level'. Bush had little hesitation to describe India a 'global power'. The President's keenness for energy cooperation with India included 'civil nuclear energy cooperation'.[50] Dr Rice, already committed to deeper relations, in her interaction with

EAM emphasized her country's endeavour to push their relations 'to a new level' in several areas and to 'accelerate the work on the NSSP-II initiative.[51]

Natwar Singh did not agree with reports that the US was using India to counter China and neither did he expect it. He said India valued good relations with America, which it wanted to widen, deepen and broaden but it was not intended to gang up against China and neither would it work. He mentioned the visit of the Chinese Premier, Wen Jiabao, to India which he said was a 'resounding success'.[52]

But China certainly was on Washington's mind. After the collapse of the Soviet Union, the US perceived a rising China would threaten its domination in the long run. That it was the United States' investments and technology transfer in the past, which had been responsible for China's faster rise, was another story. Washington too was worried at the threats that Japan, its biggest ally in Asia, was facing from Beijing, besides its monetary policies were no less distressing. The US calculated that an unbridled China was not in its interest and started looking for a regional power which would stand up to China in a crisis. Under the circumstances, the US hedged its bets on India. The US calculated that by bolstering India's capabilities, the largest country in China's neighbourhood, and with a score to settle, could arrest the growth of Chinese influence in the Indian Ocean rimlands.[53] At this stage, China's energies were certainly focused on Asia trying to build its capacity to dominate this virgin region. It adopted a benign foreign policy aimed at projecting its rise as a peaceful one, so as not to raise any apprehensions in countries in its vicinity. Unfortunately, India's earlier policies toward its smaller neighbours were domineering, which incentivized them to welcome China's presence to counter India. That China was on Washington's mind when it decided to work with India has been confirmed by no less a person than Stephen Hadley, Bush's NSA in his second term. Speaking at the Carnegie Endowment on 15 March 2023, he said while many believed China was the rising power, Bush strongly felt it was India which had emerged as a global power and hence the need to woo it. At this point while looking for policy alternatives which would be attractive to India to walk into Washington's camp, the US policy analysts were unanimous in their belief that it was the nuclear apartheid and nuclear technology denial regime that had alienated India from the US since 1974. Now the need for a change in the old policy had become imperative to attract India which led the US to scrap the contentious policy. This change in policy was found in sync with the fact that its policy of trying to put the Indian nuclear genie back in the bottle had failed. If India needed to be propitiated, it had to be helped to continue to harness nuclear energy for its progress.[54]

This was in line with the general thinking that the tectonic shift that took place in India–US bilateral relations was born out of increasing fears in the US business and strategic circles about China.[55]

India too believed that China was a factor in Washington's calculation for its policy change. Foreign Secretary Shyam Saran confirmed this in an interview to Prof. Zoya Hasan. She quoted him to say, 'For the U.S. India can be relied upon to emerge as a counterweight to China. This was the bedrock of the India-US strategic partnership.'[56]

Ashley Tellis had warned Washington that:

[B]y integrating India into the non-proliferation order at the cost of capping the size of its eventual nuclear deterrent (the U.S. would) threaten to place New Delhi at a severe disadvantage vis-à-vis Beijing, a situation that could not only undermine Indian security but also U.S. interests in Asia in the face of the prospective rise of Chinese power over the long term.[57]

For India, at least initially, the prime mover for better relations with the US was the urgent need for nuclear power for accelerated economic progress of the country. It was presented as a panacea to the enormous energy needs of a rapidly growing economy. As the prime minister had observed, 'no government can afford to shrink the responsibility of ensuring energy security and hope to find favour with the people.'[58] Another reason for better relations with the US was to end nuclear isolation since there were problems in getting the required quantity of uranium for its existing nuclear reactors not only from the US but also from other countries because of the Nuclear Suppliers Group (NSG) restrictions applicable to non-NPT nations. India was also worried at China's resurgence which 'was altering the power balance across Asia–Pacific region' and in the absence of effective regional institutions, the region was now as volatile as during the Cold War.[59]

Already there were several India–US groups working on various items of cooperation, the most important being the Defence Policy Group. In May 2005, a new group was formed for 'dialogue and action on issues associated with civilian uses of nuclear energy and its control'.[60]

The visit of Prime Minister Dr Manmohan Singh to Washington was now scheduled for July 2005. There were hectic preparations in India a month before. Similarly, advance preparations were made between the two countries on various issues to prepare for the summit meeting. The most important meeting in this connection was the one between US Under Secretary of State Nicholas Burns and Foreign Secretary Shyam Saran. They conducted an overall review of the entire gamut of issues including NSSP and noted the progress made in that respect. Burns appreciated the legislation which India had adopted against Weapons of Mass Destruction (WMD) and to control the export of sensitive and dual-use equipment and technologies. India had also strengthened its systems to enforce it.[61]

On 28 June 2005, India and America signed the Defence Cooperation framework agreement. One of its aims was to collaborate in missile defence, to strengthen the abilities of their militaries to respond quickly to disaster situations, including in combined operations.[62]

Defence Minister Pranab Mukherjee having signed the framework agreement trashed speculation that the framework was at the expense of Russia or any other country. When asked by the media whether Washington would be a 'reliable partner' he added one had to be 'practical and realistic' given every country's own specific laws. Mukherjee again said given the geopolitical environment and India's proven track record, India should justifiably be allowed to access all the technologies and defence equipment it needed. US Defence Secretary Rumsfeld had described 'military-to-military relationship as "excellent"'.

In choosing India, the US was cognizant of its human and material resources. It was a big country both in size and population which was young. India too had a vested interest in taming China to be able to resolve its border deadlock simmering since the sixties, but had failed to keep pace with China as its development galloped over the years and military power multiplied. Since the US had shown interest in canvassing its support, and their interests appeared to converge, it was easy for them to take the new road that suddenly opened up.

Mukherjee while speaking to journalists before leaving for America rejected the insinuation that the UPA government was following the NDA agenda under Vajpayee and insisted that it was following an independent foreign policy and the framework agreement would widen India–US friendship in the important sector of defence. He too tried to allay the fears of the left parties, stating that India had 'neither signed the framework under duress, nor have we applied pressure on the other side to sign it'.[63] He insisted it was not a violation of any of the points of the Common Minimum Programme of the parties to the coalition government. Apart from the defence minister, Foreign Secretary Shyam Saran too, described the criticism due to a misunderstanding and added, 'it set out the "parameters" within which the two countries could potentially cooperate if it was in their interest.'[64] On the question of missile defence, Mukherjee insisted that there was no question of accepting a missile defence shield from 'anybody'. Calling his remarks, a welcome step back, *The Hindu* exulted: 'In one stroke Mukherjee repudiated one of the central elements of the new defence framework.'[65] Mukherjee later told the Rajya Sabha that the framework agreement updated the 'Agreed Minutes of Defence Relations' signed in January 1995 and identified global security threats that had seriously affected India's security such as terrorism and violent religious extremism and the proliferation of weapons of mass destruction etc. It was an ongoing effort to expand cooperation with the US in the field of high technology by using the US as a potential source of advanced defence equipment and technology, thereby increasing our options.[66]

The domestic political criticism and opposition to the defence framework agreement was the result of genuine surprise at the fundamental changes underway in India's external relations and national security architecture. The framework agreement was indeed a watershed in defining the new direction and strategic significance of India's defence policy, as the prime minister had elucidated in his speech in Parliament. Replying to the debate on the motion of thanks to the president's address, he had said, 'Freedom to make policy choices and pursue our enduring objectives in an increasingly inter-dependent world,' it was necessary 'to evolve responses to the changing reality of an ever-changing world.' He assured the House that while 'the instruments of our policy, tactics and strategy we adopt may change from time to time, the values in which they are embedded are universal and will remain true for all times'.[67] Speaking to the Kerala Pradesh Congress Committee on 1 November 2006, the prime minister had said that the nation could not remain tied to the past and underlined the need for flexibility of tactics by widening its horizon.

The present state of relations between India and the US was in contrast to the past when despite all India's efforts to prove its credentials as a friend, it failed to impress Washington. The US mesmerized by Beijing, strengthened its ties with China and by default denied India the needed technology. This was the point Ambassador Blackwill and his advisor and expert in security matters, Ashley Tellis, had repeatedly made to the State Department, but it fell flat on the deaf ears of its bureaucracy in the first term of President Bush. But Condoleezza Rice's initiative had its impact on the President in his second term, when he forcefully pursued his agenda of wooing India. Again, it was Rice's influence that the US decided to de-hyphenate India and Pakistan and lean toward India while not writing off Pakistan.

The Left riled at the political possibility of India aligning itself with the US, particularly in defence matters, was caught in an isolationist trap and was not open to change to meet the requirements of a new India and meet the aspirations of the young generation.[68]

Before the prime minister visited the US, there was a meeting of the India–US energy group in Washington, DC, which set up five working groups on various aspects of energy cooperation.[69]

Foreign Secretary Shyam Saran briefing journalists on the prime minister's Washington visit, said that the world looked at India as a country 'which has array of capabilities and has the potential to emerge as a very important power in the future'. This new perception had created a desire among countries to partner with India. Saran insisted that India was going into a new relationship with the US in the 'spirit of confidence' and in the sense that 'this is going to be a partnership which brings benefits to India as well as the United States of America'. Underlining the need for energy security, which was 'increasingly becoming more challenging', Saran said India was looking at major partners for 'civil nuclear energy cooperation' and for a major transformational change. India wanted to take the cooperation from the stage of dialogue to the 'level of action'. Finally, underlining the purpose of the visit, he left no one in doubt that the US and India would cooperate together in civil nuclear energy and said, 'We look at it for an affirmation at the highest level.'[70] Shyam Saran, even earlier during the visit of Dr Rice to New Delhi, had emphasized that for a partnership to mean something, you have to treat India as a partner and not a target. 'Both,' he had said, 'could not go together.'[71]

Dr Singh in his interview with the *New York Times* before his departure, said his priority in Washington would be to 'persuade the United States to share more of its nuclear technology' with India. He hoped the two countries would move from being 'estranged to engaged' on issues of mutual interest. Dr Singh, however, made it clear that 'we are an independent power, we are not a client state, nor are we supplicant.'[72] Speaking to journalists on board the flight to Washington, the prime minister made some of the most important remarks, which set at rest the journalists' doubts about his agenda in Washington. He did not share the concern of the Left parties that India was moving away from an independent foreign policy. He insisted it would be a mistake to think that 'any prime minister of the Congress party would sell India cheap'. 'India is not for sale,' he told journalists. Assuring the accompanying journalists, he said he 'would safeguard it [India's honour] till the end of his life'. He expected journalists to appreciate that India could not function in isolation and we would try to find the areas of 'convergence'. Underlying the need for technology for India's progress, he said, while the bulk of resources for development were being mobilized domestically, international finance and technology transfer were available elsewhere. Finally, he said, 'At the moment India was subjected to "discriminatory restrictions" that had affected the state of technological development in a number of areas.' He hoped the world would have a better appreciation of the country's role as a responsible nuclear power and recognize that the restrictions have outlived their utility. The technological modernization was a priority for him on this visit.[73]

From his tête-à-tête with journalists, it was clear that Dr Singh was on a transformational journey to Washington. On arrival, he was briefed by the foreign secretary, who had arrived in Washington a couple of days ahead to study the language of the draft joint statement to be signed by the two heads of government/state. While the big picture was clear, the devil was in the details and there was abundance of devilish details as the two sides discussed how to craft an actual nuclear deal.[74]

The prime minister was aware of the assurance he had given to the Left partners that he would not sign any major agreement without consulting them first. Already, the Left was upset with Defence Minister Mukherjee signing the Defence framework agreement. On the flight to Washington, when the accompanying journalists had raised the question of the Left's stand on the nuclear deal, the prime minister had responded politely, but firmly, that he did not need any lessons in patriotism from the Left parties.[75]

In Washington, the PM had certain reservations as he studied the draft and was not comfortable or inclined to go ahead, which upset Dr Rice. As it happened, before he was to meet President Bush for the meeting next morning, Dr Singh was troubled by the concerns of the Left parties, who were crucial for the government's political survival. Taking note of his reluctance, Rice told the PM:

> You and President Bush are about to put U.S.-India relations on a fundamentally new footing. I know it is hard for you, but it is hard for the President too. I didn't come here to negotiate the language— only ask you to tell your officers to get this done; and let us get it done before you see the President.[76]

In the hurried last-minute negotiations, an agreeable language for the joint statement was found which enabled the prime minister to meet the president next morning. Dr Rice's efforts did help in restoring the PM's confidence, since at his arrival ceremony at the White House, his remarks were so effusive that it left no one in any doubt about the outcome of the meeting which was to take place in the next few minutes. He said:

> I am confident that from our talks today will emerge an agenda of cooperation that reflects a real transformation of our relationship [and] its realisation would help India meet the expectations of its people for a better quality of life, a more secure future and greater ability to participate in global creativity.[77]

That the prime minister was quite happy and satisfied with his discussions with the president and the results it achieved was evident from his remarks made at the banquet hosted by the president and Mrs Bush that night. Quoting Bernard Shaw about America and England as 'two countries divided by one language', he said that 'this held true for America and India as well'. He credited Bush for an improvement in their relations and added India was indebted to him and his 'sustained support for the transformational India–US relationship'.[78]

The landmark joint statement of 18 July 2005 which was regarded as the basic document on which the agreement for nuclear energy was built, over the next three years, began by underlining the need to combat terrorism, and creating an 'international environment conducive to promotion of democratic values'. It had five subtexts—(i) promotion of economic dialogue with a view to deepen economic relationship; (ii) strengthening of energy security for sustainable development; (iii) promotion of Global Democracy; (iv) non-proliferation to prevent the proliferation of Weapons of Mass Destruction, and (v) Science and High Technology Cooperation to strengthen non-proliferation commitments undertaken in NSSP.

The statement specifically recognized the importance of civilian nuclear energy in development and 'discussed India's plans to develop its civil nuclear energy programme'. President Bush recognized India as a country strongly committed to non-proliferation and against use of WMDs and accepted that India should 'acquire the same benefits and advantages as other such states'.

Apart from the generalities of the statement, the president undertook to seek an agreement from the Congress to: (i) adjust US laws and policies; (ii) work with friends and allies to adjust international regimes to enable full civil nuclear energy cooperation and trade with India including, but not limited to, expeditious consideration of fuel supplies for safeguarded nuclear reactors at Tarapur (suspended since India's peaceful nuclear explosion of 1974); and (iii) consult with its partners to accommodate India's request to join the International Thermonuclear Experimental Reactor (ITER).

The prime minister reciprocally agreed to (i) assume same responsibilities to acquire the now offered benefits; (ii) identify and separate civil and military nuclear facilities and programmes in a phased manner; (iii) file a declaration regarding civilian facilities with the International Atomic Energy Agency (IAEA) under its safeguards; (iv) sign and adhere to an Additional Protocol with respect to civilian nuclear facilities; (v) continuing India's unilateral moratorium on nuclear testing; (vi) work with the US for conclusion of a Multilateral Fissile Material Cut-off Treaty; (vii) refrain from transfer of enrichment reprocessed technologies to states that do not have them and supporting international efforts to limit their spread, and (viii) ensure necessary steps to secure nuclear materials and technology through comprehensive export control legizlation and through harmonisation and adherence to Missile Technology Control Regime (MTCR) and Nuclear Suppliers Group (NSG) guidelines.[79]

The joint statement laid down the roadmap which enabled India to exit the nuclear ghetto and end the apartheid regime in which it had found itself since 1974. In superficial terms, India's obligations were more but for the US they were onerous. US Secretary of State Dr Rice, the most enthusiastic supporter, like the defence secretary, saw in India a customer for military hardware. This was an exciting prospect for its defence industry. The 'Vulcans' (friends of India) were seemingly convinced by Rice's views.[80] However, the State Department bureaucracy fixated by the non-proliferation lobby, was not excited or helpful.

There could have been no more potent symbol of PM Manmohan Singh's and President George W. Bush's determination to forge a new India–US strategic partnership. The larger ramifications of what was proposed were immediately clear to friends and foes alike. The traditional non-proliferation ayatollahs in the US think tanks and elsewhere, particularly China, saw their assumptions about India's foreign policies shaken. As Shivshankar Menon said China immediately began a form of guerrilla warfare against the initiative.[81]

In India, the initiative quickly caught the imagination of the emerging young aspirational generation. In the long months of internal politics that followed, every poll consistently showed strong popular support, and this, buttressed by the determination of Prime Minister Manmohan Singh, sustained the Civil Nuclear Initiative in India.[82]

The PM's satisfaction with the talks was reflected in his statement that 'they were very productive and focused on the future direction of transformation in our multi-faceted relations'.[83] The immediate result of the joint statement was available in the statement issued in Washington the same day. It said, 'The successful completion of this initiative clears the way for even greater engagements in a number of key areas in which cooperation had previously been limited or non-existent.'[84]

Along with the signing of the joint statement, many other areas of cooperation were discussed on the same day in other forums— Global Democracy Initiative; Economic Dialogue—strengthening Information and Communication Technology Cooperation; Energy Dialogue; Disaster Relief Initiative; Initiative in the fight against HIV/AIDS; Chief Executive Officers' Forum for Enhancing Economic Dialogue; Trade Policy Forum and Initiative on Agriculture, Education, Teaching, Research, Service and Commercial Linkages, etc.[85]

In the next two days that Prime Minister Manmohan Singh spent in Washington, he had a number of speaking engagements including the one to the US Congress where he referred to their common heritage which made them 'natural partners' in peace and prosperity. Speaking to the India Caucus he called for not only the removal of misperceptions and stereotypes of the past but also 'in pooling our efforts to realise the hope with which our two countries now view this partnership'. Speaking to the guests at the Indian ambassador's reception, Prime Minister Singh expressed his satisfaction at the success of his visit which laid the groundwork for a new relationship. At the National Press Club, he told his audience that his interaction with President Bush, his senior colleagues and the Congress had convinced him that the journey on which they had embarked upon toward the future would make the people of the two countries friends and partners.[86]

> His message during the visit was simple and substantive that the government and the people of India are ready and willing for substantive engagement with the United States; there are enough commonalities and shared concerns which should have ensured such engagement earlier. The absence of such an ongoing engagement has been a gap and both sides should try to fill it; we on our part are doing everything we can in that direction.[87]

The US believed and it was also accepted on all hands that the outcome of the visit was wholly in favour of India. It allowed India to continue to produce material needed to sustain its strategic and military programme unchanged by the guidelines outlined in the joint statement. In the nature of things, it was now for India to adopt a separation plan to trigger other steps to breast the tape.[88]

In his report card to Parliament, the PM expressed his happiness that the US had agreed for the resumption of 'bilateral civilian nuclear energy cooperation' which had been frozen for some time and which would help India meet its energy requirements for its development'. He underlined the responsibilities, both domestic and international, that the US had undertaken to make the nuclear cooperation work and also stated what was expected of India in this regard. Describing the Indian nuclear programme as unique, he said it encompassed a complete range of activities that characterized an advance nuclear power including generation of electricity, advanced research and development and India's strategic programme, predicated on our modest uranium resources and vast reserves of thorium. Underlining the principle of reciprocity, he said it was expected that there would be a close symbiotic relationship between the actions of India and the US. Stressing this point the prime minister said, 'Indian action will be contingent at every stage on action taken by the other side [and] should we not be satisfied that our interests are fully secured, we shall not feel pressed to move ahead in a pre-determined manner.' He assured the House that while India had been accepted as a responsible nuclear power with an impeccable record on nuclear non-proliferation, India's strategic policies and assets are a source of national security 'and will continue to be so and will remain outside the scope of our discussion with any external interlocutor'. Concluding, he said, his visit to the US was 'undertaken solely with the purpose of enhancing relations with the world's preeminent power, so as to widen our developmental options'.[89]

The impact of the new relationship with the US did not take much time to reflect on the Indian attitude. In September 2005, India voted against Iran with the US at the IAEA, though it could have got away with an abstention. India's decision was an internal one, but it did placate the US. Again, India voted for a western-sponsored resolution in November 2005 for a referral of Iran's nuclear programme at the Security Council for minor breaches of IAEA rules. Yet again, the government showed willingness to go with the American demand not to proceed with Iran–Pakistan–India gas pipeline, which in any case was hazardous given the security problems in the region. People generally believed that India's vote on Iran was the condition for the nuclear deal. This gave rise to the thinking that the strategic consideration was the main reason the US favoured India.[90] Later, it was clarified that the US was prepared to concede Iran the right to develop civil nuclear energy but not the right 'to become a nuclear weapon state'.[91] Foreign Secretary Shivshankar Menon clarifying the Indian position had said that India had told Iran that it needed to address the international community's concerns about its nuclear programme.[92]

In specific terms, the final journey of the proposed agreement had to cross several stages, which seriatim in brief were:

i.   India to separate its nuclear reactors from civilian use to military use;

ii. The US to pass legislation to enable it to undertake cooperation with India on civil nuclear energy which it had banned since 1974;

iii. India to approach the International Atomic Energy Agency for a safeguard agreement for its civil reactors;

iv. India to apply to the Nuclear Suppliers' Group (NSG) for a waiver to undertake nuclear trade with member countries, and

v.   When all the above steps had been successfully accomplished, United States to amend Section 123 of the US Atomic Energy Act of 1954.

The US anxiety to acquaint itself on the progress in implementation of the stages of the 18 July statement was reflected in President Bush's call to Dr Singh within two months of the signing of the statement.[93]

Within three days of the President's call, Nicholas Burns, Under Secretary for Political Affairs, (the point man for negotiations with India) landed in New Delhi to carry out a detailed review of the implementation of the Civil Nuclear Energy Agreement. He even mentioned that the US had initiated consultations with the NSG in Vienna and asked for modification of its practices that would enable all members to engage in civil nuclear trade with India. The foreign secretary was in agreement with Burns on the progress achieved by both sides.[94] The prime minister, in the meantime, told journalists accompanying him on the flight to Kuala Lumpur for the East Asian summit that the exercise for separating India's civil and military nuclear facilities was at a fairly advanced stage.[95] The foreign secretary reacted strongly to a *Reuters* report that Nicholas Burns had presented India with a plan for separation of civil and military facilities. Trashing the report, the foreign secretary said, he had received no such blueprint. It was made known in New Delhi that separation was India's prerogative and it was competent to do it. Washington too, clarified, that no such plan was given to India.[96]

Meanwhile, domestic politics were getting shriller. The Left parties who traditionally saw the US as the world's bully, including India's, was getting impatient with the government on getting closer to the US on a daily basis. As pointed out earlier, they had even taken exception to the Defence framework agreement but had decided to live with it. This perhaps encouraged the government on the nuclear deal too. It was felt that the Left would make the necessary noises but finally resign itself and not bring down the government of which they were important partners.

Awaiting President Bush's reciprocal visit to India, two reviews were conducted on the implementation of the agreement; one in December and another in January 2006. They confirmed that significant progress had been achieved. But all was not smooth sailing. Both were aware that some contentious issues remained but there was confidence that these would be resolved before the President's visit to India.[97]

The National Security Advisor, M.K. Narayanan, acknowledged that 'many contentious issues regarding the nuclear deal remained' but he was confident that they would be resolved before Bush's visit.[98] The sticking points were on both the sides. In Washington, serious division, particularly on the non-proliferation issue, had cropped up within the State Department bureaucracy. The US too had run into problems with the NSG to get a waiver for India, and the law to allow cooperation with India had yet to go through the US Congress. On the Indian side, the Left parties claimed the deal had limited India's options and firmly put India in the American camp. It may be recalled that due to the US attack on Iraq, public sentiments against the Bush administration were not friendly. India had yet to separate its civil and military facilities. Even the Bhartiya Janata Party (BJP) which had initiated the deal by signing the NSSP now had turned against it. The BJP's opposition was essentially part of the politics that parties in India generally play against each other to make the life of the ruling party difficult.[99]

President Bush was expected in India in early March and there were issues which needed resolution before his arrival for which Burns had arrived in advance and held discussions with the foreign secretary on 23 and 24 February to resolve the sticking points. It was claimed that the talks were 'productive' without giving details.[100]

Briefing the media on the president's visit, Foreign Secretary Shyam Saran frankly said there were still some sticking points with regard to the civil nuclear energy. Terming it a complex issue, he said, 'I can only report that we have managed to make considerable progress [but] we have some distance to go.' He recounted the other areas on which considerable progress had been made and gave the example of 'licencing of high technology products which had become much more 'liberal as well as predictable'. Regarding the PM's statement a day earlier, expressing disappointment on the US failure to supply fuel for the Tarapur plant as promised, he said the PM had called Secretary of State Rice, (which was not in keeping with protocol) presumably to clear his position on his own statement. Rice's response, as Shyam Saran put it, was 'we are close and we need to work hard in order to close whatever gaps there are' and added that, 'Foreign Secretary Mr Shyam Saran should put extra effort with Under Secretary Burns in order to achieve closure.'[101] In the interim, to bypass the US law until it was amended, India was allowed stockpiling of fuel and the promise of alternative supplies from France, Russia and other countries was made.[102]

On arrival, the prime minister told the President that India had 'finalised the identification of civilian facilities' for separation from the military. The President said he would now approach the Congress to amend the US laws and the NSG to adjust its guidelines. Bush conceded it was not easy for the PM to have achieved this agreement but it was necessary to do so, since it would help both countries. Replying to a question, Bush again conceded that earlier the two countries were divided and there was not much of a relationship, but now, he said, the relationship was changing 'dramatically' and also alluded to the contribution of the Indian diaspora in changing the relationship.[103]

Bush's visit produced the most positive narrative which left little doubt that the deal was as good as done. India had taken the first and most important step of separating its nuclear facilities into civil and military parts, which in turn put pressure on the Bush administration to convince the Congress to amend a key law that had barred nuclear cooperation with India since its first nuclear explosion of 1974.

On 11 May 2006, the government formally submitted to Parliament a 'Separation Plan' of its nuclear facilities to kick-start the full civilian nuclear energy cooperation. It was affirmed that India would also enter into an India-specific safeguard agreement with the IAEA which would provide insurance against any withdrawal of safeguarded nuclear material from civilian use at any time, as well as providing for corrective measures that India might enter into, to ensure uninterrupted operation of its civilian nuclear reactors in the event of disruption of foreign fuel supplies. India would place civilian nuclear facilities under India-specific safeguards in perpetuity and negotiate an appropriate safeguard agreement to this end with the IAEA. Parliament was assured that the Separation Plan was in conformity with the commitments made to Parliament by the government.[104]

The announcement of the separation plan caused commotion in the country, particularly from the Left parties, and the government was accused of 'surrender' to Washington since it was feared it would result in a gap in fissile material availability for the weapons' programme. The BJP's criticism was that by placing two-thirds of its civil reactors under perpetual safeguard of the IAEA, India had lost nuclear autonomy. The prime minister remaining unmindful of the criticism went ahead on the nuclear path.

To follow up on the productive outcome of the President's visit, Foreign Secretary Shyam Saran found himself in Washington. The bonhomie now witnessed in their relations was oozing out of foreign secretary's lecture that he delivered at the Heritage Foundation in Washington. He described the new relationship as one between 'engaged democracies' unlike in the past when it was described between 'estranged democracies'. He too expected that as long as the US legislation was within the perimeters and bounds of the understanding which had been worked out bilaterally after 'painstaking and complex negotiations, India would not have any problem'. The foreign secretary too was emphatic that even if India had not signed the NPT, it had always been in the mainstream of the non-proliferation regime.[105] Saran had noted the widespread support for India in the US Congress during his visit to Washington. But he also realized that there were some concerns being expressed on account of the civil nuclear energy cooperation.

To dispel any of their doubts, Saran met a number of Congressmen individually and found them 'impressed by the very broad ranging relationship that was emerging'. After meeting a cross-section of Congressmen who mattered, he said:

> [T]he only country that will shape India's strategy is India itself. However, we do believe that choices that India will make or actions that India will take in its own best interest, given its own assessment of the global situation will in certain cases be convergent to United States's interests also.

In those cases, he agreed to work with the US, which was normal.[106] One has to remember that an agreement between two sovereign nations is essentially a compromise on their sovereignties in a particular area since it represents synergy of interests with different objectives. And the nuclear cooperation was in that league.

Referring to a report in the *Telegraph* of Kolkata that India would sign an agreement with the US on 'No further Nuclear testing', a spokesperson of the MEA clarified that 'such a proposal had no place in the proposed bilateral agreement and that India is bound only by what is contained in the July 18 Joint Statement that is continuing its commitment to a unilateral moratorium on nuclear testing.'[107]

It was going to be a year since the PM's visit to Washington and the signing of the joint statement on 18 July. Foreign Secretary Shyam Saran speaking to a gathering at the India Habitat Centre had said that in seeking to enter into an agreement on civil nuclear cooperation, we sought to 'synchronize our diplomacy much more closely with the changes that have taken place in India over the last fifteen years', which essentially was to catch up with the world. Adding, he said the proposal for nuclear cooperation was 'our determination to put behind us an era of defensive diplomacy'. He insisted that 'our foreign policy must reflect our national aspirations and express our confidence as an emerging global player'. In an emphatic voice he said, 'We cannot duck the difficult issues of the day and display an aversion to risk taking. July 18 is in some ways an effort to usher in a change in mindset.'[108]

In a lengthy statement in the Rajya Sabha on 17 August 2006, Prime Minister Manmohan Singh documented India's position, listing what was acceptable and what was not. The Bill coming out of the US Senate required the US president to make an annual report to the Congress, and among other things, that India remained in full compliance of non-proliferation and other commitments. The prime minister now said India had cautioned the US that though these provisions were not binding on India, such certification would diminish a permanent waiver authority into an annual one and was not acceptable to India.[109]

To clear the necessary legislation from the Congress, two bills had already been introduced in the two Houses of the Congress on 27 and 29 June and some discussions had taken place. Secretary of State Rice had also appeared before the Congress. The PM had some apprehensions about the two legislations and told President Bush his concerns when the two met in St Petersburg on 17 July. Dr Singh said he hoped constructive solutions would be found to Indian concerns.[110]

The two bills emerging from the Senate and House of Representatives were not identical and the prime minister had said the process of reconciling them 'would have to take on board our concerns' before the process of cooperation in the nuclear field began.[111]

During the debate in the Lok Sabha, the Left parties had raised certain doubts and the PM took care to reply to their concerns so as to create confidence in them that India had in no way compromised national interest in agreeing to go in for this agreement. Similarly, he referred to divergent views expressed by some scientists and responded to them as well. At the end, he assured the Lok Sabha that given some divergence in the two bills before the Senate and the House of Representatives, if the final reconciled product was not consistent with the assurance given to us, or the NSG guidelines imposed extraneous conditions, the government would draw necessary conclusions consistent with its commitments to Parliament.[112]

Pranab Mukherjee, who had since taken over the ministry of external affairs, welcomed the passage of the bill in the Senate but was somewhat worried because the Democrats had in the meantime gained a majority in the Senate.[113]

On 6 December in answering a question in the Lok Sabha on the specific areas relating to joint research, the EAM said, 'An amendment to the waiver Bill passed by the US Senate to enable full civil nuclear energy cooperation with India envisaged setting up of a cooperative threat reduction programme to further the common non-proliferation goals. India's agreement to this agency, yet to be taken, would be done after fully taking into account all aspects of our national security.' He was concerned that the final legislation of the Congress adhered as closely as possible to the understanding contained in the India–US Joint Statement of July 2005 and India's Separation Plan of May 2006.[114]

The US pointsman, Nicholas Burns, along with the new Foreign Secretary Shivshankar Menon carried out a review of the progress made and expressed confidence that the final document emerging from the Congress would be favourable to Indian views. Underlining the uniqueness of the proposed agreement, he said what was happening in India–US relations was unprecedented since there never had been a deal like this before. India had been welcomed in the non-proliferation community by breaking down the barriers of the last three decades. Foreign Secretary Menon endorsing Burns remarks said this would not have happened twenty or thirty years ago.[115]

On 9 December 2006, President Bush appreciated the Congress for its support for the legislation which enabled the two countries to work together 'to meet their energy needs in a manner that does not increase air pollution and green-house gas emissions, promotes clean development, support non-proliferation and advances trade interests'.[116] EAM Pranab Mukherjee on 12 December in a statement in the Lok Sabha welcomed the bipartisan support in the Congress and recognized the initiative that President Bush had taken to make these exceptions to India.[117] On 18 December 2006, President Bush signed the reconciled Bill into a law, the 'Henry J. Hyde United States-India Peaceful Atomic Energy Cooperation Act', which cleared the way for the two countries to go ahead on the journey which had begun in

July of the previous year. It exempted India from American domestic legislation. Senator Henry Hyde, had told Shyam Saran prior to the signing ceremony that he was 'hugely honoured' to have his name associated to this piece of legislation. For Saran, this indicated that 'the American lawmakers were coming round to nuclear cooperation'.[118]

The Government of India did express satisfaction at the reconciled Bill but the prime minister still found areas of concern in 'certain extraneous and prescriptive provisions' and said that 'no legislation enacted in a foreign county can take away our sovereign right to conduct foreign policy determined solely by our national interests'.[119]

Repeating his concerns, Dr Singh added he had been assured that they [the US] will be able to fully comply with their commitments' and remained appreciative of the efforts put in by the US administration and the Congress for the present legislation which had several positive features that took into account Indian concerns. But the PM still insisted that, 'I will be the last one to deny that there are areas which continue to be a cause for concern and we will need to discuss them with the US Administration before the bilateral cooperation agreement can be finalised.'[120]

The US negotiating the implementation of the nuclear cooperation with India had to face critics who apprehended that it would accelerate the nuclear arms race in South Asia. The administration assured critics that India while expanding energy production would be under the watch of the IAEA to prevent diversion of technology. Similarly, the administration did not agree with critics that it would effectively make India a nuclear weapons state, since India did not come under the definition of NPT to qualify for that status.[121]

President Bush while signing the Henry Hyde Act gushed, 'the relationship between the US and India has never been more vital—and this bill will help us to meet the energy and security challenges of 21st century.' He paid fulsome tributes to Secretary of State Condoleezza Rice and said but for her leadership, this would not have been possible. He was frank to admit the rivalries of the past which had kept India and the US apart but were now no more. He counted the four goals that this Act would achieve, which he said were:

   i.   Strengthen cooperation between the US and India and help to achieve the most important challenge of 21st century which was 'energy';

   ii.   It will help economic growth and open new markets for American business;

  iii. Help India to reduce emissions—and improve its environment, and

  iv. It will help keep America safe by paving the way for India to join the global efforts to stop the spread of nuclear weapons.[122]

The Hyde Act gave India three waivers to enable the US to enter into nuclear cooperation with India despite (i) India having conducted a series of nuclear tests; (ii) India had a strategic programme and all its nuclear facilities would not be subjected to full safeguards, and (iii) because there was no freezing or capping of India's strategic weapons programme.

The fact sheet that the White House issued on the day the president signed the Hyde Act repeated the 'four key goals', which he had underlined before signing the legislation that would benefit the US.[123]

Crucially, the Act exempted India from clauses embedded in the US Atomic Energy Act of 1954. It was for the first time in American Constitutional history, at least since the 1954 Act was passed, that the US Congress authorised the executive branch to enter into a 'proposed agreement for cooperation with India', a state that had not signed the NPT and had tested nuclear weapons.[124] Notably, it took nine rounds and 300 hours of talks over two years to arrive at this point.[125]

Though the prime minister was happy at the signing of the Act, he still told the president of his concerns, while joining him in expressing the hope that the remaining concerns would also be 'addressed in the next stage of negotiations'.[126]

Foreign Secretary Menon later speaking at the Carnegie Endowment emphasized the theme that 'we, today, together have capabilities that we didn't have before' and even added that the world around us had changed so rapidly and so quickly that wherever he looked, whether in India's immediate neighbourhood, or the Asian subcontinent, or on the bigger global issues, he saw 'convergence'. Burns, emphasizing the importance of India's cooperation to the US said Americans '20 or 30 years from now' would recognize India 'as one of the two or three most important partners in the world'.[127]

While the negotiations appeared to proceed smoothly there were tensions which were simmering underneath, particularly on the question of any future nuclear test by India. News agency Press Trust of India quoting *U.S. Today* suggested on 13 April that the nuclear accord risked collapse due to the Indian demand for right to continue testing of nuclear weapons. Americans felt Indians were being 'greedy' and were delaying conclusion of the agreement by the time Bush left office at the end of his term. Nicholas Burns, normally positive in his remarks, acknowledged that 'three rounds of talks produced little'. Not questioning India's goodwill, he said, 'There is a fair degree of frustration in Washington that the Indian Government has not engaged seriously enough or quickly enough.' He said India wanted permission to buy uranium enrichment and plutonium reprocessing technology from the US, but since both have military applications, the sale was prohibited in most cases by US laws. New Delhi did not want any limits on testing nuclear weapons and had been told should India test one, the deal would fall through. However, the under secretary for Commerce sounded hopeful and insisted that the two countries were engaged in finalizing the 123 agreement and making efforts towards understanding each other. Meanwhile the Brazilian foreign minister on a visit to Delhi told a press conference that Brazil, as chairman of the NSG, had had discussions with India and found it committed to non-proliferation and that the attitude of NSG members towards India was changing.[128] In the light of these developments, the visit of Foreign Secretary Menon to Washington to discuss 'India-U.S. bilateral agenda including the bilateral civil nuclear energy cooperation agreement' raised some positive hopes of breakthrough.[129]

The foreign secretary after a two-day discussion with Burns was positive that the agreement would be finalized. Questions were raised how the American 'frustration' had been converted into positivity'. Menon without disclosing any details insisted that the agreement be finalized during the course of the month of May itself, while Burns was in India. It was apparent from the answers given by Menon that Secretary of State Rice had played a positive role. Menon said, 'A lot of it wouldn't have been possible without her guidance and help to the relationship.'[130]

Menon's visit was followed by the President's call to the prime minister when among other things they reviewed the matters related to the civil nuclear energy agreement. Despite Menon's positive note, in Washington's perception there were apparently still some issues which had not been resolved. A spokesperson of the State Department, when asked about the schedule of Burns' visit to India said, 'Burns will go to New Delhi when we are ready to seal the deal [and] we are not at that point yet.' Dodging a straight answer to further questions, the State Department spokesperson said he was not aware of his travel plans but added work was in progress and 'it is not complete yet'. Finally, he gave some positive indication saying, 'Over the course of the past several weeks there have been some positive discussions on concluding the agreement,' and the Indian government too wanted to conclude the agreement and that 'we would like to do it sooner than later.'[131] It was clear that there was no chance of finalizing the agreement by the end of May as Menon had hinted earlier.

Finally, Burns made it to New Delhi on 31 May and held discussion for three days, which contrary to earlier expectation were not conclusive despite being 'intense, productive and constructive'. The foreign secretary in his media briefing did not wish to enter into any detailed discussions, except claiming that these discussions had enabled them to come 'much closer' in their understanding of the issues.[132]

The contentious issues were said to be: US refusal to allow India the right to reprocess spent fuel produced by American manufactured reactors and the US insistence on including a 'right of return' over any nuclear equipment or material such as the strategic nuclear reserve sold to India, in the event of an Indian nuclear test. The media described the talks as 'hard-nosed negotiations' and said the two had 'hit an impasse with no real progress registered on the major issues separating them'. While the official Indian sources quoted by the media declined to characterize the situation as 'deadlock', it was said 'more time was needed to sort out the issues'. But if there was no reprocessing consent then we simply can't proceed, media said quoting an official source. It was stressed that reprocessing was integral to India's indigenous civil nuclear programme of converting the spent fuel produced by a nuclear reactor into fresh fuel for use in a fast breeder reactor. Despite all these uncertainties, the US embassy's press note issued on the night of 2 June gave some hope when it said they had made 'some progress' on the 123 but 'some work remains to be done to complete arrangements that will permit a civil nuclear agreement to be finalised'.[133] In sum, India insisted that there should be no ambiguity in 123 Agreement for India's right to reprocess spent fuel. India insisted while lack of explicit consent might be acceptable to China, India needed its rights to be recognized upfront. 'Reprocessing is integral to our entire three-stage programme,' said an Indian official adding, 'without reprocessing, there is nothing.' India was guided by its experience of Tarapur where huge pools of spent fuel produced by the American-built reactor had accumulated over the years with Washington neither agreeing to take it back nor granting India the right to reprocess it. This was the main reason India was insisting on a clear, right-based approach. The US was reminded that guaranteeing adequate fuel, including a strategic reserve for India's reactor, was a key provision in the 2 March 2006 Separation Plan agreed by the US and India. India, based on past experience, this time, was more explicit than in the past that the ownership of any nuclear fuel it imported under the India–US agreement was a red line which could not be crossed under any circumstances.[134] When Nicholas Burns made a courtesy call to the prime minister, Dr Singh made it clear to him 'in the clearest manner possible' that the deal would not be acceptable to either Parliament or the people if it did not insulate India's nuclear facilities from supply disruptions and granted the right to reprocess spent fuel. The media quoted senior officials to say that the PM's message was intended to convey that the government had no intention of backing off on these and other red lines drawn by him in Parliament in August 2006 and the government's determination was not 'negotiating tactics' but a reflection of domestic political reality. *The Hindu* quoted a senior official to say that 'no prime minister of India can stand up and tell Parliament that he is going ahead with this deal even though we haven't got reprocessing rights and there is no security of fuel supplies'. Burns was exasperated: 'we are doing such a big deal for India; why the hell are you not taking it? Why are you making such a big deal about reprocessing and strategic reserve?' Despite the irritation, media reports said that for the first time it appeared to the Americans that it was a political issue which had to be resolved and India was 'not bluffing'.[135] Clarifying, it was said on India's behalf that full civil nuclear energy cooperation included four separate spheres: (i) reactors; (ii) fuel; (iii) reprocessing rights; and (iv) fuel cycle equipment and technology. And it was very important to get these elements in the 123 Agreement. If there was a problem on the American side, it was their problem. Regarding nuclear testing by India, the Indian officials were of the view that they were focused on ensuring that any consequences that allow an Indian nuclear test should not compromise the country's ability to ride out any cut-off in fuel supplies.[136] India too had a problem with the Hyde Act that sought to limit not only its own fuel supplies in the event of it ending the nuclear cooperation but also lobby to end supplies from other sources as well.[137]

Despite these developments, the foreign secretary was positive that 'considerable progress' toward the goal of an agreement had been reached, as reflected in the 18 July 2005 statement and the 2 March 2006 Separation Plan. The PM did not gloss over the fact that 'there were issues where there was a gap'.[138] The prime minister had a brief conversation with President Bush in Berlin where he had gone to attend the Outreach Conference of G-8 and found him quite understanding of India's difficulties. The PM was, however, satisfied that the president had positive feelings towards India, but qualified it to say that he could not claim that he had got a final answer to India's concerns. He said all we were interested in was that the substance of the 123 agreement would conform to 'what I had told the people of India, what I told Parliament'. He had little doubt that there was no finality to those concerns and there was no light at the end of the tunnel.[139]

The telephonic talk the PM had with President Bush led to media speculation that it represented the urgency on the part of Washington to clinch the issue. The inclusion of Anil Kakodkar, Secretary Department of Atomic Energy, and the National Security Advisor, in the Indian delegation to Washington was taken as a significant development which kindled the hope that it might lead to finalisation of the agreement. The media speculated that the visit of Ambassador Ronen Sen to New Delhi for consultation was yet another indication on the need to clinch the agreement.

The *Indian Express* on 11 July said though atmospherics were in place for the talks, the key hurdle in the 123 talks, that of US extending India's right to reprocess spent fuel, still remained unresolved. While this was an absolute must for India, the American bureaucracy continued to grapple with the reality that a blanket 'programmatic consent' had not been given even to Russia and China. Indian hope, however, rested on the White House. It was well known whenever India got stuck with the State Department, it quietly and successfully activated its contacts in the White House to resolve any sticking issue. The second sticking point was follow-up action by the US if India exploded a nuclear device after the agreement had been signed.[140] In Washington, after four days of intense talks between the Indian and US delegations, a text of the '123 civil nuclear cooperation agreement' was finalized.[141] New Delhi approved the text at the joint meeting of the Cabinet Committee on Political Affairs (CCPA) and the Cabinet Committee on Security (CCS) on 25 July. To allay the Left's apprehensions, the prime minister met the Left leaders on the night of 25 July, after which EAM Pranab Mukherjee told the media that all concerns of India had been 'adequately addressed' in the 123 Agreement.[142] President Bush, in his statement welcoming the conclusion of the talks, said it marked 'another step in the continued progress that is deepening strategic partnership with India, a vital world leader'.[143] A joint statement issued after talks between EAM Pranab Mukherjee and Secretary of State Dr Rice now outlined the next step to complete the process. It was for India to negotiate a safeguard agreement with the IAEA and support for nuclear trade with India from the forty-five-member Nuclear Suppliers Group. Once these steps had been completed successfully, President Bush would be required to submit the text to the US Congress for its final approval.[144]

On 27 July, the Ministry of External Affairs issued a fact sheet on the 123 Agreement which claimed that the finalized document met the concern of both sides and

> [F]ulfils all the assurances made by the Prime Minister to Parliament on 17 August 2006 including three basic principles—that the agreement would specifically provide that India's strategic nuclear programme, three-stage Nuclear Programme and R&D activities will remain unhindered and unaffected.[145]

It was understood that India would negotiate an India-specific safeguard agreement with the IAEA, but as far as NSG was concerned, it put the onus principally on the US 'to work with friends and allies in the Nuclear Supplier Group for an adjustment of their guidelines so as to enable the NSG to enter into nuclear cooperation and trade as an equal partner'. On the same day in Washington, the US too issued a similar fact sheet.[146]

Most concerned with the operational part, the scientific community expressed its satisfaction that the agreement would end India's nuclear isolation. However, a group of scientists from the Bhabha Atomic Research Centre expressed their apprehension against a hijack by the Opposition parties and expressed their unhappiness with the Left parties questioning the integrity of Prime Minister Manmohan Singh over the agreement, which they described as a 'national shame'.[147]

In Washington too, some questions were raised about the deal particularly whether India 'would have the right to explode a nuclear device'. Nicholas Burns answering said, 'India would have the sovereign right' but he hoped that such a situation would not arise and dismissed it as a hypothetical since 'they are very far from the reality of the situation'. He however added, if there was a test, then the 'American President would have to decide whether or not to ask for fuel and technology return . . . and we have preserved that legal right in our law. But it is a choice; it is not automatic'. He explained that:

> The four specific fuel assurances that President George W. Bush made to Prime Minister Manmohan Singh on 2 March 2006 had been written

verbatim in the Hyde Act. These were assurances from our Government
to Government of India that we will, as its partner, help it to provide for
a continuous supply of nuclear fuel to its power reactors . . . One of the
assurances is that U.S. will help India create a multilateral reserve fuel.
We suggested that India can work with IAEA. This makes sense for any
country that would want to have a continuous supply of fuel to power
reactors. But this did not obviate the fact that both countries have laws
that they live up to it. One of our laws is the Atomic Energy Act and we
have preserved the ability of any future President to fulfil his or her legal
obligations under it.[148]

Regarding the proposed strategic fuel reserves sourced from other
countries, the US ambassador in New Delhi, David Mulford clarified
that it would remain unaffected even if a nuclear test was conducted.
'The testing issue is not mentioned in the agreement' and there was no
regulation over India's strategic nuclear capability.[149]

While efforts were being made to resolve the sticking points in
the nuclear deal, a controversy was raised by Nicholas Burns when
addressing the Joint Business Council, where Burns questioned the
relevance of non-alignment. The MEA spokesperson then made an
official statement highlighting the role played by non-alignment and
its continued relevance. The EAM separately insisted 'we don't believe
that the movement has lost its relevance'.[150]

On the question of nuclear energy cooperation, Secretary of State
Rice described the agreement a 'key' to the bilateral relationship, and
said that 'we will be in a position to complete this deal by the end of
the year' because 'we are not quite there'.[151] On India's Independence
Day, President Bush called the PM to convey his greetings and used the
opportunity to discuss the issues related to the nuclear agreement too.[152]

While these developments were leading the way to a new
relationship with the US, the Left parties raised hell. On 8 September
2007, the Communist Party (Marxist) in an open letter cautioned that
the deal should not be seen in isolation but in the context of its impact
on India's foreign policy and strategic autonomy and bilateral relations
generally.[153]

On 8 October 2007, the four Left parties together issued a joint statement, warning that the nuclear deal was against the interests of India and that 'we need not surrender our vital interests to America'. Prakash Karat, General Secretary, CPI(M), saw the deal dragging India into a strategic alliance with the US. He warned that if it was taken forward it would 'have heavy political consequences'. For most part, all the four Left parties paddled together and shared an almost identical outlook. Sitaram Yechury, an important member of the Politburo, and a moderate, was bitten by the alarmist thinking and said it would make India a 'subordinate ally of the US'. The value of their criticism lay in their numbers, since their fifty-nine members were the mainstay of the coalition government which was being headed by Dr Manmohan Singh. The Coordination Committee that was constituted with six members from the Left to look into some aspects of the deal was not successful since they did not want to be satisfied with anything less than suspension of negotiations with the US. The government rejecting their demand for a Joint Parliamentary Committee said 'no treaty or a bilateral agreement was ever scrutinized by a JPC'.[154] The prime minister found the tone of the Left parties, harsh, and said, 'UPA–Left partnership could not be a one-sided affair'. Answering questions at the *Hindustan Times* summit on 12 October, the PM when asked if he had staked his personal prestige on the nuclear deal, replied:

[W]e are not one-issue government. We have made changes in various area…but in life one has to take certain disappointments and move on to the next…and if the deal does not come through, that is not the end of life and in politics we must survive short term battles to address long term concerns. He insisted that the nuclear deal was 'an honourable deal that is good for India and good for the world'.[155]

Mrs Sonia Gandhi, Chairperson of the National Advisory Council and Chairman of the United Progressive Alliance (an alliance of political parties, then ruling the country) did not believe that the Left were being unreasonable and that they were merely stating their point of view and the government had to understand them. Speaking of the coalition *dharma*, she added all had to work together while trying to understand and accommodate each other's views.[156]

Even a nine-hour debate in the Rajya Sabha did little to satisfy the Left. The Coordination Committee met eight times between September 2007 and June 2008 but failed to give any satisfaction to the Left.[157]

The time had come for the government to take a call on the attitude of the Left. But the Congress did vacillate because of the Left's importance for the stability of the government. Finally, the Left was told that it was not possible to renegotiate the agreement. The prime minister insisted it was an honourable deal approved by the Cabinet and it was not possible to go back on it and if they wanted to withdraw support; 'so be it'.[158] There was debate in both the Houses of Parliament when the Left reeled out its litany of problems with the nuclear deal— impact on the future of the country, the economy, relationship with other countries and energy security. The government was cautioned that 'if you go without our consultations, as we are supporting partners, we cannot be a party to it'. The Left also rejected the charge that they were 'acting on behalf of China'.[159]

BJP Leader L.K. Advani giving his reasons for the BJP's opposition said: (i) it bars our right to test; (ii) it makes India a junior partner; and (iii) that apart from IAEA inspectors, the US inspectors could also inspect the safeguarded reactors; and urged the government to come clean on these issues.[160] It may be recalled, initially, former PM and BJP senior leader Atal Bihari Vajpayee, who had initiated the process by signing the NSSP, was in fact against it. He had argued the way it was taking shape it would make India surrender its right to determine what kind of nuclear deterrent it should have in future based on its own threat perception.[161]

EAM Mukherjee in his speech, hit the nail on the head when he said, 'This agreement will provide us the passport to enter into an agreement on nuclear trade with a host of other countries' and remove all sanctions that had been imposed on India since the first and second nuclear explosion in 1974 and 1998.[162] Apart from the several rounds of discussions on the civil nuclear energy agreement in Parliament, all parties also issued their own statements elaborating their policy and stand on this issue. The Left parties issued several position papers.[163] The editorial in all national newspapers commented on the issue which had occupied the nation's attention as never before.[164]

The prevailing situation on the Opposition front was best described later by Shivshankar Menon in his book:

> Throughout the fractious domestic political process, Indian negotiators were also sustained by confidence that the Indian public understood the logic and supported the initiative. The media parsed (analysed), chittered and sensationalised, depending on the prevailing winds of the day. Politicians and political parties, even established ones like the BJP, chose to support or oppose the initiative depending on their attitude towards the Congress party government rather than on the basis of substance of the issues or their previous conduct and stance while in government.[165]

Public opinion polls in the autumn of 2007 showed that 93 per cent of the people of India supported the initiative for what it promised in terms of better relations with the US and energy supplies. He said the noise generated by the vocal minority that opposed it had an effect on the chattering classes rather than the masses.[166]

Meanwhile, Australian Prime Minister John Howard called the PM and informed him of his government's decision to sell uranium to India.[167] Addressing a press conference in Canberra, Howard said it was strange that Australia sold uranium to China but not to India and added Uranium sales would be 'one key element of a comprehensive package of measures [that Canberra] is taking to strengthen' ties with India. Hailing India as the 'world's largest democracy, he described it as an increasingly influential regional power and an important potential strategic power'.[168] The Australian Foreign Minister Alexander Downer had also held a meeting earlier with EAM Mukherjee in Manila on 31 July and conveyed his country's assurance to him. He also assured the EAM of Australia's support in NSG.[169] Later, after the change of government in Canberra, the Labour Party government led by Kevin Rudd, had a different take and said, 'If and when 123 agreement comes before either the Nuclear Suppliers' Group or the IAEA, we will give consideration to it at that point in time.'[170]

The question of testing nuclear weapons by India again retuned to haunt the deal. Some confusion was caused by the briefing of Spokesman of State Department Sean McCormack when he said there would be termination of cooperation in the event of India testing a nuclear device. When the matter was raised in the Lok Sabha, the EAM said India did not have an authentic version of the spokesperson's statement and insisted that India had 'the sovereign right to test and would do so'.[171] This position was further fortified by the statement of Anil Kakodkar that there was no prohibition on conducting a nuclear test in the 123 agreement and 'everything [about the deal] has been worked out in great detail'.[172]

On the American side, despite the intervention of Bush and Rice, it did not help in clinching the contentious issues and the pace remained sluggish. However, both countries remained hopeful that the agreement would sail through the rough waters of Indian politics. The prime minister himself was always been optimistic of the outcome.[173] The US Treasury Secretary Henry Paulson on a visit to India said the nuclear deal would be perceived by the global business community 'positively'.[174]

Rice was honest to acknowledge the web of sanctions and constraints, many dating back to India's first nuclear test in 1974, that made it impossible to engage with India in that sphere.[175]

There were concerted efforts both by the President and Dr Rice to dismantle those past barriers and move forward with India, but the high priests and protectors of NPT in Congress and 'in some corners of the State Department' would resist anything that looked like a change of US policy in that area. Rice also noted that there was an intense debate in India on the nuclear deal and the US continued to urge India to move forward, but the differences within India were for India to resolve.[176]

On 30 October 2007, EAM Mukherjee had a telephonic conversation with Secretary of State Rice and according to MEA

Spokesperson they discussed issues of mutual interest 'including the India–US agreement for cooperation on civil nuclear energy and regional issues'.[177]

As the negotiations progressed, the issue got dominated yet again by domestic politics. It divided public opinion both vertically and horizontally. It was not that the differences were confined among the political parties alone; the intellectual community too did not remain immune from it. It threatened the stability of the ruling coalition government. All this found expression in large-scale media analysis and debate. But the government's deft handling of the issue by explaining the nuances of the agreement helped clear many a cloud both grey and dark. In the US too, there certainly were occasions when some pronouncements in the Congress or media accused the Bush administration of rewarding India for violating the NPT, which did upset India and provide grist to the critics' mill.

The Hyde Act was essentially an enabling step for the US to complete the various stages of the final agreement. To Prime Minister Dr Manmohan Singh, it was a harbinger of a major change. At the dedication ceremony of Units 3 and 4 the of the Tarapur Power Plant, the PM had said, 'There is today talk the world over of a nuclear renaissance and we cannot afford to miss the bus or lag behind these global developments.'[178]

Mukherjee found his meeting with DG of IAEA, Mohamed ElBaradei, in Vienna, quite helpful. He said that since 2004 he had been expressing the need for 'India to take its rightful place as an equal partner in the global nuclear order'. Considering that there was delay from India in asking for a safeguard agreement due to lack of consensus at home, Mohamed ElBaradaei said, 'There is no deadline to start formal talks with us [for safeguards] we would be ready whenever India was ready and wanted India to be a full partner of the IAEA.' He did not attach too much importance to safeguards since he said the India-specific safeguards were already there.[179] Later, Menon did not add credibility to some reports that the negotiations with the IAEA were stumbling. On the contrary, he said they were progressing rapidly and likely to be wrapped up by end of the month.[180]

The PM, after his talks with the Chinese during his visit to Beijing, was not sure of China's support in the NSG for a clean waiver.[181] India, however, expected the US to take the initiative with the NSG for a waiver, as the principal initiator and leader of these regimes.[182]

Mukherjee's interview with the weekly magazine *Outlook* seemed to suggest he was disappointed in that he was not positive on the nuclear deal due to the differences with the Left. He posed the question, 'if the government did not exist, how could there be an agreement'. He carried his disappointment to Washington and met both President Bush and Condoleezza Rice and said, 'India would not move forward on the civilian nuclear deal until a national consensus emerged.' Throwing up her hands, Rice said though the agreement was good for both conceded, 'events have their own momentum'.[183]

The government displayed a strong desire not to let the opportunity for a nuclear energy agreement slip away after putting so much of effort. It made a strong pitch to make the Opposition relent. The prime minister appealed to the political class to allow the government to complete the process after going through the IAEA and NSG and offered to place the final outcome before Parliament for approval. He said if he could negotiate the safeguards with the IAEA and get the waiver from the NSG, he would place the whole matter before the Parliament and would not become operational unless Parliament approved it. He assured both the Left and the BJP that there would be an opportunity for a full discussion.[184]

The Left parties remained adamant and asked the government to suspend further negotiations altogether. The government, however, decided not to leave the negotiating process midway and went ahead for a Safeguard Agreement with the International Atomic Energy Agency in Vienna. This Safeguard Agreement was finalized in three rounds of discussions in November and December 2007 and in January 2008. The third round with IAEA especially, discussed issues which would satisfy the Left parties. The agreement, among other things, made it clear that the government was entering this India-specific safeguard agreement with the 'IAEA and its members with the objective of full development and use of nuclear energy for peaceful purposes on a stable, reliable and predictable basis'. Importantly, the IAEA undertook to 'implement the safeguards in a manner designed to avoid hampering India's economic or technological development' and 'not to hinder or otherwise interfere' with any activities involving the use of nuclear energy or technology by India 'for its own purposes'. But the Left parties' opposition had become congenital, which they could not disinherit, and refused to be placated. Even the BJP's attitude remained negative. The Left parties went to the extent of prejudicing Muslims by propagating that India's vote against Iran at the IAEA was the result of the Congress-led government's pro-US stand to clinch the nuclear deal.

The negative stand of the Opposition made the government look for alternatives and found the Samajwadi Party, which hitherto had been opposing the agreement along with other parties, willing to reconsider its stand if the government could 'convince' it of its national importance and other aspects of the deal.

National Security Advisor M.K. Narayanan took upon himself to talk to the Samajwadi Party members to convince them of the need of the agreement for India's future economic development. In his meeting with some important MPs of the Samajwadi Party, he succeeded in conveying to them the import of the agreement, without sacrificing the basic values of India's non-aligned foreign policy or undermining the nuclear sovereignty or decision-making in any manner whatsoever.[185] Was it an epiphany hour for the Samajwadi Party? Keen observers were intrigued that the Samajwadi Party after a meeting of an hour or so could comprehend everything about the complex deal which it could not in the last three years when PM and EAM had had made several statements and the issue was debated in the media threadbare. People speculated on the various considerations including pecuniary which had made the mare go. The Samajwadi Party coming on board emboldened the government and the PM was able to convey to President Bush when they met on the sidelines of the G-8+5 summit in Tokyo that India was ready for the deal. The subject also came up for discussion at the summit itself, and was reflected in the chairman's executive summary, which said:

[W]e look forward working with India, the IAEA, the NSG and other partners to advance India's non-proliferation commitments and progress so as to facilitate a more robust approach to civil nuclear cooperation with India to meet its growing energy needs in a manner that enhances and reinforces the global non-proliferation regime.[186]

This enabled Dr Anil Kakodkar, chairman of the Atomic Energy Commission, to inform a press conference in Mumbai that 'this was a de facto recognition of India as a nuclear weapon state, free to pursue its own atomic weapons development with no interference from the IAEA'.[187]

The understanding with the Samajwadi Party emboldened the prime minister to seek a vote of confidence from the Lok Sabha on the nuclear agreement. Technically and Constitutionally it was not necessary for the government to do so, since agreements with foreign powers are not subject to scrutiny by the legislature. Cabinet approval is considered more than sufficient for this purpose. Nevertheless, it was considered prudent to get it accepted by the Parliament in view of the great public interest and the controversy raised by the Opposition. The two-day debate which took place on 21 and 22 July 2008 gave the government enough confidence to go ahead with the deal without looking over its shoulders.

The prime minister in his opening remarks was constrained to point out that the present session was avoidable if he had been allowed to complete the negotiations with the IAEA and the NSG. He regretted the Left's withdrawal of support. He ended his speech invoking the words of Guru Gobind Singh to not shirk to fight for the right cause.[188] While replying to the debate, he once again reiterated that there was nothing hidden from the House and categorically stated that 'except for the 123 agreement, Separation Plan and the draft of the safeguard agreement with the IAEA' there was nothing which would 'affect India's ability to pursue an independent foreign policy'. Finally, the government having won the vote of confidence was now more confident that the agreement was within reach.[189] This cleared the road to the nuclear deal of all obstacles as far as domestic politics was concerned.

It was now the turn of the Nuclear Suppliers' Group to consider the exemption for India from its guidelines to allow for full civil nuclear energy trade. It was apprehended at the very beginning that the drill at the NSG was going to be more difficult than at the IAEA.

The rules of the Nuclear Suppliers Group required endorsement of the waiver by consensus of all the member countries. It may be recalled that the NSG comprising forty-five countries was formed in the wake of India's nuclear test of 1974, with membership of only seven nations; which has since then gone up to the strength of forty-eight. India, though had applied for membership of the NSG in 2016, was denied it by the joint decision of the other member countries since India had not signed the NPT. The NSG guidelines stipulated that the countries importing nuclear material provide assurance to the NSG that the proposed deal would not contribute to the creation of nuclear weapons. Another requirement was that the importing country would not export nuclear-related dual-use items and technologies to another country.

In giving India a waiver, there were some countries which held out, and some even suggested a waiver with conditions, which was unacceptable to India. Since India was not a member, it could not present its case before the NSG when it had met on 21 August. No fewer than fifty amendments were on the table and the countries which held back were: Austria, New Zealand, Ireland, Norway, Switzerland, Netherlands, Canada and even China. Some wanted a periodic review of India's compliance. Some of these countries, who were tough with India, had shut their eyes to enable A.Q. Khan to steal nuclear technology, which made Pakistan's bomb possible. In making things difficult for India, both Pakistan and China did not sit idle either. The US when seeking to know whether India would be accommodating in some way, if necessary, was told that the prime minister would not sign a condition-laden deal.[190] Finally, it were Indian and American senior diplomats who worked overtime and logged several thousand miles to make the recalcitrant countries fall in line. China's case was sui generis. It opposed as long as there were other countries opposing, but at the same time it did not want to be the only country in opposition. It watched until all the other countries had withdrawn their reservations. Once that happened, China finding it futile to hold on, declared its support. To cover its discomfiture, the Chinese foreign ministry answering a question at its media briefing said, 'China believes that all countries are entitled to make peaceful uses of nuclear energy and added its cooperation should be conducive to safeguarding the integrity and efficacy of international nuclear non-proliferation regime.' India was upset at China's unhelpful attitude and had made a démarche to the Chinese embassy to convey India's displeasure. Media reports suggested that President Bush had called the Chinese President Hu Jintao to soften China's position, but Western reports said it was Condoleezza Rice who had rung up her counterpart. The *People's Daily*, reporting the waiver, quoted the Chinese representative at Vienna to remark that, 'It was Beijing's hope that the decision made by NSG would stand the test of time and contribute to the goal of nuclear non-proliferation and peaceful uses of atomic power.'[191] Interestingly, China hinted that Pakistan too be given the waiver, and the Chinese representative said, 'NSG will equally address the aspirations of all parties for the peaceful use of nuclear power, while adhering to the nuclear non-proliferation mechanism.' Media reports suggested that India had slammed China during the Chinese foreign minister's Delhi visit for being unwilling to support Indian entry in the NSG. National Security Advisor Narayanan reportedly said, 'We were rather disappointed because the Chinese suddenly jumped into the arena supporting—they didn't say anything themselves—the naysayers.' This enabled Dr Anil Kakodkar to tell a press conference in Mumbai that 'this was a de facto recognition of India as a nuclear weapon state, free to pursue its own atomic weapons development with no interference from the IAEA.'[192]

There was yet another furore that suddenly erupted. The chairman of the House of Representatives, Foreign Relations Committee, had released the US State Department's response to questions raised in the Congress. India's initial response was to ignore it and it said, 'We do not, as a matter of policy, comment on internal correspondence between different branches of another government' and added that 'we will be guided solely by terms of the bilateral agreement between India and the United States, the India Specific Safeguards Agreement with the IAEA and the clean waiver from the NSG, which we hope will be forthcoming in the NSG meeting on 4–5 September'.[193]

Later, when the contents were made public that US assurances would not 'insulate India against the consequences of a nuclear explosive test', they were found to be against the assurances given to India that such a requirement would not find mention in any legal format. However, it was understood that India by virtue of having unilaterally renounced nuclear tests at the very beginning, would stand by its policy commitment. Finding the discrepancies, an alert India threatened to walk out of the agreement. India wanted reopening of the agreement, but it was pronounced not possible. Finally, a compromise was struck that 'Bush would read a statement at the time of signing the agreement into law to reassure India'.[194] Later, signing the agreement to fulfil his promise the President said:

The Legislation makes no changes to the terms of the 123 agreement I submitted to the Congress. It enables me to bring that agreement into force and to accept on behalf of the United States all the obligations that are part of the agreement. The Legislation does not change the fuel assurance commitments that the United States government has made to the Government of India, as recorded in the 123 Agreement. The agreement also grants India 'advance consent to reprocessing' which will be brought into effect upon the conclusion of arrangements and procedures for a dedicated reprocessing facility under the IAEA safeguards.[195]

This requirement of the presidential statement delayed the signing of the agreement. It was expected that it would be signed when Secretary of State Rice was in Delhi on 4 October, but India had insisted that the final signing should take place only after the president had signed it and made the necessary declaration as promised. When asked about the delay, Mukherjee said that only after the president had signed the agreement, would the process be complete, and India would be in a position to sign it. Rice, however, had assured that 'the United States would stand by its commitment'.[196]

The final waiver came from the NSG at its meetings held between 4 and 5 September 2008 in Vienna. Here also, there was some problem. On the first day, some countries still raised doubts about India's commitment to non-proliferation. To set at rest their doubts, Pranab Mukherjee had made a statement on 5 September early morning, committing India to voluntary universal moratorium on nuclear testing and also on India's commitment not to subscribe to any arms race, including a nuclear arms race.[197] The statement was meant to assure the NSG and it said that India would not be a source of proliferation of sensitive technologies, including enrichment and reprocessing transfers. Finally, this enabled the NSG on 6 September to give India a clean waiver so that it would enter into full nuclear trade. (A formal communication conveying the waiver was received by India on 19 September from Germany.) The prime minister welcomed it as a 'forward looking and momentous' decision.[198] The waiver was also welcomed by the Indian nuclear scientists. Former NSA, Brajesh Mishra welcoming it, said it gave India 'lots of advantages'. The Samajwadi Party too, described it as a 'great victory for the country'. The prime minister spoke to President Bush to thank him for 'his role in taking forward the nuclear initiative and NSG adjusting its guidelines'.[199]

Later, speaking of the efforts put in by the American side in getting the waiver, Foreign Secretary Shivshankar Menon, who was in the thick of negotiations said:

> It is tribute to U.S. power and persuasion that despite the misgivings and divergences in the expressed views and interests of so many NSG members, the United States obtained a clean exemption in an acceptable form from the meeting on the 6th September, 2008. India's red lines were respected, namely no reference to testing, no discriminatory provisions, and no periodic review of India's behaviour or the exemptions, thus permitting permanent full civil nuclear cooperation—the 'clean' exemption that India had sought.[200]

As a final act in the drama, it still required President Bush to get the ratification from the Congress which he was hopeful about. President Bush, aware of India's red lines, assured the prime minister, when they met in Washington that 'we want the agreement to satisfy you and get it out of our Congress'; and that he was working hard to get it passed as quickly as possible.

The prime minister acknowledged the President's personal contributions and paid tribute to his leadership saying, it was his 'personal intervention which resolved all the difficulties'.[201]

The wavier ended three decades of nuclear technology denial regime against India. It was described as a tectonic shift in the petrified status quo world. The world had adjusted and that too at India's terms and to that extent, it was Indian diplomacy's great triumph, no doubt helped by the US, which was anxious to grab it at any cost for its own reasons.

Now, there was the 'Hill' left to climb; the adoption of the 123 Agreement by the Congress. Given the time constraint, procedural matters were circumscribed to facilitate the legislation. It was not until the House of Representatives adopted the 123 amendment of the US Atomic Energy Act, 1954 by 298 to 117 votes on 27 September 2008 and the Senate by eighty-six to thirteen votes on 1 October that the journey, which began in July 2005, came to fruition. It was then that India could break open the doors of the nuclear ghetto. As pointed out above, the president while signing the bill on 8 October had made sure all the concerns of India were met, which indeed were. India's External Affairs Minister Pranab Mukherjee happily joined Secretary of State Condoleezza Rice on 10 October in signing the 'United States–India Nuclear Cooperation Approval and Non-proliferation Enhancement Act'. The agreement was given a life of forty years with another ten-year extension unless either party gave notice of termination.

Rice, while signing the agreement, called it 'unprecedented' and a fulfilment of a vast potential which had remained 'unfulfilled for too many decades of mistrust'. Mukherjee described it not only as an enabling agreement for cooperation with the US but also the rest of the world.[202] After signing the agreement, Mukherjee said, 'It strikes a balance between the obligations and rights which we will comply with' leaving little doubt about the uninterrupted supply of nuclear fuel and pointed to the President's speech while signing the agreement unto law on 8 October.[203]

Ashley Tellis, the man who played a leading role in providing the motivation and intellectual input for the agreement from the sidelines, said, 'The deal won acceptance for India's de facto nuclear weapons state status at the NSG, the international cartel that controls trade in nuclear technology and fuel and that was established as a response to India's defiance of the global nuclear order in 1974.'

The hero of this epic is none other than President George W. Bush about whom Prime Minister Manmohan Singh at the end had said, 'When history is written, I think, it will be recorded that President George W. Bush played a historic role in bringing the two democracies closer to each other.' It was expected if this success was sustained it would portend enormous consequences for the future generations in both the countries.

Pranab Mukherjee while speaking in Parliament said that the government considered the agreement 'a historic contribution to our nation-building efforts in respect of energy, sustainable development, technology and other aspects'. Finally, the agreement acknowledged India's role as a responsible power in international affairs on the global stage.[204]

India's major gain has been that it irrevocably and irreversibly breached the nuclear barrier that had fettered it for decades. India ceased to be a nuclear pariah and all sanctions gradually melted away. India's nuclear programme now suffers no disability of any kind and it has been crucial in according it a status of a responsible nuclear power.

In the agreement, the two countries, US and India, had in their strategic relationship discovered a new convergence of both values and national interests. India was conscious of the fact that no country, other than the US could provide the two inputs India needed the most to sustain the momentum of its economic progress: investment and high technology. The relationship is strategic, covering the whole gamut of relations including political, economic, commercial, military, energy and agricultural cooperation.[205]

India's foreign policy has since then taken in its sweep a wide range of national interests including security, trade and investments, and climate change. The India–US nuclear energy agreement has in a large measure enhanced India's international profile and India has since then got a place at the high table of several organizations and countries. Most importantly, India is no longer hyphenated with Pakistan.[206]

Interestingly, since the signing of the agreement, India has not imported even a single reactor from the US and members of the US Congress 'have a sense of disappointment and some feel India took them for a ride'.[207] If the agreement had not incentivized India to get even a single reactor from the US, it was due to the differences between the two sides over the 'liability' rules relating to seeking damage from suppliers in the event of an accident.

In recent years there is renewed interest to operationalize the nuclear agreement in the face of growing global concerns over energy security triggered by the Russia–Ukraine conflict. The subject came up for discussion during the visit of US Assistant Secretary of State for Energy Resources Geoffrey R. Pyatt, in February 2023, to New Delhi. In an interview to *The Hindu*, he said he was 'very focused' on seeking a breakthrough to the 'liability' question, since that was holding up the operation of the agreement since 2008. Pyatt also attributed the slow progress due to the scare created following the 2011 accident in Japan's Fukushima nuclear power station, fears which appeared to be dissipating, but slowly. He was hopeful of reviving the interest in nuclear energy in India.[208]

The agreement did put an end to the nuclear technology denial regime, but the other most important part of the agreement—energy security—has remained a mirage even after more than a decade-and-a-half of signing of the agreement. The Chief Economic Advisor, to the Government of India, Anantha Nageswaran, while speaking at the annual session of the Confederation of Indian Industries on 25 May 2023, described energy as the 'most important worry in sustaining growth…' Describing it as an 'important driver of growth' he said it had come under a lot of pressure, thanks to 'geopolitical developments and climate change'.[209] Since then, the developments in the Middle East have added further worry on account of availability of energy if the conflict gets prolonged.

Since nuclear energy continues to elude India, the government has in recent years, laid greater stress on solar energy. Starting in 2014–15, the availability of solar power as on 30 June 2023 stood at 70.1 GW.

According to the latest solar policy, the government has allocated a total capacity of 39,600 MW of domestic solar PV module manufacturing capacity to eleven companies with a total outlay of Rs 14,007 crore under the Production Linked Incentive Scheme (PLIC) for High Efficiency Solar PV Modules (Tranche-II).

To start with, one of the important factors in the relationship was the US's long-term worries of a rising China, and India's envisaged role in that direction. That scenario has since, undergone a substantial change and confront both of them in real time. There is now a question mark whether a more confident India would play a role, if at all, to Washington's satisfaction, when it has its own problems with China to worry about. Do the US and India even see eye to eye on how to respond to the various challenges now posed by China, collectively and separately?

Finally, the need for energy security continues to be as worrisome as it was in 2005 when the deal was initiated. Unless the expectations are redeemed, it would recede in memory, which it almost has. As former Foreign Secretary and National Security Advisor, Shivshankar Menon, who was an active player in its realization said, 'Today India and the United States are victims of the initiative's success. The emotional impact of the civil nuclear initiative raised the level of ambition in the relationship so high that expectations on both sides have become hard to fulfil.'[210]

Epilogue

History, as Professor E.H. Carr, the distinguished historian put it, is 'an unending dialogue between the past and the present'. It is not a one-time event as most people think. Its impact is often felt from generation to generation. Eventually, history becomes the on-going story of a nation.

The lessons learnt and the conclusions drawn from the past often determine the course of future events. If history describes the events, historiography helps us understand them in their broader perspective and overlying characteristics that shape the events. It is important that we keep studying the phenomena, their shapes and colours, to ensure that changes do not bewilder or mislead us.

For more than two centuries before Independence, the British who ruled over us decided who would be India's friends and what would be good for us. India and its peoples' interests were subordinated to the larger interests of the colonial 'mother country'. This inevitably meant that India's foreign policy and relations with other countries, even in the neighbourhood, were seen through the prism of British interests. The starkest example was of Indians being offered as cannon fodder in battles across the world for the benefit of the imperial power.

Independence opened up new vistas and horizons. The entire foreign policy was seen through a new perspective and had a new look. India emerged into Independence in a world which was different than when they had lost it. The world that existed prior to the arrival of the British in India was one of empires and imperial rule. Colonialism, foreign control and racism were the phenomena of the eighteenth century world. Post Independence, India fought to secure independence, self-governance, freedom and non-discrimination for all colonized peoples.

It was an emerging new order that demanded a more nuanced and sophisticated diplomacy with a new lexicon of its own.

A free India found itself grappling with multiple challenges, both at the domestic and diplomatic level. Being a successor to the British Raj, India could not forsake the inherited legacy though imperialist, negative and often disruptive. The Partition of India created another country, and another challenge, in the form of Pakistan. The emergence of communist China in our neighbourhood was a most disruptive phenomenon and a new challenge to contend with. As it happened, India found itself not fully prepared to meet it.

The agreements which have been discussed in the aforementioned pages were spread over several decades. Some were rooted in history, and some, the product of history. Each one posed a new challenge, and the experience gained in each case, provided some direction for the nation's journey in diplomacy.

The India–China Agreement on Tibet, 1954, was then India's most important agreement and the first agreement of any significance that India negotiated. It exposed India's lack of preparedness and experience in negotiations. The trust displayed on the other party during negotiations was out of proportion to what was warranted. India made erroneous presumptions that it held the initiative to set the terms of the agreement and that China would pander to its diktat. No attempt was made to study and evaluate the strength of China and the extent to which it would accommodate India's agenda. Too much reliance was laid on factors which were outside India's control. The people asked to negotiate were given a vague, but negative brief, and were found deficient in experience. Relying on the friendship of another country in matters of state was a fundamental flaw which spilled over even after it was found to be misplaced. It was forgotten that an agreement is the product of give-and-take and while giving away something, it needed to be balanced with something gained which was of vital interest to us. No such attempt was made, and on the contrary, all efforts were toward gaining the goodwill of the other party.

* * *

The Soviet Union, suo moto, offered India a Treaty of Friendship, Peace and Cooperation. The Soviet Union was a superpower of the day and India was still struggling to come out of its third world status. The treaty offered by Moscow was neither for India's economic development nor social amelioration. The underlying character was defence or security. India was quietly sailing through after the disastrous events of 1962, trying to build its economy, security apparatus and the morale of the nation. It had been adjusting its relations both with the West and the East, though leaning toward the latter, while trying to maintain a balance. The Bangladesh developments were then nowhere on the horizon.

As far as the Soviet Union was concerned, its motives in offering a treaty of this kind in 1969 remained shrouded in mystery. India did drag its feet on the treaty offer for two reasons: (i) the right wing of the ruling Congress party was quite strong and would not allow it to happen, and (ii) it would be a violation of non-alignment—India's fundamental principle of foreign policy since the days of Prime Minister Jawaharlal Nehru. If India did finally accept the treaty, it was under the circumstances which developed much later, and not when the treaty was first offered.

As the narrative shows, its offer was neither unselfish nor philanthropic, but for a purpose. It wanted to involve India in its ideological and political dispute with China, taking advantage of India's strained relations with Beijing. And later, when India would not bite, the Soviets denied India vital weaponry to replenish the war losses of 1971.

If a big nation and a superpower at that, was being magnanimous toward a developing country and a less powerful country, to the extent of offering to jump into a war in its favour, it should have aroused some suspicions in Delhi. Due diligence was called for. At the end, given India's desperate need for Soviet assistance to meet a developing situation, New Delhi's reluctance for a treaty reflected in the external affairs minister's talks with the Soviet leaders, should have given some clue of Soviet intention. But it was too late and also perhaps New Delhi had been left with no option. India decided to go ahead. Such situations do arise but not too frequently.

* * *

Bangladesh, as part of Pakistan, was the product of a two-nation
theory, which had led to the Partition of India in 1947. As part of
Pakistan, its mindset remained Pakistani. It underwent a gradual
change as it became disillusioned with the idea of being part of
a larger Pakistan, since the locus of that Pakistan, was located in
an alien land with alien interests. India misunderstood Dhaka's
disenchantment as a sign of its revulsion with the old two-nation
theory and the desire for harmonious living with a people—
Indians—they had been extant for generations.

After the war, India found to its disappointment, that Bangladesh's
dilution of its Muslim identity which had metamorphosed East
Pakistan into Bangladesh, was only tactical and not a commitment
to secularism. As the situation developed in the years following the
assassination of Sheikh Mujibur Rahman, it left India little to celebrate
for its efforts.

* * *

India's disenchantment in West Pakistan or what was left of old Pakistan,
was as acute as it felt about Bangladesh. After the Simla Agreement had
been signed and the prisoners had gone home, it too returned to old
ways of antagonism. The old issues which should have been settled,
remained unresolved and the narrative of the past returned quickly.
India could only take solace in the fact that it had helped split the
partitioned Pakistan.

* * *

The India–Sri Lanka Accord was a hush-hush affair between the Sri
Lankan president and the Indian prime minister. The Lankan president
entered into this accord against the advice of his prime minister and
most of his Cabinet ministers. Indeed, they did not even attend the
signing ceremony. In signing the agreement, the president even feared
a coup against him. The entire country had observed shutdown in
protest against it. His only reason for signing it was that Prime Minister

Rajiv Gandhi had undertaken to end the ethnic conflict, something for which he had accepted responsibility, particularly when it was India which was backing the Tamil cause with misplaced enthusiasm.

In doing so, the Indian prime minister had brushed aside the opposition of Tamils both of the militant and moderate variety and for whom the agreement was being signed. He even ignored the sane and prudent advice of his cabinet colleague, Narasimha Rao. He chose to walk in where angels feared to tread. That the resentment of the Lankan people against the agreement was at boiling point was brought home to him while inspecting a guard of honour in Sri Lanka at the time of his departure. That too, did not drive home the risks of getting into the domestic problem of another country.

Rajiv Gandhi's adventurous policy met with the greatest foreign policy disaster since 1962. In the first instance, while deciding to stand with the Tamils, no study was made whether their demands were genuine. The Tamils were only 12 per cent of the population of the island against 74 per cent Sinhalese, whose language Sinhala, had been declared the official language. Tamil was a regional language since the Tamils were concentrated only in the north and east provinces. Their language was indeed declared the language of the Tamil provinces and they should have been happy. Unfortunately, the Tamils suffered from superciliousness and would not be satisfied unless their language was given a status on par with the Sinhala language. Their second-most important demand was merger of the two Tamil provinces, north and east, to create a Tamil homeland, a concept which was repugnant to the very idea of a nation state. That was as far as the Tamils were concerned. India, in the initial years, had decided to stay out of the internal problem of a neighbouring country. It was Mrs Gandhi's personal pique that was the trigger for her, and therefore, India's involvement in the affairs of the island. Once India had its foot in the door, it could not help entering its body and soul. Even having realized that it had got itself caught in the Lankan quagmire, India refused to leave with honour and dignity. That the LTTE was a terrorist organization, and Colombo was fighting a war on terror like India against Sikh separatists in

Punjab, remained beyond the understanding of the ruling group in New Delhi. The result was neither the army nor the nation could escape the self-inflicted humiliation.

* * *

India's diplomacy came to its own while negotiating a civil nuclear energy agreement with another superpower, the United States of America. It correctly perceived Washington's disquiet at China's assertiveness in Asia and the challenge it posed to America's biggest ally, Japan, in east Asia and also other countries in the region. China's refusal to abide by the rule-based verdict of the International Court of Justice on the South China Sea was a big challenge for its allies in South-East Asia. The Indian negotiators proved more than a match for their American negotiators and did not blink when under pressure. They had a clear agenda before them and met all the challenges tirelessly in negotiating the agreement.

One only hopes that future negotiators would make good use of their experience and learn the art of negotiating with foreign powers, big and small.

Acknowledgements

I would like to express my gratitude to a number of friends who very kindly spared their valuable time to go through various chapters and offered their valuable comments which enabled me to make the narrative richer.

First, I express my sincere thanks to Ambassador Shivshankar Menon, former Foreign Secretary and National Security Advisor, for general guidance and also for reading through the chapter on the India–US Civil Nuclear Energy Agreement. His comments have been most valuable and enabled me to make the narrative relevant and richer.

Ambassador T.C.A. Raghavan, former Indian High Commissioner in Pakistan, read through the chapter on the Simla Agreement. Ambassador T.C.A. Rangachari, who not only read the India–China Agreement on Tibet specifically, but at the end, read through all the five chapters and made comments and corrections, which were indeed very helpful in every manner.

Both Shri Sathiya Moorthy, a senior journalist based in Chennai who frequently comments on Sri Lankan developments, and Ambassador Sumith Nakandala, of the Sri Lankan Foreign Service read the chapter on the India–Sri Lanka Accord. Their comments from Indian and Sri Lankan perspectives were most useful in analysing the agreement.

Shri Rajiv Rajan, presently Associate Professor at Delhi University in the East Asia Department and formerly from the Shanghai University, had offered to read the India–Soviet Treaty of Peace, Friendship and Cooperation. I am grateful to him for sparing his time to offer his comments.

For the past almost twenty-five years, the Library of the India International Centre has become my base station. I am profoundly thankful to its chief librarian, Usha Mujoo Munshi, for ensuring a congenial atmosphere for academic studies and research. During my long association with the Library, I have particularly noted and have been impressed with innovations introduced by her in recent years to facilitate the work of library users.

I must confess my lack of digital knowledge and ability to handle problems which my laptop throws up rather frequently. It is Dr Kanchan Nagpal who invariably comes to my rescue. I express my grateful thanks to her for the ready help that she unhesitatingly provides to enable me to continue with my work uninterrupted.

I am equally gratful to Rajiv Mishra and Puja Puri, Hema who instinctively have been helpful and, of course, Rakesh, Jagdish and Sunil.

I use this opportunity to welcome my great-grandson Aryan Bir Singh.

However, at the end, I remain fully responsible for the narrative and the views expressed on various aspects of the agreements analysed in the book.

Appendix I

AGREEMENT BETWEEN THE REPUBLIC OF INDIA AND THE PEOPLE'S REPUBLIC OF CHINA ON TRADE AND INTERCOURSE BETWEEN TIBET REGION OF CHINA AND INDIA

The Government of the Republic of India and The Central People's Government of the People's Republic of China,

Being desirous of promoting trade and cultural intercourse between Tibet Region of China and India and of facilitating pilgrimage and travel by the peoples of China and India,

Have resolved to enter into the present Agreement based on the following principles:

1. mutual respect for each other's territorial integrity and sovereignty,
2. mutual non-aggression,
3. mutual non-interference in each other's internal affairs,
4. equality and mutual benefit, and
5. peaceful co-existence.

And for this purpose have appointed as their respective Plenipotentiaries:

The Government of the Republic of India, H.E. Nedyam Raghavan, Ambassador Extraordinary and Plenipotentiary of India; accredited to the People's Republic of China;

The Central People's Government of the People's Republic of China, H.E. Chang Han-fu, Vice-Minister of Foreign Affairs of the Central People's Government,

Who, having examined each other's credentials and finding them in good and due form, have agreed upon the following:-

Article I: The High Contracting Parties mutually agree to establish Trade Agencies:

1. The Government of India agrees that the Government of China may establish Trade Agencies at New Delhi, Calcutta and Kalimpong.

2. The Government of China agrees that the Government of India may establish Trade Agencies at Yatung, Gyantse and Gartok.
   The Trade Agencies of both Parties shall be accorded the same status and same treatment. The Trade Agents of both Parties shall enjoy freedom from arrest while exercising their functions, and shall enjoy in respect of themselves, their wives and children who are dependent on them for livelihood, freedom from search. The Trade Agencies of both Parties shall enjoy the privileges and immunities for couriers, mail-bags and communications in code.

Article II: The High Contracting Parties agree that traders of both countries known to be customarily and specifically engaged in trade between Tibet Region of China and India may trade at the following places:-

1. The Government of China agrees to specify (1) Yatung, (2) Gyantse and (3) Phari as markets for trade.
   The Government of India agrees that trade may be carried on in India, including places like (1) Kalimpong, (2) Siliguri and (3) Calcutta, according to customary practice.

2. The Government of China agrees to specify (1) Gartok, (2) Pulanchung (Taklakot), (3) Gyanima-Khargo, (4) Gyanima- Chakra, (5) Rampura, (6) Dongbra, (7) Puling-Sumdo, (8) Nabra, (9) Shangtse and (10) Tashigong as markets for trade; the Government of India agrees that in future, when in accordance with the development and need of trade between the Ari District of Tibet Region of China and India, it has become necessary to specify markets for trade in the corresponding district in India adjacent to the Ari District of

Tibet Region of China, it will be prepared to consider on the basis of equality and reciprocity to do so.

Article III
The High Contracting Parties agree that pilgrimage by religious believers of the two countries shall be carried on in accordance with the following provisions:-

1. Pilgrims from India of Lamaist, Hindu and Buddhist faiths may visit Kang Rimpoche (Kailas) and Mavam Tso (Manasarovar) in Tibet Region of China in accordance with custom.
2. Pilgrims from Tibet Region of China of Lamaist and Buddhist faiths may visit Banaras, Sarnath, Gaya and Sanchi in India in accordance with custom.
3. Pilgrims customarily visiting Lhasa may continue to do so in accordance with custom.

Article IV
Traders and Pilgrims of both countries may travel by the following passes and routes:

(1) Shipki La pass, (2) Mana pass, (3) Niti pass, (4) Kungri Bingri pass, (5) Darma pass and (6) Lipu Lekh pass.

Also, the customary route leading to Tashigong along the valley of the Shangatsangpu (Indus) River may continue to be traversed in accordance with custom.

Article V
For travelling across the border, the High Contracting Parties agree that diplomatic personnel, officials and nationals of the two countries shall hold passports issued by their own respective countries and visas by the other Party except as provided in Paragraphs 1, 2, 3 and 4 of this Article.

1. Traders of both countries known to be customarily and specifically engaged in trade between Tibet Region of China and India, their wives and children who are dependent on them for livelihood and

their attendants will be allowed entry for purposes of trade into India or Tibet Region of China, as the case may be, in accordance with custom on the production of certificates duly issued by the local government of their own country or by its duly authorised agents and examined by the border check-posts of the other Party.

2. Inhabitants of the border districts of the two countries who cross the border to carry on petty trade or to visit friends and relatives may proceed to the border districts of the other Party as they have customarily done heretofore and need not be restricted to the passes and route specified in Article IV above and shall not be required to hold passport, visas or permits.

3. Porters and mule team drivers of the two countries who cross the border to perform necessary transportation services need not hold passports issued by their own country, but shall only hold certificates good for a definite period of time (three months, half a year or one year) duly issued by the local government of their own country or by its duly authorised agents and produce them for registration at the border check-posts of the other Party.

4. Pilgrims of both countries need not carry documents or certification but shall register at the border check-posts of the other Party and receive a permit for pilgrimage.

5. Notwithstanding the provisions of the foregoing paragraph 2 of this Article, either Government may refuse entry to any particular person.

6. Persons who enter the territory of the other Party in accordance with the foregoing paragraphs of this Article may stay within its territory only after complying with the procedures specified by the other Party.

Article VI

The present Agreement shall come into effect upon ratification by both Governments and shall remain in force for eight (8) years. Extension of the present Agreement may be negotiated by the two Parties if either Party requests for it six (6) months prior to the expiry of the Agreement and the request is agreed to by the other Party.

DONE in duplicate in Peking on the twenty-ninth day of April, 1954, in Hindi, Chinese and English languages, all texts being equally valid.

(Sd.) NEDYAM RAGHAVAN,
 Plenipotentiary of the Government of
India of the Republic of India

> **(Sd.) CHANG HAN-FU.**
> **Plenipotentiary of the Central People's**
> **Government, People's Republic of China.**

* * *

NOTES EXCHANGED

Peking, April 29, 1954

<u>NOTE</u>

Your Excellency Mr. Vice-FOREIGN MINISTER,

In the course of our discussions regarding the Agreement on Trade and Intercourse Between Tibet Region of China and India, which has been happily concluded today, the Delegation of the Government of the Republic of India and the Delegation of the Government of the People's Republic of China agreed that certain matters be regulated by an exchange of notes. In pursuance of this understanding, it is hereby agreed between the two Governments as follows:

1. The Government of India will be pleased to withdraw completely within six (6) months from date of exchange of the present notes the military escorts now stationed at Yatung and Gyantse in Tibet Region of China. The Government of China will render facilities and assistance in such withdrawal.

2. The Government of India will be pleased to hand over to the Government of China at a reasonable price the postal, telegraph and public telephone services together with their equipment operated by the Government of India in Tibet Region of China. The concrete measures in this regard will be decided upon through further negotiations between the Indian Embassy in China and the Foreign

Ministry of China, which shall start immediately after the exchange of the present notes.

3. The Government of India will be pleased to hand over to the Government of China at a reasonable price the twelve (12) rest houses of the Government of India in Tibet Region of China. The concrete measures in this regard will be decided upon through further negotiations between the Indian Embassy in China and the Foreign Ministry of China, which shall start immediately after the exchange of the present notes. The Government of China agrees that they shall continue as rest houses.

4. The Government of China agrees that all buildings within the compound walls of the Trade Agencies of the Government of India at Yatung and Gyantse in Tibet Region of China may be retained by the Government of India. The Government of India may continue to lease the land within its Agency compound walls from the Chinese side. And the Government of India agrees that the Trade Agencies of the Government of China at Kalimpong and Calcutta may lease lands from the Indian side for the use of the Agencies and construct buildings thereon. The Government of China will render every possible assistance for housing the Indian Trade Agency at Gartok. The Government of India will also render every possible assistance for housing the Chinese Trade Agency at New Delhi.

5. The Government of India will be pleased to return to the Government of China all lands used or occupied by the Government of India other than the lands within its Trade Agency compound walls at Yatung. If there are godowns and buildings of the Government of India on the above mentioned lands used or occupied and to be returned by the Government of India and if Indian traders have stores, godowns or buildings on the above-mentioned lands so that there is a need to continue leasing lands, the Government of China agrees to sign contracts with the Government of India or Indian traders, as the case may be, for leasing to them those parts of the land occupied by the said godowns, buildings or stores and pertaining thereto.

6. The Trade Agents of both Parties may, in accordance with the laws and regulations of the local governments, have access to their nationals involved in civil or criminal cases.

7. The Trade Agents and traders of both countries may hire employees in the locality.
8. The hospitals of the Indian Trade Agencies at Gyantse and Yatung will continue to serve personnel of the Indian Trade Agencies.
9. Each Government shall protect the person and property of the traders and pilgrims of the other country.
10. The Government of China agrees, so far as possible, to construct rest houses for the use of pilgrims along the route from Pulanchung (Taklakot) to Kang Rimpoche (Kailas) and Mavam Tso (Manasarover); and the Government of India agrees to place all possible facilities in India at the disposal of pilgrims.
11. Traders and pilgrims of both countries shall have the facility of hiring means of transportation at normal and reasonable rates.
12. The three Trade Agencies of each Party may function throughout the year.
13. Traders of each country may rent buildings and godowns in accordance with local regulations in places under the jurisdiction of the other Party.
14. Traders of both countries may carry on normal trade in accordance with local regulations at places as provided in Article II of the Agreement.
15. Disputes between traders of both countries over debts and claims shall be handled in accordance with local laws and regulations.

On behalf of the Government of the Republic of India I hereby agree that the present Note along with Your Excellency's reply shall become an agreement between our two Governments which shall come into force upon the exchange of the present Notes.

I avail myself of this opportunity to express to Your Excellency Mr. Vice-Foreign Minister, the assurances of my highest consideration.

(Sd.) N. RAGHAVAN
Ambassador Extraordinary and
Plenipotentiary of the Republic of India.

His Excellency Mr. CHANG HAN-FU,
Vice-Minister of Foreign Affairs, Central People's Government, People's Republic of China, Peking.

NOTE

Your Excellency Mr. AMBASSADOR:

I have the honour to receive your note dated April 29, 1954 which reads: [Not reprinted] On behalf of the Central People's Government of the People's Republic of China, I hereby agree to Your Excellency's note, and your note along with the present note in reply shall become an agreement between our two Governments, which shall come into force upon the exchange of the present notes.

I avail myself of this opportunity to express to Your Excellency, Mr. Ambassador, the assurances of my highest consideration.

(Sd.) CHANG HAN-Fu. Vice Minister, Ministry of Foreign Affairs, People's Republic of China.

H.E. NEDYAM RAGHAVAN,
Ambassador Extraordinary and Plenipotentiary, Republic of India.
NOTES REGARDING RATIFICATION

Peking, the 17th August, 1954

EXCELLENCY,

I have the honour to state that
WHEREAS an agreement between the Government of the Republic of India and the Central People's Government of the People's Republic of China on trade and intercourse between Tibet region of China and India was signed at Peking on the 29th Day of April, 1954, by the respective plenipotentiaries of the two Governments, namely, **For the Government of the Republic of India, His Excellency Nedyam Raghavan, Ambassador Extraordinary and Plenipotentiary of India,**

For the Central People's Government of the People's Republic of China, His Excellency Chang Han-fu,

Which Agreement is reproduced, word for word, in the Annexure hereto, (*not reproduced*)

AND WHEREAS the Government of the Republic of India has ratified this Agreement on the 3rd June, 1954. I request you to convey information of the said ratification to the Central People's Government of the People's Republic of China.

I avail myself of this opportunity to renew to you, Excellency, the assurances of my highest consideration.

NEDYAM RAGHAVAN.
Ambassador of the Republic of India.

His Excellency Mr. CHOU EN-LAI,
Minister for Foreign Affairs, Central People's Government of the People's Republic of China, Peking.

EMBASSY OF THE PEOPLE'S REPUBLIC OF CHINA IN INDIA
(Translation from Chinese)

No. M/680/54   **17 August, 1954**

EXCELLENCY,

I have the honour to inform you that the Agreement between the People's Republic of China and the Republic-of India on Trade and Intercourse between Tibet Region of China and India, which was signed at Peking on the 29th of April, 1954, by Chang Han-fu, Vice-Minister, Ministry of Foreign Affairs, Central People's Government of the People's Republic of China, for the Central People's Government of the People's Republic of China and Nedyam Raghavan, Ambassador Extraordinary and Plenipotentiary of the Republic of India to the People's Republic, of China for the Government of the Republic of India, was subsequently ratified on the 3rd June, 1954, by the Central People's Government of the People's Republic of China. I hereby request you to convey information of the said ratification to the Government of India.

The Agreement is reproduced, word for word, in the annexure hereto (not reproduced). I avail myself of this opportunity to renew to you, Excellency, the assurances of my highest consideration.

(Sd.) YUAN CHUNG-HSIEN,
Ambassador Extraordinary and
Plenipotentiary of the People's Republic of China.

His Excellency PANDIT JAWAHARLAL NEHRU,
Minister for External Affairs, Government
of Republic of India, New Delhi.

Appendix II

Treaty of Peace, Friendship and Co-operation between the Republic of India and the Union of Soviet Socialist Republics, signed in New Delhi on August 9, 1971.

Desirous of expanding and consolidating the existing relations of sincere friendship between them,

Believing that the further development of friendship and co-operation meets the basic national interests of both the States as well as the interests of lasting peace in Asia and the world,

Determined to promote the consolidation of universal peace and security and to make steadfast efforts for the relaxation of international tensions and the final elimination of the remnants of colonialism,

Upholding their firm faith in the principles of peaceful co-existence and co-operation between States with different political and social systems,

Convinced that in the world today international problems can only be solved by cooperation and not by conflict,

Reaffirming their determination to abide by the purposes and principles of the United Nations Charter,

The Republic of India on the one side, and the Union of Soviet Socialist Republics on the other side,

Have decided to conclude the present Treaty, for which purpose the following Plenipotentiaries have been appointed:

On behalf of the Republic of India:

Sardar Swaran Singh,

Minister of External Affairs

On behalf of the Union of Soviet Socialist Republics:

Mr A. A. Gromyko,

Minister of Foreign Affairs

who, having each presented their Credentials, which are found to be in proper form and due order,

Have agreed as follows:

ARTICLE 1

The High Contracting Parties solemnly declare that enduring peace and friendship shall prevail between the two countries and their peoples. Each Party shall respect the independence, sovereignty and territorial integrity of the other Party and refrain from interfering in the other's internal affairs. The High Contracting Parties shall continue to develop and consolidate the relations of sincere friendship, good neighbourliness and comprehensive co-operation existing between them on the basis of the aforesaid principles as well as those of equality and mutual benefit.

ARTICLE II

Guided by the desire to contribute in every possible way to ensure enduring peace and security of their people, the High Contracting Parties declare their determination to continue their efforts to preserve and to strengthen peace in Asia and throughout the world, to halt the arms race and to achieve general and complete disarmament, including both nuclear and conventional, under effective international control.

ARTICLE III

Guided by their loyalty to the lofty ideal of equality of all peoples and Nations, irrespective of race or creed, the High Contracting Parties condemn colonialism and racialism in all forms and manifestations, and reaffirm their determination to strive for their final and complete elimination.

The High Contracting Parties shall co-operate with other States to achieve these aims and to support the just aspirations of the peoples in their struggle against colonialism and racial domination.

ARTICLE IV

The Republic of India respects the peace loving policy of the Union of Soviet Socialist Republics aimed at strengthening friendship and co-operation with all nations.

The Union of Soviet Socialist Republics respects India's policy of non-alignment and reaffirms that this policy constitutes an important factor in the maintenance of universal peace and international security and in the lessening of tensions in the world.

ARTICLE V

Deeply interested in ensuring universal peace and security, attaching great importance to their mutual co-operation in the international field for achieving those aims, the High Contracting Parties will maintain regular contacts with each other on major international problems affecting the interests of both the States by means of meetings and exchanges of views between their leading statesmen, visits by official delegations and special envoys of the two Governments, and through diplomatic channels.

ARTICLE VI

Attaching great importance to economic, scientific and technological co-operation between them, the High Contracting Parties will continue to consolidate and expand mutually advantageous and comprehensive co-operation in these fields as well as expand trade, transport and communications between them on the basis of the principles of equality, mutual benefit and most-favoured-nation treatment, subject to the existing agreement and the special arrangements with contiguous countries as specified in the Indo-Soviet Trade Agreement of December 26, 1970.

ARTICLE VII

The High Contracting Parties shall promote further development of ties and contacts between them in the fields of science, art, literature, education, public health, press, radio, television, cinema, tourism and sports.

ARTICLE VIII

In accordance with the traditional friendship established between the two countries, each of the High Contracting Parties solemnly declares that it shall not enter into or participate in any military alliance directed against the other Party.

Each High Contracting Party undertakes to abstain from any aggression against the other Party and to prevent the use of its territory for the commission of any act which might inflict military damage on the other High Contracting Party.

ARTICLE IX

Each High Contracting Party undertakes to abstain from providing any assistance to any third party that engages in armed conflict with the other Party. In the event of either Party being subjected to an attack or a threat thereof, the High Contracting Parties shall immediately enter into mutual consultations in order to remove threat and to take appropriate effective measures to ensure peace and the security of their countries.

ARTICLE X

Each High Contracting Party solemnly declares that it shall not enter into any obligation, secret or public, with one or more States which is incompatible with this Treaty. Each High Contracting Party further declares that no obligation exists, nor shall any obligation be entered into, between itself and any other State or States, which might cause military damage to the other Party.

AIRTICLE XI

This Treaty is concluded for the duration of twenty years and will be automatically extended for each successive period of five years unless either High Contracting Party declares its desire to terminate it by giving notice to the other High Contracting Party twelve months prior to the expiration of the Treaty. The Treaty will be subject to ratification and will come into force on the date of the exchange of Instruments of Ratification which will take place in Moscow within one month of the signing of this Treaty.

ARTICLE XII

Any difference of interpretation of any Article or Articles of this Treaty which may arise between the High Contracting Parties will be settled bilaterally by peaceful means in a spirit of mutual respect and understanding.

The said Plenipotentiaries have signed the present Treaty in Hindi, Russian and English, all texts being equally authentic and have affixed thereto their seals.

Done in New Delhi on the ninth day of August in the year one thousand nine hundred and seventy-one.

On behalf of the Republic of India	On behalf of the Union of Soviet Socialist Republics
(Sd.) Swaran Singh, Minister of External Affairs	(Sd.) A.A. Gromyko, Minister of Foreign Affairs

Appendix III

Simla Agreement on Bilateral Relations between India and Pakistan signed by Prime Minister Indira Gandhi, and President of Pakistan, <u>Z. A. Bhutto</u>, in Simla on 2 July 1972.

The <u>Government of India</u> and the <u>Government of Pakistan</u> are resolved that the two countries put an end to the conflict and confrontation that have hitherto marred their relations and work for the promotion of a friendly and harmonious relationship and the establishment of durable peace in the subcontinent so that both countries may henceforth devote their resources and energies to the pressing task of advancing the welfare of their people.

In order to achieve this objective, the Government of India and the Government of Pakistan have agreed as follows:

(i) That the principles and purposes of the <u>Charter of the United Nations</u> shall govern the relations between the two countries.

(ii) That the two countries are resolved to settle their differences by peaceful means through bilateral negotiations or by any other peaceful means mutually agreed upon between them. Pending the final settlement of any of the problems between the two countries, neither side shall unilaterally alter the situation and both shall prevent the organization, assistance or encouragement of any acts detrimental to the maintenance of peace and harmonious relations.

(iii) That the prerequisite for reconciliation, good neighbourliness and durable peace between them is a commitment by both the countries to peaceful coexistence respect for each-others territorial integrity and sovereignty and noninterference in each-others internal affairs, on the basis of equality and mutual benefit. That the basic issues and causes of conflict which have bedevilled the relations between the two countries for the last 25 years shall be resolved by peaceful means.

(iv) That they shall always respect each-others national unity, territorial integrity, political independence and sovereign equality.

(v) That in accordance with the <u>Charter of the United Nations</u>, they will refrain from the threat or use of force against the territorial integrity or political independence of each other.

Both governments will take all steps within their power to prevent hostile propaganda directed against each other. Both countries will encourage the dissemination of such information as would promote the development of friendly relations between them.

In order progressively to restore and normalize relations between the two countries step by step, it was agreed that:

(i) Steps shall be taken to resume communications, postal, telegraphic, sea, land, including border posts, and air links, including over flights;

(ii) Appropriate steps shall be taken to promote travel facilities for the nationals of the other country;

(iii) Trade and cooperation in economic and other agreed fields will be resumed as far as possible;

(iv) Exchange in the fields of science and culture will be promoted.

In this connection delegations from the two countries will meet from time to time to work out the necessary details.

In order to initiate the process of the establishment of durable peace, both the governments agree that:

(i) <u>Indian</u> and <u>Pakistani</u> forces shall be withdrawn to their side of the international border;

(ii) In <u>Jammu and Kashmir</u>, the <u>line of control</u> resulting from the ceasefire of 17 December 1971, shall be respected by both sides without prejudice to the recognized position of either side. Neither side shall seek to alter it unilaterally, irrespective of mutual differences and legal interpretations. Both sides further undertake to refrain from the threat or the use of force in violation of this line;

(iii) The withdrawals shall commence upon entry into force of this
agreement and shall be completed within a period of 30 days thereof.

This agreement will be subject to ratification by both countries in accordance
with their respective constitutional procedures, and will come into force with
effect from the date on which the instruments of ratification are exchanged.

Both governments agree that their respective heads will meet again at
a mutually convenient time in the future and that in the meanwhile the
representatives of the two sides will meet to discuss further the modalities
and arrangements for the establishment of durable peace and normalization
of relations, including the questions of repatriation of prisoners of war
and civilian internees, a final settlement of Jammu and Kashmir and the
resumption of diplomatic relations.

Indira Gandhi   Zulfiqar Ali Bhutto
Prime Minister   President
Republic of India   Islamic Republic of Pakistan
                                                      Simla, 2 July 1972

Appendix IV

Agreement between the Government of India and the Government of Sri Lanka to Establish Peace and Normalcy in Sri Lanka

Colombo, 29 July 1987

The Prime Minister of The Republic of India, His Excellency Mr. Rajiv Gandhi,
and

The president of the Democratic Socialist Republic of Sri Lanka, his excellency Mr. J.R. Jayawardene, having met at Colombo on July 29, 1987.

Attaching utmost importance to nurturing, intensifying and strengthening the traditional friendship of Sri Lanka and India, and

acknowledging the imperative need of resolving the ethnic problem of Sri Lanka, and the consequent violence, and for the safety, wellbeing and prosperity of people belonging to all communities of Sri Lanka.

Having this day entered into the following agreement to fulfil this objective;

1.1 **desiring** to preserve the unity, sovereignty and territorial integrity of Sri Lanka;

1.2 **acknowledging** that Sri Lanka is a multi-ethnic and a multi lingual plural society consisting *inter alia* of Sinhalese, Tamil Muslims (Moors) and Burghers;

1.3 **recognising** that each has a distinct cultural and linguistic identity which has to be carefully nurtured;

1.4 **also recognising** that the northern and Eastern Provinces have been areas of historical habitation of Sri Lankan Tamil speaking people, together in this territory with other ethnic groups;

1.5   **conscious** of the necessity of strengthening the forces contributing
        to the unity, sovereignty and territorial integrity of Sri Lanka and
        preserving its character as a multi-ethnic, multi-lingual and multi-
        religious plural society, in which all citizens can live in equality,
        safety, and harmony and prosper and fulfil their aspirations;

2. Resolve that:

2.1   Since the Government of Sri Lanka proposes to permit adjoining
        provinces to join to form one administrative unit and also by a
        Referendum to separate as may be permitted to the Northern and
        Eastern Provinces as outlined below:

2.2   During the period, which shall be considered an interim period
        (i.e.) from the date of the elections to the Provincial Council, as
        specified in para 2.8 to the date of the referendum as specified in
        para 2.3, the Northern and Eastern Provinces as now constituted,
        will form one administrative unit, having one elected provincial
        council. Such a unit will have one Governor, one Chief Minister
        and one Board of Ministers.

2.3   There will be a Referendum on or before 31st December 1988 to
        enable the people of the Eastern Province to decide whether:

        A)   The Eastern Province should remain linked with the Northern
             Province as one administrative unit, and continue to be
             governed together with the Northern Province as specified in
             para 2.2, or
        B)   The Eastern province should constitute a separate administrative
             unit having its own distinct Provincial Council with a separate
             Governor, Chief Minister and Board of Ministers.

The president may, at his discretion, decide to postpone such a referendum.

2.4   All persons who have been displaced due to ethnic violence or other
        reasons, will have the right to vote in such a referendum. Necessary
        conditions to enable them to return to areas from where they were
        displaced will be created.

2.5   The Referendum, when held, will be monitored by a committee headed by the Chief Justice, a member appointed by the President, nominated by the Government of Sri Lanka, and a member appointed by the president, nominated by the representatives of the Tamil speaking people of the Eastern Province.

2.6   A simple majority will be sufficient to determine the result of the Referendum.

2.7   Meetings and other forms of propaganda, permissible within the laws of the country, will be allowed before the Referendum.

2.8   Elections to Provincial Councils will be held within the next three months, in any event before 31st December 1987. Indian observers will be invited for elections to the Provincial Council of the North and East.

2.9   The emergency will be lifted in the Eastern and Northern Provinces by Aug. 15, 1987. A cessation of hostilities will come into effect all over the island within 48 hours of signing of this agreement. All arms presently held by militant groups will be surrendered in accordance with an agreed procedure to authorities to be designated by the Government of Sri Lanka. Consequent to the cessation of hostilities and the surrender of arms by militant groups, the army and other security personnel will be confined to barracks in camps as on 25 May 1987. The process of surrendering arms and the confining of security personnel moving back to barracks shall be completed within 72 hours of the cessation of hostilities coming into effect.

2.10 The Government of Sri Lanka will utilise for the purpose of law enforcement and maintenance of security in the Northern and Eastern Provinces the same organisations and mechanisms of Government as are used in the rest of the country.

2.11 The President of Sri Lanka will grant a general amnesty to political and other prisoners now held in custody under The Prevention of Terrorism Act and other emergency laws, and to combatants, as well as to those persons accused, charged and/or convicted under these laws. The Government of Sri Lanka will make special efforts to rehabilitate militant youth with a view to bringing them back into the mainstream of national life. India will co-operate in the process.

2.12 The Government of Sri Lanka will accept and abide by the above provisions and expect all others to do likewise.

2.13 If the framework for the resolutions is accepted, the Government of Sri Lanka will implement the relevant proposals forthwith.

2.14 The Government of India will under-work and guarantee the resolutions, and co-operate in the implementation of these proposals.

2.15 These proposals are conditional to an acceptance of the proposals negotiated from 4.5.1986 to 19.12.1986. Residual matters not finalised during the above negotiations shall be resolved between India and Sri Lanka within a period of six weeks of signing this agreement. These proposals are also conditional to the Government of India co-operating directly with the Government of Sri Lanka in their implementation.

2.16 These proposals are also conditional to the Government of India taking the following actions if any militant groups operating in Sri Lanka do not accept this framework of proposals for a settlement, namely,

A) India will take all necessary steps to ensure that Indian territory is not used for activities prejudicial to the unity, integrity and security of Sri Lanka.

B) The Indian navy/coast guard will cooperate with the Sri Lankan navy in preventing Tamil militant activities from affecting Sri Lanka.

C) In the event that the Government of Sri Lanka requests the Government of India to afford military assistance to implement these proposals the Government of India will cooperate by giving to the Government of Sri Lanka such military assistance as and when requested.

D) The Government of India will expedite repatriation from Sri Lanka of Indian citizens to India who are resident here, concurrently with the repatriation of Sri Lankan refugees from Tamil Nadu.

E) The Governments of India and Sri Lanka will co-operate in ensuring the physical security and safety of all communities inhabiting the Northern and Eastern Provinces.

2.17 The government of Sri Lanka shall ensure free, full and fair participation of voters from all communities in the Northern and Eastern Provinces in electoral processes envisaged in this agreement. The Government of India will extend full co-operation to the Government of Sri Lanka in this regard.

2.18 The official language of Sri Lanka shall be Sinhala. Tamil and English will also be official languages.

3. This agreement and the annexure thereto shall come into force upon signature.

In witness whereof we have set our hands and seals hereunto.

Done in Colombo, Sri Lanka, on this the twenty-ninth day of July of the year one thousand nine hundred and eighty-seven, in duplicate, both texts being equally authentic.

Rajiv Gandhi   Junius Richard Jayawardene,
Prime Minister   The President of the Democratic of
the Republic of India   Socialist Republic of Sri Lanka

* * *

Annexure To the Agreement

1. His Excellency the Prime Minister of India and His Excellency the President of Sri Lanka agree that the referendum mentioned in paragraph 2 and its sub-paragraphs of the Agreement will be observed by a representative of the Election Commission of India to be invited by His Excellency the President of Sri Lanka.

2. Similarly, both Heads of Government agree that the elections to the Provincial Councils mentioned in paragraph 2.8 of the Agreement will be observed by a representative of the Government of India to be invited by the President of Sri Lanka.

His Excellency the President of Sri Lanka agrees that the Home Guards would be disbanded and all para-military personnel will be withdrawn from the Eastern and Northern Provinces with a view to creating conditions conducive to fair elections to the Council.

3. The President in his discretion shall absorb such para-military forces, which came into being due to ethnic violence into regular security forces of Sri Lanka.

4. The Prime Minister of India and the President of Sri Lanka agree that the Tamil militants shall surrender their arms to the authorities agreed upon to be designated by the President of Sri Lanka. The surrender shall take place in the presence of one senior representative each of the Sri Lanka Red Cross and the Indian Red Cross.

5. The Prime Minister of India and the President of Sri Lanka agree that the Indo-Sri Lankan observers group consisting of representatives of the Government of India and the Government of Sri Lanka would monitor the cessation of hostilities from 31 July, 1987.

6. The Prime Minister of India and the President of Sri Lanka also agree that in terms of paragraph 2.14 and paragraph 2.16(c) of the Agreement, an Indian Peace Keeping contingent may be invited by the President of Sri Lanka to guarantee and enforce the cessation of hostilities, if so required.

* * *

Prime Minister of India

Excellency,
Conscious of the friendship between our two countries stretching over two Millenia and more, and recognising the importance of nurturing this traditional friendship, it is imperative that both Sri Lanka and India reaffirm the decision not to allow our respective territories to be used for activities prejudicial to each other's unity, territorial integrity and security.

In this spirit, you had during the course of our discussions, agreed to meet some of Indian concerns as follows:

i. Your Excellency and myself will reach an early understanding about the relevance and employment of foreign military and intelligence personnel with a view to ensuring that such presence will not prejudice Indo-Sri Lanka relations.

ii. Trincomalee or any other port in Sri Lanka will not be made available for military use by any country in a manner prejudicial to India's interests.

iii. The work of restoring and operating the Trincomalee Oil Tank Farm will be undertaken as a joint venture between India and Sri Lanka.

iv. Sri Lanka's agreement with foreign broadcasting organisations will be reviewed to ensure that any facilities set up by them are used solely as public broadcasting facilities and not for any military or intelligence purposes.

3. In the same spirit, India will:
i. Deport all Sri Lankan citizens who are found to be engaging in terrorists or advocating separatism or secessionism;
ii. Provide training facilities and military supplies for Sri Lankan security foces,

India and Sri Lanka have agreed to set up a joint consultative mechanism to continuously review matters of common concern in the light of the objectives stated in para 1 and specifically to monitor the implementation of other matters contained in this letter.

Kindly, confirm, Excellency, that the above correctly sets out the agreement reached between us.

Please accept, Excellency, the assurances of my highest consideration.

Yours Sincerely
(Rajiv Gandhi)

His Excellency,
Mr. Jayewardene,
President of the Democratic Socialist
Republic of Sri Lanka, Colombo

* * *

President of Sri Lanka

July 29, 1987

Excellency,

Please refer to your letter dated the 29th July 1987, which reads as follows:
Excellency,

"Conscious of the friendship between our two countries stretching over two Millenia and more, and recognising the importance of nurturing this traditional friendship, it is imperative that both Sri Lanka and India reaffirm the decision not to allow our respective territories to be used for activities prejudicial to each other's unity, territorial integrity and security.

In this spirit, you had during the course of our discussions, agreed to meet some of Indian concerns as follows:

i.   Your Excellency and myself will reach an early understanding about the relevance and employment of foreign military and intelligence personnel with a view to ensuring that such presence will not prejudice Indo-Sri Lanka relations.

ii. Trincomalee or any other port in Sri Lanka will not be made available for military use by any country in a manner prejudicial to India's interests.

iii. The work of restoring and operating the Trincomalee Oil Tank Farm will be undertaken as a joint venture between India and Sri Lanka.

iv. Sri Lanka's agreement with foreign broadcasting organisations will be reviewed to ensure that any facilities set up by them are used solely as public broadcasting facilities and not for any military or intelligence purposes.

3.   In the same spirit, India will:

i.   Deport all Sri Lankan citizens who are found to be engaging in terrorists or advocating separatism or secessionism;

ii. Provide training facilities and military supplies for Sri Lankan security forces,

4.   India and Sri Lanka have agreed to set up a joint consultative mechanism to continuously review matters of common concern in the light of the objectives stated in para 1 and specifically to monitor the implementation of other matters contained in this letter.

5.   Kindly, confirm, Excellency, that the above correctly sets out the agreement reached between us.

Please accept, Excellency, the assurances of my highest consideration."

This is to confirm that the above correctly sets out the understanding reached between us.

Please accept, Excellency, the assurances of my highest consideration.

(J.R. Jayewardene)
President

His Excellency Rajiv Gandhi,
Prime Minister of the Republic of India,
New Delhi

* * *

**Confidential Letters of Exchange between India and Sri Lanka regarding
Indian military assistance to ensure surrender of arms and cessation of
hostilities in the Jaffna peninsula; Colombo, July 29, 1987**

Letter of Sri Lankan Foreign Secretary:

Excellency,

Consequent upon the Agreement signed on 29th July, 1987 between the
President of Sri Lanka and Prime Minister of India, I have been directed by
the President of Sri Lanka to inform you that the Government of Sri Lanka
is in need of urgent assistance to bring about the cession of hostilities in the
Northern and Eastern Provinces.

As the terms of the Agreement referred to above stipulate a responsibility
for the Government of India as a guarantor for the implementation of its
provisions, I have been directed by the President of Sri Lanka to request your
Prime Minister and the Government of India to provide appropriate military
assistance to ensure the surrender of arms and cession of hostilities in the
Jaffna peninsula and if required, in the Eastern Province.

I have also been directed to convey that some naval vessels may be
despatched to Colombo with immediate effect to stabilise the situation and
to preserve the unity, stability and integrity of Sri Lanka.

I have been directed by the President to request that your Government
immediately responds to this request.

Yours sincerely
(W.M.P.B. Menikdiwela)
Secretary to the President

H.E. Shri K.P.S. Menon,
Foreign Secretary
Government of India

New Delhi

* * *

Reply Letter of Indian Foreign Secretary:

Confidential

K.P.S. Menon
Camp: High Commission of India
Colombo, Sri Lanka

Excellency,

I am to acknowledge your Confidential letter dated the 29th July conveying certain requirements of the Government of Sri Lanka in terms of para 2.14 and 2.16 (c) of the Indo-Sri Lanka Agreement concluded today, 29 July.

2. I have been directed to confirm that the assistance which the Government of Sri Lanka has asked for shall be rendered in full measure.

3. I have been directed by the Prime Minister of India to assure you that India shall cooperate fully in the matters touched upon in your letter.

Yours sincerely
(K.P.S. Menon)

His Excellency
Mr. W.M.P.B. Menikdiwela
Secretary to the President of the
Democratic Socialist Republic of Sri Lanka;
Colombo

Appendix V

AGREEMENT FOR COOPERATION BETWEEN THE GOVERNMENT OF THE UNITED STATES OF AMERICA AND THE GOVERNMENT OF INDIA CONCERNING PEACEFUL USES OF NUCLEAR ENERGY (123 AGREEMENT)

The Government of India and the Government of the United States of America, hereinafter referred to as the Parties,

RECOGNIZING the significance of civilian nuclear energy for meeting growing global energy demands in a cleaner and more efficient manner;

DESIRING to cooperate extensively in the full development and use of nuclear energy for peaceful purposes as a means of achieving energy security, on a stable, reliable and predictable basis;

WISHING to develop such cooperation on the basis of mutual respect for sovereignty, non-interference in each other's internal affairs, equality, mutual benefit, reciprocity and with due respect for each other's nuclear programmes;

DESIRING to establish the necessary legal framework and basis for cooperation concerning peaceful uses of nuclear energy;

AFFIRMING that cooperation under this Agreement is between two States possessing advanced nuclear technology, both Parties having the same benefits and advantages, both committed to preventing WMD proliferation;

NOTING the understandings expressed in the India - U.S. Joint Statement of July 18, 2005 to enable full civil nuclear energy cooperation with India covering aspects of the associated nuclear fuel cycle;

AFFIRMING their support for the objectives of the International Atomic Energy Agency (IAEA) and its safeguards system, as applicable to India and the United States of America, and its importance in ensuring that international cooperation in development and use of nuclear energy for peaceful purposes is carried out under arrangements that will not contribute to the proliferation of nuclear weapons or other nuclear explosive devices;

NOTING their respective commitments to safety and security of peaceful uses of nuclear energy, to adequate physical protection of nuclear material and effective national export controls;

MINDFUL that peaceful nuclear activities must be undertaken with a view to protecting the environment;

MINDFUL of their shared commitment to preventing the proliferation of weapons of mass destruction; and

DESIROUS of strengthening the strategic partnership between them;

Have agreed on the following:

ARTICLE 1 - DEFINITIONS

For the purposes of this Agreement:

(A) "By-product material" means any radioactive material (except special fissionable material) yielded in or made radioactive by exposure to the radiation incident to the process of producing or utilizing special fissionable material. By-product material shall not be subject to safeguards or any other form of verification under this Agreement, unless it has been decided otherwise by prior mutual agreement in writing between the two Parties.

(B) "Component" means a component part of equipment, or other item so designated by agreement of the Parties.

(C) "Conversion" means any of the normal operations in the nuclear fuel cycle, preceding fuel fabrication and excluding enrichment, by which uranium is transformed from one chemical form to another - for example, from uranium hexafluoride (UF_6) to uranium dioxide (UO_2) or from uranium oxide to metal.

(D) "Decommissioning" means the actions taken at the end of a facility's useful life to retire the facility from service in the manner that provides adequate protection for the health and safety of the decommissioning workers and the general public, and for the environment. These actions can range from closing down the facility and a minimal removal of nuclear material coupled with continuing maintenance and surveillance, to a complete removal of residual radioactivity in excess of levels acceptable for unrestricted use of the facility and its site.

(E) "Dual-Use Item" means a nuclear related item which has a technical use in both nuclear and non-nuclear applications.

(F) "Equipment" means any equipment in nuclear operation including reactor, reactor pressure vessel, reactor fuel charging and discharging equipment, reactor control rods, reactor pressure tubes, reactor primary coolant pumps, zirconium tubing, equipment for fuel fabrication and any other item so designated by the Parties.

(G) "High enriched uranium" means uranium enriched to twenty percent or greater in the isotope 235.

(H) "Information" means any information that is not in the public domain and is transferred in any form pursuant to this Agreement and so designated and documented in hard copy or digital form by mutual agreement by the Parties that it shall be subject to this Agreement, but will cease to be information whenever the Party transferring the information or any third party legitimately releases it into the public domain.

(I) "Low enriched uranium" means uranium enriched to less than twenty percent in the isotope 235.

(J) "Major critical component" means any part or group of parts essential to the operation of a sensitive nuclear facility or heavy water production facility.

(K) "Non-nuclear material" means heavy water, or any other material suitable for use in a reactor to slow down high velocity neutrons and increase the likelihood of further fission, as may be jointly designated by the appropriate authorities of the Parties.

(L)   "Nuclear material" means (1) source material and (2) special fissionable material. "Source material" means uranium containing the mixture of isotopes occurring in nature; uranium depleted in the isotope 235; thorium; any of the foregoing in the form of metal, alloy, chemical compound, or concentrate; any other material containing one or more of the foregoing in such concentration as the Board of Governors of the IAEA shall from time to time determine; and such other materials as the Board of Governors of the IAEA may determine or as may be agreed by the appropriate authorities of both Parties. "Special fissionable material" means plutonium, uranium-233, uranium enriched in the isotope 233 or 235, any substance containing one or more of the foregoing, and such other substances as the Board of Governors of the IAEA may determine or as may be agreed by the appropriate authorities of both Parties. "Special fissionable material" does not include "source material". Any determination by the Board of Governors of the IAEA under Article XX of that Agency's Statute or otherwise that amends the list of materials considered to be "source material" or "special fissionable material" shall only have effect under this Agreement when both Parties to this Agreement have informed each other in writing that they accept such amendment.

(M)   "Peaceful purposes" include the use of information, nuclear material, equipment or components in such fields as research, power generation, medicine, agriculture and industry, but do not include use in, research on, or development of any nuclear explosive device or any other military purpose. Provision of power for a military base drawn from any power network, production of radioisotopes to be used for medical purposes in military environment for diagnostics, therapy and sterility assurance, and other similar purposes as may be mutually agreed by the Parties shall not be regarded as military purpose.

(N)   "Person" means any individual or any entity subject to the territorial jurisdiction of either Party but does not include the Parties.

(O)   "Reactor" means any apparatus, other than a nuclear weapon or other nuclear explosive device, in which a self-sustaining fission chain reaction is maintained by utilizing uranium, plutonium, or thorium or any combination thereof.

(P) "Sensitive nuclear facility" means any facility designed or used primarily for uranium enrichment, reprocessing of nuclear fuel, or fabrication of nuclear fuel containing plutonium.

(Q) "Sensitive nuclear technology" means any information that is not in the public domain and that is important to the design, construction, fabrication, operation, or maintenance of any sensitive nuclear facility, or other such information that may be so designated by agreement of the Parties.

ARTICLE 2 - SCOPE OF COOPERATION

1. The Parties shall cooperate in the use of nuclear energy for peaceful purposes in accordance with the provisions of this Agreement. Each Party shall implement this Agreement in accordance with its respective applicable treaties, national laws, regulations, and license requirements concerning the use of nuclear energy for peaceful purposes.

2. The purpose of the Agreement being to enable full civil nuclear energy cooperation between the Parties, the Parties may pursue cooperation in all relevant areas to include, but not limited to, the following:

    a. Advanced nuclear energy research and development in such areas as may be agreed between the Parties;

    b. Nuclear safety matters of mutual interest and competence, as set out in Article 3;

    c. Facilitation of exchange of scientists for visits, meetings, symposia and collaborative research;

    d. Full civil nuclear cooperation activities covering nuclear reactors and aspects of the associated nuclear fuel cycle including technology transfer on an industrial or commercial scale between the Parties or authorized persons;

    e. Development of a strategic reserve of nuclear fuel to guard against any disruption of supply over the lifetime of India's reactors;

    f. Advanced research and development in nuclear sciences including but not limited to biological research, medicine, agriculture and industry, environment and climate change;

g. Supply between the Parties, whether for use by or for the benefit of the Parties or third countries, of nuclear material;

h. Alteration in form or content of nuclear material as provided for in Article 6;

i. Supply between the Parties of equipment, whether for use by or for the benefit of the Parties or third countries;

j. Controlled thermonuclear fusion including in multilateral projects; and

k. Other areas of mutual interest as may be agreed by the Parties.

3. Transfer of nuclear material, non-nuclear material, equipment, components and information under this Agreement may be undertaken directly between the Parties or through authorized persons. Such transfers shall be subject to this Agreement and to such additional terms and conditions as may be agreed by the Parties. Nuclear material, non-nuclear material, equipment, components and information transferred from the territory of one Party to the territory of the other Party, whether directly or through a third country, will be regarded as having been transferred pursuant to this Agreement only upon confirmation, by the appropriate authority of the recipient Party to the appropriate authority of the supplier Party that such items both will be subject to the Agreement and have been received by the recipient Party.

4. The Parties affirm that the purpose of this Agreement is to provide for peaceful nuclear cooperation and not to affect the unsafeguarded nuclear activities of either Party. Accordingly, nothing in this Agreement shall be interpreted as affecting the rights of the Parties to use for their own purposes nuclear material, non-nuclear material, equipment, components, information or technology produced, acquired or developed by them independent of any nuclear material, non-nuclear material, equipment, components, information or technology transferred to them pursuant to this Agreement. This Agreement shall be implemented in a manner so as not to hinder or otherwise interfere with any other activities involving the use of nuclear material, non-nuclear material, equipment, components, information or technology and military nuclear facilities produced, acquired or developed by them independent of this Agreement for their own purposes.

ARTICLE 3 - TRANSFER OF INFORMATION

1. Information concerning the use of nuclear energy for peaceful purposes may be transferred between the Parties. Transfers of information may be accomplished through reports, data banks and computer programs and any other means mutually agreed to by the Parties. Fields that may be covered include, but shall not be limited to, the following:

    a. Research, development, design, construction, operation, maintenance and use of reactors, reactor experiments, and decommissioning;

    b. The use of nuclear material in physical, chemical, radiological and biological research, medicine, agriculture and industry;

    c. Fuel cycle activities to meet future world-wide civil nuclear energy needs, including multilateral approaches to which they are parties for ensuring nuclear fuel supply and appropriate techniques for management of nuclear wastes;

    d. Advanced research and development in nuclear science and technology;

    e. Health, safety, and environmental considerations related to the foregoing;

    f. Assessments of the role nuclear power may play in national energy plans;

    g. Codes, regulations and standards for the nuclear industry;

    h. Research on controlled thermonuclear fusion including bilateral activities and contributions toward multilateral projects such as the International Thermonuclear Experimental Reactor (ITER); and

    i. Any other field mutually agreed to by the Parties.

2. Cooperation pursuant to this Article may include, but is not limited to, training, exchange of personnel, meetings, exchange of samples, materials and instruments for experimental purposes and a balanced participation in joint studies and projects.

3. This Agreement does not require the transfer of any information regarding matters outside the scope of this Agreement, or information that the Parties are not permitted under their respective treaties, national laws, or regulations to transfer.

4. Restricted Data, as defined by each Party, shall not be transferred under this Agreement.

ARTICLE 4 - NUCLEAR TRADE

1. The Parties shall facilitate nuclear trade between themselves in the mutual interests of their respective industry, utilities and consumers and also, where appropriate, trade between third countries and either Party of items obligated to the other Party. The Parties recognize that reliability of supplies is essential to ensure smooth and uninterrupted operation of nuclear facilities and that industry in both the Parties needs continuing reassurance that deliveries can be made on time in order to plan for the efficient operation of nuclear installations.

2. Authorizations, including export and import licenses as well as authorizations or consents to third parties, relating to trade, industrial operations or nuclear material movement should be consistent with the sound and efficient administration of this Agreement and should not be used to restrict trade. It is further agreed that if the relevant authority of the concerned Party considers that an application cannot be processed within a two-month period it shall immediately, upon request, provide reasoned information to the submitting Party. In the event of a refusal to authorize an application or a delay exceeding four months from the date of the first application the Party of the submitting persons or undertakings may call for urgent consultations under Article 13 of this Agreement, which shall take place at the earliest opportunity and in any case not later than 30 days after such a request.

ARTICLE 5 - TRANSFER OF NUCLEAR MATERIAL, NON-NUCLEAR MATERIAL, EQUIPMENT, COMPONENTS AND RELATED TECHNOLOGY

1. Nuclear material, non-nuclear material, equipment and components may be transferred for applications consistent with this Agreement. Any special fissionable material transferred under this Agreement shall be low enriched uranium, except as provided in paragraph 5.

2. Sensitive nuclear technology, heavy water production technology, sensitive nuclear facilities, heavy water production facilities and major critical components of such facilities may be transferred under this Agreement pursuant to an amendment to this Agreement. Transfers of dual-use items that could be used in enrichment, reprocessing or heavy water production facilities will be subject to the Parties' respective applicable laws, regulations and license policies.

3. Natural or low enriched uranium may be transferred for use as fuel in reactor experiments and in reactors, for conversion or fabrication, or for such other purposes as may be agreed to by the Parties.

4. The quantity of nuclear material transferred under this Agreement shall be consistent with any of the following purposes: use in reactor experiments or the loading of reactors, the efficient and continuous conduct of such reactor experiments or operation of reactors for their lifetime, use as samples, standards, detectors, and targets, and the accomplishment of other purposes as may be agreed by the Parties.

5. Small quantities of special fissionable material may be transferred for use as samples, standards, detectors, and targets, and for such other purposes as the Parties may agree.

    a. The United States has conveyed its commitment to the reliable supply of fuel to India. Consistent with the July 18, 2005, Joint Statement, the United States has also reaffirmed its assurance to create the necessary conditions for India to have assured and full access to fuel for its reactors. As part of its implementation of the July 18, 2005, Joint Statement the United States is committed to seeking agreement from the U.S. Congress to amend its domestic laws and to work with friends and allies to adjust the practices of the Nuclear Suppliers Group to create the necessary conditions for India to obtain full access to the international fuel market, including reliable, uninterrupted and continual access to fuel supplies from firms in several nations.

    b. To further guard against any disruption of fuel supplies, the United States is prepared to take the following additional steps:

        i. The United States is willing to incorporate assurances regarding fuel supply in the bilateral U.S.-India agreement on peaceful uses of nuclear energy under Section 123 of the

U.S. Atomic Energy Act, which would be submitted to the U.S. Congress.

ii. The United States will join India in seeking to negotiate with the IAEA an India-specific fuel supply agreement.

iii. The United States will support an Indian effort to develop a strategic reserve of nuclear fuel to guard against any disruption of supply over the lifetime of India's reactors.

iv. If despite these arrangements, a disruption of fuel supplies to India occurs, the United States and India would jointly convene a group of friendly supplier countries to include countries such as Russia, France and the United Kingdom to pursue such measures as would restore fuel supply to India.

c. In light of the above understandings with the United States, an India-specific safeguards agreement will be negotiated between India and the IAEA providing for safeguards to guard against withdrawal of safeguarded nuclear material from civilian use at any time as well as providing for corrective measures that India may take to ensure uninterrupted operation of its civilian nuclear reactors in the event of disruption of foreign fuel supplies. Taking this into account, India will place its civilian nuclear facilities under India-specific safeguards in perpetuity and negotiate an appropriate safeguards agreement to this end with the IAEA.

ARTICLE 6 - NUCLEAR FUEL CYCLE ACTIVITIES

In keeping with their commitment to full civil nuclear cooperation, both Parties, as they do with other states with advanced nuclear technology, may carry out the following nuclear fuel cycle activities:

i.   Within the territorial jurisdiction of either Party, enrichment up to twenty percent in the isotope 235 of uranium transferred pursuant to this Agreement, as well as of uranium used in or produced through the use of equipment so transferred, may be carried out.

ii. Irradiation within the territorial jurisdiction of either Party of plutonium, uranium-233, high enriched uranium and irradiated nuclear material transferred pursuant to this Agreement or used in or produced through the use of non-nuclear material, nuclear material or equipment so transferred may be carried out.

iii. With a view to implementing full civil nuclear cooperation as envisioned in the Joint Statement of the Parties of July 18, 2005, the Parties grant each other consent to reprocess or otherwise alter in form or content nuclear material transferred pursuant to this Agreement and nuclear material and by-product material used in or produced through the use of nuclear material, non-nuclear material, or equipment so transferred. To bring these rights into effect, India will establish a new national reprocessing facility dedicated to reprocessing safeguarded nuclear material under IAEA safeguards and the Parties will agree on arrangements and procedures under which such reprocessing or other alteration in form or content will take place in this new facility. Consultations on arrangements and procedures will begin within six months of a request by either Party and will be concluded within one year. The Parties agree on the application of IAEA safeguards to all facilities concerned with the above activities. These arrangements and procedures shall include provisions with respect to physical protection standards set out in Article 8, storage standards set out in Article 7, and environmental protections set forth in Article 11 of this Agreement, and such other provisions as may be agreed by the Parties. Any special fissionable material that may be separated may only be utilized in national facilities under IAEA safeguards.

iv. Post-irradiation examination involving chemical dissolution or separation of irradiated nuclear material transferred pursuant to this Agreement or irradiated nuclear material used in or produced through the use of non-nuclear material, nuclear material or equipment so transferred may be carried out.

ARTICLE 7 - STORAGE AND RETRANSFERS

1. Plutonium and uranium 233 (except as either may be contained in irradiated fuel elements), and high enriched uranium, transferred pursuant to this Agreement or used in or produced through the use of material or equipment so transferred, may be stored in facilities that are at all times subject, as a minimum, to the levels of physical protection that are set out in IAEA document INFCIRC 225/REV 4 as it may be revised and accepted by the Parties. Each Party shall record such facilities on a list, made available to the other Party. A Party's list

shall be held confidential if that Party so requests. Either Party may make changes to its list by notifying the other Party in writing and receiving a written acknowledgement. Such acknowledgement shall be given no later than thirty days after the receipt of the notification and shall be limited to a statement that the notification has been received. If there are grounds to believe that the provisions of this sub-Article are not being fully complied with, immediate consultations may be called for. Following upon such consultations, each Party shall ensure by means of such consultations that necessary remedial measures are taken immediately. Such measures shall be sufficient to restore the levels of physical protection referred to above at the facility in question. However, if the Party on whose territory the nuclear material in question is stored determines that such measures are not feasible, it will shift the nuclear material to another appropriate, listed facility it identifies.

2. Nuclear material, non-nuclear material, equipment, components, and information transferred pursuant to this Agreement and any special fissionable material produced through the use of nuclear material, non-nuclear material or equipment so transferred shall not be transferred or re-transferred to unauthorized persons or, unless the Parties agree, beyond the recipient Party's territorial jurisdiction.

ARTICLE 8 - PHYSICAL PROTECTION

1. Adequate physical protection shall be maintained with respect to nuclear material and equipment transferred pursuant to this Agreement and nuclear material used in or produced through the use of nuclear material, non-nuclear material or equipment so transferred.

2. To fulfil the requirement in paragraph 1, each Party shall apply measures in accordance with (i) levels of physical protection at least equivalent to the recommendations published in IAEA document INFCIRC/225/Rev.4 entitled "The Physical Protection of Nuclear Material and Nuclear Facilities," and in any subsequent revisions of that document agreed to by the Parties, and (ii) the provisions of the 1980 Convention on the Physical Protection of Nuclear Material and any amendments to the Convention that enter into force for both Parties.

3. The Parties will keep each other informed through diplomatic channels of those agencies or authorities having responsibility for ensuring that levels of physical protection for nuclear material in their territory or under their jurisdiction or control are adequately met and having responsibility for coordinating response and recovery operations in the event of unauthorized use or handling of material subject to this Article. The Parties will also keep each other informed through diplomatic channels of the designated points of contact within their national authorities to cooperate on matters of out-of-country transportation and other matters of mutual concern.

4. The provisions of this Article shall be implemented in such a manner as to avoid undue interference in the Parties' peaceful nuclear activities and so as to be consistent with prudent management practices required for the safe and economic conduct of their peaceful nuclear programs.

ARTICLE 9 - PEACEFUL USE

Nuclear material, equipment and components transferred pursuant to this Agreement and nuclear material and by-product material used in or produced through the use of any nuclear material, equipment, and components so transferred shall not be used by the recipient Party for any nuclear explosive device, for research on or development of any nuclear explosive device or for any military purpose.

ARTICLE 10 - IAEA SAFEGUARDS

1. Safeguards will be maintained with respect to all nuclear materials and equipment transferred pursuant to this Agreement, and with respect to all special fissionable material used in or produced through the use of such nuclear materials and equipment, so long as the material or equipment remains under the jurisdiction or control of the cooperating Party.

2. Taking into account Article 5.6 of this Agreement, India agrees that nuclear material and equipment transferred to India by the United States of America pursuant to this Agreement and any nuclear material used in or produced through the use of nuclear material, non-nuclear material, equipment or components so transferred shall be subject

to safeguards in perpetuity in accordance with the India-specific Safeguards Agreement between India and the IAEA [*identifying data*] and an Additional Protocol, when in force.

3. Nuclear material and equipment transferred to the United States of America pursuant to this Agreement and any nuclear material used in or produced through the use of any nuclear material, non-nuclear material, equipment, or components so transferred shall be subject to the Agreement between the United States of America and the IAEA for the application of safeguards in the United States of America, done at Vienna November 18, 1977, which entered into force on December 9, 1980, and an Additional Protocol, when in force.

4. If the IAEA decides that the application of IAEA safeguards is no longer possible, the supplier and recipient should consult and agree on appropriate verification measures.

5. Each Party shall take such measures as are necessary to maintain and facilitate the application of IAEA safeguards in its respective territory provided for under this Article.

6. Each Party shall establish and maintain a system of accounting for and control of nuclear material transferred pursuant to this Agreement and nuclear material used in or produced through the use of any material, equipment, or components so transferred. The procedures applicable to India shall be those set forth in the India-specific Safeguards Agreement referred to in Paragraph 2 of this Article.

7. Upon the request of either Party, the other Party shall report or permit the IAEA to report to the requesting Party on the status of all inventories of material subject to this Agreement.

8. The provisions of this Article shall be implemented in such a manner as to avoid hampering, delay, or undue interference in the Parties' peaceful nuclear activities and so as to be consistent with prudent management practices required for the safe and economic conduct of their peaceful nuclear programs.

ARTICLE 11 - ENVIRONMENTAL PROTECTION

The Parties shall cooperate in following the best practices for minimizing the impact on the environment from any radioactive, chemical or thermal contamination arising from peaceful nuclear activities under this Agreement and in related matters of health and safety.

ARTICLE 12 - IMPLEMENTATION OF THE AGREEMENT

1. This Agreement shall be implemented in a manner designed:
    a. to avoid hampering or delaying the nuclear activities in the territory of either Party;
    b. to avoid interference in such activities;
    c. to be consistent with prudent management practices required for the safe conduct of such activities; and
    d. to take full account of the long term requirements of the nuclear energy programs of the Parties.
2. The provisions of this Agreement shall not be used to:
    a. secure unfair commercial or industrial advantages or to restrict trade to the disadvantage of persons and undertakings of either Party or hamper their commercial or industrial interests, whether international or domestic;
    b. interfere with the nuclear policy or programs for the promotion of the peaceful uses of nuclear energy including research and development; or
    c. impede the free movement of nuclear material, non nuclear material and equipment supplied under this Agreement within the territory of the Parties.
3. When execution of an agreement or contract pursuant to this Agreement between Indian and United States organizations requires exchanges of experts, the Parties shall facilitate entry of the experts to their territories and their stay therein consistent with national laws, regulations and practices. When other cooperation pursuant to this Agreement requires visits of experts, the Parties shall facilitate entry of the experts to their territory and their stay therein consistent with national laws, regulations and practices.

ARTICLE 13 - CONSULTATIONS

1. The Parties undertake to consult at the request of either Party regarding the implementation of this Agreement and the development

of further cooperation in the field of peaceful uses of nuclear energy on a stable, reliable and predictable basis. The Parties recognize that such consultations are between two States with advanced nuclear technology, which have agreed to assume the same responsibilities and practices and acquire the same benefits and advantages as other leading countries with advanced nuclear technology.

2. Each Party shall endeavour to avoid taking any action that adversely affects cooperation envisaged under Article 2 of this Agreement. If either Party at any time following the entry into force of this Agreement does not comply with the provisions of this Agreement, the Parties shall promptly hold consultations with a view to resolving the matter in a way that protects the legitimate interests of both Parties, it being understood that rights of either Party under Article 16.2 remain unaffected.

3. Consultations under this Article may be carried out by a Joint Committee specifically established for this purpose. A Joint Technical Working Group reporting to the Joint Committee will be set up to ensure the fulfilment of the requirements of the Administrative Arrangements referred to in Article 17.

ARTICLE 14 - TERMINATION AND CESSATION OF COOPERATION

1. Either Party shall have the right to terminate this Agreement prior to its expiration on one year's written notice to the other Party. A Party giving notice of termination shall provide the reasons for seeking such termination. The Agreement shall terminate one year from the date of the written notice, unless the notice has been withdrawn by the providing Party in writing prior to the date of termination.

2. Before this Agreement is terminated pursuant to paragraph 1 of this Article, the Parties shall consider the relevant circumstances and promptly hold consultations, as provided in Article 13, to address the reasons cited by the Party seeking termination. The Party seeking termination has the right to cease further cooperation under this Agreement if it determines that a mutually acceptable resolution of outstanding issues has not been possible or cannot be achieved

through consultations. The Parties agree to consider carefully the circumstances that may lead to termination or cessation of cooperation. They further agree to take into account whether the circumstances that may lead to termination or cessation resulted from a Party's serious concern about a changed security environment or as a response to similar actions by other States which could impact national security.

3. If a Party seeking termination cites a violation of this Agreement as the reason for notice for seeking termination, the Parties shall consider whether the action was caused inadvertently or otherwise and whether the violation could be considered as material. No violation may be considered as being material unless corresponding to the definition of material violation or breach in the Vienna Convention on the Law of Treaties. If a Party seeking termination cites a violation of an IAEA safeguards agreement as the reason for notice for seeking termination, a crucial factor will be whether the IAEA Board of Governors has made a finding of non-compliance.

4. Following the cessation of cooperation under this Agreement, either Party shall have the right to require the return by the other Party of any nuclear material, equipment, non-nuclear material or components transferred under this Agreement and any special fissionable material produced through their use. A notice by a Party that is invoking the right of return shall be delivered to the other Party on or before the date of termination of this Agreement. The notice shall contain a statement of the items subject to this Agreement as to which the Party is requesting return. Except as provided in provisions of Article 16.3, all other legal obligations pertaining to this Agreement shall cease to apply with respect to the nuclear items remaining on the territory of the Party concerned upon termination of this Agreement.

5. The two Parties recognize that exercising the right of return would have profound implications for their relations. If either Party seeks to exercise its right pursuant to paragraph 4 of this Article, it shall, prior to the removal from the territory or from the control of the other Party of any nuclear items mentioned in paragraph 4, undertake consultations with the other Party. Such consultations shall give

special consideration to the importance of uninterrupted operation of nuclear reactors of the Party concerned with respect to the availability of nuclear energy for peaceful purposes as a means of achieving energy security. Both Parties shall take into account the potential negative consequences of such termination on the on-going contracts and projects initiated under this Agreement of significance for the respective nuclear programmes of either Party.

6. If either Party exercises its right of return pursuant to paragraph 4 of this Article, it shall, prior to the removal from the territory or from the control of the other Party, compensate promptly that Party for the fair market value thereof and for the costs incurred as a consequence of such removal. If the return of nuclear items is required, the Parties shall agree on methods and arrangements for the return of the items, the relevant quantity of the items to be returned, and the amount of compensation that would have to be paid by the Party exercising the right to the other Party.

7. Prior to return of nuclear items, the Parties shall satisfy themselves that full safety, radiological and physical protection measures have been ensured in accordance with their existing national regulations and that the transfers pose no unreasonable risk to either Party, countries through which the nuclear items may transit and to the global environment and are in accordance with existing international regulations.

8. The Party seeking the return of nuclear items shall ensure that the timing, methods and arrangements for return of nuclear items are in accordance with paragraphs 5, 6 and 7. Accordingly, the consultations between the Parties shall address mutual commitments as contained in Article 5.6. It is not the purpose of the provisions of this Article regarding cessation of cooperation and right of return to derogate from the rights of the Parties under Article 5.6.

9. The arrangements and procedures concluded pursuant to Article 6(iii) shall be subject to suspension by either Party in exceptional circumstances, as defined by the Parties, after consultations have been held between the Parties aimed at reaching mutually acceptable resolution of outstanding issues, while taking into account the effects of such suspension on other aspects of cooperation under this Agreement.

ARTICLE 15 - SETTLEMENT OF DISPUTES

Any dispute concerning the interpretation or implementation of the provisions of this Agreement shall be promptly negotiated by the Parties with a view to resolving that dispute.

ARTICLE 16 - ENTRY INTO FORCE AND DURATION

1. This Agreement shall enter into force on the date on which the Parties exchange diplomatic notes informing each other that they have completed all applicable requirements for its entry into force.
2. This Agreement shall remain in force for a period of 40 years. It shall continue in force thereafter for additional periods of 10 years each. Each Party may, by giving 6 months written notice to the other Party, terminate this Agreement at the end of the initial 40-year period or at the end of any subsequent 10-year period.
3. Notwithstanding the termination or expiration of this Agreement or withdrawal of a Party from this Agreement, Articles 5.6(c), 6, 7, 8, 9, 10 and 15 shall continue in effect so long as any nuclear material, non-nuclear material, by-product material, equipment or components subject to these articles remains in the territory of the Party concerned or under its jurisdiction or control anywhere, or until such time as the Parties agree that such nuclear material is no longer usable for any nuclear activity relevant from the point of view of safeguards.
4. This Agreement shall be implemented in good faith and in accordance with the principles of international law.
5. The Parties may consult, at the request of either Party, on possible amendments to this Agreement. This Agreement may be amended if the Parties so agree. Any amendment shall enter into force on the date on which the Parties exchange diplomatic notes informing each other that their respective internal legal procedures necessary for the entry into force have been completed.

ARTICLE 17 - ADMINISTRATIVE ARRANGEMENT

1. The appropriate authorities of the Parties shall establish an Administrative Arrangement in order to provide for the effective implementation of the provisions of this Agreement.

2. The principles of fungibility and equivalence shall apply to material and non-nuclear material subject to this Agreement. Detailed provisions for applying these principles shall be set forth in the Administrative Arrangement.

3. The Administrative Arrangement established pursuant to this Article may be amended by agreement of the appropriate authorities of the Parties.

IN WITNESS WHEREOF the undersigned, being duly authorized, have signed this Agreement.

DONE in Washington (D.C.), this 10th day of October, 2008, in duplicate.

For the Government of India

(Pranab Mukherjee)
Minister of External Affairs
Government of India

For the Government of
United States of America
(Condoleezza Rice)
Secretary of State,
Government of the
United State of America

AGREED MINUTE

During the negotiation of the Agreement for Cooperation Between the Government of the United States of America and the Government of India Concerning Peaceful Uses of Nuclear Energy ("the Agreement") signed today, the following understandings, which shall be an integral part of the Agreement, were reached.

Proportionality

For the purposes of implementing the rights specified in Articles 6 and 7 of the Agreement with respect to special fissionable material and by-product material produced through the use of nuclear material and non-nuclear material, respectively, transferred pursuant to the Agreement and not used in or produced through the use of equipment transferred pursuant to the Agreement, such rights shall in practice be applied to that proportion of special fissionable material and by-product material produced that represents the ratio of transferred nuclear material and non-nuclear material, respectively, used in the production of the special fissionable material and by-product material to the total amount of nuclear material and non-nuclear material so used, and similarly for subsequent generations.

By-product material

The Parties agree that reporting and exchanges of information on by-product material subject to the Agreement will be limited to the following:

1. Both Parties would comply with the provisions as contained in the IAEA document GOV/1999/19/Rev.2, with regard to by-product material subject to the Agreement.
2. With regard to tritium subject to the Agreement, the Parties will exchange annually information pertaining to its disposition for peaceful purposes consistent with Article 9 of this Agreement.

For the Government of India

(Pranab Mukherjee)
Minister of External Affairs
Government of India

For the Government of
United States of America
(Condoleezza Rice)
Secretary of State,
Government of the
United State of America

Notes

I: The India–China Agreement on Tibet, 1954

1   Bhasin, *India–China*, Nehru to Panikkar, 16 June 1952, Vol. II, p. 723.

2   Shakabpa, W.D., *Tibet, A Political History*, Potala Publications, New York, 1984, p. 198, quoted in Warren Smith's *Tibetan Nation*, HarperCollins, New Delhi, 1996, p. 153.

3   Smith, Warren, *Tibetan Nation: A History of Tibetan Nationalism and Sino–Tibetan Relations*, HarperCollins, New Delhi, 1997, p. 156.

4   Lamb, Alastair, *The McMahon Line: A Study in Relations between India, China and Tibet*, Routledge and Kegan Paul/ University of Toronto Press, 1966, p. 49.

5   Lamb, *The McMahon Line*, p. 93.

6   Lamb, *The McMahon Line*, p. 3.

7   Lamb, *The McMahon Line*, p. 6.

8   Lamb, *The McMahon Line*, p. 27.

9   Lamb, *The McMahon Line*, p. 149.

10 Smith, *Tibetan Nation*, pp. 168–69.

11 Lamb, *The McMahon Line*, p. 199.

12 Maxwell, Neville, *India's China War*, Jaico Publishing House, Bombay, 1970, p. 42.

13 Maxwell, *India's China War*, p. 46.

14 Mehra, P., *North–Eastern Frontier*, Vol. I, Oxford University Press, 1979, pp. 66–67, memorandum from British Minister Jordan to Chinese Foreign Office, 12 August 1912.

15 Smith, *A History of Tibetan Nationalism and Sino–Tibetan Relations*, p. 183.

16   Lamb, *The McMahon Line*, p. 468.

17   Lamb, *The McMahon Line*, p. 524.

18   Woodman, Dorothy, *Himalayan Frontiers: A Political Review of British, Chinese, Indian and Russian Rivalries*, Barrie and Jenkins, 1969, p. 176; Barrie and Rockliff, The Cresset Press, London, 1969, p. 176.

19   Bhasin, *India–China*, p. 3.

20   Bhasin, *India–*, p. 11, Letter from Foreign Secretary Anthony Eden to Chinese Ambassador T.V. Soong, 5 August 1943.

21   Bhasin, *India–China*, p. 12, Letter from GoI to Secretary of State for India, 3 April 1944; *India–China*, Vol. I, p. 12.

22   Reid, Robert, *History of the Areas Bordering Assam*, Republished by Eastern Publishing House, Delhi, 1983, p. 294–95, original published by Assam G24 Maxwell, p. 56.

23   Reid, *History of the Areas Bordering Assam*, p. 295.

24   Maxwell, *India's China War*, p. 56.

25   Reid, *History of the Areas Bordering Assam*, p. 295.

26   Reid, *History of the Areas Bordering Assam*, p. 295.

27   Maxwell, *India's China War*, pp. 57–58.

28   Maxwell, *India's China War*, p. 58, quoting Political External Dept, Collection No. 36, File 23, letter dt. 23 March 1939.

29   Gould's Memorandum No. 77-P. 44, dated camp–Lhasa, 7 December 1944, External Dept File No. 157-CA/44-Secret.

30   Foreign Dept File No. 7/2/NEF/48-Secret.

31   Mansergh, Nicholas and Moon, Penderel, *Transfer of Power*, ed., HMSO Vol. X, 1981, p. 156.

32   Mansergh and Moon, *Transfer of Power*, p. 156.

33   Letter from LAC Fry, Deputy Secretary, Government of India to Political Officer in Gangtok, 8 April 1947. *India–China*, Vol. I, p. 38.

34   Gopal, S.W.J.N., Vol. 2, p. 176, Parliamentary Debates, 1950, Vol. 5, Part-I, pp. 155–56.

35   MEA file No. 713/NEF/49-pt. II-Secret.

36   'Journal of the Royal Society for Encouragement of Art', JSTOR, Vol. 84, No. 4330, pp. 2–16.

37   Lamb, *The McMahon Line,* p. 548.

38   Letter from Ambassador K.P.S. Menon to Foreign Dept 21 October 1947, File No. 124 NEF/47-Secret.

39   Mansergh and Moon, *Transfer of Power*, p. 156, Foreign Dept to Political Officer, 8 April 1947.

40   Sen, Tansen, *India, China and the World: A connected history*, New Delhi, OUP, 2018, p. 340.

41   Tibet Govt. letter to PM Nehru, 16 October 1947, Foreign Dept F. No. 124NEF/47-NAI.

42   Nehru Letter to Zhou, 26 September 1959, para. 14, White Paper-II, pp. 35–46.

43   Panikkar, K.M., *In Two Chinas, Memoire of a Diplomat*, Allen Unwin, London, 1955, p. 220.

44   Note by F.S., 12 November 1949, MEA File No. 7/13/NEC/49-Secret.

45   Foreign Dept File No. 7/13/NEF/49; Part II-Secret.

46   Nehru's letter to the premiers of the Indian provinces, 1 December 1949, *Selected Works of Jawaharlal Nehru*, Vol. No. 14, Part-I, p. 367.

47   Foreign Relations of the United States (FRUS), April 1949, Vol. IX, pp. 1065–68.

48   P.O. to the Ministry of External Affairs (MEA), 17 August 1950, 'Nehru Papers', Folio No. 52-I, p. 181.

49   P.O. to MEA of Tibet, 17 August. 1950; Nehru Papers, Folio No. 52-I, p.181.

50   Bhasin, *Nehru, Tibet and China*, p. 46; Foreign Dept File No. 7/13/NEF/49-secret (NAI).

51   Article by a Chinese Jurist; *People's Daily*, 13 September 1949; *India–China*; Vol. I, p. 147.

52   FS note, 19 November 1949, Foreign Dept File No. 7/13/NEC/49-Secret.

53   MEA File No. 7/13/NEF/1949-Part. II-Secret.

54   Bhasin, A.S., *Nepal's Relations with India and China*, Geetika Publishers, New Delhi, 2005, Vol. V, p. 3042.

55   MEA File No. 7/13/NEF/49-Part.II, Secret.

56   *Selected Works of Jawaharlal Nehru*; Vol. 15; Part II, 20 November
      1950, p. 349.

57   PM's letter to chief ministers of states, 17 November 1950.;
      Selected Works of Jawaharlal Nehru, Vol. 15; Part II, p. 342.

58   Foreign Dept File No. 7/2/NEF/48 –Secret.

59   PM's note from 8 November 1950; Nehru's Note on Recent
      Developments in East and South Asia; *Selected Works of Jawaharlal
      Nehru*, Vol. 15, Part II, p. 407.

60   'Nehru Papers', Folio No. 120-I, 10 March 1952, p. 79.

61   'Nehru Papers', Indian Embassy to MEA, 21 August 1950, Folio
      No. 52-I, p. 215–17.

62   'Nehru Papers', Mission Lhasa to MEA, 11 March 1951, Folio
      No. 76-II, p. 338.

63   'Nehru Papers', Indian Embassy to MEA, 15 June 1952, Folio
      No. 134-I, pp. 148–49.

64   'Nehru Papers', 20 August 1953, Folio No. 196-I, p. 15.

65   Nehru Papers, Folio No. 138–II, 14 July 1952, pp. 273–74.

66   Nehru's Remarks at a press conference; 21 June 1952; *Selected
      Works of Jawaharlal Nehru*, Vol. 18, p. 376.

67   'Nehru Papers', 20 August 1953, Folio No. 196-I, p. 15 and
      Folio No. 199-I, p. 1.

68   'Nehru Papers', 11 February 1952, Folio No. 117-I, p. 183.

69   Indian Embassy telegram, 13 February 1952.

70   'Nehru Papers', Folio No. 138-I, p. 114 and 114a.

71   'Nehru Papers', 18 July 1952, Folio No. 139-I, p. 113.

72   'Nehru Papers', Folio No. 117-I, p. 183.

73   'Nehru Papers', Indian Embassy's telegram to the PM, 15 June
      1952, Folio No. 134-I, pp. 148–49.

74   'Nehru Papers', 15 June 1952, Folio No. 134-I, pp. 148–49.

75   'Nehru Papers', 16 June 1952, Folio No.134-II, p. 202.

76   'Nehru Papers', 17 June 1952, Folio No. 134-II; pp. 222–23.

77   'Nehru Papers', 17 June 1952, Folio No. 134-II, pp. 222–23.

78   Nehru Papers, 18 June 1952; Folio No. 135-I, p. 8.

79   MEA Telegram to Embassy in Beijing, 31 July 1952.

80   Goldstein, Melvyn, *A History of Modern Tibet*, 1913–51,
      University of California Press, Berkeley, 1991,Vol. II, p. 23.

81   'Nehru Papers', 31 July 1952, Folio No. 140-II, pp. 328–29.

82   'Nehru Papers', Letter from Panikkar to Governor of Bombay, 4 August 1952, Folio No. 142-I, pp. 106–07.

83   'Nehru Papers', 7 August 1952, Folio No. 142-I, p. 108.

84   It was a comprehensive note of all the difficulties and problems faced by the Indian establishment in Tibet since Chinese occupation of Tibet was handed over to the Assistant Foreign Minister of China Chiao Kuan-Hua by the Foreign Secretary. A note on problems being faced by Indian Agencies in Tibet; 28 August 1953; *India–China*; Vol. II, p. 928.

85   Note by Nehru, 30 August 1953, *Selected Works of Jawaharlal Nehru*, Vol. 23, p. 484.

86   *Selected Works of Jawaharlal Nehru*, August,1953; Vol. 23/24, pp. 482–83.

87   Madan, Tanvi, *Fateful Triangle*, Penguin, Gurugram, 2019, p. 59.

88   'Nehru Papers', Folio No. 140-II, pp. 328–29 and Folio No. 141-I, p. 77.

89   'Nehru Papers', Nehru's message to Zhou, 1 September 1953. Folio No. 199-I, p. 274.

90   'Nehru Papers', 15 June 1952, Folio No. 134-I, p. 148–49.

91   PM's minute on the note by the Ministry of External Affairs; *India–China*, 28 August 1953. Vol. II, p. 930.

92   Note by T.N. Kaul; *India–China*, Vol. II, p. 859.

93   Internal notes in the Ministry of External Affairs, 26 September 1953, Bhasin, *India–China*, pp. 955–63.

94   Zhou's letter to Nehru, 19 October 1953, *Selected Works of Jawaharlal Nehru*, Vol. 24, p. 595, fn.

95   'Nehru Papers', Folio No. 199-I, pp. 274–80.

96   *Selected Works of Jawaharlal Nehru*, Vol. 24; foot note No. 3, p. 596.

97   PM's Note, 25 October 1954, *Selected Works of Jawaharlal Nehru*, Vol. 24, p. 596–97.

98   PM's Note, 25 October 1954, *Selected Works of Jawaharlal Nehru*, Vol. 24, p. 596–97.

99   'Nehru Papers', Indian mission in Lhasa to MEA, 27 November 1953, Folio No. 217-I, p. 23.

100   'Nehru Papers', 31 October 1953, Folio No. 210-II, p. 303–06.

101   'Nehru Papers', 31 October 1953, Folio No. 210-II, pp. 303–06.

102   Note by the MEA on main points for discussion with China; 3 December 1953; *India–China*; Vol. II; p. 970.

103   Note by the MEA on main points for discussion with China; 3 December 1953; *India–China*; Vol. II; p. 970.

104   Note by the MEA on main points for discussion with China; 3 December 1953; *India–China*; Vol. II; p. 970.

105   Note by the MEA on main points for discussion with China; 3 December 1953; *India–China*; Vol. II; p. 970.

106   Note by the MEA on main points for discussion with China; 3 December 1953; *India–China s*; Vol. II; p. 970.

107   'Nehru Papers', MEA Brief, 3 December 1953, Folio No. 218, pp. 200–08.

108   'Nehru Papers', 3 December 1953, Folio No. 218, pp. 200–08.

109   'Nehru Papers', MEA to Lhasa consulate, 27 January 1954, Folio No. 232-I, p. 80.

110   'Nehru Papers' Indian Embassy Beijing to MEA, 2 January 1954, Folio No. 226-I, pp. 14–15.

111   'Nehru Papers' Indian Embassy Beijing to MEA, 2 January 1954, Nehru Papers, Folio No. 226-I, pp. 14–15.

112   Telegram from Beijing; 31 December 1953; Nehru Papers; Folio No, 226-I, pp. 14–15; in *India–China*, Vol., II, p. 993.

113   *India–China*, Vol. II, 8 January 1954, p. 1000 (Nehru Papers, Folio. 227-II, p. 190)

114   'Nehru Papers', 8 January 1954, Folio No. 227-II, p. 190.

115   'Nehru Papers', 9 January 1954, Folio No. 228, p. 52.

116   'Nehru Papers', Telegram from Embassy in Peking to MEA, 12 January 1954, Folio No. 228, pp. 215–18.

117   'Nehru Papers', PM to Ambassador, 31 December 1953, Folio No. 225, p. 119.

118   'Nehru Papers', Indian Embassy in Beijing to MEA, 11 January 1954, Folio No. 228, pp. 127–30.

119 'Nehru Papers', Indian Embassy to MEA, 18 March 1954, Folio No. 241-I, pp. 96–97.

120 'Nehru Papers', MEA to Indian Embassy Beijing, 21 March 1954, Folio No. 241-II, p. 272.

121 'Nehru Papers', Indian Embassy Beijing to MEA, 23 March 1954, Folio No. 241-II, p. 418.

122 'Nehru Papers', MEA to Indian Embassy, 19 March 1954, Folio No. 241-I, p. 160.

123 'Nehru Papers', Indian Embassy to MEA, 22 March 1951, Folio No. 78-I, p. 8.

124 *India–China*, Vol. II, 888; Nehru Papers, Folio. 161-II, p. 315.

125 'Nehru Papers', MEA to Raghavan, 21 January 1954, Folio No. 230-II, pp. 269–70.

126 'Nehru Papers', Raghavan to MEA, 23 January 1954, Nehru Papers, Folio No. 231, p. 82.

127 'Nehru Papers', MEA to Indian Embassy, 25 January 1954, Folio No. 231, p. 216.

128 'Nehru Papers', Folio No. 241-II, pp. 475–78.

129 'Nehru Papers', FS to Ambassador, 2 April 1954, Folio No. 244-I, p. 120.

130 'Nehru Papers', Ambassador to FS, 3 April 1954, Folio No. 244-II, p. 202.

131 Second, third and fourth parts of telegram. No. 23 dated 11 January 1954; *India–China*, Vol. II, p. 1006.

132 'Nehru Papers', Indian Embassy to MEA, 3 April 1954, Folio No. 244-II, p. 202.

133 'Nehru Papers', Folio. No. 245-II, p. 191 and 245-II, p. 189.

134 Kaul, T.N. *Diplomacy in Peace and War*, Vikas Publishing House, Uttar Pradesh, 1979, p. 102.

135 'Nehru Papers', Folio No. 246-I, p. 70.

136 P.M. telegram to Amb. Raghavan, 16 April 1954; *India–China*, Vol. II, p.1071; Nehru Papers, Folio 247; p. 19.

137 'Nehru Papers', PM to Ambassador, 16 April 1954, Folio No. 247, p. 19.

138 'Nehru Papers', PM to Ambassador Raghavan, 16 April 1954, Folio No 247, p. 19.

139   'Nehru Papers', MEA to Indian Embassy, 20 April 1954, Folio No. 247, p. 231

140   'Nehru Papers', Indian Embassy to MEA, 23 April 1954, Folio No. 248-I, p. 185.

141   Gopal, S., *Jawaharlal Nehru*, Vol. II, Oxford University Press, New Delhi, 1979, p. 180.

142   Gopal. S, speech in the Lok Sabha on the agreement, 15 May 1954, p. 180.

143   PM's Statement in Parliament; 3 May 1954; *India–China*, Vol. II, p. 1108.

144   Bhasin, *India–China*, Vol. II, p. 1109.

145   Gopal, P., Nehru's note to SG and FS, 2 May 1954, p. 468.

146   PM to Ambassador in Rangoon, 9 March 1954.

147   Gopal, S., *Nehru's Biography*, OUP, New Delhi, 1979, Vol. II, p. 181.

148   Gopal, *Nehru's Biography*, p. 181.

149   White Paper, 4 November 1959, No. 2, p. 24.; Gopal. S., *Jawaharlal Nehru: A Biography*, Vol. II, New Delhi, 1979, p. 181.

150   'Nehru Papers', Mao at the Credential ceremony of Panikkar, 20 May 1950, Folio No. 44-II, p. 282.

151   PM's note to SG. 18 June 1954.

152   Woodman, Dorothy, *Himalayan Frontier: A Political Review of British, Chinese, Indian and Russian Rivalries*, Barrie & Jenkins, 1969, p. 226.

153   Woodman, *Himalayan Frontier*, p. 226.

154   Woodman, *Himalayan Frontier,* p. 226.

155   Bhasin, A.S., PM's note on policy toward east and south Asia, 8 November 1950, Doc. No. 266, p. 452 in Vol. I of the five volume study of *India–China*.

156   Nehru's letter to G.L. Mehta, Indian Ambassador in USA, 29 June 1954, *Selected Works of Jawaharlal Nehru*, Vol. 26, p. 356.

157   'Nehru Papers', Kaul's Report, Folio No. 252-II, pp. 358–65.

158   T.N. Kaul's Report, 12 May 1954; Nehru's Papers; Folio 252-II, pp. 358–65.

159   'Nehru Papers', 1 July 1954, Folio No. 265-I, pp. 34–36.

160   *India–China*, Vol. III, p. 2767.

161   *India–China*, Vol. IV, p. 3286.

162   Nehru's note on Tibet, 18 June 1954, *Selected Works of Jawaharlal Nehru*, Vol. 26, p. 477.

163   Nehru's speech in the Lok Sabha; Nehru, Jawaharlal, *India's Foreign Policy*, Publication Division, 1961, p. 57.

II: Indo–Soviet Treaty of Peace, Friendship and Cooperation, 1971

1   Jawaharlal, Nehru, *India's Foreign Policy*, The Publication Division, Ministry of Information and Broadcasting, New Delhi, 1961, p. 24.

2   Nehru replying to the debate on foreign affairs in the Lok Sabha, 12 June 1952. Nehru, *India's Foreign Policy*, p. 57.

3   Nehru, Jawaharlal, *Selected Works of Jawaharlal Nehru*, Nehru's letter to Ambassador S. Radhakrishnan in Moscow, 5 March 1950 and letter dated 26 February 1950, Vol. 14, Part I, p. 543.

4   Letter from the PM to the Ambassador in Moscow, 3 December 1962, *India–China*, Vol. IV, p. 4087.

5   This is part of the famous Pakistan Resolution of 24 March 1940.

6   Aziz, K.K., *The Making of Pakistan: A Study in Nationalism*, Sang-e-Meer Publications, Lahore, 1998, p. 56.

7   Dil, Anwar S. and Dil Afia, *Bengali Language Movement in Bangladesh*, Intellectual Forum, 2000, p. 82.

8   Transfer of Power, 20 June 1947, Vol. XI, pp. 244–45.

9   Transfer of Power, Proceedings of League's Convention, 10 June 1947, Vol. IX, pp. 244–45.

10   Bhasin, A.S., *India–Bangladesh Relations: 1971–2002*, Geetika Publishers, New Delhi, Vol. I, p. xiii.

11   Menon, S., quoted in *Geopolitics of Asia*, Penguin, Gurugram, p. 123.

12   Zakaria, Anam, *A People's History from Bangladesh, Pakistan and India*, Penguin (Vintage) Gurugram, 2019, p. 69.

13   Zakaria, *A People's History from Bangladesh*, p. 70.

14   Jones, Owen Bennett, *Pakistan: Eye of the Storm*, Viking, New Delhi, 2002, p. 153.

15   Babar, Ayaz, *What's Wrong with Pakistan?* Hay House, New Delhi, p. 64.

16   Jaffrelot, Christophe, *A History of Pakistan and Its Origins*, Anthem Press, London, 2002, p. 51.

17   Babar, *What's Wrong with Pakistan?* p. 64.

18   Jones, *Pakistan*, p. 158.

19   Jaffrelot, *A History of Pakistan and Its Origin,* p. 51.

20   Rahman, Sheikh Mujibur, *Unfinished Memoirs*, The University Press, Dhaka, p. xxii, cited in Zakaria, *A People's History from Bangladesh*, p. 89.

21   Dixit, J.N., *Liberation and Beyond*, Konark, New Delhi, 1999, p. 28.

22   Jaffrelot, *A History of Pakistan and Its Origin,* p. 53.

23   Khan, Roedad, *The American Papers, Secret and Confidential: India–Pakistan–Bangladesh Documents, 1965–1973*, OUP, Karachi, 1999, p. 274.

24   Choudhury, G.M., *The Last Days of United Pakistan*, Hurst & Co., London, 1974, p. 85.

25   Choudhury, *The Last Days of United Pakistan*, p. 85.

26   Salik, Siddiq, *Witness to Surrender*, University Press, Dhaka, 1997, p. 32.

27   Zaheer, Hasan, *The Separation of East Pakistan: The Rise and Realization of Bengali Muslim Nationalism*, OUP, Karachi, p. 134.

28   Choudhury, *The Last Days of United Pakistan,* p. 149.

29   Choudhury, *The Last Days of United Pakistan,* p.146.

30   Choudhury, *The Last Days of United Pakistan,* p.151.

31 Lt Gen. Niazi, A.A.K., Lt Gen., *The Betrayal of East Pakistan*, OUP, Karachi, 1999, p. xxiv and p. xxv.

32   Bhasin, *India–Pakistan*, Vol. III, 26 March 1971, p. 1351.

33   Statement by Yahya Khan, 26 March 1971, *India–Pakistan*, Vol. III, p. 1351.

34   Menon, Shivshankar, *India and Asian Geopolitics*, Penguin, Gurugram, 2021, p. 127.

35 Kaul, T.N., *Diplomacy in Peace and War*, Vikas Publishing House, Ghaziabad, UP, 1979, p. 181.

36 Kow, R.N., director R&AW's note and intelligence assessment, 14 January 1971, *India–Pakistan*, Vol. III, p. 1317.

37 Indian External Affairs Minister's message to Pakistan Interior minister, 1 February 1971, *India–Pakistan*, Vol. III, p. 1325.

38 Statement by the PM in the Lok Sabha on 27 March 1971, *India–Pakistan*, Vol. III, p. 1357.

39 *India–Pakistan*, Vol. III, p. 1368.

40 Circular letter from the MEA to Indian missions abroad, 17 April 1971, *India–Pakistan*, Vol. III, p. 1372.

41 *The American Papers*, President Nixon's letter to Yahya, 7 May 1971, p. 564.

42 *The American Papers*, Memorandum of Conversation from 10 May 1971, p. 577.

43 Raghavan, Srinath, *Bangladesh*, Permanent Black, Ranikhet Cantt., 2013, p. 156.

44 Note on the meeting between the foreign secretary and American Ambassador Chester Bowles, 1 April 1968, *India–Pakistan*, Vol. III, p. 1780.

45 Kaul, T.N., Note of 24 November 1970.

46 The EAM's statement in the Lok Sabha, 6 July 1971, *India–Pakistan*, Vol. VI, p. 4392.

47 Record of discussions between Foreign Secretary T.N. Kaul and Chairman Kosygin, 25 May 1970, *India–Pakistan*, Vol. III, p. 1307.

48 Note by Foreign Secretary T.N. Kaul on his talks with Kosygin in Moscow, 25 May 1970, *India–Pakistan*, Vol. III, p. 1307.

49 *The American Papers*, US Senior Review Group assessment, 16 April 1971, p. 544.

50 Top-secret telegram from DHC, Dhaka via Cabinet Sect., 14 March 1971, *India–Pakistan*, Vol. III, p. 1349.

51 Top-secret telegram from Dhaka via Cabinet Sect., 14 March 1971, *India–Pakistan*, Vol. III, p. 1349.

52 Pakistan's note of 22 March 1971, *India–Pakistan*, Vol. III, pp. 1350–51.

53   Foreign Relations of the United States (FRUS), Office of the Historian, United States Department of State, 27 March 1971, Vol. IX/12.

54   Bhasin, A.S., *India and Pakistan: Neighbours at Odds*, Bloomsbury, New Delhi, 2018, p. 218.

55   Ambassador Dhar's Letter No. MOS/Amb/378/71-Haksar Papers. NMML.

56   *The American Papers*, American Embassy, Kabul, telegram to the State Dept, 30 August 1971, p. 648.

57   'Haksar Papers', Nehru Memorial Museum and Library (NMML; renamed the Prime Ministers' Museum and Library Society), New Delhi.

58   Marker, Jamsheed, *Quiet Diplomacy*, Oxford, New Delhi, 2010, pp. 119–20.

59   Marker, *Quiet Diplomacy,* p. 121.

60   Marker, *Quiet Diplomacy,* p. 122.

61   'Haksar Papers', NMML.

62   'Haksar Papers', NMML.

63   Note of the conversation between Kosygin and Arshad Hussain, top-secret letter marked 'strictly personal' from Haksar to Ambassador Dhar containing the above conversation, 22 May 1971, Haksar File No. 166.

64   Marker, *Quiet Diplomacy,* p. 123.

65   Marker, *Quiet Diplomacy,* p. 124.

66   'Haksar Papers', Telegram from Ambassador Dhar to the MEA, No. 378, CCB No. 06152, 28 April 1971.

67   Marker, *Quiet Diplomacy,* p. 129.

68   Marker, *Quiet Diplomacy,* p. 130.

69   'Haksar Papers', NMML.

70   Letter No. MOS/AMB/378/71 from Ambassador Dhar, 4 April 1971.

71   'Haksar Papers', Ambassador's Dhar letter to the FS, No. 518-Amb/71, 29 April 1971.

72   Article by the *People's Daily,* 11 April 1971, Bhasin, A.S., *India–China Relations, 1947–2000*, Vol. V, p. 4841.

73   Zhou's message to Yahya Khan, 12 April 1971, *India–China*, Vol. V, p. 4843.

74 Record of conversation at the State Dept. about the conflict, 20 September 1965, *India–Pakistan*, Vol. VI, p. 5195.

75 'Appa Pant Papers', NMML.

76 Bhutto's speech on 24 July 1963, *India–Pakistan*, Vol. II, p. 937.

77 Statement of Bhutto in the National Assembly, 17 July 1963, *India–Pakistan*, Vol. II, p. 925.

78 Letter from High Commissioner Parathasarthi to Foreign Secretary, 23 July 1963, *India–Pakistan*, Vol. II, p. 933.

79 US Foreign Policy Documents, No. 317, Vol. XIX.

80 US Foreign Policy Documents, No. 322, Vol. XIX.

81 Talks between Defence Minister Jagjivan Ram and Kissinger, 13 July 1971, *India–Pakistan*, Vol. III, pp. 1409–13.

82 *The American Papers*, discussions in the White House, 11 August 1971, p. 658.

83 Menon, Shivshankar, *India and Asian Geopolitics*, Penguin, Gurugram, 2021, p. 130.

84 Sultan Khan, *Memories and Reflections of a Pakistani Diplomat*, Centre for Pakistan Studies, London, p. 188, quoted in Raghavan, *Bangladesh*, p. 184.

85 Menon, *India and Asian Geopolitics*, p. 130.

86 Raghavan, Srinath, *1971: A Global History of the Creation of Bangladesh*, Harvard University Press, London, 2013, p. 184, quoting Sultan Khan, *Memories and Reflections of a Pakistani Diplomat*, p. 344.

87 'Haksar Papers', High Commissioner to FS, 6 November 1971.

88 Menon, *India and Asian Geopolitics*, p. 132.

89 'Haksar Papers', Letter No. PAR/104/2/71, 6 July 1971, NMML.

90 Record of talks between the EAM and Kissinger, 7 July 1971, *India–Pakistan*, Vol. III, p. 1408.

91 Letter from Pakistan Minister of Foreign Affairs, 24 July 1971, *India–Pakistan*, Vol. III, pp. 1415–16.

92 'Haksar Papers'.

93 Letter No. Par/104/2/71, 6 July 1971.

94 Record of discussions between President Nixon, Kissinger and Bhutto, 18 September 1973, *India–Pakistan*, Vol. III, p. 2189.

95 Shankar, Kalyani, *Nixon, Indira: Politics and Beyond*, Macmillan, New Delhi, p. 233.

96   Top-secret letter No. 282-Min/69, 27 March 1969.; Bhasin, *India and Pakistan*, p. 214.

97   Menon, *India and Asian Geopolitics*, p. 127.

98   Bhasin, *India and Pakistan,* p. 217.

99   Haksar's letter to Ambassador Dhar, 7 April 1971, *India–Pakistan,* p. 220.

100 Mrs Gandhi's letter of 27 April 1971, Bhasin, *India–Pakistan*, p. 220 (Text in Haksar Papers).

101 Dhar's top secret letter to FS T.N. Kaul, No. 519/AMB/71, 29 April 1971, *India–Pakistan* (Text in Haksar Papers).

102 Dhar's top secret letter to Haksar, No. 518-Amb/71, 29 April 1971.

103 Record of call by Dhar on Soviet defence minister, 5 June 1971, *India–Pakistan*, Vol. III, p. 1387.

104 Record of call by Dhar on Soviet defence minister, 5 June 1971, *India–Pakistan*, Vol. III, p. 1387

105 Ambassador Dhar's top-secret letter D.O. No. 677-AMB/71, 5 June 1971, *India–Pakistan*, Vol. III, p. 1385.

106 Ambassador Dhar's top-secret letter to Foreign Secretary, D.O. No. 677-AMB/71, 5 June 1971, *India–Pakistan*, Vol. III, p. 1385.

107 *India–Pakistan*, 6 July 1971, Vol. III, p. 1395.

108 Talks between Haksar and Kissinger, 6 July 1971, *India–Pakistan*, Vol. III, p. 1395.

109 Dasgupta, C., *India and the Bangladesh Liberation War*, Juggernaut, New Delhi, 2021, p. 139.

110 Letter from Nixon to Mrs Gandhi, 1 July 1971, *India–Pakistan*, Vol. III, p. 1394.

111 Mrs Gandhi's letter to Nixon, 7 August 1971, *India–Pakistan*, Vol. III, pp. 1444–46.

112 Kaul, T.N., *Diplomacy in Peace and War: Recollections and Reflections*, Vikas, 1979, p. 183.

113 'Haksar Papers', discussions between Swaran Singh and Soviet leaders and subsequent discussion on the draft of the treaty, third instalment, Sub. File 203.

114 Record of discussions between Dhar and Kosygin on 5 August 1971, *India–Pakistan*, Vol. III, pp. 1417–38.

115   Yahya's letter to Kosygin, 6 August 1971, *India–Pakistan*, Vol. III, pp. 1441–44.

116   EAM's statement in Rajya Sabha, 21 June 1971, *India–Pakistan*, Vol. III, p. 1414.

117   'Haksar Papers', top-secret letter from Lt Governor Tripur to PM, No. 11/LG/RN/71 of 27 April 1971.

118   The EAM's statement in the Lok Sabha, 9 August 1971, *India–Pakistan*, Vol. III, p. 1448.

119   Menon, *India and Asian Geopolitics,* p. 131.

120   Talks between Gromyko and Mrs Gandhi, 10 August 1971, *India–Pakistan*, Vol. III, pp. 1453–54.

121   Indian Embassy, Boon telegram conveying message from Beijing, 8 November 1971, *India–Pakistan*, Vol. III, p. 1503.

122   *The Hindu,* 4 September 1971.

123   Radio Peking Broadcast, 5 December 1971.

124   *The American Papers*, State Dept Memorandum on situation report, 16 September 1971, p. 665.

125   *The American Papers*, telegram from American Embassy, Islamabad, to State Dept., 21 September 1971, p. 669.

126   *The American Papers*, US Bureau of Intelligence and Research report, 27 September 1971, p. 679.

127   *The American Papers*, American Embassy in Colombo telegram, 1 October 1971, p. 732.

128   Record of meeting of Bhutto with Nixon and Kissinger, 18 September 1973, *India–Pakistan*, Vol. III, p. 2189.

129   Shankar, Kalyani, *Nixon, Indira and India: Politics and Beyond*, Macmillan, New Delhi, p. 233.

130   Message of PM Indira Gandhi to Zhou Enlai on China's admission to the UN, 27 October 1971, *India–China*; Vol. V. p. 4846.

131   Huang Hua's Speech in the UNSC, 4 December 1971, *India–China*, Vol. V, p. 4848.

132   Huang Hua's Speech in the UNSC, 5 December 1971, *India–China*, Vol. V, p. 4850.

133   Statement in the UNGA, 7 December 1971, *India–China*, Vol. V, p. 4851.

134   Mrs Gandhi's letter to the Chinese premier, 11 December 1971, *India–China*, Vol. V, p. 4855.
135   Chinese statement of 16 December 1971, *India–China*, Vol. V, p. 4858.
136   D.P. Dhar's meeting with Kosygin, 24 February 1972, Vol. III, p. 1606.
137   Discussions between D.P. Dhar and Chief of Army Staff and Soviet General Staff, *India–Pakistan*, Vol. III, p. 1624

III: The Simla Agreement, 1972

1   Marker, Jamsheed, *Quiet Diplomacy*, Oxford University Press, New Delhi, 2010, p. 149.
2   Marker, *Quite Diplomacy*, p. 152.
3   Subramaniam, Arjun, *India's Wars: 1947–71*, HarperCollins, Noida, 2016, p. 427.
4   Singh, K. Natwar, *One Life Is Not Enough*, Rupa Publications, New Delhi, 2014, p. 155.
5   Prasad, S.N. and Thapliya, U.P. (eds), *The India–Pakistan War of 1971: A History*, Natraj Publishers, Dehradun, New Delhi, 2014, p. 427.
6   Note of the Sri Lankan High Commissioner, 17 February 1972, *India–Pakistan*, Vol. III, pp. 1651–52.
7   Messages exchanged between New Delhi and Colombo, 25 February 1972, *India–Pakistan*, Vol. III, pp. 1651–53.
8   Indian note of 17 February 1972 to Pakistan via the Swiss embassy, *India–Pakistan*, Vol. III, p. 1650.
9   Indian note of 17 February 1972 to Pakistan through the Swiss Embassy, *India–Pakistan*, Vol. III, p. 1650.
10   Note of Swiss Ambassador on 27 February 1972 on behalf of Pakistan; Bhutto's interview to journalists of the *Times of India* and the *Indian Express* in Larkana on 14 March 1972. *India–Pakistan*, Vol. III, pp. 1644–45.
11   Message from Douglas-Home to the PM, 20 March 1971, *India–Pakistan*, Vol. III, pp. 1648–49.

12   Note of the Secretary (East) in the MEA S.K. Banerjee to the Principal Secretary to the PM on 21 March 1972, *India–Pakistan*, Vol. III, pp. 1649–59.

13   Swiss embassy's note of 28 February 1972, *India–Pakistan*, Vol. III, p. 1651.

14   Record of discussion between Foreign Secretary and Swiss Ambassador, 26 March 1972, *India–Pakistan*, Vol. III, pp. 1654–56.

15   The EAM's letter of 7 June 1972, *India–Pakistan*, Vol. III, p. 1674.

16   Note on the conversation by Ambassador Chatterjee, 21 February 1972, *India–Pakistan*, Vol. III, p. 1602.

17   Mrs Gandhi's letter to the French President, 12 June 1972, *India–Pakistan*, Vol. III, pp. 1675–77.

18   Telegram from Ambassador in Belgian on his meeting with the Head of Asia Dept, 26 June 1972, *India–Pakistan*, Vol. III, pp. 1680–81.

19   Letters exchanged between the Sudanese President and PM Indira Gandhi on 9 April 1972, *India–Pakistan*, Vol. III, pp. 1659–61.

20   Kosygin–Dhar Talks, 24 February 1972, *India–Pakistan*, Vol. III, p. 1606.

21   Dhar's top-secret note on his talks in Moscow and Paris, undated, *India–Pakistan*, Vol. III, p. 1630.

22   Record of discussions between Kosygin and D.P. Dhar, 24 February 1972, *India–Pakistan*, Vol. III, p. 1609.

23   Note recorded by D.P. Dhar on meeting with Marshal Grechko, 25 February 1972, *India–Pakistan*, Vol. III. p. 1624.

24   Record of discussions between Soviet defence minister and Indian delegation on 25 February 1972, *India–Pakistan*, Vol. III, p. 1624.

25   D.P. Dhar to P.N. Haksar, 26 February 1972, *India–Pakistan*, Vol. III, p. 1629.

26   Mrs Gandhi's letter to Brezhnev, 26 April 1972.

27   Top-secret records of the meeting, 25 April 1972.

28   Mrs Gandhi's letter to Brezhnev, 26 April 1972, 'Haksar Papers'.

29   The PM's top-secret note to the defence minister, 13 May 1972.

30   Top-secret note of the defence minister, 22 May 1972.

31   S. Dutt's Note, 11 May 1972, *India–Pakistan*, Vol. III, p. 1667.

32   Mrs Gandhi's letter to Bhutto, 1 April 1972. P.N. Haksar (III
      Instl.) Sub. File No. 180 (This was a copy of the letter written by
      Mrs Gandhi to Bhutto, but in the present case, a copy of it was
      sent by Haksar to Ambassador in Moscow.)

33   'Haksar Papers', D.P. Dhar's top-secret note to the PM on his
      meeting with the Soviet ambassador, 12 March 1972.

34   D.P. Dhar's top-secret note to the PM on his meeting with the
      Soviet ambassador, 12 March 1972.

35   Dhar–Kosygin Talks, 24 February 1972, *India–Pakistan*, Vol.
      III, p. 1606.

36   Marker, *Quiet Diplomacy*, p. 158.

37   Marker, *Quiet Diplomacy*, pp. 158–60.

38   Marker, *Quiet Diplomacy*, pp. 158–60.

39   'Haksar Papers', Mrs Gandhi's letter to Brezhnev, 26 April 1972.

40   'Haksar Papers', Mrs Gandhi's letter to Brezhnev, 26 April 1972.

41   *The American Papers*, Nixon's letter to Bhutto, 22 March 1972,
      p. 825.

42   Note of discussions between the FS and Swiss Ambassador, 28
      March 1972, *India–Pakistan*, Vol. III, pp. 1654.

43   Text of the five points, 29 April 1972, *India–Pakistan*, Vol. III,
      p. 1664.

44   Text of the ten points, 29 April 1972, *India–Pakistan*, Vol. III,
      p. 1165.

45   Joint statement issued by the two emissaries, 30 April 1972,
      India–Pakistan, Vol. III, p. 1666.

46   *The American Papers*, American Ambassador in Islamabad,
      telephonic conversation, 27 March 1972, p. 828. It is a note of
      US Embassy in Islamabad to State Department.

47   Telegram from Moscow, 26 June 1972, *India–Pakistan*, Vol. III,
      pp. 1682–83.

48   Soviet Memorandum for India reporting Aziz Ahmed's meeting with
      Soviet leaders, 27 June 1972, *India–Pakistan*, Vol. III, p. 1686.

49   Text of Soviet memorandum, *India–Pakistan*, Vol. III, p. 1686.

50   Record of discussions between the EAM and Soviet ambassador Pegov, 27 June 1972, *India–Pakistan*, Vol. III, pp. 1683–85.

51   Note to Sheikh Abdullah, 25 August 1952, *Selected Works of Jawaharlal Nehru*, Vol. 19, p. 324.

52   Nehru's telephone to Patel, 30 October 1948, *India–Pakistan*, Vol. I. p. 117.

53   Pakistani PM's radio broadcast, 8 November 1948, *India–Pakistan*, Vol. I, p. 118.

54   Nehru to Krishna Menon, 20 February 1948, *India–Pakistan*, Vol. VI, p. 4819.

55   Bhutto's speech, 27 June 1972, *India–Pakistan*, Vol. III, pp. 1691–96.

56   Speech at plenary, 28 June 1972, *India–Pakistan*, Vol. III, p. 1710.

57   Note by Haksar, 28 June 1972, *India–Pakistan*, Vol. III, pp. 1698–1700.

58   Note recorded by P.N. Dhar, 28 June 1972, *India–Pakistan,* Vol. III; pp. 1697–98.

59   Telegram from Paris, 27/28 June 1972, *India–Pakistan*, Vol. III, p. 1701.

60   Text of PM's press conference on 1 July 1972, *India–Pakistan*, Vol. III, pp. 1702–10.

61   Remarks of PM and Bhutto, 28 June 1972, *India–Pakistan*, Vol. III, pp. 1710–11.

62   Summary of discussions between official delegations, 28 June 1972, *India–Pakistan*, Vol. III, pp. 1711–18.

63   Text of Joint Statement, 28 June 1972, *India–Pakistan*, Vol. III, p. 1719.

64   Record of discussions on 30 June 1972, *India–Pakistan*, Vol. III, p. 1733.

65   Pakistani draft of the agreement, 30 June 1972, *India–Pakistan*, Vol. III, pp. 1730–31.

66   *India–Pakistan*, 1 July 1972, Vol. III, pp. 1747–48.

67   Record of full meeting of the Indian and Pakistani delegation, *India–Pakistan*, Vol. III, Document No. 0710-H; p. 1738.

68   Kaul, T.N., *Diplomacy in Peace and War*, Vikas Publishers, Ghaziabad, 1979, p. 191.

69   Record of discussions at the full delegations meeting on 1 July 1972, *India–Pakistan*, Vol. III, pp. 1738–44.

70   Veena Datta nee Veena Sikri's note, 3 July 1972, *India–Pakistan*, Vol. III, p. 1758.

71   Bakshi, K.N., *The Ambassadors' Club*, ed. Rajan, Krishna V., HarperCollins, Noida, 2012, p. 17.

72   Bhutto's farewell message, 3 July 1972, *India–Pakistan*, Vol. III, p. 1756.

73   Bhutto's second message, 3 July 1972, *India–Pakistan*, Vol. III, p. 1757.

74   Dixit, J.N., *Anatomy of A Flawed Inheritance, Indo–Pak Relations: 1970–94*, Konark, Delhi, 1995, pp. 323–28.

75   Mrs Gandhi's letter to Sirimavo Bandaranaike, 7 August 1972, *India–Pakistan*, Vol. III, p. 1797.

76   Mrs Gandhi's letter to President Bhutto, 19 August 1972, *India–Pakistan*, Vol. III, p. 1805.

77   *Journal of Peace Studies*, Vol. II, No. 9/10; pp. 33–39.

78   Briefing by FS, 4 July 1972, *India–Pakistan*, Vol. III, p. 1762.

79   Bhutto's speech in the National Assembly, 14 July 1972, *India–Pakistan*, Vol. III, pp. 1764–83.

80   The PM's speech on 31 July 1972, *India–Pakistan*, Vol. III, pp. 1788–94.

81   The EAM's speech in Lok Sabha debate, 31 July 1972, *India–Pakistan*, Vol. III, pp. 1786–87.

82   MEA Aide-memoire, 9 November 1973, *India–Pakistan*, Vol. III, pp. 2211–12.

83   The EAM's letter to Aziz Ahmed, 21 November 1973, *India–Pakistan*, Vol. III, p. 2213.

84   Aziz's letter to the EAM, 29 November 1973, *India–Pakistan*, Vol. III, p. 2217.

85   The EAM's speech, 6 December 1973, *India–Pakistan*, Vol. III, p. 2222.

86   The EAM's letter to Aziz Ahmed, 8 January 1974, *India–Pakistan*, Vol. III, p. 2228.

87   Aziz Ahmed's letter to the EAM, 24 January 1974, *India–Pakistan*, Vol. III, p. 2231.

88   Annexure to text of discussions between Indian ambassador S.K. Lambah and Pak FS on 7 December 1978, *India–Pakistan*, Vol. IV, p. 2449.

89   The PM's speech on 31 July 1972, *India–Pakistan*, Vol. III, pp. 1788–94.

90   Pakistan spokesperson statement, 5 April 1995, *India–Pakistan*, Vol. V, p. 3501.

91   Marker, *Quiet Diplomacy*, p. 162.

92   Marker, *Quiet Diplomacy*, p. 161.

93   Menon, *India and Asian Geopolitics*, p. 136.

94   Bhutto speaking in the National Assembly, 14 July 1972, *India–Pakistan*, Vol. III, p. 1764.

95   Dixit, J.N., *Liberation and Beyond*, Konark, New Delhi, 1999, p. 164.

96   Record of meeting between Bhutto with Nixon and Kissinger, 18 September 1973, *India–Pakistan*, Vol. III, p. 2189.

IV: India–Sri Lanka Accord, 1987

1   Bhasin, A.S. (ed), *India–Sri Lanka Relations and Sri Lanka's Ethnic Conflict*, Vol. I, India Research Press, New Delhi, 2001, p. lxix.

2   Wilson, A. Jeyaratnam, *Politics in Sri Lanka, 1947–79*, Macmillan, London, 1979, Second edition, p. 38.

3   Wilson, *Politics in Sri Lanka*, p. 42.

4   James Manor's contributory chapter in ed. John Clifford Holt's *The Sri Lanka Reader*, Duke University Press, Durham and London, 2011, p. 602.

5   Federal Party Convention, 18–19 August 1956, Trincomalee, Bhasin, Vol. III, p. 1045.

6   Text of joint statement of Bandaranaike and Chelvanayakam Pact, 26 July 1957, *India–Sri Lanka*, Vol. III, p. 1048.

7   See footnote to the Bandaranaike–Chelvanayakam Pact, *India–Sri Lanka*, Vol. III, p. 1048.

8   Report on Tamil Opposition, 9 April 1958, *India–Sri Lanka*, Vol. III, p. 1049.

9   Bandaranaike's statement on 4 July 1958, *India–Sri Lanka*, Vol III, p. 1052.

10 Wilson, *Politics in Sri Lanka*, p. 21.

11 Wilson, *Politics in Sri Lanka*, p. 22.

12 Gundevia, Y.D., *Outside the Archives*, Sangam Books, Hyderabad, 1984, p. 183.

13 PM's speech at a banquet, 30 December 1960, *India–Sri Lanka*, Vol. I, p. 32.

14 Question in Lok Sabha, 6 May 1976, *India–Sri Lanka*, Vol. I, p. 101.

15 Text of Vaddukoddai Resolution, 15 May 197, *India–Sri Lanka*, Vol. III, p. 1070.

16 Mehrotra, Lakhan, contributory chapter in 'Hope and Despair in Sri Lanka', in *Ambassadors' Club,* ed. K.V. Rajan, HarperCollins, Noida, 2012, p. 170.

17 Wickramasinghe, Nira, *Sri Lanka in the Modern Age*, C. Hurst & Co., London, 2006, p. 282.

18 Wickramasinghe, *Sri Lanka in the Modern Age*, p. 282.

19 Prabhakaran's interview to Anita Pratap, *Sunday* magazine, 11 March 1984.

20 Text of document released by the LTTE, 'The Struggle for Tamil Eelam', November 1978, *India–Sri Lanka*, Vol. III, p. 1079.

21 *India–Sri Lanka*, August 1977, Vol. III, p. 1075.

22 Text of speeches, *India–Sri Lanka*, Vol. I, pp. 106–08.

23 Text of speeches at the banquet and Morarji's speech in SL Parliament on 6 February 1979, *India–Sri Lanka*, Vol. I, pp. 122–32.

24 Mrs Gandhi's letter to the Tamil Coordination Committee in London, 27 August 1979, *India–Sri Lanka*, Vol. III, p. 1425.

25   Gharekhan, Chinmaya, *Centres of Power*, Rupa, New Delhi, 2023, p. 80.

26   Discussion on Calling attention to the notice in Lok Sabha, 9 August 1981, *India–Sri Lanka*, Vol. III, p. 1428.

27   Text of discussions, 22 March 1983, *India–Sri Lanka*, Vol. III, p. 1435.

28   Deshmukh, B.G., *Cabinet Secretary looks back*, HarperCollins, New Delhi, 2004, p. 334.

29   Text of Jayewardene's interview, 9 July 1983, *India–Sri Lanka*, Vol. III, p. 1086.

30   *The Times,* London, 8 August 1983, p. 31.

31   *India Today*, New Delhi, 31 August 1983.

32   Tambiah, S.J., *Ethnic Fratricide and the Dismantling of Democracy*, OUP, New Delhi, 1986, p. 27.

33   Text of interview, 9 July 1983, *India–Sri Lanka*, Vol. III, p. 1086.

34   Wickramasinghe, *Sri Lanka in the Modern Age,* p. 287.

35   Text of press conference, 5 August 1983, *India–Sri Lanka*, Vol. III, p. 1092.

36   Text of Jayewardene's broadcast, 20 August 1983, *India–Sri Lanka*, Vol. III, p. 1102.

37   India–Sri Lanka Vol. I, p. lxxxix

38   Press release, 29 July 1983, for text see: *India–Sri Lanka*, Vol. III, p. 1154-Annexure 'A'-1.

39   Lankan PM's statement in Parliament, 24 May 1984, *India–Sri Lanka*, Vol. III, p. 1131.

40   *India–Sri Lanka* Vol. I, P. XCI.

41   *India–Sri Lanka* Vol. I, P. XCI.

42   President's brother's interview on return from India, for text see India–Sri Lanka, Vol. III, Annexure A-2, p. 1155.

43   Gharekhan, Chinmaya, *Centres of Power*, Rupa, New Delhi, 2023, p. 82.

44   Gharekhan, *Centres of Power*, p. 83.

45   Gharekhan, *Centres of Power*, p. 86.

46   Text of Speech of TULF president Amirthalingum at the all-party Conference, 30 September 1984, Bhasin, Vol. III, p. 1140.

47   Text of Jayewardene's speech and the footnote on p. 1145, 14 December 1984, India–Sri Lanka, Vol. III, p. 1145.

48   Text of proposals from the President, *India–Sri Lanka*, Vol. III, p. 1106–19.

49   Gharekhan, *Centres of Power*, p. 87.

50   Swamy, Narayan M.R., *Inside an Elusive Mind,* Konark, New Delhi, 2003, p. 91.

51   Bose, Sumantra, *State, Nation, Sovereignty: Sri Lanka, India and Tamil Eelam Movement,* New Delhi, 1994, p. 84, Cited in Wickramasinghe, Nira, *Sri Lanka in Modern Age*, Foundation Books, New Delhi, 2006, p. 252.

52   Prabhakaran's interview to Anita Pratap for *Sunday* magazine, 11 March 1984, *India–Sri Lanka*, Vol. III, p. 1124.

53   Bhasin, A.S., *India-Sri Lanka Relations and Sri Lanka's Ethnic Conflict*, Indian Research Press, New Delhi, 2001, Vol. I, p. xcv.

54   Singh, K. Natwar, *One Life Is Not Enough,* p. 254.

55   Dixit, *Assignment Colombo*, p. 24.

56   Rajiv Gandhi's letter of 20 November 1984 to Jayewardene, *India–Sri Lanka*, Vol. III, p. 163.

57   Rajiv Gandhi's statement, 11 December 1984, *India–Sri Lanka*, Vol. III, p. 1636.

58   Statement of Lankan foreign minister, 13 December 1984, *India–Sri Lanka*, Vol. III, p. 1636.

59   Joint statement issued at the end of Jayewardene's visit to New Delhi, *India–Sri Lanka*, Vol. III, p. 1680.

60   SL govt. statement, 21 June 1985, *India–Sri Lanka*, Vol. III, pp. 1682–84.

61   Bhasin, Vol. III, p. 1168.

62   Report of the Thimphu Conference, *India–Sri Lanka*, Vol. III, p. 1171.

63   Tamil response in Thimphu, 13 July 1985, India–Sri Lanka, Vol. III, p. 1168 and TULF letter to PM, 9 September 1985, India–Sri Lanka, Vol. III, p. 1207.

64   Dixit, *Assignment Colombo,* p. 43.

65   Dixit, *Assignment Colombo,* p. 37.

66   Dixit, *Assignment Colombo,* p. 45.

67 Lankan President's letter to PM Rajiv Gandhi, 1 March 1985, *India–Sri Lanka*, Vol. III, p. 1642.

68 Jayewardene's letter to Gandhi, 3 October 1985, *India–Sri Lanka*, Vol. III, p. 1685.

69 Letter from Zia to Jayewardene, 22 May 1985, *India–Sri Lanka*, Vol. I, p. 151.

70 EAM statement, 15 March 1985, India–Sri Lanka, Vol. III, p. 1644.

71 SL communiqué on Bhandari's visit, 27 March 1985. *India-Sri Lanka*, Vol. III, p. 1645.

72 PM statement in LS, 25 April 1985; *India-Sri Lanka*, Vol. III, p. 1662

73 PM in LS, 3 May 1985; *India–Sri Lanka*, Vol. III, p. 1675.

74 PM's letter to Jayewardene on 7 May 1985, *India–Sri Lanka*, Vol. III, p. 1678.

75 Joint press statement, 3 June 1985, *India–Sri Lanka*, Vol. III, p. 1680.

76 Lankan statement in Parliament, 21 June 1985, *India–Sri Lanka*, Vol III, p. 1683.

77 President's letter to PM, 3 October 1985, *India–Sri Lanka*, Vol. III, p. 1685.

78 PM's press conference on 11 October 1985, *India–Sri Lanka*, Vol. III, p. 1686.

79 PM's interview in October 1985, *India–Sri Lanka*, Vol. III, p. 1686.

80 PM's press conference on 15 November 1985, *India–Sri Lanka*, Vol. III, p. 1688.

81 PM's remarks to *PTI*, 24 December 1985, *India–Sri Lanka*, Vol. III, p. 1700.

82 TULF letter to PM, 17 January 1986, *India–Sri Lanka*, Vol. III, p. 1700.

83 Statement of Indian High Commission, Colombo, 21 February 1986, *India–Sri Lanka*, Vol. III, p. 1705.

84 EAM statement, 26 February 1986, *India–Sri Lanka*, Vol. III, p. 1705.

85 Proceedings in the Indian Parliament on 26 and 27 February 1986 and Colombo's statement on 1 March 1986, *India–Sri Lanka*, Vol. III, pp. 1705–24.

86 Spokesman's statement, 19 May 1986, India–Sri Lanka, Vol. III, p. 1779.

87 Bhasin, Vol. III, p. 1779.

88 Jayewardene's interview with Radio Australia, 18 April 1986, *India–Sri Lanka*, Vol. III, p. 1284.

89 Jayewardene's speech, 1 May 1986, *India–Sri Lanka*, Vol. III, p. 1286.

90 Question in the Rajya Sabha, 23 March 1992, *India–Sri Lanka*, Vol. I, p. 211.

91 *India–Sri Lanka,* Vol. III, pp. 1780–81.

92 *Newsweek*, 11 August 1986; *India–Sri Lanka*, Vol. III, p. 1304.

93 Footnote on p. 1301, *India–Sri Lanka*, 20 May 1986, Vol. III, p. 1301.

94 The PM's statement in Delhi, 19 May 1986, *India–Sri Lanka*, Vol. III, p. 1780.

95 India–Sri Lanka, Vol. III, p. 1781, fn.

96 Final proposals, 4 May 1986, *India–Sri Lanka*, Vol III, p. 1287.

97 Jayewardene's speech at UNP Convention, 3 June 1986, *India–Sri Lanka*, p. 1303.

98 Question in SL Parliament, 6 January 1987, *India–Sri Lanka*, Vol. III, p. 1360.

99 Discussions in SL Parliament, 8 January 1987, *India–Sri Lanka*, p. 1365.

100 Speech in SL Parliament, 19 February 1987, *India–Sri Lanka*, Vol. III, p. 1377.

101 Sri Lanka's final proposals for a political settlement, 4 May 1986, *India–Sri Lanka*, Vol. III, p. 1287.

102 *India–Sri Lanka*, Vol. III, pp. 1824–33.

103 Singh, K. Natwar, *One Life Is Not Enough*, Rupa & Co., New Delhi, 2014, p. 252.

104 Jayewardene statement at SAARC summit, Bangalore, 15 November 1986, Bhasin, Vol. III, p. 1834.

105 Singh, *One Life Is Not Enough,* p. 253.

106 Singh, *One Life Is Not Enough,* p. 256.

107 Press release of Indian High Commission, 16 December 1986, *India–Sri Lanka*, p. 1838.

108 Proposals emerging from the discussions between SL President and Indian ministers, 19 December 1986, *India–Sri Lanka*, Vol. III, p. 1838.

109 National Security Minister Athulathmudali's statement, *India–Sri Lanka*, Vol. III, p. 1840.

110 Gandhi's letter to Jayewardene, 12 February 1987, *India–Sri Lanka*, Vol. III, p. 1841.

111 Singh, *One Life is Not Enough,* p. 256.

112 Discussion in SL Parliament, 8 January 1987, Vol. III pp. 1365–76.

113 UNP resolution, 23 April 1987, *India–Sri Lanka*, Vol. III, p. 1419.

114 *India–Sri Lanka*, Vol. III, pp. 1790–91.

115 *India–Sri Lanka*, footnote, Vol. III, p. 1790.

116 Annex to President's speech, 19 February 1987, *India–Sri Lanka*, Vol. III, p. 1377.

117 Deshmukh, B.G., *A Cabinet Secretary Looks Back*, HarperCollins, New Delhi, 2004, p. 329.

118 Deshmukh, *A Cabinet Secretary Looks Back*, p. 329.

119 Discussions in SL Parliament on 6 and 8 January 1987, *India–Sri Lanka*, Vol. III, p. 1360 and 1365.

120 TULF letter to PM, 1 April 1987, Bhasin, p. 1868.

121 India's message to Colombo, 9 February 1987, Bhasin, footnote on pp. 1839–40.

122 PM Rajiv Gandhi's message to President Jayewardene, 12 February 1987, *India–Sri Lanka*, Vol. III, p. 1841.

123 PM's statement in both houses of Parliament, *India–Sri Lanka*, Vol. III, pp. 1843–44.

124 Secret message from the PM to Jayewardene, 13 March 1987, *India–Sri Lanka*, Vol. III p. 1848.

125 PM's speech in Lok Sabha, Bhasin, p. 1843.

126 TULF letter to the PM, 6 March 1987, *India–Sri Lanka*, Vol. III, p. 1844.

127 Gandhi's message to President Jayewardene, 15 March 1987, *India–Sri Lanka*, Vol. III, p. 1848.

128 *India–Sri Lanka*, Vol. III, p. 1848.

129   TULF letter to PM, 1 April 1987, *India–Sri Lanka*, Vol. III, p.
      1868.

130   Indian spokesman statement, 18 April 1987, *India–Sri Lanka*,
      Vol. III, p. 1871.

131   Speech of Premadasa in Parliament, 24 April 1987, *India–Sri
      Lanka,* Vol. III, p. 1871.

132   Statement by the MEA, 26 April 1987, *India–Sri Lanka*, Vol.
      III, p. 1873.

133   Sri Lanka President to the PM, 5 May 1987, *India–Sri Lanka*,
      Vol. III, p. 1874.

134   Discussion in the Rajya Sabha, 8 May 1987, Bhasin, Vol. III, p.
      1874.

135   *India–Sri Lanka*, discussion in the Lok Sabha, 11–12 May 1987,
      Vol. III, p. 1886.

136   *India–Sri Lanka*, Vol. III, p. 1890, fn.

137   *India–Sri Lanka*, Vol. III, p. 1901, fn.

138   *India–Sri Lanka*, Vol. III, p. 1890, fn.

139   Statement of the EAM, 26 May 1987, *India–Sri Lanka*, Vol. III,
      p. 1900.

140   Deshmukh, B.G., *A Cabinet Secretary Looks Back*, HarperCollins,
      New Delhi, 2004, p. 330.

141   Statement of Gandhi, 28 May 1987, *India–Sri Lanka*, p. 1901.

142   Dixit, *Assignment Colombo*, p. 98.

143   Dixit, *Assignment Colombo*, p. 106.

144   GoI message, 1 June 1987, *India–Sri Lanka*, Vol. III, p. 1902.

145   *India–Sri Lanka*, Vol. III, p. 1902.

146   *India–Sri Lanka*, Vol. III; p. 1903.

147   *India–Sri Lanka,* Vol. III; p. 1903.

148   *India–Sri Lanka*, Vol. III; p. 1903.

149   Jayewardene's message to Gandhi, 2 June 1987, *India–Sri
      Lanka*, Vol. III, p. 1904.

150   The PM's message to Jayewardene, 2 June 1987, *India—Sri
      Lanka*, p. 1904.

151   Jayewardene's message to Gandhi, 2 June 1987, *India–Sri
      Lanka*, Vol. III, p. 1904.

152 *India–Sri Lanka*, Vol. III, p. 1904, fn.

153 Briefing by the official spokesman of the MEA, 2 June 1987, Bhasin, Vol. III, p. 1905.

154 Lankan PM's speech in Parliament, 2 June 1987, *India–Sri Lanka*, Vol. III, p. 1906.

155 *India–Sri Lanka*, Vol. III, p. 1911.

156 *India–Sri Lanka*, Vol. III, p. 1913–14.

157 *India–Sri Lanka*, Vol. III, p. 1912, fn.

158 *India–Sri Lanka*, Vol. III, p. 1913, fn.

159 MEA spokesperson's statement, 4 June 1987, *India–Sri Lanka*, Vol. III, p. 1914.

160 Singh, *One Life Is Not Enough*, pp. 257–58.

161 Deshmukh, *A Cabinet Secretary Looks Back*, p. 330.

162 Press release of SL high commission, 4 June 1987, *India–Sri Lanka*, Vol. III, p. 1915.

163 Dixit, *Assignment Colombo*, pp. 107–08.

164 UNP's Statement, 9 June 1987, *India–Sri Lanka*, Vol. III, p. 1919.

165 Swamy, M.R. Narayan, *Inside an Elusive Mind*, Konark Publishers, New Delhi, 2003, p. 154.

166 *India–Sri Lanka*, Vol. III, p. 1917, fn.

167 Press release of Sri Lanka Government, 5 June 1987, *India–Sri Lanka*, Vol. III, p. 1918.

168 *India–Sri Lanka*, Vol. III, p. 1918, fn.

169 Hameed's interview, 21 June 1987, *India–Sri Lanka*, Vol. III, p. 1924.

170 Reaction of Colombo to Gandhi's remarks, 21 June 1987, *India–Sri Lanka*, p. 1923.

171 Rajiv Gandhi's remarks, 29 June 1987, *India–Sri Lanka*, Vol. III, p. 198.

172 Press release of the high commission. 6 July 1987, *India–Sri Lanka*, Vol. III, p. 1933.

173 *India–Sri Lanka*, Vol. III, p. 1933.

174 Press Release of the high commission, 17 July 1987, *India–Sri Lanka*, Vol. IV, p. 1937.

175 Speech of Athulathmudali at the Executive Committee of UNP, 27 July 1987, *India–Sri Lanka*, Vol. IV, p. 1937.

176 TULF letter to PM, 28 July 1987, *India–Sri Lanka*, p. 1939.

177 Statement of Premadasa, 27 July 1987, *India–Sri Lanka*, Vol. IV, p. 1940.

178 *India–Sri Lanka*, Vol. IV, p. 1944–45, fn.

179 LTTE press release, 29 July 1987, *India–Sri Lanka*, Vol. IV, p. 1944.

180 Swamy, *Inside an Elusive Mind*, pp. 151–64.

181 Dixit, *Assignment Colombo*, p. 158.

182 *India–Sri Lanka*, Vol. IV, p. 1944.

183 TULF letter to the PM, 28 July 1987, *India–Sri Lanka*, Vol. IV, p. 1939

184 Bhasin, Vol. IV, p. 1945, fn.

185 Deshmukh, *A Cabinet Secretary Looks Back*, p. 331.

186 Dixit, *Assignment Colombo*, p. 119.

187 Dixit, *Assignment Colombo*, p. 189.

188 Dixit, *Assignment Colombo*, p. 161 and p. 163.

189 Speeches of Gandhi and Jayewardene on Sri Lanka TV, 29 July 1987, *India–Sri Lanka*, p. 1955.

190 Joint Press conference on 29 July 1987, *India–Sri Lanka*, Vol. IV, p. 1956.

191 *India–Sri Lanka*, Vol. IV, p. 1966.

192 Rajiv Gandhi's statement in the Lok Sabha on the Accord, 30 July 1987, *India–Sri Lanka*, p. 1969.

193 Speech of the PM in Parliament, 30 July 1987, *India–Sri Lanka*, p. 1969.

194 Letter from Bandaranaike to Gandhi, 28 July 1987, *India–Sri Lanka*, Vol. III, p. 1945.

195 Interview, 30 July 1987, *India–Sri Lanka*, p. 1974.

196 The PM's speech in Chennai, 2 August 1987, Bhasin. Vol. IV, p. 1977.

197 Jayewardene's address to the nation, 6 August 1987, *India–Sri Lanka*, Vol. IV, p. 1986.

198 Natwar's speech on 6 and 18 August 1987, Bhasin, Vol. IV, p. 1987 and p. 2034.

199   Dixit, *Assignment Colombo,* p. 219.

200   Prabhakaran's speech in Jaffna, 4 August 1987, *India–Sri Lanka,* Vol. IV, p. 1984.

201   Debate in Parliament, 11, 17, 18, 19 August 1987, *India–Sri Lanka,* Vol. IV, pp. 1996–2008, pp. 2012–36, pp. 2040–65.

202   Spokesman's statement, 20 September 1987, *India–Sri Lanka,* Vol. IV, p. 2077.

203   Joint press conference on 23 September 1987, *India–Sri Lanka,* Vol. IV, p. 2078.

204   Prabhakaran's letter to the HCI, 27 September 1987, *India–Sri Lanka,* Vol. IV, p. 2080.

205   Athulathmudali's interview to Reuter, at Nuwara Eliya, Sri Lanka, 28 September 1987, *India–Sri Lanka,* Vol. IV, p. 2085.

206   Spokesman's statement, 2 October 1987, India–Sri Lanka, Vol. IV, p. 2086.

207   Statement of the spokesman and its footnotes, 14 October 1987, *India–Sri Lanka,* Vol. IV, p. 2094.

208   Rajiv Gandhi's press conference in Washington, 20 October 1987, Bhasin, Vol. IV, p. 2102.

209   Discussion in the Rajya Sabha, 6 November 1987, India–Sri Lanka, pp. 2112–17.

210   Statement by Lankan minister Gamini Jayasuriya, 9 October 1987, Bhasin, Vol. IV, p. 2091.

211   Short duration discussion in Rajya Sabha, 6 November 1987, *India–Sri Lanka,* Vol. IV, p. 2112.

212   Debate in Rajya Sabha, 6 November 197, *India–Sri Lanka,* Vol. IV, p. 2112.

213   Statement of PM, 9 November 1987, *India–Sri Lanka,* Vol. IV, p. 2119.

214   Prabhakaran's statement in Jaffna, 18 November 1987, *India–Sri Lanka,* Vol. IV, p. 2153.

215   MEA spokesman's statement, 26 November 1987, *India–Sri Lanka,* Vol. IV, p. 2166.

216   MEA spokesman's statement, 26 November 1987, *India–Sri Lanka,* Vol. IV, p. 2166.

217   Gandhi's statement, 21 December 1987, *India–Sri Lanka*, Vol. IV, p. 2183.

218   Hameed in SL Parliament, 3 December 1987, *India–Sri Lanka*, Vol. IV, p. 2171.

219   Questions raised by Gandhi and Jayewardene's response, 13 January 1988, *India–Sri Lanka*, Vol. IV, p. 2184.

220   Interview with N. Ram of *The Hindu*, 8 February 1988, *India–Sri Lanka*, Vol. IV, p. 2196.

221   Jayewardene's address, 25 February 1988, *India–Sri Lanka*, Vol. IV, p. 2204.

222   High Commissioner's briefing, 27 February 1988, *India–Sri Lanka*, Vol. IV, p. 2206.

223   Gandhi's speech, 2 March 1988, *India–Sri Lanka*, Vol. IV, p. 2208.

224   Jayewardene message, 5 March 1988, *India–Sri Lanka*, Vol. IV, p. 2.

225   Prabhakaran to Gandhi, 9 March 1988, *India–Sri Lanka*, p. 2213.

226   Statement of Natwar Singh, 18 March 1988, *India–Sri Lanka*, Vol. IV, p. 2217.

227   Statement of Indian Tamil leaders, 21 March 1988, *India–Sri Lanka*, Vol. IV, p. 2224.

228   LTTE statement, 5 April 1988, *India–Sri Lanka*, Vol. IV, p. 2227.

229   Press briefing by Jayewardene, 30 January 1988, *India–Sri Lanka*, Vol. IV, p. 2191.

230   Statement of Sirimavo Bandaranaike, 26 January 1988, *India–Sri Lanka*, Vol. IV, p. 2189.

231   Premadasa's answers to questions, 28 September 1988, *India–Sri Lanka*, Vol. IV, p. 2317.

232   Bhasin, Vol. IV, p. 2319.

233   Text of two drafts, 7 March 1989, *India–Sri Lanka*, Vol. IV, p. 2359.

234   Dixit, *Assignment Colombo*, p. 229.

235   Statement of SLFP, 8 April 1988, *India–Sri Lanka*, Vol. IV, p. 2230.

236 *India–Sri Lanka*, Vol. IV, p. 2235.

237 Athulathmudali's statement, 22 April 1988, *India–Sri Lanka*, Vol. IV, p. 2234.

238 Top-secret message sent through R&AW sources, *India–Sri Lanka*, Vol. IV, p. 2236.

239 Note of the SL govt, 19 June 1988, *India–Sri Lanka*, Vol. IV, p. 2258.

240 Dixit, *Assignment Colombo*, p. 206.

241 Dixit, *Assignment Colombo*, p. 215.

242 Statements of the LTTE, 9 July and 26 October 1988, Bhasin, p. 2271 and p. 2326.

243 Statement of Jaffna University teachers, October 1988, India–Sri Lanka, Vol. IV, p. 2330.

244 Special press release of the High Commission, 27 October 1988, India–Sri Lanka, Vol. IV, p. 2329.

245 MEA Spokesman's statement, 13 January 1989, *India–Sri Lanka*, Vol. IV, p. 2341.

246 Press release of HCI on Dixit's meeting with the new President, 18 January 1989, *India–Sri Lanka*, Vol. IV, p. 2341.

247 LTTE letter to the 45th session of the UN Commission on Human Rights, 7 February 1989, *India–Sri Lanka*, Vol. IV, p. 2342.

248 Press Release of the LTTE's Political Committee, 21 March 1989, *India–Sri Lanka*, Vol. IV, p. 2355.

249 *India–Sri Lanka*, Vol. IV, pp. 2366–67, fn.

250 Message to LTTE, 16 April 1989, *India–Sri Lanka*, Vol. IV, p. 2367.

251 Bhasin, Vol. IV, p. 2367, fn.

252 *India–Sri Lanka*, Vol. IV, p. 2368, fn.

253 Spokesman statement, 17 April 1989, *India–Sri Lanka*, Vol. IV, p. 2368.

254 *India-Sri Lanka*, Vol. IV, p. 2370, fn.

255 *India-Sri Lanka*, Vol. IV, p. 2370, fn.

256 Press release of the HCI, 3 May 1989, *India–Sri Lanka*, Vol. IV, p. 2372.

257 *India–Sri Lanka*, Vol. IV, p. 2373, fn.

258 Press conference of Lankan FM, 4 May 1989, *India–Sri Lanka*, Vol. IV, p. 2375.

259 Press conference of Lankan FM, 4 May 1989, *India–Sri Lanka*, Vol. IV, p. 2375.

260 Presidential press release, 16 May 1989, *India–Sri Lanka*, Vol. IV, p. 2378.

261 Press release of the HCI, 17 May 1989, *India–Sri Lanka*, Vol. IV, p. 2378.

262 Press release of LTTE, 20 May 1989, *India–Sri Lanka*, Vol. IV, p. 2380.

263 Statement of the official spokesman of the MEA, 23 May 1989, *India–Sri Lanka*, Vol. IV, p. 2381.

264 Statement of the official spokesman of the MEA, 12 July 1989, *India–Sri Lanka*, Vol. IV, p. 2389.

265 Karthikeyan, D.R., and Raju, Radhavinod, *Triumph and Truth—Rajiv Gandhi Assassination: The Investigation*, New Dawn Press, 2004, p. 194.

266 Mehrotra, Lakhanlal, contributory chapter in the book, *The Ambassadors' Club: The Indian Diplomats at Large*, ed. Rajan, Krishna, HarperCollins, New Delhi, 2012, p. 178.

267 President's address, 18 September 1989, *India–Sri Lanka*, Vol. IV, p. 2397.

268 *India–Sri Lanka*, Vol. IV, 3 December 1989, p. 2428.

269 Press release of MEA, 7 December 1989, *India–Sri Lanka*, Vol. IV, p. 2429.

270 Lankan FM's call on Indian EAM, 7 December 1989, *India–Sri Lanka*, Vol. IV, p. 2429, fn.

271 Balasingham interview with *Sunday Observer*, 10 December 1989, *India–Sri Lanka*, Vol. IV, p. 2430.

272 The PM's interview with the BBC, 1 November 1987, *India–Sri Lanka*, Vol. IV, p. 2111.

273 Remarks in the Lankan Parliament, 10 December 1987, *India–Sri Lanka*, Vol. IV, p. 2180.

274 Question in Lok Sabha, 16 March 1988, *India– Sri Lanka*, Vol. IV, p. 2214.

275 Statement of Natwar Singh in the Rajya Sabha, 18 March 1988, *India–Sri Lanka*, Vol. IV, p. 2217.

276 HC's interview, 27 March 1988, *India–Sri Lanka*, Vol. IV, p. 2225.

277 Press conference on 13 May 1988, *India–Sri Lanka*, Vol. IV, p. 2441.

278 MEA official spokesperson's statement on 13 May 1988, *India–Sri Lanka*, Vol. IV, p. 2442.

279 Lankan home minister's letter, 28 May 1988, *India–Sri Lanka*, Vol. IV, p. 2254.

280 The LTTE's press release, 9 July 1988, *India–Sri Lanka*, Vol. IV, p. 2271.

281 Joint statement, 1 June 1988, *India–Sri Lanka*, Vol. IV, p. 2443.

282 Press Release of the MEA, 7 June 1988, Bhasin, Vol. IV, p. 2444.

283 Statement of Lankan deputy defence minister, 8 June 1988, *India–Sri Lanka*, Vol. IV p. 2447.

284 Jayewardene's interview to BBC, 13 December 1988, *India–Sri Lanka*, Vol. IV, p. 2339.

285 Speech of Premadasa at the Pinnacle Ceremony, 1 June 1989, *India–Sri Lanka*, Vol. V, p. 2449.

286 President's letter to Gandhi, 2 June 1989, *India–Sri Lanka*, Vol. V, p. 2456.

287 Informal discussions between N. Ram and Premadasa, 5 June 1989, *India–Sri Lanka*, Vol. V, p. 2469.

288 *India–Sri Lanka*, Vol. V, p. 2480.

289 Resolution of the UNP, 7 June 1989, *India–Sri Lanka*, Vol. V, p. 2472.

290 Question in SL Parliament, 9 June 1989, *India–Sri Lanka*, Vol. V, p. 2475.

291 Press release of the Indian High Commission, 7 June 1989, *India–Sri Lanka*, Vol. V, p. 2471.

292 Question in Parliament, 9 June 1989, *India–Sri Lanka*, Vol. V, p. 2475.

293 Wijeratne's statement, 15 June 1989, *India–Sri Lanka*, Vol. V, p. 2481.

294 Special message of President, 16 June 1989, *India–Sri Lanka*, Vol. V, p. 2483.

295 PM's letter, 20 June 1989, India–Sri Lanka, Vol. V, 2457.

296 Mehrotra, Lakhan, *My Days in Sri Lanka*; Har-Anand, New Delhi, 2011, p. 106.

297 Premadasa's message on the occasion of Gam Udawa, 26 June 1989, *India–Sri Lanka*, Vol. V, p. 2488.

298 Telegram from the President to the PM, 28 June 1989, *India–Sri Lanka*, Vol. V, p. 2458.

299 President's letter to the Indian PM, 30 June 1989, *India–Sri Lanka*, Vol. IV, p. 2458.

300 Press briefing by MEA spokesman, 29 June 1989, *India–Sri Lanka*, Vol. V, p. 2499.

301 Wijeratne's telephonic interview with *Telegraph*, Calcutta, 2 July 1989, *India–Sri Lanka*, Vol. V, p. 2502.

302 The LTTE's response to PM's letter of 20 June and 2 July 1989, *India–Sri Lanka*, Vol. V, p. 2503.

303 The PM's message to Premadasa, 11 July 1989, *India–Sri Lanka*, Vol. V, p. 2463.

304 Premadasa's letter to PM, 12 July 1989, *India–Sri Lanka*, Vol. V, p. 2464.

305 Mehrotra, *My Days in Sri Lanka*, p. 115.

306 Mehrotra, *My Days in Sri Lanka*, p. 122.

307 Joint communiqué issued in Colombo, 28 July 1989, *India–Sri Lanka*, Vol. V, p. 2505.

308 Spokesman's statement, 28 July 1989, *India–Sri Lanka*, Vol. V, p. 2505.

309 Joint communiqué at the end of foreign ministers' talks, 18 September 1989, *India–Sri Lanka*, Vol. V, p. 2567.

310 *India–Sri Lanka*, 18 September 1989, Vol. V, p, 2567, fn.

311 Official briefing in Delhi, 3 December 1989, *India–Sri Lanka*, Vol. V, p. 2572.

312 Joint press communiqué, 9 December 1989, *India–Sri Lanka*, Vol. V, p. 2573.

313 Bhasin, Vol. V, p. 2576, fn 311, *India–Sri Lanka*, Vol. V, p. 2576, fn.

314 Joint press release, 6 January 1990, *India–Sri Lanka*, Vol. V, p. 2578.

315 Press briefing by Wijeratne, 12 January 1990, *India–Sri Lanka*, Vol. V, p. 2579.

316 Official spokesman statement, 17 February 1990, *India–Sri Lanka*, Vol. V, p. 2580.

317 Press release of Lankan foreign minister Wijeratne, 22 February 1990, *India–Sri Lanka*, Vol. V, p. 2581.

318 Statement of Stanley Dominic, LTTE political wing leader 21 February, 1990, *India–Sri Lanka*, Vol. V, p. 2581.

319 Press release of Indian High Commission, 24 March 1990, *India–Sri Lanka*, Vol. V, p. 2583.

320 Prabhakaran's statement;1 April, 1990, *India–Sri Lanka*, Vol. V, p. 2586.

321 Prabhakaran's statement;1 April, 1990, *India–Sri Lanka*, Vol. V, p. 2586.

322 Gandhi's letter to former President Jayewardene, 23 June 1990, *India–Sri Lanka*, Vol. V, p. 2626.

323 Jayewardene's letter, 29 June 1990, *India–Sri Lanka*, Vol. V, p. 2630.

324 Wickramasinghe, Nira, *Sri Lanka in the Modern Age: A History*, C. Hurst & Co, Foundation Books, South Asia Edition, 2006, p. 149.

325 Lambah, Satinder Kumar, *In Pursuit of Peace: India–Pakistan Relations under Six Prime Ministers*, Penguin, Gurugram, 2023, p. 55.

326 'Sri Lanka–China Relations: Analysing Sri Lankan, Chinese and Indian Perspectives'. Article by Rajiv Rajan, who taught at the College of Liberal Arts, Shanghai University, and Asantha Senevirathna, Department of Strategic Studies, Sir John Kotlewala Defence University, Sri Lanka, *Economic and Political Weekly*, Vol. LVII, No. 7, pp. 31–36.

V: India–United States Civil Nuclear Energy Agreement, 2008

1   Chari, P.R., *Indo–US Nuclear Deal: Seeking Synergy in Bilateralism*, Routledge, New Delhi, 2009, p. 14.
2   Bhasin, A.S., *India and Pakistan: Neighbours at Odds*, Bloomsbury, New Delhi, 2018, pp. 361–62.
3   Letter from PM Atal Behari Vajpayee to President Clinton, 12 May 1998, https://www.nytimes.com.world.
4   Sirohi, Seema, *Friends with Benefits: The India–US Story*, HarperCollins, Gurugram, 2023, p. 95.
5   *Foreign Affairs*, published by the US Council on Foreign Affairs, September–October 1998, Vol. 77, No. 5, pp. 41–62.
6   Tellis, Ashley, *India as a New Global Power, An Action Agenda for the United States*, Carnegie, Washington, DC, July 2005, quoted by Swapna Kona Nayudu in her chapter in *Indo–US Nuclear Deal*, ed. P.R. Chari, Routledge, New Delhi, 2009, p. 168.
7   Talbott, Strobe, *Engaging India: Diplomacy, Democracy, and the Bomb*, Brookings, 2004, pp. 96–97.
8   *Foreign Affairs*, published by the Council on Foreign Affairs, Vol. 79, No. 1 (January–February 2000), pp. 45–62.
9   Rice, Condoleezza, *No Higher Honour*, Simon & Schuster, London, p. 128.
10 Ganguly, Sumit, Review Article, 'Behind India's Bomb', *Foreign Affairs*, Vol. 80, No. 5 (September–October 2001), p.136.
11 Mohan, Raja, *Impossible Allies: Nuclear India, the United States and the Global Order*, quoting Blackwill's speech at the Indian Chamber of Commerce, Kolkata on 27 November 2002, India Research Press, New Delhi, 2006, p. 102.
12 Ambassador Rakesh Sood at the discussion at the Carnegie Endowment in 2015 while making an appraisal of the nuclear deal.
13 Rice, *No Higher Honour*, p. 129.
14 Chaudhuri, Rudra, *Forged in Crisis: India and the United States since 1947*, Hurst, London, 2014, pp. 221–22.
15 Mohan, *Impossible Allies*, pp. 102–03.
16 Sirohi, *Friends with Benefits*, p. 169.

17 India spokesman's statement, 20 March 2004, ed. Bhasin, India's Foreign Relations: 2004, New Delhi, 2005, p. 629

18 Joint statement issued at the end of India–US talks on High Technology, 13 November 2002, India's Foreign Relations, 2002, p. 1219.

19 Statement of principles of High Technology Commerce, 6 February 2003, IFR-2003, pp. 1174–77.

20 Speech of Foreign Secretary Kanwal Sibal at the Carnegie Endowment for Peace, Washington, 4 February 2003, ed. *India's Foreign Relations–2003*, Geetika, New Delhi, 2006, p. 1158.

21 Menon, Shivshankar, *India and Asia's Geopolitics*, Penguin, Gurugram, 2021, p. 55.

22 Sirohi, *Friends with Benefits*, p. 177.

23 Mansingh, Lalit, contributory chapter on 'India–US Nuclear Deal and Indian Foreign Policy', in *Indo–US Nuclear Deal*, ed. P.R Chari, Routledge, New Delhi, 2009, pp. 171–88.

24 Statement of Principles for High Technology Commerce, 6 February 2003, Bhasin, A.S., *India's Foreign Relations–2003*, Geetika Publishers, New Delhi, 2006, p. 1174.

25 'Statements on Next Step in Strategic Partnership between India and the US', 13 January 2004, IFR-2004, p. 1140.

26 Joint press statement, 17 September 2004, IFR-2004, p. 1170.

27 Mohan, *Impossible Allies*, p. 134.

28 Mohan, *Impossible Allies*, p. 230.

29 IFR-2004, 21 September 2004, p. 1171, fn.

30 Joint press conference, 6 June 2004, IFR-2004, p. 1157.

31 Gopalakrishnan, 'India–US Nuclear cooperation: A non-starter', *Economic and Political Weekly*, 2 July 2005, quoted in Raja Mohan, p. 138.

32 N. Ravi. 'Missing the Wood for the Trees', *The Hindu*, 19 July 2008.

33 Menon, Shivshankar, *Choices, Inside the Making of India's Foreign Policy*, Penguin, Gurugram, 2016, p. 51.

34 Menon, Shivshankar, *India and Asian Geopolitics: The Past, Present*, Penguin, Gurugram, 2021, p. 215.

35   Joint statement at the end of talks between the PM and President, 21 September 2004, IFR-2004, p. 1171.

36   Speech of the PM, 24 September 2004, IFR-2004, p. 1173.

37   Pant, Harsh V., *The US–India Nuclear Pact: Policy, Process, and Great Power Politics*, Oxford University Press, New Delhi, 2011, p. 51.

38   PM's letter, 4 November 2004, IFR-2004, p. 1185.

39   IFR-2004, p. 1186, fn.

40   Press release issued by the PM's office on the meeting with Rumsfeld, 9 December 2004, IFR-2004, p. 1199.

41   Media briefing, 16 March 2005, IFR-2005, p. 1278.

42   Pant, *The US–India Nuclear Pact*, p. 40.

43   Sirohi, *Friends with Benefits*, p. 178.

44   Kazi, Reshmi. 'The process of Negotiations', contributory chapter in *Indo–US Nuclear Deal*, ed. P.R. Chari, Routledge, New Delhi, 2009, p. 78.

45   Aiyar, Vidya Shankar. Contributory chapter 'Prime Time Deal', in *Indo–US Nuclear Deal*, p. 32.

46   Pant, *The US–India Nuclear Pact*, p. 49.

47   IFR-2005, p. 1293.

48   IFR-2005, p. 1297, fn.

49   Hasan, Zoya, *Congress after Indira*, in the chapter on 'India–US Nuclear Deal and Great Power Ambitions', OUP, New Delhi, 2012, p. 195.

50   Media briefing by FS Shyam Saran on EAM's meeting with the President, 14 April 2005, IFR-2005, p. 1295.

51   Bhasin (ed), *India's Foreign Relations*, Ministry of External Affairs, New Delhi, 2005, p. 1296.

52   52 IFR-2005, p. 1298, fn.

53   Sirohi, *Friends with Benefits*, p. 188.

54   'Did the India Civil-Nuclear Deal Work?' Carnegie Endowment, https://www.youtube.com/live/nVYtVS9pJXE?feature+shar

55   Varadarajan, Siddharth, 'Truth Behind the Deal', *The Hindu*, 29 July 2005.

56   Hasan, *Congress after Indira*, p. 198.

57   'India as a New Global Power', Carnegie, 2005, quoted in *The Hindu* by Varadarajan, see No. 55.

58   Hasan, Zoya, p. 199, quoting Venkitesh Ramakrishnan in *Frontline*, Vol. 24, No.17, 25 August 2007.

59   Pant, Harsh, p. 26, quoting Subramanyam K., 'The Nuclear Pact and Minimum deterrent', *Times of India*, 12 December 2006.

60   Joint statement on meeting of Energy Dialogue, 31 May 2005, IFR-2005, p. 1312.

61   Media briefing on the meeting between the US Under Secretary of State and the Indian Foreign Secretary, 24 June IFR-2005, p. 1315.

62   Defence Cooperation framework agreement, 28 June 2005, IFR-2005, p. 1316.

63   IFR-2005, p. 1320.

64   IFR-2005, p. 1320, fn.

65   Mohan, *Impossible Allies*, p. 126.

66   Statement of the defence minister, 2 August 2005, Bhasin, IFR-2005, p. 1399.

67   PM's speech, 23 February 2006, Bhasin, IFR-2006, p. 147.

68   Mohan, *Impossible Allies,* p. 129.

69   Joint statement, 31 May 2005, Bhasin, IFR-2005, p. 1312.

70   Media briefing by FS on the eve of the PM's visit to the US on 14 July 2005, IFR-2005, p. 1324.

71   Chaudhuri, *Forged in Crisis*, p. 228.

72   PM's interview with the *New York Times*, 15 July 2005, IFR-2005, p. 1335.

73   IFR-2005, p. 1339, fn.

74   Sirohi, *Friends with Benefits,* p. 182.

75   Mohan, *Impossible Allies,* p. 148.

76   Sirohi, *Friends with Benefits*, p. 184.

77   IFR-2005, 18 July 2005, pp. 1339–40.

78   PM's banquet speech, 18 July 2005, IFR-2005, pp. 1340–42.

79   Text of the joint statement, 18 July 2005, IFR-2005, pp. 1342–46.

80   Chaudhuri, *Forged in Crisis,* p. 223.

81   Menon, *Choices*, p. 53.

82   Shivshankar, *Choices*, p. 53.

83 PM's opening statement at the joint press conference, 18 July 2005, IFR-2005, p. 1348.

84 Statement issued on 18 July 2005, IFR-2005, p. 1347.

85 IFR-2005, pp. 1348–62.

86 IFR-2005, pp.1363–79.

87 PM's remarks to Indian journalists, 20 July 2005, IFR-2005, pp. 1380–81.

88 Chaudhuri, *Forged in Crisis*, p. 233.

89 PM's speech in Parliament, 29 July 2005, Bhasin, IFR-2005, pp. 1383–89.

90 Hasan, *Congress after Indira*, p. 196.

91 Burns, Nicholas, 22 February 2007, IFR-2007, p. 1887.

92 FS's press conference on 23 February 2007, IFR-2007, p. 1907.

93 Call by the President, 18 October 2005, IFR-2005, p. 1448.

94 Joint press conference on 21 October 2005, IFR-2005, p. 1450.

95 IFR-2005, 11 December 2005, p. 1458, fn.

96 IFR-2005, p. 1461, fn.

97 Joint press interaction between FS and US Under Secretary of State, 20 January 2006, IFR-2006, p. 140.

98 TV interview with a private TV channel, 22 December 2006, IFR-2005, p. 1516.

99 Sirohi, *Friends with Benefits*, p. 193.

100 Press briefing by the official spokesman, 22/24 February 2006, IFR-2006, p. 1461.

101 Briefing by the FS, 28 February 2006, IFR-2006, p. 1483.

102 Menon, *Choices*, p. 63.

103 Joint press interaction of PM and President, 2 March 2006, IFR-2006, p. 1494.

104 Separation Plan, 11 May 2006, IFR-2006, p. 446.

105 FS Shyam Saran's lecture to Heritage Foundation, 30 March 2006, IFR-2006, p. 1528.

106 Shyam Saran at press conference in Washington, D.C., 31 March 2006, IFR-2006, p. 1541.

107 MEA spokesperson's clarification, 17 April 2006, IFR-2006, p. 1551.

108   FS's speech to mark one year of signing of the joint statement, 14 July 2006, IFR-2006, p. 1558.

109   PM's speech in the Rajya Sabha, 17 August 2006, IFR-2006, p. 461.

110   Meeting between President and PM, 17 July 2006, IFR-2006, p. 1567.

111   Telephonic conversation between US President and Indian PM, 16 November 2006, IFR-2006, p. 1590.

112   The PM's speech in the Lok Sabha, 17 August 2006, IFR-2006, p. 461.

113   Pranab Mukherjee's remarks, 17 November 2006, IFR-2006, p. 1592.

114   Statement of the EAM, 17 November 2006, IFR-2006, p. 487, fn.

115   Joint press conference, 7 December 2006, IFR-2006, p. 1593.

116   IFR-2006, p. 1604, fn.

117   EAM statement in Lok Sabha, 12 December 2006, IFR-2006, Part-I, p. 594.

118   Chaudhuri, *Forged in Crisis*, p. 236.

119   MEA spokesperson's statement, 8 December 2006, IFR-2006, p. 1604.

120   The PM's speech in Lok Sabha, 18 December 2006, IFR-2006, p. 496.

121   IFR-2006, Part-I, Appendix-I, p. 523.

122   Remarks of President Bush while signing the Henry Hyde Act, 18 December 2006, IFR-2006, Part. I, Appendix-4, p. 590.

123   Factsheet issued by the White House, IFR-2006, Part-I, Appendix-6, p. 594.

124   Chaudhuri, *Forged in Crisis*, p. 236.

125   Chaudhuri, *Forged in Crisis*, p. 237.

126   Press release issued by the PM's office, 21 December 2006, IFR-2006, p. 1603.

127   IFR-2007, 22 February 2007, p. 1879.

128   IFR-2007, p. 1917.

129   Press release of the MEA, 24 April 2007, IFR-2007, p. 1916.

130   The FS's press conference, 1 May 2007, IFR-2007, p. 1918.

131   IFR-2007, p. 1936, fn.

132   Press conference of FS, 2 June 2007, IFR-2007, p. 1937.

133   IFR-2007, p. 434, fn.

134   IFR-2007-Part-I, p. 435, fn.

135   IFR-2007, p. 436, fn.

136   IFR-2007, p. 436, fn.

137   IFR-2007, p. 436, fn.

138   The FS's press briefing, 2 June 2007, IFR-2007, p. 434.

139   The PM's briefing to journalists accompanying him on the flight returning home from Berlin, IFR-9, June 2007, p. 442.

140   IFR-2007, Part-I, p. 449.

141   Joint press statement on the Nuclear Cooperation Agreement, 21 July 2007, IFR-2007, Part-I, p. 450.

142   IFR-2007, Part-I, p. 450, fn.

143   Bush's statement, 27 July 2007, IFR-2007, Part-I, p. 470.

144   Joint statement issued after talks between Rice and Mukherjee, 27 July 2007, IFR-2007, Part-I, p. 471.

145   MEA's factsheet, 27 July 2007, IFR-2007, Part-I, p. 472.

146   MEA's factsheet, 27 July 2007, IFR-2007, Part-I, p. 472.

147   IFR-2007, Part-I, p. 479.

148   IFR-2007, Part-I, p. 481, fn.

149   IFR-2007, Part-I, p. 489.

150   Spokesman's statement, 29 June 2007, IFR-2007, p. 1947.

151   IFR-2007, Part-II, 29 June 2007, p. 1947, fn.

152   MEA press release, 14 August 2007, IFR-2007, Part-II, p. 1948.

153   Text of the letter, IFR-2007, Part-I, Appendix XII, p. 707.

154   IFR-2007, Part-I, p. 534.

155   IFR-2007, Part-I, p. 548,

156   IFR-2007, Part-I, p. 549.

157   Chaudhuri, *Forged in Crisis*, pp. 238–3.

158   PM's interview with *Telegraph*, Kolkata, 11 August 2007, IFR-2007, Part-I, p. 499.

159   Speech of CPM member Roopchand Pal in Lok Sabha, 28 November 2007, IFR-2007, Part-I, pp. 574–3.

160   Advani's speech in the Lok Sabha, 28 November 2007, IFR-2007, Part-I, pp. 583–95.

161   Tellis, Ashley, contributory chapter: 'Transforming US-India Relations and Its Significance for American interests', in *India's Foreign Policy*, ed, Kanti Bajpai and Harsh V. Pant, Oxford, New Delhi, 2013, p. 326.

162   Speech of EAM, 28 November 2007, IFR-2007, Part-I, pp. 114–609.

163   For text of these statements please see: IFR-2007, Part-I, pp. 670–724.

164   For text of all the editorials please see: IFR-2007, Part-I, pp. 727–38.

165   Menon, *Choices*, p. 79.

166   Menon, *Choices*, p. 79.

167   MEA spokesman's reply to a question, 16 August 2007, IFR-2007, Part-I, p. 519.

168   IFR-2007, Part-I. p 519, fn.

169   IFR-2007, Part-I, p. 520.

170   Media report on the EAM's visit to Canberra, 23 June 2008, p. 1478, IFR-2008, Part-II, p. 1478.

171   Statement of the EAM in the Lok Sabha, 16 August 2007, IFR-2007, Part-I, p. 521.

172   IFR-2007, Part-I, p. 522.

173   IFR. 2007-Part-I; p. 596 and p. 647.

174   IFR-2007, Part-I, 2007, p. 549, fn.

175   Rice, p. 129.

176   IFR-2007, Part-I, p. 559.

177   India's Foreign Relations-2007, p. 558

178   The PM's speech, 31 August 2007, IFR-2007, Part-I, p. 530.

179   MEA spokesman's briefing, 10 October 2007, IFR-2007, Part-I, p. 547.

180   Media briefing, 11 January 2008, IFR-2008, Part-I, p. 363.

181   *The Hindu*, 17 January 2008.

182   Shyam Saran, special envoy of the PM, while speaking at the India International Centre, 18 February 2008, IFR-2008, Part-I, p. 375.

183   Media report on Mukherjee's visit to Washington, 25 March 2008, IFR-2008, Part-I, p. 392.

184   IFR-2008, part-I, p. 411.

185   Press release from PMO on the meeting with Samajwadi Party, 2 July 2008, IFR-2008, Part-I, p. 411.

186   IFR-2008, Part-I, 9 July 2008, p. 417, fn.

187   Kakodkar's press conference, 10 July 2008, IFR-2008, Part-I, p. 555, fn.

188   The PM's speech in Lok Sabha, 21 July 2008, Bhasin, IFR-2008, Part-I, pp. 449–50.

189   The PM's reply speech in Lok Sabha, 22 July 2008, IFR-2008, Part-I, pp. 504–09.

190   Sirohi, *Friends with Benefits*, pp. 207–08.

191   Media Briefing by Chinese Ministry of Foreign Affairs, 8 Sept. 2008; IFR.2008, Pt. I, p. 578 and footnotes on pages 578 and 579.

192   Kakodkar's press conference, 10 July 2008, IFR-2008, Part-I, p. 555, fn.

193   Official spokesman's response to item in the *Washington Post* of 3 September, IFR-2008, Part-I, p. 569.

194   Sirohi, *Friends with Benefits*, p. 213.

195   Speech of President Bush while signing the Agreement, 8 October 2008, IFR-2008, Part-I, p. 753.

196   EAM and Secretary of State at the joint press conference, 4 October 2008, IFR-2008, Part-II, p. 2159.

197   The EAM's statement, 5 September 2008, IFR-2008, Part-I, p. 570.

198   The PM's statement, 6 September 2008, IFR-2008, p. 572.

199   Press release by the MEA, 6 September 2008, IFR-2008, Part-I, p. 577.

200   Menon, *Choices*, p. 77.

201   IFR-2008, 6 September 2008, Part-I, p. 577, fn.

202   Remarks at the signing ceremony, 10 October 2008, IFR-2008, Part-I, pp. 596–619.

203   The EAM's press conference, IFR-2008, Part-I, p. 620.

204 The EAM's statement in Parliament, 20 October 2008, IFR-2008, Part-I, p. 627.

205 Former foreign secretary Lalit Mansingh's contributory chapter in *India–US Nuclear Deal* (ed. P.R. Chari, Routledge, New Delhi, 2009, p. 183).

206 Ashley Tellis' contributory chapter in the book *India's Foreign Policy* (ed. Kanti Bajpai and Harsh Pant, Oxford University Press, New Delhi, 2013, pp. 309–10).

207 Sirohi, *Friends with Benefits*, p. 214.

208 *The Hindu*, 19 February 2023.

209 *Indian Express*, 26 May 2023.

210 Menon, *Choices*, p. 86.

Scan QR code to access the
Penguin Random House India website